Resident-owned Flats:
A guide to company purchase and management of freehold

AUSTRALIA
The Law Book Company
Brisbane • Sydney • Melbourne • Perth

CANADA
Carswell
Ottawa • Toronto • Calgary • Montreal • Vancouver

Agents:
Steimatzky's Agency Ltd., Tel Aviv;
N.M. Tripathi (Private) Ltd., Bombay;
Eastern Law House (Private) Ltd., Calcutta;
M.P.P. House, Bangalore;
Universal Book Traders, Delhi;
Aditya Books, Delhi;
MacMillan Shuppan KK, Tokyo;
Pakistan Law House, Karachi, Lahore

Resident-owned Flats:
A guide to company purchase and management of freehold

by

S. J. Tabbush, *M.A. (Oxon)*
of the Middle Temple, Barrister

LONDON
SWEET & MAXWELL
1994

Published in 1994 by
Sweet & Maxwell Limited of
183 Marsh Wall, London E14
Computerset by P.B. Computer Typesetting, Pickering, N. Yorks.
Printed in Great Britain by Butler and Tanner Ltd.,
Frome and London.

British Library Cataloguing in Publication Data

A Catalogue record
for this book is
available from the
British Library

ISBN 0421–472–006

No natural forests were destroyed to make this product; only farmed timber was used and re-planted.

To J.K.

PREFACE

This is an age of home ownership. Apart from the great increase in the number of owner-occupiers over the last few decades, it has been government policy to remove public sector estates and blocks of flats from the ownership of local councils and vest them in housing associations, with the tenants themselves as members.

In a parallel move, tenants of private estates and blocks of flats, whether purpose-built or converted from houses, have increasingly bought out the landlord and vested the estate or block in a company owned by themselves. Until now, it has only been possible to do this with the agreement of the landlord. Since the passing earlier this year of the Leasehold Reform, Housing and Urban Development Act 1993 it has become possible for a suitable majority of the tenants to compel the landlord to sell his interest for its market value.

Increasingly, therefore, tenants will face the task of managing their own blocks, with all the responsibilities for repairs and insurance that that implies; increasingly, also, they will be faced with complicated and burdensome (but essential) administrative duties imposed by the Companies Acts. They will usually be without professional guidance in this, unless by chance one of the tenants happens to be a lawyer or an accountant.

The books available on relevant subjects are usually either heavy works of reference designed for practising lawyers or the secretaries of large public companies, or slim guides that give a cursory description of the activities of a company without any of the references needed to give practical help to those who need to carry out these activities for themselves. Also, so far as I know there is no work dealing with both the property law side and the company side of the problem.

The present volume is designed to fill this gap. The first three Parts set out the basis of flat ownership, describe different methods of buying out the landlord, and give guidance on running the building and the company from then on. As far as possible they are written in non-technical language, but through the apparatus of footnotes it is possible to follow up references and find the necessary piece of legal machinery for dealing with any particular problem. The fourth Part follows an imaginary example of a building bought and managed by the tenants through a company, and takes the form of a complete company file. It should be possible to find examples of almost all the forms and documents which will need to be used.

The book is designed so that the secretary of an ownership and management company, or others concerned in the management of blocks of flats owned by the tenants, should be able to use it as a comprehensive guide without needing to consult any other book. It does not however replace the need for professional advice. In particular the part dealing with accounting concepts is intended purely as a guide to understanding what a company's accountants do: it should not be used as an instruction manual for do-it-yourself accountancy.

The law is stated as at July 20, 1993, when the Leasehold Reform, Housing and Urban Development Act 1993 became law. The forms given in Part Four are therefore the ones in force at that date, rather than the ones in force at the relevant dates in the imaginary history, as they are intended to be helpful for the future rather than historically authentic.

Thanks are due to officials at the Department of Trade and Industry, Companies House, the Lord Chancellor's Department and Lloyds Bank plc for answering my questions; to Oyez law stationers for allowing me to use their forms; and to Adrian Mundy for reading part of the text in draft. I must also thank Linda McCann, Josephine Flood, Jane Harrison, Paula Jarvis and the other residents of 67 Clapton Common, who participated in the practical experience on which this book is based, and to assist whom the first germ of it was conceived. Finally, I must thank my wife for her encouragement and James and Anna for occasionally letting me do the actual writing.

Simon Tabbush
September 1993

Table of Contents

Part Four: The Story of a Company

Table of Cases

Table of Statutes

Table of Statutory Instruments

PART ONE: INTRODUCTION

A. The System of Leasehold

Landlords and Tenants

Most people who live in flats own them on long leases. This means that when buying or selling the flat, or arranging for repairs or insurance, they have to deal with a ground landlord. This book is about how to eliminate the ground landlord so that the residents can own and manage their own building.

Houses and flats are usually owned in one of these three ways. The simplest situation is that of **owner occupation**. In this case there is one owner, called the freeholder, who owns the house outright. His interest is called a "freehold in possession".[1] A house can also be owned jointly by two or more freeholders, such as a husband and wife.[2] At the other extreme, the house or flat can be let to tenants on a **periodic tenancy**.[3] This can be either by a written document or by word of mouth.[4] The landlord is the freeholder; the tenant has a limited ownership which renews itself weekly, monthly, quarterly or yearly, until he gives, or is given, notice to quit. In the third situation the tenant has a **long lease**—99 years, for example (and that is not renewable). In this case he has limited ownership throughout that term[5] to the extent that he can also sell the term or mortgage it. He has a written document called a lease, signed by both landlord and tenant.

With a long lease, the freeholder's rights are to the rent (which is usually nominal) and to recover the house or flat at the end of the term; for this reason, his interest is sometimes called the "reversion" (or "freehold reversion"). It is still possible to speak of "landlord" and "tenant" in this context, but more usual to speak of "freeholder" and "leaseholder". It is possible for a leaseholder to grant a sub-lease provided that this is timed to come to an end before his own lease; he

[1] *Littleton's Tenures* §1; Law of Property Act, s.1(1)(*a*).
[2] *Littleton's Tenures* §277–291; Law of Property Act 1925, ss.34–37.
[3] *Bowen* v. *Anderson* [1894] I Q.B. 164; see also *Prudential Assurance Co. Ltd.* v. *London Residuary Body* [1992] 2 A.C. 386.
[4] Law of Property Act 1925, s.54(2).
[5] *Littleton's Tenures* §58–67.

can also let to periodic tenants. References in this book to "landlord" and "tenant" cover all these situations.

Houses are usually thought of as being freehold and flats as being leasehold, but this is not invariable. It is quite common for houses on a large estate to be let on long leases by the estate owner to the individual residents; it is also possible (though unusual and undesirable) for flats to be owned freehold by owner-occupiers. In the rest of this Part, however, we shall be speaking of the typical example, which is of a house or block owned by a freeholder, and divided into flats, each let to its occupier on a long lease.

The Lease

The parties to a lease are the *lessor* who is the original freehold owner who makes ("grants") the lease and the *lessee* who is the first leaseholder, in whose favour the lease is made. If the lessor later sells the freehold, or the lessee the lease, the new freeholder or leaseholder steps into his shoes;[6] but the original lessor and lessee retain a certain fall-back responsibility if the new freeholder or leaseholder does not fulfil his obligation.[7]

The *term* is the length of time for which the lease is made. It starts at a fixed time (usually but not always the same day as the lease was signed) and goes on for a fixed number of years, the most usual periods being 21, 50, 99 or 999 years.

The *premium* is the price originally paid by the lessee to the lessor for the lease. This is usually the full value of the flat, or a little less. The *rent* may be paid quarterly, half-yearly or yearly. Where the lease is at a full premium, the rent will be nominal: £50 per year, £10 per year or a peppercorn. This kind of rent under a lease is often called a "ground rent".

The lease contains a number of undertakings, or *covenants*, made by the lessee to the lessor ("tenant's covenants") and by the lessor to the lessee ("landlord's covenants"). When a new freeholder or leaseholder comes in, he is automatically bound to observe these undertakings even though he has never personally promised to do so; similarly he is entitled to make sure that the other party observes his undertakings. This is the great advantage of the leasehold system, since in most other situations, agreements only bind, or help, the people who originally made them.[8]

The tenant's covenants are usually to pay the rent, not to use the flat for illegal or immoral purposes and not to be a nuisance to the other

[6] *Spencer's Case* (1583) 5 Co. Rep. 16a.

[7] *Thursby* v. *Plant* (1670) 1 Wms. Saund. 230; Law of Property Act 1925, s.79.

[8] *Spencer's Case* (1583) 5 Co. Rep. 16a; for exceptions, see *Tulk* v. *Moxhay* (1848) 2 Ph. 774. The effect of covenants other than in leases is one of the most complicated areas of the law. For a detailed discussion, see *Megarry's Law of Real Property* (5th ed). pp. 760–798.

occupiers. Sometimes there are detailed rules such as that he must not carry on a business from home or play gramophones or musical instruments after a given time at night. The landlord's covenants are usually not to disturb the tenant in his possession of the flat and to make sure that the other tenants keep their own obligations under the other leases.

The most important covenants are those concerning repairs and insurance. Any number of systems are found here. In some blocks, each tenant is responsible for repairs on his own flat, but repairs to the block are carried out by the landlord, who then levies a service charge on all the tenants to cover the cost. In others, the tenants between them are bound to carry out all the repairs—this is an extremely awkward system, as if one tenant does not co-operate the other tenants have no remedy except to sue the landlord, in order to compel the landlord in his turn to sue the uncooperative tenant. In yet others, a management company is set up (usually owned by all the tenants) which is responsible for repairs; quite often this company is a third party to the lease. In the case of very short leases (seven years or less) the landlord is liable for all repairs. Even when the landlord is not *bound* to carry out the repairs, he is usually given the *right*, on giving reasonable notice to the tenants, to do them and charge the tenants.[9]

There is a similarly wide range of provisions for *insurance*. Sometimes the landlord insures the whole block, and the tenants' interests are noted on the policy; the landlord then reclaims the premiums from the tenants (this is sometimes called an "insurance rent"). Sometimes the tenants arrange this kind of policy between them. Sometimes each tenant is left to insure his own flat and there is a separate policy for the common parts.[10]

The last type of covenant concerns the tenant's *power to sell* his lease. Usually the tenant has the unrestricted right to sell his lease, though he must inform the landlord when this is done. Sometimes (for example in a small house or block where the landlord lives in one of the flats) he may not do so without the consent of the landlord. This kind of provision is more usual in business leases, so will not be discussed further.

Finally, a lease usually contains *provisos for re-entry*. These are provisions that if a tenant does not pay his rent, or does not observe his covenants, the landlord may claim the flat back without compensation: this is called "forfeiture" of the lease. There are detailed procedures laid down by law for giving the tenant the opportunity to pay the arrears, or remedy the broken covenant, before the forfeiture becomes final.[11]

[9] For further discussion on repairs, see p. 60 *et seq.*

[10] For further discussion on insurance, see p. 65 *et seq.*

[11] For relief against forfeiture for unpaid rent, see *Howard* v. *Fanshawe* [1895] 2 Ch. 581, and Common Law Procedure Act 1852 s.210. For relief in other cases, see Law of Property Act 1925, s.146 and pp. 74–75 *post.*

B. Advantages and Disadvantages of Leaseholds

Advantages

The advantages of the leasehold system lie in the existence of covenants and provisos for re-entry. Dwellers in flats in the same house or block are so dependent on each other for their happiness or misery, and for the reasonable maintenance of the building, that without this kind of restraint on the residents' behaviour, life could easily become impossible.

It is for this reason that it is not recommended that flats be owned freehold. An old superstition had it that only "land" could be owned freehold, so that the freehold of a building could never be divided into slices one above the other, but this was never soundly based in law and it is fully established that so-called "flying freeholds" are possible. However, the law only provides the most basic protection for freehold flats: for example, that if you own an upstairs flat, the owners of the downstairs flat may not demolish the central supports so that your flat crashes to the ground. It is also possible for the owners of the flats to make an agreement among themselves establishing rules for the management of the building. The problem is that, when the flats are sold, many of these rules will not bind the new owners; conversely the new owners cannot take advantage of these rules in dealings with the owners of the other flats. (The negative rules, forbidding particular uses of the flats, may in some circumstances be passed on to the new owners, but the positive ones, such as ones requiring repairs, are not).[12]

The leasehold system, as we have seen, is free of these disadvantages, as all the covenants, both positive and negative, are passed on to the new landlords and tenants. It does however have several disadvantages of its own.

Disadvantages

One disadvantage is the fact that a lease decreases in value. The typical lease is granted for a term of 99 years; after the first 20 years, its value is already significantly less and many will warn against buying it; when there are less than 70 years to run it is still harder to re-sell, unless there is some prospects of the freehold being for sale as well.

The second disadvantage is that the system of repairs, whatever structure is contained in the lease, necessarily depends on the landlord,

[12] See note 8 to this section.

either to do the repairs or to compel the tenants to do them. The landlord may live far away, or have no assets, or be a shell company; or it may be a large company with many other properties and little staff time to devote to any one building. In any case, since all the building is worth to the landlord is the value of a number of fairly insignificant ground rents, he has little interest in the state of the building and still less incentive to become enmeshed in litigation with the tenants for its sake.

The landlord then, will never be the active, willing promoter of change, who takes the burden and responsibility of looking after the building off his tenants' shoulders. At best, he will be the clearing house for the tenants' initiatives and the instrument by which the more responsible tenants enforce the house rules against the less responsible tenants; at worst he will himself be the obstacle to all schemes of improvement. In the end, both the responsibility for initiating repairs and the cost of the repairs fall just as firmly on the tenants with a landlord as without one.

The third disadvantage is that the tenants' control over the landlord only extends to necessary repairs. If the tenants want to carry out an improvement, or to re-decorate the common parts in a particular way, the landlord's consent is needed and he can refuse without giving reasons. Similarly he can himself carry out alterations to or re-decorations of the common parts at his own cost, which the tenants cannot object to, however much they dislike them.

A final disadvantage is that some landlords will abuse their position. Leases where the landlord has the responsibility for repairs often contain very wide powers to levy service charges, so that instead of doing the repairs and presenting the tenants with the bill he can estimate the cost in advance. By manipulating this kind of clause, some landlords can make a considerable profit out of the service charge. Further, some landlords who are builders by trade may have the work done by associated companies at an inflated charge. There are however safeguards against these abuses in the Landlord and Tenant Act 1985, which limits the service charge to costs reasonably incurred.[13]

Many landlords, of course, have no such malicious intentions, and find the ownership of the building a burden which they would be glad to be without. The best of both worlds, then, is found where the occupants of the flats have long leases, and also jointly control the freehold of the building. There is just as powerful a mechanism of control, through the tenants' covenants and the provisos for re-entry, as there is where the building is owned by a landlord, without the trouble of having to involve the landlord every time a tenant does not meet his obligations. Further, the running down of the time left on the leases is not a problem, as the tenants' association will always grant extensions of the individual leases on request.

[13] See further, p. 67 *et seq.*

It should be noted that in certain circumstances, buying out the landlord may not be a sensible option, that is if some of the flats are let, not on long leases, but on periodic tenancies. Owning flats let to periodic tenants can be a full-time occupation, and there is frequently personal bitterness between the landlord and the periodic tenants. It is therefore perhaps better that the thankless role of landlord be left with the absentee freeholder than that it be assumed by the general body of long leaseholders, who have to live in the same building as the periodic tenants and see them daily.

The cost, divided among the long leaseholders, is seldom great and the Leasehold Reform, Housing and Urban Development Act 1993 now gives the tenants power to purchase the freehold compulsorily from the landlord at a market price.[14]

[14] See further, p. 12 *et seq.*

PART TWO: HOW TO PURCHASE YOUR FREEHOLD

A. Systems of Ownership

When purchasing the freehold of their building from a landlord, the tenants must first decide upon the method by which they will jointly own the property.

Tenancy in Common

One option is for the freehold to be put directly into the joint names of all the leaseholders, to be owned as so-called "tenants in common". (This is not possible if there are more than four of them.) In this case it should be agreed in what shares the freehold shall be owned: whether all should have equal shares, or the tenants of large flats should have greater shares than the tenants of small flats.

This arrangement has two problems: First, whenever one of the tenants sells his flat, he must also arrange for his share of the freehold to be transferred with it, which adds to the cost of conveyancing: the purchaser's solicitor will have two separate sets of enquiries about the title to make and there will be two separate sets of deeds. Secondly, and more importantly, whenever the owners decide to do anything belonging to their role as collective landlord, they must decide unanimously: there is no way in which the majority can overrule a minority. Since the main point of a collectively owned freehold is to enable the majority of responsible tenants to enforce the house rules against a recalcitrant fellow tenant, to give that tenant a power of veto over their actions is clearly foolish.

Direct common ownership of the freehold is only appropriate in the case of a house converted into two flats, where it is agreed that the owner of the upper flat has sole responsibility for repairs to everything above the dividing line, including the roof, and that the owner of the lower flat has sole responsibility for repairs to everything below the dividing line, including the foundations.

Ownership Through a Company

The overwhelming favourable option, to which the rest of this book is devoted, is for the tenants to form or acquire a company, which then owns the freehold. This kind of company will, in this book, be called an "ownership and management company". This option has the advantage that the company will continue to own the freehold without anything having to be done about it, no matter how often the tenants come and go; also decisions can be made by a majority. The one disadvantage is that running a company involves tedious and time-consuming formalities, such as annual accounts and returns, audit and annual general meetings, all of which are designed to ensure some degree of public accountability. The underlying reason for the formalities is that the company system was devised for trading enterprises — for which the benefits of company status are so great, and so open to abuse, that it is considered necessary for the State to be able to keep a close watch on a company's affairs and for most of the important information about companies to be available to the public. The burden of these arrangements, much of which can be passed on to the company's accountants, should therefore be reckoned a small price to pay for the convenience of this form of ownership.

Commonhold

One further option is due to become available in the next few years. There is a proposal by the Law Commission (*Commonhold: A Consultation Paper,* Cm.1345 (1990)), due to be introduced into Parliament as a Bill in the next few years, which will, if and when it becomes law, set up a wholly new kind of ownership called "commonhold". On this system, each flat owner will have permanent ownership of his flat, equivalent to a freehold; there will also be a "commonhold association" which will be a legal entity in the same way as a company, and which will own the common parts. The entire package will come into being as soon as the necessary documents have been filed at the Land Registry and the first flat has been sold: Companies House will not be involved. It will be possible for a developer to set up the commonhold arrangements before selling the flats; it will also be possible for the tenants in an existing building, having compelled the landlord to sell the freehold at its market price, to set up a commonhold from there. If the flat owners put an end to the commonhold (for example in order to sell the block) the entire block will become the property of the association, and each owner, instead of owning one flat, will own a percentage share in the association's assets. The association must hold meetings and prepare simple accounts, but will not have as complicated a set of requirements as a normal company.

The association will have a constitution agreed by the owners at the time when it is formed; they will be able to agree house rules which can be enforced in the same way as covenants in a lease. However, the room for flexibility, both in types of constitution and in house rules, will be very limited, as the proposals are intended to import a high degree of standardization.

It should be emphasized that the commonhold system, once it becomes law, will not in any way supersede the existing option of ownership through a company. Existing ownership and management companies will not be turned into commonhold associations, and after the new system has come into force, there will still be nothing to stop ownership and management companies from being set up in the same way as before. Even after the introduction of the proposed power to compel the landlord to sell the freehold, it will still be at the tenants' option whether to set up a commonhold association or to vest the freehold in an ownership and management company. In America, where the condominium system has been in existence for many years, condominia (equivalent to commonholds) and cooperatives (leasehold flats where the freehold is owned by the leaseholders through a company) both remain popular.

It is not yet possible to make a proper comparison of the merits of the commonhold system and the existing ownership and management company system. Many details of the commonhold system will have to be decided during the Bill's passage through Parliament, and much will depend on the administrative regulations that will need to be made under the powers of the new law. Further, there will undoubtedly be teething troubles and litigation during the first few years of the commonhold system's existence, as the new law is tested and ambiguities in it are discovered and resolved; whereas the details of company law and landlord and tenant law have both been clear for a long time, making similar problems unlikely to arise within the existing system.

The main advantage of the proposed commonhold system is that the paperwork involved in setting up and running the association will be considerably simplified and standardized and that guidance on running the association will be available from the relevant government departments. As against this, the company system offers far greater flexibility, and will appeal far more to independent-minded tenants who wish to devise their own system for running their building.

It should be noted that it could in theory be possible to have the freehold owned through a tenants' association. An association (other than a company) is not a legally existing entity, and cannot own anything, so two, three or four of the tenants would own the freehold as trustees for the others, and it would be dealt with according to the association's rules. However, this would be complicated and rather cumbersome.

B. Obtaining the Landlord's Agreement

The first step after the tenants in a block have decided to purchase their freehold is to persuade or compel the landlord to sell. There are three ways in which this can be done.

First, if the landlord proposes to sell the freehold to anyone other than the tenants, the tenants can insist on having it offered to them at the same price. Second, if the landlord is seriously in default in his duties of managing the property, the tenants can compel a sale to them at a "fair price" fixed by a rent assessment committee. Third, it is now (since the Leasehold Reform, Housing and Urban Development Act 1993 became law on July 20, 1993) possible for the tenants to claim "collective enfranchisement": this involves the compulsory purchase of the freehold from the landlord at a market value. This market value is estimated rather more generously than the "fair price" under the second procedure. It is therefore still in the interest of landlords to manage their properties well; and a group of tenants wishing to purchase their freehold should consider carefully which of the two procedures to use.

First Refund

In more detail, the three procedures are as follows:

If the landlord proposes to sell the freehold to someone else, he must give the tenants the **right to first refusal**.[1] The way this works is that he must give each of them a notice explaining what he proposes to sell and for what price[2], offering to sell the same interest to the tenants collectively for the same price. The tenants then have two months (longer if the notice allows a longer period) in which to accept that offer: they can do this by a simple majority. Alternatively they can offer a different price, which the landlord accepts or rejects[3].

Once a price is agreed, the tenants have two more months (which, again, can be made longer by the landlord's original notice) in which to name a person to take the freehold. In practice, this means that they have that long in which to form or acquire a company for the purpose.

After that the landlord and the company have three months in which to exchange contracts for the sale of the freehold[4].

If this procedure fails at any point (*e.g.*, no price is agreed; no company or other person is nominated; no contract is entered

[1] Landlord and Tenant Act 1987, s.1.
[2] Landlord and Tenant Act 1987, s.5.
[3] Landlord and Tenant Act 1987, s.7.
[4] Landlord and Tenant Act 1987, s.6.

into within the three months), the landlord has a period of a year in which he can sell the freehold to his chosen purchaser as originally planned, or to another purchaser; but he may not do so at a lower price than he has specified in his offer to the tenants.[5] After that year if he still wishes to sell the freehold he must go through the notice procedure all over again.

The High Court or a county court can make an order requiring any person to comply with any step in the procedure,[6] but the main restraint on the landlord from deviating from it is that, if he sells the freehold without going through the notice procedure, the tenants have the automatic right to buy the freehold from the purchaser for the same price as he paid for it.[7]

Every new landlord has the duty to notify the tenants of the change.[8] If the freehold has been sold without going through the notice procedure as described, the tenants (or a majority of them) have two months after that notice in which to ask for further details of the sale, including the price paid.[9] Within three months after receiving those details (or after the period for receiving them has expired) they can demand to buy the reversion at the same price the new landlord paid for it[10]; if there is any dispute as to the terms of the sale, it is resolved by a rent assessment committee.[11] If the new landlord sells the freehold again, the tenants can still continue the process in the same way as before: the third landlord has stepped into the shoes of the second landlord in all respects.[12]

Landlord in Default

The tenants also have the **power to buy the landlord's freehold compulsorily** if he is not fulfilling his duties under the lease relating to repairs, maintenance, insurance or management.

The first step is to give the landlord a "preliminary notice".[13] This must be given by the tenants of a majority of the flats; it must say what the fault is in the repairs or management arrangements, and (where possible) give the landlord a reasonable time in which to put them right. The notice further says that, if the landlord does not put these matters right within the time mentioned, the tenants will apply for an acquisition

[5] Landlord and Tenant Act 1987, s.6(3).
[6] Landlord and Tenant Act 1987, s.19.
[7] Landlord and Tenant Act 1987, s.12.
[8] Landlord and Tenant Act 1987, s.3.
[9] Landlord and Tenant Act 1987, s.11.
[10] Landlord and Tenant Act 1987, s.12.
[11] Landlord and Tenant Act 1987, s.13.
[12] Landlord and Tenant Act 1987, s.16.
[13] Landlord and Tenant Act 1987, s.27.

order. (An example of such a notice is given in Part Four on page 93).

If the fault has not been put right in the time mentioned, or it is one that in its nature cannot be put right, the tenants (again, the tenants of a majority of the flats) may apply to the court for an acquisition order.[14] The court has to be convinced of the existence of the fault, and that it has not been put right. Even then, the court will not automatically make an order: it will generally only do so where the fault is serious, and it is not sufficient to appoint a manager for the building.

If the court does make an acquisition order, there must be a "nominated person" to take the freehold; again, usually a company formed or acquired by the tenants. If the landlord and the tenants cannot agree on a price, a fair price is fixed by a rent assessment committee; this also settles the other terms of the sale.[15]

Collective Enfranchisement

This option was given by the Leasehold Reform, Housing and Urban Development Act 1993, which came into force on November 1, 1993.[16]

The Right to Buy

Briefly, in the case of any building divided into flats, the Act gives the tenants the right to buy the freehold provided that at least two thirds of the flats are held on long leases and at low rents.[17] A long lease is one for more than 21 years;[18] the definition of a low rent depends on when the lease was entered into.[19] The decision to purchase must be taken by at least two thirds of the qualifying tenants[20] (that is, tenants with long leases at low rents); and these must between them own at least half of the flats in the building.

The right to buy the freehold carries with it the right to buy all other landlords' interests in the building.[21] Thus, if the immediate landlord of the block or of any part of it is himself a leaseholder, the tenants can buy

[14] Landlord and Tenant Act 1987, ss.28–30.
[15] Landlord and Tenant Act 1987, s.31.
[16] The Act received the Royal Assent on July 20, 1993. It was brought into force by the Leasehold Reform, Housing and Urban Development Act 1993 (Commencement and Transitional Provisions (No. 1) Order 1993 (S.I. 1993 No. 2134).
[17] Leasehold Reform, Housing and Urban Development Act 1993, s.5(1).
[18] Leasehold Reform, Housing and Urban Development Act 1993, s.7(1).
[19] Leasehold Reform, Housing and Urban Development Act 1993, s.8.
[20] Leasehold Reform, Housing and Urban Development Act 1993, s.13(2).
[21] Leasehold Reform, Housing and Urban Development Act 1993, s.2.

both his lease and the freehold owned by the ultimate landlord; and the same is true however long the chain of landlords. Similarly if one of the flats is sub-let, it is only the tenant at the bottom of the chain (always supposing that he has a long lease at a low rent) who counts as a "qualifying tenant" and has the right to join in the purchase; all the tenants higher up the chain have their interests bought from them at the same time as the landlords.

Nominee Purchaser and the Reversioner

In any purchase under the Act, there are therefore two groups involved: the "participating tenants", who are those of the qualifying tenants who are claiming their right to buy,[22] and the "relevant landlords", whose interests are being bought from them.[23] Once the participating tenants have set the process in motion by giving their initial notice,[24] the negotiations are between just two people: the "nominee purchaser", who acts on behalf of the tenants, and the "reversioner", who acts on behalf of the landlords.

The nominee purchaser is appointed by the participating tenants.[25] They may appoint one of themselves, or someone else, or a company; they can also replace the nominee purchaser as often as they like. Normally, at the time of the initial notice they will choose one of themselves as nominee purchaser; when the purchase looks imminent, they will acquire a company (as described in the next section) and appoint the company as nominee purchaser in place of their original choice.

The reversioner is usually the freeholder; but the court can in certain circumstances appoint one of the other relevant landlords, or someone else entirely, instead.[26]

The Notice Procedure

After the participating tenants have given their initial notice, the reversioner gives a counter-notice.[27] In this, he may either accept that the participating tenants have the right to buy but propose his own terms for the sale, or refuse to accept that the participating tenants have the right to buy. Any dispute about whether there is a right to buy is decided by the

[22] Leasehold Reform, Housing and Urban Development Act 1993, s.14.
[23] Leasehold Reform, Housing and Urban Development Act 1993, s.9.
[24] Leasehold Reform, Housing and Urban Development Act 1993, s.13.
[25] Leasehold Reform, Housing and Urban Development Act 1993, s.15.
[26] Leasehold Reform, Housing and Urban Development Act 1993, s.9.
[27] Leasehold Reform, Housing and Urban Development Act 1993, s.21.

County Court[28]; any dispute about the terms of the sale (*e.g.*, the price) is decided by a rent assessment committee, known for this purpose as a leasehold valuation tribunal.[29]

The Price

A separate price is set for the interest of each relevant landlord.[30] The price of the freehold consists of three parts[31]:

(i) the price that the freehold would fetch it it were being sold on the open market[32];
(ii) an assessed proportion (never less than half) of the "marriage value", that is, of the amount by which the freehold is more valuable to the participating tenants than it would have been to a third party purchaser[33];
(iii) compensation for loss of value of other property of the freeholder caused by the sale.[34]

The price paid to the other relevant landlords is fixed either by market values[35] or (in some cases) by a complicated formula depending on the rent which each landlord receives and the length of time left on the lease.[36]

Comparison of These Methods

After the Leasehold Reform, Housing and Urban Development Act 1993, the freeholds of residential blocks will not be a very attractive proposition for outside purchasers looking for an investment, so the occasion for exercising the right of first refusal will seldom arise. The second method, however (that of compulsory purchase from a landlord in default), will remain of importance. The advantage of the second method is that the price will be cheaper than in the case of the third method, as the landlord will not be able to claim anything for marriage value or loss of value of other property. The disadvantage is the uncertainty of success: the court may decide that the landlord is not in default, or that though he is in default the appointment of a manager will be an adequate

[28] Leasehold Reform, Housing and Urban Development Act 1993, ss.22, 90.
[29] Leasehold Reform, Housing and Urban Development Act 1993, ss.24, 91.
[30] Leasehold Reform, Housing and Urban Development Act 1993, s.32 and Sched. 6.
[31] Leasehold Reform, Housing and Urban Development Act 1993, Sched. 6, para. 2(1).
[32] Leasehold Reform, Housing and Urban Development Act 1993, para. 3.
[33] For the assessed proportion, see *ibid.*, paras. 4(1). For the marriage value, see *ibid.*, paras. 4(2) and (3).
[34] Leasehold Reform, Housing and Urban Development Act 1993, para. 5.
[35] Leasehold Reform, Housing and Urban Development Act 1993, para. 6(1)(*b*).
[36] Leasehold Reform, Housing and Urban Development Act 1993, para. 7(2) to (10).

remedy. The third method, collective enfranchisement, is more expensive but more certain to succeed. It also has the advantage of ensuring the purchase of all of the different landlords' interests.

It will often be possible to purchase the freehold from the landlord by voluntary agreement, without the use of any of these procedures. Even in this case, the existence of the procedures is a useful negotiating point, both as providing a measure of the suitable price and as a means of applying pressure if the landlord is dilatory.

C. Acquiring a Company

Once the landlord's agreement has been obtained and a price has been fixed, the next step is usually for the tenants either to form, or to acquire, a company.

What Is a Company?

A company is a society of persons which the law recognises as having a personality of its own, separate from that of its members.[37] It can have property of its own: the members do not in any sense own that property, only their interest in the company, which in turn derives its value from that property. The company can also have debts: as long as the company exists, the creditors can only reach the property of the company, and not the property of the members. No matter how often the membership of the company changes, it remains the same body and continues with all its rights and liabilities.

The most usual sort of company is a company limited by shares.[38] This means that the ownership of the company is divided into proportional shares, each with a nominal cash value: thus, a normal small company is owned in 100 shares of £1 each. Every member has one or more shares, so that "member" and "shareholder" are synonymous.[39] On being issued with a share, the member pays (or owes) its nominal value to the company, and may or may not pay (or owe) a premium as well.[40] It often happens that only a few of the available shares are issued at first, the rest being left vacant until the occasion arises. When the company is insolvent, so that all its property will have to be paid to its creditors, each member must contribute the amount he still owes on his shares:[41] after that, the company is dissolved and he is free. That is what is meant by saying that the company is one with limited liability.

[37] Companies Act 1985, s.1(1).
[38] Companies Act 1985, s.1(2)(a).
[39] Companies Act 1985, s.22.
[40] Companies Act 1985, s.99.
[41] Insolvency Act 1986, s.74(2)(d).

There are three ways of becoming a **shareholder** in a company:

(a) By being one of the founder members, called subscribers. These sign the original formation documents of the company, and automatically become shareholders as soon as the company is formed;[42]

(b) By allotment. After the company is formed, all the shares, except the subscriber shares, remain unissued, and many remain so as long as the company wishes. At any time, the existing shareholders can authorise the directors to allot these shares: this permission can last any time up to five years;[43]

(c) By transfer. Any shareholder can transfer his shares to another person:[44] depending on the rules of the particular company, he may or may not need the directors' permission.

In every case, the company must keep a register of members,[45] in which all shareholders must be entered as soon as they receive their shares.[46]

In principle, all the tenants should be shareholders of the company. When a flat is jointly owned, the owners should decide which of them should hold the share: it causes unnecessary complications for a share to be owned by more than one person. Where the flats are widely different in size, it may be preferred to reflect this in the shareholding arrangements: *e.g.*, to allot three shares to the owners of each large flat and two shares to the owners of each small flat.

Directors

A company's affairs are managed by **directors**,[47] who may or may not also be shareholders.[48] They are responsible to the shareholders, and explain their actions every year in an annual general meeting.[49] A company must also have a **secretary**,[50] who is responsible for the meetings and the paperwork. A register of the directors and secretaries must be kept:[51] this can be done by keeping copies of certain Companies

[42] Companies Act 1985, s.22(1).
[43] Companies Act 1985, s.80.
[44] Companies Act 1985, s.182(1)(*b*).
[45] Companies Act 1985, s.352(1).
[46] Companies Act 1985, s.352(2).
[47] Companies Act 1985, s.282.
[48] Companies Act 1985, s.291.
[49] See Chapters 5 and 6.
[50] Companies Act 1985, s.283.
[51] Companies Act 1985, s.288(1). This requirement is probably sufficiently complied with if copies of the form 10 (statement of first directors and secretary) and of all forms 288 (notification of change of director or secretary) sent to the Registrar of Companies are kept at the registered office of the company. In the rest of the book I shall assume that this is the method chosen.

House forms. The directors are collectively called the Board, and meet every so often to run the company; one of them is elected Chairman of the Board. In the case of an ownership and management company, before the company is formed or acquired it should be decided who the directors and secretary are to be.

Who should be the directors may vary. In the case of a small house (say six flats or fewer), it is best for all the tenants to be directors; managing the house will then be a task in which all participate. Again, where a flat is jointly owned, only one of the joint owners should be a director. This is so that the voting power is in proportion to the number of flats. It is more convenient for the director to be the same person as the shareholder for that flat.

In the case of a large block, it will be found more convenient to elect a small committee to carry out the day to day management; the committee members will be directors, and meet monthly or every other month, while the remaining tenants will only meet at the annual general meeting, to elect the directors.

The **secretary** will be whichever tenant is willing to spend the most time on the company's affairs, handle the paperwork and be the contact for the company's accountants and Companies House. In the case of a company with a very large membership, such as one covering a whole estate, a professional person, not necessarily one of the tenants, will be engaged at a salary. The secretary may also be a director; but there must be at least one director other than the secretary,[52] and the secretary should not also be the chairman.

From a practical point of view it should be clearly agreed with all the tenants that, when a flat has several residents and one of them becomes a shareholder or director, only that person need be consulted about the affairs of the flat, and that it is for him — not the company secretary — to make sure that the others agree. There can be little more frustrating for a company secretary than to make what appears to be a watertight arrangement with one tenant only to be told it has to be cancelled because another person living in the same flat was not consulted and does not agree.

Company or Association in Existence

There may already be in existence a management company set up by a developer, which is a third party to all the leases in a block, and there will be provisions, first, that whenever anyone takes a lease he will also take a share in the management company, and secondly that as soon as all the flats are sold the freehold will be transferred to that management company, for a nominal price or for no payment at all.

[52] Companies Act 1985, s.283(2).

The typical developer will usually arrange the shares in such a way that he keeps overall control until the last flat is sold.

After all the shares have been transferred to the tenants, they can hold a meeting in which they elect themselves, or a committee of themselves, directors and one of themselves the secretary of the management company.

It sometimes happens that although it was the developer's intention to do these things, both the issue of the shares and the transfer of the freehold are delayed for years. It is unlikely that this is because the developer has changed his mind and decided to hang on to the freehold: since his original intention was to transfer it, he will not normally have had the leases drafted in such a way as to make the landlord's position particularly advantageous. It is far more likely that the developer has duly executed the share transfers and the conveyance of the freehold, and that one of the tenants, through inertia, or through some mistaken notion that he will be able to avoid contributing to the cost of repairs, had delayed registering the share transfer and notifying the Land Registry of the conveyance. In that case the other tenants should force the process through. Each one has the right to require the company secretary to register the transfer of his destined share[53]; once a majority of willing tenants have come to own their shares, they (together with the landlord) control the company and have the right to require the transfer of the freehold to be sent in to the Land Registry.

The usual catalyst for this action on the part of the tenants is when one of them sells his flat. Since the flat will have been advertised as "with share of freehold" the buyer will, quite rightly, refuse to exchange contracts until the share transfers and the transfer of the freehold are complete.

There may be a situation in which although there is already a management company, owned by the tenants, there is no specific provision for it to purchase the freehold.

In this case, the tenants can decide to buy by a simple majority; although if there is a substantial minority of unwilling tenants it is unlikely that the majority will be willing to bear the minority's share of the price as well as their own. (An arrangement for deferred payment is possible: (see pages 25–26).

There may also be a situation where there is no company, but there is a tenants' association. This association may be "recognised"[54] (by the landlord or through the local Rent Assessment Panel) or it may not: the only difference this makes is that the landlord must inform the secretary of a "recognised" association of how the service charge is made up[55]. The existence of an association (recognised or not) does not provide any machinery for acquiring the freehold, since an association cannot own

[53] Companies Act 1985, s.135.
[54] Landlord and Tenant Act 1985, s.29.
[55] Landlord and Tenant Act 1985, s.21(2).

property: it will therefore be necessary to form or acquire a company as if no association existed. The advantage of there being an association is simply that there is a forum in which the question of purchasing the freehold can be discussed, and that the same group of people who used to meet as an association will continue to do so as a company.

Lastly, there may be no association at all. In this case it will be necessary to canvass all the tenants individually to persuade them to join in the purchase of the freehold. That done, one of the tenants should be appointed to negotiate with the landlord.

How to Form a Company

The two essentials for forming a company are

(1) that the members agree to be formed into a company; and
(2) that the State, in the form of the Registrar of Companies, recognise the company.[56]

Documents and Registration

Standard forms for all the formal documentation may be obtained from Companies House or legal stationers. Specimens are also set out in Part Four of this book.

The agreement to form a company must be in writing, and is called the **Memorandum of Association**. It must cover the following points[57] in numbered paragraphs:

(1) The name of the company. This must end with "Limited" (or the Welsh equivalent, if the company is to be in Wales).[58] It is usual, in the case of an ownership and management company, to use the name of the house, thus: "999 Acacia Avenue Limited" or "Willow Court Limited";
(2) The country in which the registered office is to be situated, thus: "the Company's registered office is to be situated in England" (or Wales or Scotland as the case may be[59]: Northern Ireland has its own Companies Acts, which are not covered in this book). It is not usual to put the exact address of the registered office in the Memorandum of Association; that is dealt with in a separate form;
(3) The objects of the company: one of the main differences between the position of a company and the position of an

[56] Companies Act 1985, s.1(1).
[57] Companies Act 1985, s.2.
[58] Companies Act 1985, s.25(2).
[59] Companies Act 1985, ss.2(1)(*b*), 2(2).

individual is that, while an individual may do anything which is not specifically restrained by the law, a company can only do what it is specifically authorised to do by its constitution; that is, by the Memorandum of Association. This rule is no longer as important as it was: since February 4, 1991[60] the Companies Act 1989 provides that the rule does not mean that an act done outside the company's objects is invalid, but only that any shareholder has the right to forbid it in advance.[61]

Nevertheless, it is usual (and advisable) for a company's objects to be drawn as widely as possible. They will include not only the main purpose of the company, in this case the ownership and management of a house divided into flats, but also everything which the company may conceivably wish to do at some time in the future such as buying and selling property, borrowing money, amalgamating with other companies, and investing its funds;

(4) "The liability of the members is limited". The effect of this has already been explained; (see page 15)

(5) The company's shareholding arrangements. In the typical case, this will read "The company's share capital is £100 divided into 100 ordinary shares of £1 each". These may be shares with values other than £1, and there may be more or fewer than 100 shares, but the total share capital is never normally less than £100.

The Memorandum is signed by two or more of the intended members of the company (called the "subscribers") and states how many shares are to be taken by each.[62] Once the company is formed, these shares are automatically allotted to the subscribers to the Memorandum, who become the first members of the company.[63]

Together with the Memorandum of Association there must be another document, called the **Articles of Association**, which contains the company's rules.[64] These cover the issue and transfer of shares, shareholders' meetings, appointment and powers of directors, directors' meetings and accounts. For a company limited by shares there is a standard set of Articles provided by regulations called Table A.[65] It is

[60] Companies Act 1989 (Commencement No. 8 and Transitional and Saving Provisions) Order 1990 (S.I. 1990 No. 2569).

[61] Companies Act 1985, ss.35, 35A, 35B, as inserted by Companies Act 1989, s.108.

[62] Companies Act 1985, s.2(5) and (6).

[63] Companies Act 1985, s.22(1).

[64] Companies Act 1985, s.7(1).

[65] Companies (Tables A to F) Regulations 1985 (S.I. 1985 No. 805), made under Companies Act 1985, s.8. They apply so far as not expressly excluded: ibid. s.8(2). The version that applies is that in force at the time of the company's registration: *ibid.* s.8(3).

therefore usual for a company's Articles to state that Table A is incorporated in full, and then set out all the changes and modifications to Table A required by the particular company (Table A is set out in Appendix A, and a form of Articles appropriate to an ownership and management company is set out at pages 114–117). The Articles are signed by the subscribers to the Memorandum.[66]

After the Memorandum and Articles have been agreed and signed, the next step is to register the company. To do this, the people forming the company must send the Memorandum and Articles, with a fee of £50, to the Registrar of Companies.[67] For a company to be registered in England or Wales, the correct address is:

The Registrar of Companies
Companies House
Crown Way
Maindy
Cardiff
CF4 3UZ.

For a Scots company, the address is:

The Registrar of Companies
Exchequer Chambers
102 George Street
Edinburgh
EH2 3DJ.

Together with the Memorandum and Articles, they must send the following further documents:

(1) A statement of the first directors, secretary and intended situation of the **registered office** of the company[68] (Form 10). The registered office is the official address of the company. In the case of an ownership and management company, the registered office will usually be at the house itself; where there are separate letter boxes for the different flats, one of the flats (probably that where the secretary lives) will be the registered office. Sometimes it may be preferred to have the registered office at the office of the company's accountants.

The statement also shows the **first directors and secretary**. Every company must have at least one director and one

[66] Companies Act 1985, s.6(3)(*c*).
[67] Companies Act 1985, s.10(1). For the fee, see *ibid.*, s.708 and Companies (Fees) Regulations 1991 (S.I. 1991 No. 1206).
[68] Companies Act 1985, s.10(2), (6). Form 10 is prescribed with effect from 1 October 1990 by Companies (Forms Amendment No. 2 and Company's Type and Principal Business Activities) Regulations 1990 (S.I. 1990 No. 1766).

secretary, who must not be the same person.[69] The statement contains one section for each new director and secretary, containing his name and address[70] and his willingness to be appointed; each section is signed[71] by the relevant director (or secretary). The whole document is signed by the subscribers to the Memorandum.[72] A copy of this document should be kept by the company secretary in a special file, which becomes the Register of Directors and Secretaries.

Sometimes (such as when the company needs to raise money immediately) the shares are issued for more than their face value: this is called issuing shares at a premium.[73] It is never permitted to issue shares at a discount, *i.e.*, for less than their face value.[74]

(2) A declaration that the requirements of the Companies Act have been complied with (Form 12).[75] This is signed either by one of the directors or by a solicitor engaged in the formation of the company; it is signed in the presence of an independent solicitor and is called a **"statutory declaration"**.

On receiving all these documents, the Registrar of Companies issues a **Certification of Incorporation**:[76] it is at this point that the company comes into existence.[77]

It is also at this point that each subscriber either pays or, with the agreement of the directors, leaves owing, the price of his shares. Usually this will be the same as their face value.

First Meeting

The subscribers will usually only be two in number, and on the incorporation of the company they will hold one share each. The next step after incorporation is therefore to allot more shares to the remaining tenants until the desired shareholding pattern is reached. This is done in a directors' meeting. (The manner of entering the shares in the Register of Members and issuing share certificates is described on pages 56–57).

The meeting will deal with the following matters:

[69] Companies Act 1985, ss.282(3), 283(1), (2).
[70] Companies Act 1985, s.10(2).
[71] Companies Act 1985, s.10(3).
[72] *Ibid.*
[73] Companies Act 1985, s.99(1).
[74] Companies Act 1985, s.100.
[75] The declaration is not essential, but is there to convince the registrar that all the requirements have been complied with: Companies Act s.12(3). The form is prescribed by Companies (Forms) Regulations 1985 (S.I. 1985 No. 854).
[76] Companies Act 1985, s.13(1).
[77] Companies Act 1985, s.13(3), (4).

(a) To note the Certificate of Incorporation of the new company.
(b) To issue shares to all the intended members other than the subscribers; share certificates are issued and entries made in the Register of Members.
(c) To approve the company seal (if any; since July 31, 1990[78] new companies need not have seals).[79] Where there is a seal, it takes the form of a stamp making an impression in paper: this must include the company's name.[80]
(d) To appoint a firm of accountants (known as auditors) to vet the annual accounts of the company.[81]
(e) To set up the company's bank account. The bank will have provided, in advance, mandate forms and all the necessary resolutions.
(f) To decide on the company's accounting year. Traditionally this runs from April 1 to March 31: it may be preferred to use the anniversary of the date of incorporation (for example, if the certificate of incorporation was received in August 1992, the directors may decide on August 1 to July 31[82]).

Once the extra shares have been allotted, the company secretary must complete a form called a Return of Allotments (Form 88(2))[83] and send it to Companies House. This must be done within one month from the date of the allotment. He must then send in a Form 224, specifying the accounting year.[84]

Ready Made Companies

It is possible, and indeed more usual, to short-cut the process of acquiring a company by buying one "off the shelf" from a company formation agent. Company formation agents, as their name implies, can be instructed to form a company from scratch; but most agents have a large stock of ready-made companies. Usually such a company will have an arbitrary (and often absurd) name, articles in the form of Table A and

[78] Companies Act 1989, (Commencement No. 6 and Transitional and Saving Provisions) Order 1990 (S.I. 1990 s.1392).
[79] Companies Act 1985, s.36A(3), as inserted by Companies Act 1989, s.130.
[80] Companies Act 1985, s.350(1), as substituted by Companies Act 1989, Sched. 17, para. 7.
[81] On auditors, see Part Three, Section B.
[82] For more details of companies' accounting years, see Part Three, Section B and notes 90 to 97 thereto.
[83] Companies Act 1985, s.88(2). The current form presented by Companies (Forms) (Amendments) Regulations 1988 (S.I. 1988 No. 1359) with effect from August 1, 1988.
[84] Companies Act 1985, s.224. The form is presented by Companies (Forms) (Amendments) Regulations 1990 (S.I. 1990 No. 572) with effect from April 1, 1990.

a share capital of £100 divided into 100 shares of £1 each: two of these shares will be issued to employees of the agents who are the original subscribers, while the rest remain unissued.

Thus, the purchase of the company is, in form, the purchase of the two issued shares. After that, the company must change its name and registered office and alter its Articles to the desired form, and issue as many further shares as are needed to bring ownership of the company into the pattern required. The proposed company's accountant or the company formation agent will, for a fee, assist in all these processes. A detailed example of the procedure is set out in Part Four, pages 77–82.

D. Raising the Purchase Money

In our account we have now reached the point where the landlord has agreed to sell the freehold and a company owned by the tenants is in place to receive it. The next step is to raise the money to pay the price of the freehold.

The transfer of the freehold will take place following a contract between the landlord and the new company. The price should therefore come from the company, and not from the tenants directly.

Set out below are ways of raising the price of the freehold; but some of these methods can also be used to raise money for other large capital expenses, such as replacing a roof.

There are five ways in which the company can raise the price from its members. In each case, different consequences will follow when a tenant sells his flat.

(1) Direct Contribution

The members can simply give the money to the company without any formality at all, contributing in proportion to their shareholdings. This will be appropriate when the total amount is small, so that no tenant has to contribute more than a few hundred pounds. When a flat is sold on, the tenant's shares will be sold with it, for their nominal value only: the rest of the price of the flat will be treated as the price of the lease.

(2) Issue of Shares at a Premium

If a company is being formed by the tenants from scratch, all the shares can be issued at a premium, so that enough is raised to pay for the freehold. Thus, supposing that there are six flats and that the freehold is being purchased for £1,800, each share will be issued at a price of £300, consisting of £1 nominal value and £299 premium. In this case, when a flat is sold, some of the purchase price will be attributed to the share, to represent the appropriate proportion of the value of the freehold. The precise split between the price of the lease and the price of the share will be a matter for negotiation between the buyer and the seller.

If the company is acquired off the shelf, this option is not available, as the first two shares (the subscriber shares) have already been issued at par, that is to say for their face value only. In this case it will be necessary, first, to issue further shares at par so that all the tenants have the desired number of shares, and then to issue further shares to all the tenants, in proportion to their existing shares, but at a premium sufficient to cover the price of the freehold.

Unequal Contributions

The method just described is appropriate when the freehold costs more than a merely nominal amount, so that each tenant would wish to have a piece of paper representing the value of his contribution to the price. However, it is not appropriate when there is any difficulty about one or more of the tenants contributing their share of the price; the effect of this would be that the willing tenants will acquire the further shares while the unwilling ones do not. Arguably, this destroys the entire point of the company structure, which is that the freehold should be controlled by all the tenants equally or in proportion to the sizes of their flats. If one accepts that it is right that the uncooperative tenants should be penalized by the dilution of their interest, endless arguments will rage about the appropriate degree of dilution.

Assume, to take one example, that three out of six tenants are able and willing to bear the £1,800 cost of the freehold, that the others are not, and that the six basic shares have been issued at par. At one extreme, the three willing tenants could each acquire one share at a premium of £599: the willing tenants will then be able to outvote the unwilling tenants by six votes to three. At the other extreme, the three willing tenants could each acquire 600 shares at par: they will then be able to outvote the unwilling tenants by 1803 votes to three. And there could be any number of intermediate positions. In conclusion, there is sometimes a very strong temptation to manipulate the share structure of the company as a means of raising funds and of pursuing house politics; but it should be resisted with complete firmness.

Deferred Payment of Premium; Calls

In cases where the tenants cannot all immediately afford their share of the price, a variant of this method can be used. Shares are often issued at a premium on terms that so much of the premium is to be paid on allotment and the rest "when called for". The way in which the company calls for the rest of the premium is laid down in the Articles[85] (and if these do not contain such a procedure they should be amended by special resolution at the same time as the shares are issued). A call can be for as much or as little of the outstanding premium as the company decides.

Suppose that there are six flats, that the price of the freehold is £30,000 and that each tenant can afford to contribute £1,000 straight away. In that case, the company will need to borrow £24,000 from a bank or elsewhere, and repay this loan by instalments over the next five years, together with interest.

In this case, each tenant will be issued with a £1 share at a premium of £4,999, on terms that £999 (together with the £1 nominal value of the share) is payable on allotment and £4,000 when called for. At the end of year one, the company needs to repay £4,800 of the capital, plus interest: it raises the capital by making a call of £800 on each member, and the interest comes out of the service charge. At the end of years two, three, four and five the same happens; so that by the end of year five each member has paid £4,000 in calls, his share is fully paid up and the loan is repaid. During all this time, the company has been paying interest to the lender: this comes out of the service charges. (More practically, the company will make a call of £800 on each member at the beginning of each year, to be paid in equal instalments over the next twelve months: this will then keep pace with the company's own repayments).

It is important to keep the calls distinct from the service charge, and to make sure that all the company's capital repayments are covered by calls. The reason for this is that a company is, in principle, taxable on its service charges except when these are spent on allowable expenses; and repaying the capital of a loan is not an allowable expense. On the other hand, a company is not taxable on its calls, as these are part of the price of its shares and not a form of income.

When a flat is sold, the shares going with it will be sold as well, for their face value plus so much of the premium as has so far been paid. If another call is made, it will be the new shareholder and not the old who is liable to contribute.

(3) Loans From Members

Another possibility is for the tenants to lend the money to the company. The loan from each tenant should be acknowledged in a formal document called a **debenture**. This states how much was lent by the particular tenant, and how it is to be paid back. It may also impose a

[85] See for example Arts. 12 to 18 of Table A (Appendix A).

"floating charge" on the company's property. This is a clause stating that, if the company defaults on the repayment or certain other events occur, all the property of the company is frozen to allow the lender to pursue his claim. (A specimen debenture is given in Part Four.) The document is sealed with the company's seal (if any) and signed by two directors.[86] A copy of the debenture must be kept at the registered office (usually by the company secretary)[87]; a copy must also be sent to Companies House, together with form 395 (particulars of mortgage or charge), within 21 days.[88] When more than one tenant is making a loan there needs to be a separate debenture and a separate form 395 for each lender; where the number of lenders is large, this can be done as a numbered series of debentures: the whole series then represents a single transaction, recorded on a single form, called form 397. Legal advice should always be sought before debentures are issued.

The secretary must keep a register of charges[89]; that is, an index book in which the names of all debenture holders are recorded alphabetically, together with the amounts lent: repayments of the loan should also be recorded. A special form (form No. 401) is provided for the pages of the corresponding register which is kept at Companies House[90]; but the secretary may keep his own register in any form he pleases. Where all the tenants contribute their share, the loans can be interest free and not repayable until the company is wound up. In this case, when a flat is sold the buyer takes over the loan, and part of the price is attributed to it. Thus, if each tenant has lent £1,000 and a flat is sold for £100,000, it will probably be agreed that £98,999 will be called the price of the lease, £1 the price of the share and £1,000 the price of the debenture. (Realistically, the value of the debenture will be rather less than this, and some vendors will prefer to have this reflected in the apportionment of the price.)

Another time the loans can be repaid is the next time the leases are extended: each loan can be set against the price of the extended lease. Thus, if each tenant has lent the company £1,000 and the leases are being extended from 60 to 99 years for £20,000 each, each tenant will pay £19,000 in cash for the extension, and the loans will be cancelled.

[86] Companies Act 1985, s.36A(4), inserted by Companies Act 1989, s.130.

[87] Companies Act 1985, s.406. Where a series of debentures is issued, a single entry is made in both the Companies House register and the Company's own register of charges: Companies Act 1985, s.397(1); but a separate Register of Debenture Holders may be kept in respect of the debentures in the series. This is not a legal requirement; but if such a register is kept, it facilitates the transfer of individual debentures, which is then carried out in the same way as a transfer of shares.

[88] Companies Act 1985, s.395. The form is prescribed by Companies (Forms) Regulations 1985 (S.I. 1985 No. 854).

[89] Companies Act 1985, s.407.

[90] Companies Act 1985, s.401. The form is prescribed by Companies (Forms) Regulations 1985 (S.I. 1985 No. 854).

Unequal Contributions

If some of the tenants cannot contribute their full share, but the others are willing to cover for them temporarily, the loans should be at commercial rates of interest, and repayable by instalments. These instalments and the interest come out of the service charge, to which all contribute equally; or, if the amounts are significant, the capital repayments could be raised by issuing further shares at a premium "to be called for" and making a call each year, in the same way as described before. Thus in the end, the freehold will have been paid for equally by all the tenants.

In Part Four, pages 121–132, an example is provided of a transaction of this kind, where two of the tenants advance £24,000 towards the cost of a new roof, the loans are secured by debentures and the company repays them in instalments by making calls. As this is a combination of the methods in (2) and (3), all the necessary documents for both methods are included.

(4) Loan From Third Party

If the tenants between them cannot raise the price of the freehold, the balance will have to be borrowed from outside. It will need to be assessed carefully whether the best plan is for the individual tenants to borrow by increasing their mortgages, for the company to borrow from the bank in the form of a small business loan guaranteed by the directors, or for the company to borrow by mortgaging the freehold. In this last case a copy of the mortgage deed must be kept at the registered office, and another copy sent to Companies House together with form 395.[91] The mortgage must also be noted on the company's own register of charges.[92] For more about bank loans, see pages 68 to 70 below.

(5) Extension of Leases

The last way of raising the price is appropriate in such a case where the time left on the leases has run down to such an extent that to renew them, or to purchase the freehold, would cost serious money, so that none of the tenants could contribute his share out of his own savings. Suppose that the leases have only 45 years to run, and that the landlord requires £120,000 for the freehold. In that case, the best arrangement is that, on the same day as the purchase of the freehold, the

[91] See n. 67.
[92] See n. 68.

company will extend all the leases back to 99 years, for a price of £20,000 for each flat. Each tenant will raise his £20,000 by increasing his mortgage. The lenders ought in reason to be willing to do this as it improves their security, given that a flat with only 45 years left on its lease is virtually unsaleable. However, the lenders may insist on re-surveying the flats and charging the same fees as for a new mortgage. The money will then enter the company's account and leave it on the same day as part of a carefully synchronized operation. In practice, of course, the amount charged to each tenant will be slightly more than one sixth of the price of the freehold, so as to cover legal costs and leave the company with a small float. If the money is raised this way, when a flat is sold the share will be transferred for its nominal value.

Sometimes lenders will be reluctant to cooperate in synchronized purchase of the freehold and extensions of leases, as they will prefer to see the transfer of the freehold go through and be registered before considering making loans on the strength of the lease. In a perfect world, the remedy would be to put the solicitors for the lenders in direct contact with the solicitors for the landlord, who would then provide whatever assurance the lenders require. Failing that, it may be necessary for the company to raise a short-term loan for the purpose of buying the freehold, extend the leases some months later, and then pay off the loan with the money paid for the extended leases.

Finally, the actual transfer of the freehold goes through. This is done in exactly the same way as the sale of a house, *i.e.* by contract of sale followed by land transfer, registered at the Land Registry, and will almost always be carried out by solicitors or licensed conveyancers on both sides.

The procedures described apply equally when the landlord does not own the freehold but a superior lease, and the tenants purchase this. Once the tenants have done this they can go on to try to purchase the freehold from the superior landlord; machinery for this is provided by the Leasehold Reform, Housing and Urban Development Act 1993.

PART THREE: RUNNING THE COMPANY

A. Meetings

The company has now been formed or acquired, and owns the freehold of the house, and directors have been duly appointed. We now need to speak of the purpose for which the company exists, namely running the building.

Every decision of any importance has to be taken in a meeting. Most meetings are called by the secretary on the instructions of a director, usually the chairman.[1] It is best to consult with the other members before setting a date. One way of doing this is for a table of dates to be placed on the house notice board, asking each member to tick the dates that he can do. There is no need for the meeting to be conducted with any degree of formality: quite often, it starts in the flat of one member and ends up in the pub. In theory, every decision takes the form of a resolution, that is a formal motion proposed by one member and put to the vote, and then recorded in the minutes. In practice, of course, the taking of decisions is done in a much more informal manner, and it is the task of the company secretary to extract a list of specific decisions from the welter of proposals, counter-proposals, arguments relevant and irrelevant, interruptions and significant silences. Thus, however small the group of residents and however informal the procedure, it is essential to have proper minutes of each meeting, recording exactly what was decided.[2]

There are two important points to watch. One is that the minutes of a meeting should be a list of decisions, not an account of everything that was said. If there was a discussion of whether to paint the hallway, this should not be recorded blow by blow: it is sufficient to record "It was decided that we would paint the hall".

The other point is that every decision should be taken in such a form that immediate action can follow, not in the form of a vague aspiration. If

[1] For directors' meetings, see Art. 88 of Table A (Appendix A). Shareholders' meetings are called by "the directors" as a body (Article 37 of Table A), usually by a decision taken at a previous directors' meeting.

[2] Companies Act 1985, s.382.

after discussion, they agreed not to paint the hall themselves, but to bring in decorators, there is no point in deciding "The hall should be painted"; the decision should read "Belinda and Charles each to obtain two estimates for the repainting of the hall by the next meeting".

The minutes should be drafted by the company secretary, and preferably typed, as soon as possible after the meeting. At the next meeting, the first business is that the secretary reads out the minutes, the others discuss them, the secretary amends them if necessary and the chairman signs them. In practice the secretary may well accumulate minutes of meetings and give them to the chairman to sign in batches, only putting them before the other members if there is anything controversial in them. However, the full procedure should be gone through if there is any resolution affecting the company's relations with the outside world, such as setting up a bank account, raising a loan or replacing the auditors.

It is often a good idea for the company secretary to keep a running list of all the things agreed to be done and not so far done, so that he can bring them to the attention of each meeting.

House meetings should in general be held every month or every other month. However, not all meetings are exactly the same: meetings, and resolutions, fall into various categories with different requirements about who attends, about notice and about what majority is required.

Types of Meeting

The first great division is into directors' meetings and company meetings. A company as a body of persons consists of all the shareholders, and they have the ultimate right of control. However, all the ordinary functions of the company are delegated to the directors, who are spoken of as constituting the governing mind of the company. Thus, in general, whenever one speaks of the company deciding or doing anything, it is the directors who are meant.

For this reason, all the ordinary decisions of the company are taken at directors' meetings. Specific types of decision of high importance are reserved, by the law or by the Articles of the company, to meetings of the whole company, to which all the shareholders are invited. These are called company meetings, or general meetings.

Annual General Meeting

Company meetings, in turn, are classified into annual general meetings and extraordinary general meetings. (The annual general meeting is described in detail on pages 42–43.) The purpose of this is for the company's accounts to be laid before the members,[3] for the auditors to be re-appointed or replaced,[4] and for the directors to report to the shareholders on the events of the year and receive any complaints. In the case of a small association, where all the shareholders are directors, this is a formality; in the case of a large association it is of far more importance, as it is the only chance that the residents at large have of influencing the management of the house. The annual general meeting is also the usual time for the election of directors to take place.[5]

The annual general meeting must always be on at least 21 days' notice:[6] copies of the accounts should also be sent with the notice.[7] There must be an annual general meeting in every calendar year;[8] the first annual general meeting must be within the first eighteen months of the company's existence,[9] and no annual general meeting should be more than fifteen months from the previous one.[10]

Extraordinary General Meetings

Every meeting of the shareholders other than the annual general meeting is an extraordinary general meeting. Such a meeting is needed when there are annual formalities which, for reasons of timing, cannot be fitted into the annual general meeting; for example, when accounts are several years in arrears. It will also be needed when there are important resolutions affecting the company structure, such as the creation of new shares.

An extraordinary general meeting only needs to be called at 14 days' notice,[11] unless there are resolutions ("special resolutions" and "extraordinary resolutions", see below) which need 21 days' notice.

Either type of general meeting is called by the directors; the date is fixed in the previous directors' meeting.[12] Any group of members holding a least one tenth of the shares (counted by their nominal values) can require the directors to call an extraordinary general meeting,[13] or call it themselves if the directors do not call it within 21 days of being required to do so.[14]

[3] Companies Act 1985, s.241(1), as inserted by Companies Act 1989, s.11.
[4] Companies Act 1985, s.384(1).
[5] See for example Article 73 of Table A (Appendix A).
[6] Companies Act 1985, s.369 (1)(*a*), (2)(*a*); Art. 38 of Table A (Appendix A).
[7] Companies Act 1985, s.238(1), as inserted by Companies Act 1989, s.10.
[8] Companies Act 1985, s.366(1).
[9] Companies Act 1985, s.366(2).
[10] Companies Act 1985, s.366(3).
[11] Companies Act 1985, s.369(1)(*b*), (2)(*b*); Art. 38 of Table A (Appendix A).
[12] See Art. 37 of Table A (Appendix A).
[13] Companies Act 1985, s.368(1).
[14] Companies Act 1985, s.368(4).

Directors' Meetings

Most ordinary business may be dealt with in directors' meetings. Examples are: allotment of shares (so far as authorised by the Articles or by previous company resolutions); raising loans; deciding on repairs or improvements; deciding about house insurance; setting, or altering, the tenants' monthly service charges; registering the transfer of shares when a flat is sold;[15] deciding on dates of annual or extraordinary general meetings.[16] The Articles may also give the directors power to appoint new directors,[17] though without taking away the power of the membership to do this in a general meeting: such a provision is useful in the case of a small association, where all the flat-owners are directors, as it enables a new owner to be appointed a director without the need for an extraordinary general meeting. In a large association such a provision is undesirable: the election of directors should be left to the membership in their annual meeting. In either type of company it is usual for the directors, rather than the membership, to have the power of appointing the secretary.

In a small association, a meeting may turn from a directors' meeting to an extraordinary general meeting or vice-versa at a moment's notice, provided that all the members are present. In such a case two separate sets of minutes must be drawn up, one for all the business appropriate to a directors' meeting and the other for the business appropriate to an extraordinary meeting. The last item in the minutes of the directors' meeting will be a resolution to call an extraordinary general meeting to take place immediately; the first item in the minutes of the minutes of the extraordinary general meeting will be a resolution to dispense with the requirement of notice for that meeting.[18] In some cases, such as where it is decided to create and allot new shares, the minutes will need to be written in such a way as to show the directors' meeting taking place after the extraordinary general meeting.

The signed copies of the minutes of all meetings must be kept by the company secretary in a safe place and chronological order. The traditional practice is to write out the fair copy of the minutes by hand in a bound minutes book; alternatively the minutes may be typed and pasted to the pages of the book. If it is desired to keep the minutes in looseleaf form, some sort of ring binder with a locking device should be used.

Properly, the minutes of directors' meetings and the minutes of company meetings should be kept in two separate books; and certainly

[15] Companies Act 1985, ss.22, 183, 352; Arts. 23 to 28 of Table A (Appendix A). For the sale of flats generally.

[16] See Art. 37 of Table A (Appendix A).

[17] See Art. 79 of Table A (Appendix A). For another example of such a regulation, see Art. 16 of the specimen Articles (p. 117).

[18] For this kind of resolution, see Companies Act 1985, s.369(3), (4).

this practice should be followed in the case of a large association. In the case of a small association it may be convenient to keep all the minutes in a single book; this is unobjectionable provided that each individual set of minutes makes it clear whether it relates to a directors' meeting or a company meeting, and all the minutes are in chronological order.

Types of Resolution

All resolutions passed at a general meeting (whether annual or extraordinary) are of four types: ordinary resolutions, extraordinary resolutions, special resolutions and elective resolutions. Each of these types of resolution has different formalities, and each is required for different purposes.

Elective Resolutions

Elective resolutions were introduced by the Companies Act 1989. They are required for any of the following purposes:

- (a) to allow the directors to be given authority lasting more than five years to issue shares;[19]
- (b) to dispense with the requirement of laying accounts before the annual general meeting;[20]
- (c) to dispense with annual general meetings;[21]
- (d) to alter the rule about how many votes are required to shorten the notice needed for a meeting;[22]
- (e) to dispense with the annual re-appointment of auditors.[23]

These all form part of a "de-regulation package"[24] which can be adopted in whole or in part.

The requirement for an elective resolution is that all the shareholders of the company must adopt it unanimously.[25] If it is to be passed at a

[19] Companies Act 1985, s.80A, as inserted by Companies Act 1989, s.115(1).
[20] Companies Act 1985, s.252, as inserted by Companies Act 1989, s.16.
[21] Companies Act 1985, s.366A, as inserted by Companies Act 1989, s.115(2).
[22] Companies Act 1985, ss.369(4) and 378(3), paragraph inserted by Companies Act 1989, s.115(3).
[23] Companies Act 1985, s.386, as inserted by Companies Act 1989, s.119.
[24] Institute of Directors report "Deregulation for Small Private Companies", published November 1986.
[25] Companies Act 1985, s.379A(2)(*b*), as inserted by Companies Act 1989, s.116.

meeting, there must be 21 days' written notice, and the exact terms of the resolution must be circulated with the notice.[26] Otherwise the resolution can be put in writing and signed by all the shareholders:[27] in this case, no notice or meeting is needed.

Once an elective resolution is passed, it can usually be disapplied by any one member for a given year: for example, any member can require there to be an annual general meeting.[28] It can be revoked permanently by an ordinary resolution.[29]

(More will be said of elective resolutions on page 46) and examples are given in Part Four on pages 136–137.

Special Resolutions

Special resolutions are needed for any fundamental change to the company structure; for example, changing the name of the company,[30] or making alterations to its Memorandum[31] or Articles.[32] A special resolution is also needed to authorise the directors to allot shares, except where the allotment is in proportion to the existing holdings;[33] in other words, a special resolution is needed to allow any allotment that makes a real change in the ownership of the company as opposed to an allotment made only to raise money from the existing shareholders. In the case of an ownership and management company, this power will be needed when the company is first acquired, so as to allot the right number of shares to the owner of each flat, but it is most unlikely to be needed ever again in the life of the company. It is therefore usually sufficient for this power of the directors to be conferred by the Articles for a limited period, and not renewed thereafter.

A special resolution must be passed at a company meeting by a 75 per cent. majority of those present. The meeting must be called at at least 21 days' notice, and the exact words of the proposed resolution, mentioning that the resolution is to be a special one, must be circulated with the notice.[34] The notice period may be shortened, even retrospectively; but to do this needs the consent of 95 per cent. of the members (reckoned by

[26] Companies Act 1985, s.379A(2)(*d*), as inserted by Companies Act 1989, s.116.
[27] Companies Act 1985, s.381A, as inserted by Companies Act 1989, s.113.
[28] Companies Act 1985, s.366A(3), as inserted by Companies Act 1989, s.115(2).
[29] Companies Act 1985, s.379(3), as inserted by Companies Act 1989, s.116.
[30] Companies Act 1985, s.28(1).
[31] Companies Act 1985, s.4.
[32] Companies Act 1985, s.9.
[33] The authority to allot shares, as such, is conferred by ordinary resolution: Companies Act 1985, s.80(8). However, the existing shareholders have the right to have the shares offered to them first, in the same proportions as their existing shareholdings, and at the same price: *ibid.*, s.89. This rule may be excluded by the Articles: *ibid.*, s.91, or by special resolution: *ibid.*, s.95.
[34] Companies Act 1985, s.378(2).

the nominal value of their shares).[35] Alternatively, the resolution may be put in writing and signed by all the members of the company without any notice or meeting; but in this case the decision must be unanimous.[36]

Extraordinary Resolutions

Extraordinary resolutions are of rare occurrence, and are usually only required for purposes connected with the winding up of the company. The procedure is the same as for special resolutions except that only 14 days' notice is required.[37]

Copies of all elective, special and extraordinary resolutions must be sent to Companies House within 15 days of being passed;[38] further copies must be kept by the company secretary together with the company's Articles, and every copy of the Articles supplied to any person must include copies of all elective, special and extraordinary resolutions passed to date.[39] All this also applies to ordinary resolutions by which elective resolutions are revoked.[40]

Ordinary Resolutions

Ordinary resolutions cover the rest of the business of a company meeting. They are used to adopt the annual accounts; to elect directors;[41] to appoint the auditors;[42] to create new shares;[43] to authorise the directors to allot unissued shares[44] (to the existing shareholders in proportion to their existing shares, as a way of raising money for the company).

An ordinary resolution may be passed at any company meeting by a simple majority. The meeting must be called with the proper length of notice (21 days for the annual general meeting,[45] 14 days for an extraordinary general meeting),[46] but the proposed resolution need not be circulated with the notice, though it is usual to mention it in a general

[35] Companies Act 1985, s.378(3).
[36] Companies Act 1985, s.381A, as inserted by Companies Act 1989, s.113.
[37] Companies Act 1985, s.378(1).
[38] Companies Act 1985, s.380(1).
[39] Companies Act 1985, s.380(2).
[40] Companies Act 1985, s.380(4)(*bb*), as inserted by Companies Act 1989, s.116(3).
[41] Companies Act 1985, s.292; Art. 78 of Table A (Appendix A).
[42] Companies Act 1985, s.384(1), (4). For the power to remove an auditor in the middle of the year, see ibid. s.386(1).
[43] Companies Act 1985, s.121(1), (2)(*a*), (4).
[44] Companies Act 1985, s.80(8).
[45] Companies Act 1985, s.369(1)(*a*), (2)(*a*); Art. 38 of Table A (Appendix A).
[46] Companies Act 1985, s.369(1)(*b*), (2)(*b*); Art. 38 of Table A (Appendix A).

way in the form of an agenda.[47] Once more, a general resolution can be passed by being signed by all the members without a meeting.[48]

It is possible for these rules to be altered by the Articles of the company, but only in the direction of greater strictness. For example, the Article may provide that all business must be transacted by way of special resolution except the basic annual formalities; but they may not provide that the Articles may be altered by ordinary resolution.

B. End of Year Formalities

Preparing and presenting accounts and returns at the end of the each financial year is the most tedious and time-consuming part of a company secretary's duties, and the need for these formalities is the one real disadvantage of choosing to have the leaseholders' association in the form of a company. The law requires all companies — large, medium-sized, or small — to supply accounts[49] and an annual return[50] to Companies House every year. In the case of a large trading company, this is valuable and necessary, so as to compel the directors to keep the shareholders properly informed of the state of the business in which they have invested, and so that anyone wishing to do business with the company can find all the relevant information on public record (all Companies House documents are open to public inspection).[51] However, in the case of a small leaseholders' association, where the directors and the shareholders are the same people, and those with whom it does business (such as builders and decorators) are usually paid on the spot and have no need to investigate the association's probity, it can seem a little farcical. Nevertheless it is important to keep these documents up to date, if only because a company that fails to comply with these obligations is eventually struck off the register.[52]

Much of this work can be shifted to the company's accountants. In any case they will do the bulk of the work as concerns accounts and audits, and they should always be asked for advice on points of doubt. Nevertheless it is important for the company secretary (to whom this

[47] For the members' right to demand advance notice of the resolutions to be proposed at an annual general meeting, see Companies Act 1985, s.376. Certain resolutions require special notice: *ibid.*, s.379.

[48] Companies Act 1985, s.381A, as inserted by Companies Act 1989, s.113.

[49] For the duty to keep accounts, see Companies Act 1985 s.221, as inserted by the Companies Act 1989, s.2. For the duty to deliver them to the registrar of companies, see Companies Act 1985, s.242(1), as inserted by Companies Act 1989, s.11.

[50] Companies Act 1985, s.363, as inserted by Companies Act 1989, s.139.

[51] Companies Act 1985, s.709.

[52] The registrar of companies does this if he believes that the company has ceased all activities and receives no answer to his enquiries: Companies Act 1985, s.652.

section is largely addressed) to have an understanding of the process. Accountants, like all other professionals, need to be supervised, and the secretary is responsible both for explaining to the directors what the accountants are doing and for making sure that all the statutory formalities are complied with: if Companies House does ask questions, it is no answer to say that the secretary believed that the accountant had it all in hand.

The law also requires the company to hold an annual general meeting,[53] at which the accounts are laid before the company[54] and the auditors are re-appointed;[55] but a change in the law in 1989, which came into effect on April 1, 1990, allows a private company to dispense with these formalities by a unanimous resolution of all its shareholders (an "elective resolution").[56]

The annual formalities are as follows:

(1) Every company must keep accounts.[57] This means that a profit and loss account and a balance sheet must be prepared for each financial year.[58] The preparation of accounts is strictly speaking the duty of the directors;[59] in practice they are producted in draft by the company secretary in consultation with the company's accountants and then approved in a directors' meeting;

(2) The accounts must be audited.[60] This means that they must be sent to the company's accountants (who, for this purpose, are called its auditors), who sign a certificate saying that in their opinion the accounts present a true and fair view of the company's affairs;

[53] Companies Act 1985, s.366.

[54] Companies Act 1985, s.241(1), as inserted by Companies Act 1989, s.11.

[55] Companies Act 1985, s.384(1).

[56] For the right to dispense with the annual general meeting, see Companies Act 1985, s.366A, as inserted by Companies Act 1989, s.115(2); for the right to dispense with the laying of accounts, see Companies Act 1985, s.252, as inserted by Companies Act 1989, s.16; for the right to dispense with the re-appointment of auditors, see Companies Act 1985, s.386, as inserted by Companies Act, 1989, s.119. For the procedure for an elective resolution, see Companies Act 1985, s.379A, as inserted by Companies Act 1989, s.116. These provisions all came into force on April 1, 1990: Companies Act 1989, (Commencement No. 4, Transitional and Saving Provisions) Order 1990, (S.I. 1990 No. 355).

[57] Companies Act 1985, s.221, as inserted by Companies Act 1989, s.2. Accounts generally are dealt with in Companies Act 1985, ss.221–262A and Scheds. 4 to 11, and Companies Act 1989, ss.2–23 and Scheds. 1 to 10.

[58] Companies Act 1985, s.226(1) as inserted by Companies Act 1989, s.4 and Sched. 4.

[59] Companies Act 1985, s.226(1), as inserted by Companies Act 1989, s.4.

[60] Companies Act 1985, s.235, as inserted by Companies Act 1989, s.9. For the auditors' signature, see *ibid.*, s.236(1).

(3) There must be an annual general meeting.[61] The purpose of this is for the directors to report to the shareholders on the events of the year. Where, as in the case of a small leaseholders' association, the directors and the shareholders are the same people, this is largely a formality. The company may dispense with the holding of an annual general meeting by an elective resolution;[62]

(4) The audited accounts must be laid before the company in a general meeting,[63] either the annual general meeting or an extraordinary general meeting called for the purpose. This too may be dispensed with by an elective resolution;[64]

(5) At that general meeting, a resolution must be proposed either re-appointing or replacing the auditors until the next meeting at which accounts are laid.[65] This too may be dispensed with by an elective resolution;[66]

(6) A signed copy of the accounts must be sent to Companies House;[67]

(7) The company must prepare a document called the annual return and send it to Companies House,[68] together with a cheque for £32.[69]

The Typical Case

In the most usual case, where the financial year of the company ends on March 31, and no elective resolutions have been passed, the order of operations will be as follows:

Preparing the Accounts

The company's financial year ends on March 31, and bank statements usually come quarterly: say in April, July, October and January. It will

[61] Companies Act 1985, s.366.
[62] Companies Act 1985, s.366A, as inserted by Companies Act 1989 s.115(2).
[63] Companies Act 1985, s.241(1), as inserted by Companies Act 1989, s.11.
[64] Companies Act 1985, s.252, as inserted by Companies Act 1989, s.16.
[65] Companies Act 1985, s.384(1).
[66] Companies Act 1985, s.386, as inserted by Companies Act 1989, s.119.
[67] Companies Act 1985, s.242(1), as inserted by Companies Act 1989, s.11. For the requirement of signing, see Companies Act 1985, s.233, as inserted by Companies Act 1989, s.7.
[68] Companies Act 1985, s.363, as inserted by Companies Act 1989, s.139.
[69] Companies Act 1985, s.708; Companies (Fees) Regulation 1991 (S.I. 1991 No. 1206). This regulation came into force on July 1, 1991. The mention of "£25" on the annual return form (form 363a) is therefore obsolete and should be ignored.

therefore not be in a position to prepare the accounts until the April bank statement has come in, usually in early May.

In theory, the directors prepare and approve the accounts, and then the auditors decide whether they are acceptable or not. In practice, the secretary and the auditors always make sure that the accounts are acceptable to the auditors before presenting them to the directors' meeting: this saves the accounts' going back and forth between the directors and auditors until agreed, with another directors' meeting each time. So the first step is for the secretary either to prepare a first draft of the accounts for the auditors to revise, or to provide the auditors with the raw materials and let them prepare the first draft.

It will usually be found convenient to have the auditors do most of the work of preparation of the accounts. They will not usually charge more for this than for the basic audit, as going through a draft set of accounts together with the raw materials to ensure accuracy is just as laborious as preparing a new set of accounts. In this case the company secretary will send them the raw material, together with as much explanation as is needed to make sense of it.

The auditors will usually need the following:

(a) the last five quarterly bank statements;
(b) a commentary, explaining each item in the bank statement and showing what it was paid for;
(c) all invoices for items due or paid for within the financial year;
(d) a list of all transactions creating a debt (*e.g.*, whenever a leaseholder falls behind in his monthly service charge; whenever a leaseholder lends money to the company, either by paying money into the float or by paying a bill on the company's behalf: all work done for the company during the year and not yet paid for).

When the auditors have received all this, they prepare a draft set of accounts in a form which they will be prepared to certify later. They will also ask the company's bank for confirmation of the balance in the account at the end of the financial year: the bank usually makes a small charge to the company for providing this information. They usually supply the draft in several copies, each with an audit certificate typed but not yet signed.

Directors' Meeting

Once the draft accounts are received, the chairman and the secretary call a directors' meeting, in exactly the same way as the other meetings throughout the year. The secretary shows the draft accounts to those present and answers any questions. (The next section includes a brief explanation of some accounting concepts: this is not sufficient to enable a complete set of accounts to be prepared, but should allow the secretary to understand the accounts which the auditors prepare, ask questions of the auditors and give a satisfactory explanation to the other leaseholders.)

At the directors' meeting a resolution should be recorded approving the draft accounts (assuming that the directors *do* approve them). Also at that meeting the chairman should sign the page headed "directors' report" and any one director should sign the balance sheet.[70] The auditors will normally mark spaces for signature. At least two, and preferably all, of the copies of the accounts should be signed in this way.

Audit

After the directors' meeting the secretary sends all the signed copies of the accounts back to the auditors. They then sign the audit certificate on each copy, which states that they believe the accounts provide a true and fair view of the company's position.[71] Since they have done all the work on the accounts before the directors' meeting, this is a formality and does not require any further investigation by the auditors. They then send all the copies back to the secretary, retaining one for their own records. The secretary should ensure that at least two of the copies signed by a director have signed audit certificates attached.

Annual General Meeting

The chairman and the secretary then call the annual general meeting. This requires 21 days' written notice given to all the shareholders,[72] unless they all agree to accept a shorter period of notice.[73] (All, here, means all: it is not sufficient for a majority of them to attend the meeting and retrospectively agree to accept short notice.) Copies of the accounts must also be sent out at least 21 days before the meeting to all shareholders.[74] (In the case of a small association, these copies can be distributed at the directors' meeting after the accounts are approved.) If there are debentures in existence, the debenture-holders must also be sent copies.

At the meeting the following business is transacted:

(a) One copy of the accounts, signed by one director as described, and with a signed audit certificate, is shown to those present,

[70] Companies Act 1985, s.233, as inserted by Companies Act 1989, s.7.
[71] Companies Act 1985, ss.235–237, as inserted by Companies Act 1989, s.9.
[72] Companies Act 1985, ss.369(1)(*a*) and 369(2)(*a*), and Art. 38 of Table A (in Appendix A).
[73] Companies Act 1985, s.369(3)(*a*).
[74] Companies Act 1985, s.238(1), as inserted by Companies Act 1989, s.10.

who have the opportunity to see it and ask questions. In the case of a small association, where all the shareholders are directors, this is a pure formality, as the substantial discussion has already taken place at the directors' meeting. In the case of a large association, this is the one chance the shareholders have of finding out what is happening. This process is called "laying" the accounts before the company, and must take place within 10 months of the end of the financial year for which the accounts were drawn up.[75] The copy of the accounts which has been used at the meeting is retained by the secretary, and becomes the official copy of the accounts. The minutes of the meeting must record that accounts have been laid before the company;

(b) The auditors are either replaced or re-appointed. The new, or as the case may be the re-appointed, auditors then remain in the post until the next meeting at which the accounts are laid.[76] This decision too must be recorded in the minutes;

(c) The decision is taken whether to appoint new directors. In the case of a large association, there will be an election of directors at the meeting, similar to the election of a committee of any club or other association. (The exact details will depend on what the company's Articles say about whether all the directors retire annually or one-third of them in rotation, or some other arrangement.) In the case of a small association, there will be a resolution that all the existing directors are re-appointed. In either case, the decision taken must be recorded in the minutes.

The meeting is also a convenient opportunity for the secretary to make sure that all the particulars about shareholders and directors which he needs for the annual return are up to date.

Delivery of Accounts

A signed and audited copy of the accounts (but not the one used at the annual general meeting) must be sent to Companies House.[77] There is no need to wait until after the annual general meeting before doing this, and it must always be done within 10 months of the end of the financial year.[78] Thus, the entire process which I have described will be completed within those 10 months.

[75] Companies Act 1985, s.244(1)(*a*), as inserted by Companies Act 1989, s.11.

[76] Companies Act 1985, s.384(1).

[77] Companies Act 1985, s.242(1), as inserted by Companies Act 1989 s.11. For the requirement of signing see Companies Act 1985, s.233, as inserted by Companies Act 1989, s.7.

[78] Companies Act 1985, s.244(1)(*a*), as inserted by Companies Act 1989, s.11.

Annual Return

The annual return must be prepared and sent to Companies House.[79] The annual return is a printed form prescribed by the Companies Acts and their associated rules and regulations.[80] The information required in it is who the directors and secretary are, who the shareholders are, how many shares of what kind and values they hold and whether any of these facts have changed since the previous annual return.[81]

The timing of the return is quite independent of that for the accounts and the annual general meeting. One return must be sent each year: it is always made up to a particular date, and the information must be accurate as at that date.[82] This date must not be later than 12 months after the date to which the previous return was made up.[83] In the case of a company formed after October 1, 1990,[84] the first return must be made up to a date not later than 12 months after the formation of the company;[85] in the case of a company formed before then, the first return after October 1, 1990 must be made up to a date not later than 12 months after the date of the last return sent before then,[86] when different rules applied.[87] The return must be sent to Companies House within 28 days of the date to which it should be made up. (Thus, if one return is made up to December 31, 1991, the next one may be made up to any date before December 31, 1992, but must in any case be sent in before January 28, 1993.)

The form must be signed by a director or the secretary in the space shown,[88] as soon as possible after the date to which it is made up, and sent to Companies House together with a cheque for £32 payable to the Registrar of Companies.[89]

[79] Companies Act 1985, s.363(1), as inserted by Companies Act 1989, s.139.
[80] Companies Act 1985, s.363(2)(*a*), as inserted by Companies Act 1989, s.139; the current form is called form 363a and is prescribed with effect from October 1, 1990 by the Companies (Forms Amendment No. 2 and Company's Type and Principal Business Activities) Regulations 1990 (S.I. 1990. No. 1766).
[81] Companies Act 1985, s.364(1), as inserted by Companies Act 1989, s.139. The current form allows the choice of stating that the shareholders have not changed since the last return, providing a list of the changes are providing a full list of the shareholders; but a full list must be provided at least every third year.
[82] Companies Act 1985, ss.363(1) and 364(1), as inserted by Companies Act, 1989 s.139.
[83] Companies Act 1985, s.363(1)(*b*), as inserted by Companies Act 1989, s.139.
[84] Companies Act 1989, (Commencement No. 7, Transitional and Saving Provisions) Order 1990, (S.I. 1990 No. 1707).
[85] Companies Act 1985, s.363(1)(*a*), as inserted by Companies Act 1989, s.139.
[86] Companies Act 1985, s.363(1)(*b*), as inserted by Companies Act 1989, s.139.
[87] For these rules, see Companies Act 1985, s.365(1), as originally enacted.
[88] Companies Act 1985, s.363(2)(*c*), as inserted by Companies Act 1989, s.139.
[89] See note 69 on p. 40.

It is possible to arrange for the auditors to fill in and send annual returns as well as the accounts, but it is perhaps better for the company secretary to do this personally, both because it saves expense and because it gives him more control over the process: also, he is more likely to have correct and up-to-date particulars concerning changes of shareholders, directors, or secretary.

If the return or the accounts are inadequate, Companies House will send them back together with a printed form containing a box for each of the things that can go wrong, with the relevant boxes ticked. It is worth keeping this form as a checklist for future occasions.

Before sending in the return, the secretary should make sure of the following:

(a) does the return give complete lists of shareholders and directors?
(b) does the return accurately set out all the changes of shareholders, directors or secretary since the last return?
(c) is it signed in all the right places?
(d) is the cheque for £32 enclosed?

Companies House intends to introduce a scheme soon whereby it sends each company a draft return form already completed: the company then will only have to show any corrections or changes to the details shown, and send back the form as altered.

Special Cases

This basic pattern may need to be varied for a number of reasons. The most important are as follows:

Financial Year Different

The financial year of a company depends on when it was formed. If it was formed before April 1, 1990[90] the financial year always ends on March 31[91] (with flexibility of one week either way)[92] unless it specifically chooses another date.[93] If it was formed after April 1, 1990 the financial year ends one year after it was formed, at the end of the

[90] Companies Act 1989 (Commencement No. 4, Transitional and Saving Provisions) Order 1990 (S.I. 1990 No. 355).
[91] Companies Act 1985, s.224 (3)(*a*), as inserted by Companies Act 1989, s.3.
[92] Companies Act 1985, s.223(3), as inserted by Companies Act 1989, s.3.
[93] For the choice of date within nine months of incorporation, see Companies Act 1985, s.224(2), as inserted by Companies Act 1989, s.3. For a change of date thereafter, see Companies Act 1985, s.225(1), as inserted by Companies Act 1989, s.3.

month;[94] once more with flexibility of one week either way[95] and with the option to choose another date.[96] Thus if a company is formed on August 15, 1991, its financial year will end on August 31 of every year from 1992 on. For both old companies and new companies, if the date is changed Companies House must be informed.[97]

If the financial year ends on a date other than March 31, this can have two effects. First, the work of preparing accounts obviously has to start at a different time. Secondly, it may not be possible to arrange the timing so that the accounts can be laid before the annual general meeting of that year.

The reason for this is that accounts must be laid before a general meeting within 10 months of the end of the financial year.[98] On the other hand, annual general meetings go by calendar years: the annual general meeting for 1991 must take place in 1991.[99] Thus, if the financial year ends in, say, November, there is no possibility of the accounts' being ready in time for the annual general meeting of the same year: either they must be laid before the annual general meeting of the following year, which must then be early enough in the year to fall within the 10 month limit, or, if this is impossible, an extraordinary general meeting must be called specifically to deal with the accounts. This frequently has to happen when the preparation of accounts is running late and more than one year's accounts have to be prepared, audited and laid before the company to bring matters up to date: it is not possible to have more than one annual general meeting in one year.

It should be noted that when accounts have to be laid before a meeting other than the annual general meeting, or an annual general meeting is held without accounts being laid, the auditors hold office, not from one annual general meeting to the next, but from one meeting in which accounts are laid to the next.[1]

Elective Resolutions Passed

The Companies Act 1989 contains a number of measures for the deregulation of private companies, including the simplification of the

[94] Companies Act 1985, s.224(3)(*b*), as inserted by Companies Act 1989, s.3.
[95] See n. 44 to this chapter.
[96] See n. 45 to this chapter.
[97] Companies Act 1985, s.225(1), as inserted by Companies Act 1989, s.3. The change is notified on Form 225(1), prescribed by the Companies (Forms) (Amendment) Regulations 1990 (S.I. 1990 No. 572) with effect from April 1, 1990.
[98] Companies Act 1985, s.244(1)(*a*), as inserted by Companies Act 1989, s.11.
[99] Companies Act 1985, s.366(1).
[1] Companies Act 1985, s.384(1).

burdensome formalities I have described. Among other things, it allows the company to pass resolutions to dispense with any of the three requirements to re-appoint the auditors annually, to lay accounts before a general meeting and to hold an annual general meeting.[2] These three kinds of resolutions are all independent of each other: they must be passed separately, and one may be passed without the others (see Part Four, pages 136–137 for specimen forms of resolution for these purposes).

The resolutions must be "elective resolutions". That is to say, they must be unanimous resolutions of all the shareholders. The resolution must be agreed to at a general meeting of the company; at least 21 days' notice of the resolution must be given to all the shareholders, together with notice of the meeting; and all the shareholders must agree to the resolution. That does not mean only the shareholders present at the meeting, but all of them: thus, each must either attend the meeting or sign a form of proxy instructing another shareholder to attend on his behalf and vote in favour of the resolution.[3] Alternatively, the resolution can be agreed to without a meeting by all the shareholders signing it.[4]

Once such a resolution is passed, it applies to all future years.[5] Obviously, if passed at an annual general meeting it cannot apply to the business of that meeting, nor can it ever be used in respect of years which are in arrear. The election may be cancelled at any time by an ordinary resolution:[6] that is to say in a general meeting by a simple majority of those present.

To examine the three types of resolution individually:

(a) *To dispense with the annual re-appointment of auditors.* If this resolution is passed, the existing auditors automatically continue in office until the company, by an ordinary resolution, decides to replace them[7];

(b) *To dispense with the laying of accounts.* If this resolution is passed, accounts must be sent to all the shareholders at least 28 days before the end of the 10 month period for laying accounts[8]: any shareholder, within 28 days of receiving them, has the right to require that a meeting be arranged and that

[2] See n. 56 on p. 39.
[3] Companies Act 1985, s.379A, as inserted by Companies Act 1989, s.116.
[4] Companies Act 1985, s.381A, as inserted by Companies Act 1989, s.113.
[5] For the application of a resolution to dispense with current general meetings, see Companies Act 1985, s.366A(2), as inserted by Companies Act 1989, s.115(2). For the application of a resolution to dispense with the laying of accounts, see Companies Act 1985, s.252(2), as inserted by Companies Act 1989, s.16. For the application of a resolution to dispense with the re-appointment of auditors, see Companies Act 1985, s.386(2), as inserted by Companies Act 1989, s.119.
[6] Companies Act 1985, s.379A(3), as inserted by Companies Act 1989, s.116.
[7] Companies Act 1985, s.386(2), as inserted by Companies Act 1989, s.119.
[8] Companies Act 1985, s.253(1), as inserted by Companies Act 1989, s.16.

accounts be laid before it.[9] When the accounts are sent out to the shareholders, notice of this right must be included[10];

(c) *To dispense with the annual general meeting.* Once more, if this is passed, any shareholder has the right to insist on an annual general meeting being held in any particular year[11]: if he does so, he must give notice at least three months before the end of the calendar year.

If the company decides to dispense with the annual general meeting but not with the other two requirements, the effect of this will be that the company holds an extraordinary general meeting every year at which accounts and the re-appointment of auditors are considered. As this is virtually the same as an annual general meeting (but without such narrow constraints on time), this course will almost never be adopted. Similarly, if it dispenses with the laying of accounts but not with the annual re-appointment of auditors, it will be necessary to hold a general meeting to consider re-appointment of the auditors: this too is no real saving. A company will not therefore usually dispense with the annual general meeting unless it also dispenses with the other two requirements.

A company may well wish to dispense with the annual re-appointment of auditors without dispensing with the other requirements: this saves one formal step within each meeting at which accounts are laid. A leaseholders' association which has had satisfactory experience of its auditors over two or three years will probably decide on this kind of resolution.

Whether it is advisable to adopt the whole deregulation package by passing all three resolutions at once is more debatable. A small association, where all the shareholders are also directors, will wish to do this as soon as it is assured that its auditors are satisfactory, as there is nothing that can be achieved at the annual general meeting that is not equally capable of being dealt with at a directors' meeting. However, a large association ought to have an annual general meeting, as that is the only occasion on which the membership at large can influence the policy of the association, have the accounts explained to them and elect directors.

The whole end of year procedure, as described, sounds extremely daunting, but once a company secretary has completed it for one year, taking full advantage of the advice of the auditors and of any reminder notes sent by Companies House, it will feel like a matter of comparatively simple routine to do so for all the future years. Two great principles need to be kept in mind. First, it is necessary to keep the procedural requirements fulfilled punctiliously and up to date, no matter

[9] Companies Act 1985, s.253(2), as inserted by Companies Act 1989, s.16.
[10] Companies Act 1985, s.253(1)(*b*), as inserted by Companies Act 1989, s.16.
[11] Companies Act 1985, s.366A(3), as inserted by Companies Act 1989, s.115(2).

how unpopular this makes the secretary with his fellow residents. The advantages of company status are a privilege and not a right, and it is at this price that they are available. As with most other tasks, it is when they are allowed to slide into arrears that they become really complicated. The secretary will need to emphasize that he is insisting on these formalities because otherwise the company will be struck off, and not because it pleases him officiously to magnify the paperwork of his own private empire. Secondly, it is not for the purpose of fulfilling these requirements that the company exists. The association is there to keep the building safe, sound and pleasant to live in, and must never so lose sight of this object as to degenerate into a mere society for the discussion of its own constitution.

C. Accounts

The annual accounts of a company consist of two documents: the profit and loss account and the balance sheet.[12]

In the case of a trading company, these together constitute an abstract of the substantial books of account, which together are called the **ledger**. In the case of a small company such as an ownership and management company, the ledger has no existence outside the accountants' working papers, but it is still this notional ledger which forms the basis of the accounts.

The Double Entry System

Every transaction represents a transfer of value from one account to another; there are therefore two entries in the ledger, to denote the positive and negative aspects of the transaction. For example, if a Mr Smith lends £1000 to the company, there will be one entry on the credit side of the account called "Mr Smith", to show that the company now has a debt of £1000 to Mr Smith, and another entry on the debit side of the cash account, to show that the company now has £1000 more in cash than it did before.

A purchase or sale is a little more complicated, as the transfer of the goods and the payment of money for them are two different transactions, and there are therefore (in principle) four entries, like this:

[12] Companies Act 1985, s.226(1), as inserted by Companies Act 1989, s.4(1). The form of accounts is dealt with at length in Scheds. 4 to 11 of the Companies Act 1985, as amended by Scheds. 1 and 2 of the Companies Act, 1989; Scheds. 3 to 10 of the 1989 Act are also relevant.

MR SMITH (the seller)

Dr.			Cr.
Payment	£1000	By goods purchased	£1000

PURCHASES

Dr.			Cr.
To goods purchased from Mr Smith	£1000		

CASH

Dr.			Cr.
		By payment to Mr. Smith	£1000

In the case of a cash sale, where the goods are paid for at the same time as they are bought, the two entries in the "Mr Smith" account would cancel each other out and therefore do not need to be made: the transaction therefore looks like a single transfer from the "cash" account to the "purchases" account. If the sale is on credit, the entries in the "Mr Smith" account will be made, thus showing the sale in its true character of one transfer from Mr Smith to "purchases" and another from "cash" to Mr Smith. The "Mr Smith" account will show how much money at any one time the company owes to Mr Smith or Mr Smith owes to the company. All such accounts in the names of individuals or companies are added up to show total debtors and total creditors.

A little thought should show that as every transaction involves equal debit and credit entries, the total of all the debit entries in the ledger during any period will always come to the same as the total of all the credit entries. This calculation is always made at the end of the year as a check, and is called a *trial balance*.

Different Types of Accounts

A distinction is drawn between accounts containing periodic items, such as purchases, sales and expenses, and accounts containing items of permanent interest, such as buildings or equipment. The reason for this is that it is rarely of interest to know the total of all purchases made since the company was formed; it is of far more interest to know the total of purchases for the current year. The "purchases" account (and, similarly, the "sales" account and the "expenses" account and, in the case of an ownership and management company, the service charge account), is therefore returned to zero at the beginning of each accounting year. The net effect of all the changes in these revenue accounts over the year represents the total profits of the company for that year. There is therefore a special account for accumulated profits, to which the profit figure is added after the end of each year: this compensates for the zeroing of the various revenue accounts.

For example, supposing that 999 Acacia Avenue Ltd. has imposed a service change of £50 per flat per month (thus receiving £3,600 in total for the year) and has expenses of £3,000 in a given year, just before the end of the year, the "service charge" account will be £3,600 in credit and the "expenses" account will be £3,000 in debit. Immediately after the end of the year, both accounts return to zero, but a credit of £600 (which is the net profit) is added to the "accumulated profits" account.

The Profit and Loss Account

The profit and loss account is the summary of all the accounts for revenue items, that is, the accounts which are turned back to zero after the end of the year, and it represents the calculation of the net profit figure from these items. In the imaginary case given above, it may well look like this:

999 ACACIA AVENUE LIMITED
TRADING AND PROFIT AND LOSS ACCOUNT
FOR YEAR ENDED AUGUST 31, 1992

	£	£
Service charge		3,600
Legal fees	200	
Heating (gas)	400	
Entryphone	100	
Insurance	600	
Repairs	1,200	
Accountant's fees	300	
Electricity	200	
Administrative expenses		(3,000)
Net profit		600

Accumulated profits are £600 as this is the first year of trading

The Balance Sheet

The balance sheet is the summary of all the accounts other than the ones represented in the profit and loss account. I have explained that the total of all the debit items in the accounts is the same as the total of all the credit items. I have also explained that the profit for the year is the difference between the total credit and the total debit items in the revenue accounts (as represented in the profit and loss account), immediately before the end of the year. It follows that the same profit figure also represents the difference between the total debit and the total credit items in the remaining (*i.e.*, capital) accounts, immediately before the end of the year, but on the opposite side of the equation. Thus, after the end of the year, when the profit figure is added in to the capital accounts, these will balance; and that is what a balance sheet shows.

999 ACACIA AVENUE LIMITED
BALANCE SHEET AT AUGUST 31, 1992

	£	£
Land and buildings	1,600	
Fixed assets		1,600
Cash at bank	704	
Sundry debtors	202	
less Sundry creditors	(100)	
Current assets		806
Total assets		2,406

Represented by:

Share capital	12
Share premium account	1,794
Accumulated profit	600
	2,406

The explanation of these items would be as follows:

Land and Buildings

This represents the freehold, as purchased from the landlord at £1,600.

Cash at Bank

The company started with the £4 paid by the members for their original shares (numbered three to six) the other £2, which was for the subscriber shares, was treated as paid up but in fact was left owing. The company then raised £1,800 by issuing shares seven to 12; £6 represented the face value of these shares and the other £1,794 represented the premium. It then spent £1,600 on the freehold and £200 on legal fees.

During the year it charged £3,600 in service charges, but one of the members fell £200 behind on his payments, so only £3,400 was actually received. It received bills of £2,800 (apart from the £200 legal fees already mentioned), but has not yet paid the entryphone bill of £100, so it has only actually paid out £2,700.

As a result of all these transactions, the company has £704 at the bank.

Sundry Debtors

This represents the member who is £200 in arrears with his service charge, plus £2 for the two subscribers' shares which was treated as paid up but never in fact paid.

Sundry Creditors

This is the entryphone company, which is still owed £100.

Share Capital

This is the nominal value of the 12 shares so far issued.

Share Premium Account[13]

Shares seven to 12 were issued for £300 each, representing £1 nominal value and £299 premium: the six premiums added together come to £1,794.

Accumulated Profit

Explained in the profit and loss account.

It should be noted that the entries for "expenses" in the profit and loss account represent, not the money actually paid out, but the amount due for the year. This is because the account it represents in the (notional) ledger is not that for cash paid out (which is represented in the "cash at bank" figure) but that for services received. The difference, being the

[13] For the share premium account, see Companies Act 1985, s.130.

£100 still owed for the entryphone, is shown in the account for debts owed to the entryphone company, which is represented in the "sundry creditors" entry.

Similarly, the entry for "service charge" represents, not the money actually received, but the company's right to receive the charge from its members. The difference, being the £200 still unpaid, represents the debt on the personal account of the defaulting member, which appears as "sundry debtors".

Accruals and Prepayments

As explained above, the entry for "expenses" really represents the services received. Where a bill is for services over a period, the expense is therefore treated as spread out over that period even though it was all paid at the beginning or the end of it.

Thus, suppose that a telephone bill for £70 was received on August 1, 1992 and paid immediately. Of this, £50 represents calls made in the quarter from May 1 to July 31: this falls entirely within the accounting year and no problem arises. The other £20 is the standing charge for the quarter from August 1 to October 30. Only one-third of this falls within the accounting year, namely the month of August. Therefore only £6.67 is treated as belonging to this year; the other £13.33 belongs to the next accounting year.

Thus, though the whole £70 will appear in the account for cash paid out, only £56.67 will be included in "expenses". The other £13.33 is treated as an over-payment to the telephone company: it will therefore appear immediately after "Sundry debtors" and be described as "Prepayments".

In the following year's accounts, the same difference will make itself shown, as the £13.33 prepayment will be treated as part of the "expenses" in the profit and loss account, though it will not appear as a payment out of cash.

The same concept also works the other way round. Suppose that the next telephone bill, for £80, was received on November 1, 1992 and also paid immediately. The £20 standing charge is for the quarter from November 1, 1992 to January 31, 1993, and therefore does not appear in the 1991/92 accounts at all. The other £60 is for calls made in the quarter from August 1 to October 30, 1992; one-third of this, £20, therefore counts as expenses of the year to August 31, 1992. As none of this was actually paid in that year, it is treated as a debt to the telephone company, and appears after "Sundry Creditors" as "Accruals". In the next year's accounts, £20 out of the £80 payment is treated as the payment of this imaginary debt; only the other £60 will count as "expenses".

The most important application of this concept is to insurance. The insurance year might well not coincide with the accounting year. Suppose that in our example the insurance year begins on January 1. All the premium for the calendar year 1992 is paid on January 1, 1992 in advance, but only two-thirds of it, representing the months from January to August, is included in the expenses for the year ended August 31, 1992: the other third appears as a prepayment. Similarly, one third of last year's premium is included in the expenses for this year. (If the premium has not changed, these two facts will cancel each other out and leave the "expenses" entry the same as the premium actually paid; if it has changed, the "expenses" entry will be a weighted average of the premiums for the two insurance years).

Where a major expense is likely to become payable after the end of the accounting year, a prudent accountant will often treat it as incurred within the accounting year and reduce the profits figure accordingly. This works in the same way as an accrual, and is called a "provision."

D. When a Flat Changes Hands

When a flat is sold, the substance of the transaction is the transfer of the lease from the old tenant to the new tenant. This is handled by the solicitors or conveyancers for the vendor and purchaser, and registered by them at the Land Registry; none of this requires the participation of the company in any way, though the solicitor for the purchaser always sends a form of notification to the company, in its role as landlord. This should always be sent to the company secretary: the vendor's solicitor should tell the purchaser's solicitor who this is.

Once the transfer of the lease is complete, a number of other steps are needed to allow the tenant to play his full part, and these steps are largely the responsibility of the company secretary. Briefly, these are:

(a) the transfer of the share or shares;
(b) the transfer of the debenture if any;
(c) the appointment of a new director, if appropriate;
(d) the alteration of the bank mandate;
(e) notification of the insurers.

Transfer of Shares

The old tenant will have been one of the shareholders in the company; his share certificate will usually be held by his mortgagees. Upon sale of the flat, the mortgage will be repaid, and the share certificate will be given back to the vendor's solicitor. At the same time as the sale is completed, this share certificate will be given to the purchaser's solicitor, together with a share transfer form signed by the vendor and stating that the shares have been sold by the vendor to the purchaser.[14] The purchaser's solicitor then sends both documents to the company secretary, asking him to register the transfer.

Checking the Transfer Form

Before he does this, the secretary must make certain checks. He must check that the serial numbers of the shares on the transfer correspond to those on the certificate, and that they represent all the shares held by the vendor; also that both parties are called by their correct names. If the share transfer has been sent in blank, that is to say the name of the purchaser is not filled in at all, he must fill it in.

A problem arises where a flat is being sold to more than one person, such as a married couple or two friends sharing, and the names of both are shown on the share transfer. As stated earlier, it is undesirable for shares to be held in joint names; the secretary should therefore write back to the solicitor explaining that it is not company policy to register shares in joint names, and asking for a share transfer in favour of one of the purchasers only.[15] If the purchasers still insist on joint registration, the secretary must give way, unless the Articles contain a provision forbidding joint shareholdings, as it is highly desirable that they should.

Registering the Transfer

Assuming that the share transfer form is in correct order, the next step is to register the transfer. This is done at the next directors' meeting. A resolution is passed in the form "It was resolved that the transfer of the £1 ordinary shares in the company numbered four, nine and 15 from Charles Crawford to Sardanapalus Snooks be approved and that the common seal of the company be duly affixed to share certificate number nine in respect of the said shares". The secretary then enters, under the entry for "Charles Crawford" in the Register of Members, "On [date of meeting] he transferred those shares to Sardanapalus Snooks"; then in the appropriate alphabetical place in the Register he enters "Sardanapalus Snooks of 999 Acacia Avenue on [date of meeting] acquired three £1

[14] The machinery for transferring shares including the share transfer form is provided by Stock Transfer Act 1963. This is made mandatory by Companies Act 1985, s.183(1).

[15] This notice of refusal must be sent within two months of the receipt of the share transfer form: Companies Act 1985, s.183(2).

Ordinary Shares numbered four, nine and 15 by transfer from Charles Crawford". He then draws two lines across the old share certificate, with the word CANCELLED, and prepares a new share certificate[16] in the names of the purchaser but otherwise in the same form as the old one. This is signed by two directors and the secretary in the places shown on the certificate, and sealed with the company seal: that is, the sealing device is used to stamp a red wafer seal, which is then stuck to the certificate. The certificate is given to the new tenant, who will usually give it to his mortgagee together with a share transfer in blank: the mortgagee then holds these documents together with the land certificate or other title deeds for the flat.

When there are several shares being transferred to the same person, it is purely a matter of taste whether to issue one certificate for them all or an individual certificate for each share. It is usual to have one certificate for a series of shares consecutively numbered.

Transfer of a Debenture

This will only be relevant if the vendor or one of his predecessors has lent the company money, for example for the cost of the freehold, and there is a debenture recording this.

The transfer of the debenture from the vendor to the purchaser will be a simple document prepared by the solicitors on both sides[17]; the company secretary plays no part in this. Once the transfer has been signed, the company secretary is notified: he makes any necessary entries in the company's Register of Charges (and the Register of Debenture Holders if there is one).

Appointment of New Director

If the vendor was a director of the company, it may be necessary to replace him. In any case, he should send a letter of resignation immediately after completion of the sale.

In the case of a small association, where all the shareholders are directors, this is done at the next directors' meeting. A resolution is passed to appoint the purchaser a director in place of the vendor; the purchaser then fills in and signs a Form 288, giving his name, address

[16] Companies Act 1985, s.185; Arts. 6 and 7 of Table A (Appendix A). For the manner of signing or sending, see Companies Act 1985, s.36A, as inserted by Companies Act 1989, s.130.

[17] The form provided by Stock Transfer Act 1963 may be used, and is especially appropriate when the debenture is one of a series recorded in a Register of Debentures: Companies Act 1985, s.183.

and willingness to be a director, and this form is sent to Companies House.[18] A copy is kept and added to the Register of Directors and Secretaries.[19]

In the case of a large association, there is usually no need to replace the resigning director, provided that there are enough directors left to carry on running the block until the next annual general meeting. If the Articles give the directors power to fill a casual vacancy, and it is thought desirable to do so, the directors at their next meeting follow the same procedure as the one described in the case of a small association. The new director may be whichever one of the tenants the continuing directors choose: there is no need to choose the purchaser of the old director's flat (unless the residents have such a taste for feudalism that they wish certain flats, regardless of who occupies them, to owe suit of court to the company).

As in the case of shareholders, no more than one resident of any one flat should be appointed a director; it saves trouble if this is the same person as the shareholder. It should be made absolutely clear that the shareholder/director chosen has full authority to speak for everyone in his flat and that while he should of course consult them before agreeing to any major decision, it is no part of the duty of the secretary, or of the other directors, to make sure that he has done so.

If the old tenant was the chairman or secretary of the company, a new chairman or secretary is appointed at the next directors' meeting. It is of course the new secretary and not the old who will look after all the formal requirements in relation to the transfer.

Alteration of the Bank Mandate

This is only necessary where the vendor was a director.

The terms of the bank mandate are usually that any two directors have authority to sign. Thus where there is a change of directors there is strictly no need to alter the mandate: it is sufficient for the secretary to write to the bank informing them that X has ceased to be a director and that Y has been appointed in his place, enclosing a signature card for Y. (The bank should be asked to provide a signature card in time for the directors' meeting at which the new appointment is made). Most banks, however, like to have a new mandate form completed after every few changes, so that they have all the current signatures on the same document. Every new mandate requires a resolution by the directors to adopt it and to revoke the old one.

[18] Companies Act 1985 s.288(2). The current form is prescribed by Companies (Forms Amendment No. 2 and Company's Type and Principal Business Activities) Regulations 1990, with effect from October 1, 1990.
[19] For this register, see Companies Act 1985, s.288(1).

There are two other pieces of bank business that may need doing when there is a new tenant. First, the new tenant needs to sign a standing order for his service charge. The second arises if there is a bank loan outstanding which was guaranteed by the directors, and the old tenant was one of the directors who signed the guarantee. In that case the bank will release the old tenant from liability, or freeze his liability to what it was at the date of completion of the sale, and take a guarantee from the new tenants (or, in the case of a large association, the new director). The old tenant will probably insist on the new tenant's giving him an indemnity against any liability under the guarantee, but this is arranged between the solicitors for the old and the new tenants, and does not involve the company. (See further page 70).

Notification to the Insurers

How this takes place depends on the form of insurance in the house. If the flats are separately insured, the new tenant will arrange his own policy, remembering to note the interest of the company as landlord. If there is a single house policy in the company's sole name, with the tenants' interests noted, it is sufficient to inform the insurance company of the names of the new tenant and his mortgagee; the insurance company will add these to the policy in the form of an endorsement. If there is a joint policy in the name of the company and all the tenants, the insurance company will be informed of the change, and will alter the policy accordingly; but it may need information about the new tenant's insurance history.

It is in all cases the duty of the new tenant's solicitor to ascertain the form of insurance the house has and make sure that the new tenant is covered in conformity with it. It occasionally happens that the solicitor assumes that insurance will be looked after by the mortgagee, while the mortgagee assumes that it will be looked after by the residents' company as landlord, so that the new tenant remains uninsured.

To sum up, when a flat changes hands the company secretary must do the following:

(a) make sure the share transfer is correct;
(b) have a resolution passed approving the transfer;
(c) issue a new share certificate;
(d) register the transfer in the Register of Members;
(e) record the transfer of the debenture (if any);
(f) arrange the appointment of a new director (if necessary);
(g) notify Companies House of the appointment;
(h) obtain a signature card for the bank;
(i) obtain a standing order for the service charge;

(j) make the necessary arrangements about any bank guarantee;
(k) notify the insurers.

E. Insurance

One of the most important duties of an ownership and management company is to arrange insurance on the building; contents insurance is arranged by the tenants of the individual flats, and the company is not generally concerned with this. Most insurance problems are the same whether the building is owned by a private landlord or an ownership and management company, so references to the "landlord" include an ownership and management company.

There are many possible systems for insuring a house divided into flats. The basic permutations are as follows: insurance can be on the whole house or on individual flats; it can be arranged by the landlord or by the tenants; the landlord, the tenants or both may be the persons assured; whoever is not assured may or may not have his interest noted on the policy.

Insurable Interest

The fundamental principle is that a policy of insurance only covers the interest of the person assured, though he may insure that interest for any sum he pleases. Thus, if the landlord insures the building in his own name and not on behalf of the tenants, and the building is damaged, the landlord can only recover that proportion of the value of the building which represents the loss which he suffers as landlord, and the tenants cannot recover at all. If the building is totally destroyed, he will recover the "sum assured" stated in the policy, which is usually fixed at the estimated cost of re-building[20] Similarly, if a tenant insures in his own name, and not on behalf of the landlord or the other tenants, even if the

[20] There is a distinction between "indemnity policies" and "valued policies". In an indemnity policy, the assured can recover only the loss he actually suffers. In a valued policy, the value of the building is fixed at an agreed sum: if the building is destroyed, the assured recovers that sum; if it is partially damaged, he recovers the same proportion of that sum as the real damage bears to the real value of the building. (This rule is derived from the analogy of marine insurance: Marine Insurance Act 1906, s.69(3); *Elcock* v. *Thomson* [1949] 2 K.B. 755.) In either kind of policy, there may be a "sum assured": this is simply the ceiling for any claim, and need not be the same as the agreed value, though it usually is.

policy refers to the whole building, he can only recover the cost of rebuilding or repair of his own flat, plus whatever part of the communal repair cost he is legally bound to contribute; neither the landlord nor the other tenants are entitled to anything beyond this. Moreover, it is in principle possible for the landlord (or tenant, if it is his policy) to keep the insurance money and not use it on repairing the building, unless the lease specifically provides otherwise[21] (there are special rules about damage by fire,[22] to which I refer later).

Insurance on Behalf of Others

It is however possible to insure on behalf of another person. Thus, if the tenant agrees, the landlord can take out an insurance policy on behalf of both of them: any money recovered by the landlord is then held for both of them.[23] The tenant's agreement does not have to be obtained before the landlord takes out the policy: the tenant can ratify the policy at any time before he makes his claim.[24] Whether the landlord has in fact made this kind of arrangement depends only on his intentions when he took out the policy:[25] it is not necessary for him to tell the insurance company or put the tenant's name on the policy. (If the tenants are bound by the lease to pay the landlord's cost of insuring the house, it will generally be presumed that the policy is for the benefit of both).[26] Similarly, the tenant can insure his own flat on behalf of himself and the landlord. Where there is this kind of insurance, as any money paid by the insurance company belongs to both landlord and tenant, either of them can insist on the money being used for rebuilding.[27]

The special rule about fire is this: if a building is destroyed or damaged by fire, any person with an interest in the building (whether he is one of the persons insured or not) can compel the insurance company to use the insurance money in rebuilding or repair.[28] Thus if the building is insured by the landlord alone, the tenant can require the insurance company to use the money in rebuilding instead of paying the landlord. Similarly if a flat is insured by the tenant alone, the tenant's mortgagee (bank or

[21] *Leeds* v. *Cheetham* (1829) 1 Sim. 146.
[22] Fires Prevention (Metropolis) Act 1774.
[23] There is some doubt whether this can be so except to the extent that the landlord is liable to the tenant for repairs: *Re King* [1963] Ch. 459. The existence of the special rule about fire means that he could be liable up to the full value of the property, so he is allowed to insure for this amount: *Andrews* v. *The Patriotic Insurance Co.* (1886) 18 L.R. Ir. 355.
[24] *Routh* v. *Thompson* (1811) 13 East 274.
[25] *P. Samuel & Co.* v. *Dumas* [1924] A.C. 431.
[26] *Mumford Hotels Ltd.* v. *Wheler* [1964] Ch. 117; *Mark Rowlands Ltd.* v. *Berni Inns Ltd.* [1986] Q.B. 211.
[27] See n. 26.
[28] Fires Prevention (Metropolis) Act 1774.

building society) can insist on this. It must be noted that this is a duty of the insurance company and not of the landlord; if the insurance company does pay the money to the landlord, the landlord need not use the money for rebuilding unless the lease says so.

The Noting of Interests

Finally, it is possible for the insurance to be in the name of the landlord alone, but with the tenants' interests noted on the policy. This last phrase is one which often conveys reassurance rather than illumination; an uninsured tenant who is told "your interest is noted on the policy" will go away without any very clear understanding, but with the vague impression that his interests are fully protected and that he is somehow insured on the landlord's policy. It must be emphasized that this is not the case. All that the noting of a tenant's interest on a policy means is that, before the insurance company pays a claim, it must inform the tenant. This gives the tenant the opportunity to insist on the money being used for re-building, provided that the lease, or the special rule about fire, gives him this right; but the right is not conferred by the mere fact of having his interest noted.

Requirements of the Lease

To sum up, there are four possible arrangements for insuring the building: there can be a single policy on the building for both landlord and tenants (whether arranged by the landlord or by one of the tenants), or each tenant can take out a policy on his own flat for himself and the landlord, leaving the landlord to insure the common parts. The landlord can take out a policy on the building for himself alone, with the interests of the tenants noted, or each tenant can take out a policy on his own flat for himself alone, with the interest of the landlord noted. In all cases the tenants' mortgagees will insist on having their interests noted.

The lease of a flat usually specifies which of these four systems is to be used. It also specifies who is to pay for the insurance: for example, many leases provide that the landlord must arrange insurance, but that he recoups the premiums from the tenants as an "insurance rent". In drafting a lease, it is advisable to make sure that the person with the duty to repair in the case of destruction or major damage is the same as the person with the duty to insure. Otherwise one can easily have a situation where the landlord recovers the insurance money and uses it to repair the building, thus resolving the immediate crisis, but the tenants, because they have the eventual liability for repairs, then have to reimburse the insurance company.

This situation is avoided if the landlord's insurance also covers the tenants; and if a lease states that the landlord is to insure, but can recover the premiums from the tenants, it will usually follow that the landlord's insurance is also intended to cover the tenants. To put the matter beyond doubt, the lease should provide that, where the damage is covered by the landlord's policy, the landlord must use the insurance money in repairs and that the tenant's obligation to repair then ceases.[29]

Block Policies

Where the building is owned by a private landlord, the question of whether it is better to have one policy on the building or separate policies on the flats is fairly evenly balanced. Where there is a block policy, it is difficult for a tenant to make sure that the landlord has kept the insurance up to date, that the sum insured is large enough to cover all the flats and that the insurance is on behalf of the tenants as well as the landlord; he also has no control over which insurance company the landlord uses.

Where there are individual policies, each tenant can always make sure that he is properly insured, but he cannot be sure that all the other flats are insured, so that if the building is destroyed or heavily damaged it will be re-built. From the landlord's point of view, the disadvantage is that all the flats will be insured with different companies for disparate amounts and with different risks covered, though this problem can be reduced if the lease requires all the tenants to insure for amounts and with a company approved by the landlord. On either system, problems can arise about claims by one tenant against another, such as where water from one flat damages another flat, or the contents of another flat. Partly because of the difficulties about cross-claims of this kind, some brokers will refuse to arrange single flat insurance altogether.

Where the building is owned by an ownership and management company, the balance of convenience shifts heavily towards having a single block policy, as each tenant can ensure that the policy is satisfactory by attending the company meetings and raising the point.

Arranging the Policy

Usually when an ownership and management company first acquires the freehold, it takes over an existing system from the previous landlord rather than setting one up from scratch. The lease will have been granted some time ago, and the insurance arrangements will, quite rightly, have been made with a view to what is required by the leases rather than with

[29] See *Mark Rowland Ltd.* v. *Berni Inns Ltd.* [1986] 1 Q.B. 211.

a view to what would have been ideally satisfactory. However, it is always possible for the company, with the agreement of all the tenants, to ignore the system provided by the leases and make different arrangements. The problem with this is that, after the sale of one of the flats, the new tenant may well require that the new arrangements be cancelled and the system provided by the leases be restored. Also, the new arrangements may not fit the provisions of the lease about repairs.

Therefore, if it is desired to change the system provided by the leases, the safest course is to execute a **Deed of Variation**. This is a document, signed by the tenants and sealed on behalf of the company with the same formalities as a lease, which states that from a given date the terms of the lease are to be altered and sets out the new repair and insurance provisions. Usually there will be a separate Deed of Variation for each tenant (see Part Four, pages 119–120). The Deeds of Variation should be drawn up by a solicitor.

A purchaser of a flat has two dangers to avoid. One is that, by some misunderstanding, he ends up with no insurance all all; for example, if the purchaser's solicitor thinks that the building society will arrange it while the building society thinks that the landlord will arrange it. The other is that he cheerfully accepts insurance on his flat alone through the building society, and then finds that his policy does not fit in with the other flat policies or that there is already insurance on the whole house.

Where the house is owned by an ownership and management company, the arrangements for insurance will usually be made by the company secretary. An insurance policy usually lasts exactly a year; at the end of the year it is always open to the company either to renew with the same insurance company or to find another: if it is proposed to change companies, this should be agreed in a directors' meeting. Different insurance companies often have very different premiums for policies of the same type: for the same sum assured, one company may charge twice or three times the premium that another company charges. It is therefore worth shopping around when first setting up the policy, and reviewing the position every two to three years. For this purpose, it is best to instruct an insurance broker.

Other points to watch are the type of building and the risks covered. Most insurance companies have different types of policy for purpose-built blocks and for converted houses, and in all cases the broker or insurance company should be given as much information as possible: if any information that is relevant is withheld, the company can cancel the policy. Also, the cover afforded under a proposed policy should be scrutinized carefully, to ensure that all the normal risks are covered, such as damage by fire, thieves or subsidence, and public liability. A third point is the value for which the property is to be insured. This should represent the cost of re-building, and will be something like the value of the house minus the value of the site. A builder or a surveyor will be the best person to advise on this. Some insurance companies (and building societies) will apply a rule of thumb based on the number of rooms: it is best not to accept their estimate uncritically.

Whichever quotation is accepted, it is necessary first to obtain the approval of the mortgagees of all the flats. In the case of a house still owned by a landlord it may (if the lease says so) also be necessary to obtain the consent of the landlord. Once these consents have been obtained, the company secretary can inform the broker or the insurance company, and the policy will be issued.

Claims

Anyone whose interest is covered by the policy can claim under it if he suffers a loss of the kind covered by the policy. It is however best for all the claims to be channelled through the company secretary, as all the claims will involve common questions. It is important to obtain the insurance company's approval before carrying out any repairs to the damaged property: otherwise the cost of repairs may well not be covered.

F. Repairs

As with insurance, it is necessary to consider both the possible systems which may be incorporated in a lease, and how the system should be run once the lease is in existence.

If the lease says nothing at all about repairs, neither the landlord nor the tenant has any special duty to repair; except that the tenant must keep his flat wind and water tight,[30] and the landlord must keep the house structurally sound so as to support the tenant's flat. Thus it does not follow, if the tenant is given certain liabilities to repair, that whatever is not covered by these is the responsibility of the landlord, or vice versa; it is possible that many items have been left out of account and are therefore nobody's responsibility. It is therefore important, in drafting a lease, to make sure that this does not happen and that everything is somebody's responsibility.

Individual Flats

In most leases, the tenant has the responsibility for all repairs inside his own flat; the lease also defines the boundaries of the flat exactly, so that it is clear how far his area of responsibility extends, such as below floor level or above ceiling level, and whether the outside surfaces of doors

[30] *Proudfoot* v. *Hart* (1890) 25 Q.B.D. 42.

and windows are included. He is also given specific duties to decorate, such as repainting and repapering every seven years.

Repairs to the Building

The variations are in what happens about the rest of the house: corridors, stairs, lift, entrance hall ("the common parts"), the outside of the house, foundations, roof and grounds. The best and most usual system is for the landlord to be responsible for these. Sometimes specific parts are allotted to the tenants: for example, a tenant may be responsible for re-painting the outsides of his window-frames, or the tenant of the top flat may be responsible for the roof. Sometimes all the tenants are jointly responsible for the whole house, which is highly undesirable, as there is unlikely to be any coordination between them and there is no machinery for them to act together. The other possibility is for these repairs to be the responsibility of a management company owned by the tenants, which is a third party to the lease (Part Four contains an example of a lease of this kind on pages 94 to 106).

Enforcement

Whatever the system, it is desirable that the landlord be given the duty, at the request of any one tenant, to compel any other tenant to meet his responsibilities. Usually there is also a provision that if the landlord gives a tenant notice to repair, and the tenant does not do the repairs within a certain number of days, the landlord may have the repairs done himself and charge the tenant for them. The tenants may be given similar rights against the landlord, or against each other.

The landlord also has the right (whether the lease says so or not) to carry out improvements to the house, though he has no duty to do so; a tenant may only do so with permission of the landlord.

When the freehold has been bought by an ownership and management company, the company inherits the role of the landlord in every particular. It may decide, by a majority of the directors, to do anything which the landlord has the right to do under the leases; it may be compelled, by any one tenant, to do anything which the landlord has the duty to do under that tenant's lease.

As already stated, it is important that the provisions for repairs tally with those for insurance, so that when any part of the building is damaged, the person who receives the insurance money is the person with the duty to repair. It is also important that they tally with the provisions about service charges, which will be discussed in the next section. If these provisions do not tally, or are unsatisfactory for some other reason (such as leaving some types of repairs uncovered, or not placing the liability for repairs to common parts on the landlord or a management company) it is worth changing the leases by Deeds of Variation, for which solicitors should be instructed. In particular, this question should be looked at as soon as it has been arranged for an ownership and management company to purchase the freehold.

G. Finances

Service Charges

As with repairs, there is no general right for the landlord to levy service charges, unless this is stated in the lease. The same is true of a management company.

Expenses to be Covered

It is usual for a lease to contain a list of types of expense for which the landlord (or management company) is entitled to charge. There is no automatic rule that the landlord may charge for everything which the lease obliges him to do[31]; conversely, it does not follow that if he has the right to do a repair and charge for it the repair is one which he is obliged to do.[32]

It is therefore important to make sure that all the repairs which the landlord is obliged to do, and all his other compulsory expenses, such as insurance premiums, are covered; there is often a sweeping-up clause giving him the right to charge for "the cost of complying with the lessor's covenants under this lease and under the leases of the other flats". Similarly, when a tenant is in default and the landlord exercises the right to do the work himself, it is important to ensure that he can recoup the cost from that tenant. On the other hand, he should not be given the right to charge for any improvement which he chooses to carry out; one possibility is to give the right to charge for improvements provided that he majority of the tenants agree. This problem does not arise in the case of a management company, as it will in any case only carry out improvements if the majority of the tenants agree. The landlord, or management company, should also be given the right to recoup management expenses (such as accountancy fees and the cost of Companies Act formalities) and interest on loans. Other costs, such is the

[31] *Rapid Results College Ltd.* v. *Ansell* (1986) 277 E.G. 856; *Riverplate Properties Ltd.* v. *Paul* [1975] 1 Ch. 133.

[32] *Sleafer* v. *Lambeth Borough Council* [1960] 1 Q.B. 43.

cost of heating and lighting the common parts, should also be included if appropriate. Where there are expensive items of equipment, such as lifts, that need periodic replacement, there should be the right to set up a sinking fund over its expected life.

Systems of Collection

There are various possible ways of levying service charges. The most elementary system is for the landlord, at the end of the year, to calculate the total of his expenses and divide it equally among the tenants. If the sizes of the flats are widely different, different proportions may be specified. More usually, the landlord has the right to estimate his expenses at the beginning of the year; these are then paid in instalments (say quarterly or monthly), and any difference between the estimate and the actual expenses is adjusted at the end of the year. There will usually be a provision that any dispute must be referred to a surveyor (or sometimes an accountant). In the case of a management company (still more an ownership and management company), the company usually sets a monthly service charge which enables it to keep a small float.

Some additional protection is given by the Landlord and Tenant Acts 1985 and 1987. They provide[33] that service charge costs can only be recovered if "reasonably incurred"; any estimate in advance must be reasonable; the work must be done to a reasonable standard. Where the cost of work exceeds a certain amount, two estimates must be obtained. Any tenant can require a written summary of the costs incurred in the preceding period[34] and the service charges paid are held on trust for the tenants.[35] All the tenants are entitled to see copies of the estimates, and of the written summary, unless there is a "recognised tenants' association", in which case only the secretary of the association need see the documents. Such an association may or may not be a company, and may be "recognised" by either the landlord or a rent assessment committee.[36]

Bank Loans

Where an ownership and management company has some major expense, such as replacing the roof, and has not got sufficient money by way of a sinking fund and cannot raise it from the tenants in any of the ways described in Part Two, Section D, it will be necessary to borrow the

[33] Landlord and Tenant Act 1985, s.19, as amended.
[34] Landlord and Tenant Act 1987, s.21.
[35] Landlord and Tenant Act 1987, s.42, with effect from April 1, 1989.
[36] Landlord and Tenant Act 1985, s.29.

money from a bank. There are very few generalizations that can be made about bank loans, as the terms will be imposed by the bank in accordance with its policy for the time being. Here are some variations.

Types of Loan

The loan may be either by way of loan account or by way of overdraft. If it is by way of loan account, a second account will be opened which is in debit by the amount of the loan; the loan is repaid by regular instalments paid from the current account into the loan account; interest will also be charged against the loan account. If it is by way of overdraft, no separate loan account is opened, but the company's current account is permitted to go into debit to the extent of the agreed overdraft limit, and interest is charged on the amount by which the account is in debit from time to time. Usually a loan account will be opened if the loan is for a large amount, and an overdraft will be chosen if the amount is small.

When the loan is by way of loan account, it is important to distinguish between the part of the monthly payment that represents interest and the part that represents repayments of capital. As explained on page 26, the interest should be paid out of the service charge; the capital should be repaid out of calls. For this reason, as soon as the loan is taken out the company should allot more shares to its members for an amount equal to that of the loan, to be paid "when called for"; it will then make a call each year to cover the capital repayments for that year.

Security

The loan may be secured in various ways. The most frequent is for all the directors to sign personal guarantees; this means that if the company cannot repay the money the directors must find the difference out of their own resources. Alternatively, or in addition, the company may mortgage the freehold of the house to the bank. Another possibility is to give the bank a **floating charge** over all the property of the company. This means that in certain events (*e.g.*, the payments falling behind by a given number of instalments) the charge crystallizes: from then on, it is as if all the property of the company at that time were mortgaged to the bank. If a mortgage or a floating charge is used, a copy of the instrument must be sent to Companies House together with a form 395 within 21 days,[37] and the appropriate entries made in the company's Register of Charges.[38]

[37] Companies Act 1985, s.395. The form is prescribed by Companies (Forms) Regulations 1985 (S.I. 1985, No. 854).
[38] Companies Act 1985, s.407.

If the directors sign guarantees, these must be carefully worded to show whether they are only guaranteeing the particular loan or whether they are guaranteeing all debts of the company to the bank at any time in the future up to a certain amount.[39] The second will always be true where the loan is by way of overdraft.

Complicated questions may arise when the loan is guaranteed by the directors and one of the directors sells his flat. The bank will not simply release that director from his guarantee; that would have the effect of increasing the burden on the other directors, which will make their guarantees void.[40] The departing director will usually have the right to revoke his guarantee; the effect of this is not to cancel it completely, but to freeze his liability at the amount which the company owed at the date of revocation.[41] The new tenant, if he is to be a director, will give the old director an indemnity against liability under the guarantee; this will be arranged by the solicitors acting in the sale of the flat. The new tenant may also be asked to sign a fresh guarantee to the bank. In some cases the bank will prefer to cancel all the guarantees and take a fresh set from all the current directors.

H. Extension of Leases

The Need for Extension

The main disadvantage of the leasehold system, as explained in Part One, is the fact that a lease runs down. A lease may be granted for an original term of 99 years, but after 20 or 30 years, when there is significantly less time left to run, the lease becomes far less valuable and is much harder to sell. It is at this stage that a leaseholder begins to think about negotiating with the landlord for an extended lease.

When the landlord is an ownership and management company, this effect is far less significant. The tenant's share in the company represents his proportion of the value of the freehold; so to the extent that the value of the lease goes down, the value of the share go up. There is still however a certain psychological effect on a potential purchaser, in that

[39] Rowlatt on *Principal and Surety*, (20th ed.), pp. 51 to 55 and cases there cited.

[40] At any rate to the extent of the departing director's share of the liability: *Ex p. Gifford* (1802) 6 Ves. 805.

[41] This only applies to a continuing guarantee: where the guarantee is for one particular loan only, the amount owing can never increase, and the problem does not arise. By revoking a continuing guarantee, the guarantor is saying "I have guaranteed all the loans so far made; but I am not covering any further advances". See *Offord* v. *Davies* (1862) 12 C.B. (N.S.) 748, *Burgess* v. *Eve* (1872) L.R. 13 Eq. 450. For one limitation, see *Lloyd's* v. *Harper* (1880) 16 Ch. D. 290.

"90 years plus share of freehold" looks better on estate agents' particulars than "60 years plus share of freehold", even though logically there should be no difference. Thus, once all the leases have run down to about 50 or 60 years, the company ought to consider extending all the leases; say to 125 years from the date of the extension.

Another situation in which leases need extending is this. It may be that, when the company is first set up so as to purchase the freehold from the landlord, some of the leases have more time left to run than others. In this case it is clearly fair that the tenants with less time left to run should contribute more to the price of the freehold. The neatest method of ensuring this is for the company, immediately after purchasing the freehold, to extend all the shorter leases to the length of the longest existing lease, charging a market price for doing so; the balance of the price of the freehold will have been raised by one of the other methods described in Part Two, Section D.

Thus, suppose that there are four flats, two with 90 years left to run and the other two with only 60 years left to run. Suppose, also, that the landlord has agreed to sell the freehold for £20,000. In this case, the company will raise (say) £10,000 of the price by issuing shares to all four tenants at a premium, and the other £10,000 on short term loan. After completing the purchase of the freehold, it will extend the two shorter leases to 90 years, charging £5,000 for each extension, and then pay off the loan.

Whatever the position when the freehold is first acquired, it is always desirable to make sure, as soon as possible, that all the leases have the same time left to run. This is because the tenants, by owing shares in the company, control the freehold in equal shares; this would create distortions if the leases were of different lengths, making the reversion on one lease significantly more valuable than the reversion on another.

The Price

There is no need for the company to charge the tenants a market price for extending their leases. The suitable price is affected by two factors.

First, the total amount raised should not much exceed the needs of the company at the time. That is, is should cover the legal costs of granting the extensions, and any large capital expenses incurred at the same time (such as the purchase of the freehold or the cost of a new roof) and leave a small float. For the company to have a substantial amount of money at its disposal has several disadvantages. It will have the choice of investing it, thus attracting tax, or returning it to the shareholders in the form of a dividend, thus attracting still more tax. Further, the tenants will probably have had to borrow the price of their extended leases; and there is no point, from the tenants' point of view, in borrowing money in order to invest it, as the interest payable on the loan will almost certainly be at a higher rate than the interest earned by the investment.

Secondly, if the leases are being extended by different numbers of years, the tenants seeking longer extensions should pay more than the tenants seeking shorter extensions. This is because the tenants have all contributed equally to the cost of the freehold, even though those who previously had shorter leases obviously benefited more from the purchase; so for them to pay more for their extensions rectifies this inequality.

The Mechanics

The mechanics of extension will always be dealt with by solicitors or licensed conveyancers; and the company should instruct a solicitor or conveyancer different from those acting for any of the tenants.

It is not possible to extend a lease simply by varying it to contain a later expiry date. There are, broadly, two possible methods.

First, a new lease can be granted to begin immediately after the expiry of the old lease. The two leases will then remain separate[42]: all the terms of the old lease remain valid until the date of expiry, and then the new lease comes into force.

Secondly, a new lease can be granted to begin immediately. If the tenant accepts this new lease, he automatically gives up his old one.[43]

The second method will almost always be the one adopted. One advantage is that it will be possible to review the provisions dealing with service charges, repairs and insurance and make any improvements which may be thought necessary.

I. Remedies Against Recalcitrant Tenants

There is no legal means of stopping one of the tenants from being generally objectionable. Nor can he be compelled to attend meetings and bear his fair share of the responsibility for running the house. This section deals with what happens when a tenant is in breach of one of his legal obligations. When relations have deteriorated this far, solicitors will usually be instructed; so I provide only the most general description of the options.

The obligations of a tenant in a building owned by an ownership and management company are generally as follows:

[42] *Doe d. Rawlings* v. *Walker* (1826) 5 B. & C. 111.
[43] *Davidson d. Bromley* v. *Stanley* (1768) 4 Burr. 2210.

(a) *at common law*
not to commit a nuisance;
(b) *under the lease*
to pay the rent;
to pay service charges and insurance premiums;
to keep his flat in repair;
to comply with the "house rules" in the lease;
(c) *as a shareholder*
to pay the premiums on his shares when called for.

Common Law Obligations

"Nuisance" is a technical term in law. Broadly it covers any way of using one's own property which unreasonably interferes with a neighbour's use of his property. Typical examples are allowing water to leak from one flat into another, carrying on a business that produces loud noises or noxious smells, and obstructing doors and windows.

The remedy for this is to sue the person making a nuisance. The court (usually the local county court) can award damages, grant an injunction or both. An injunction is an order to remove the nuisance: if it is not complied with, the court can commit to prison the person responsible. In limited cases, the person affected by a nuisance can personally remove it without going to court; this should not be done except on legal advice.

The concept of nuisance applies not only between tenants in the same building, but between neighbours of any kind. Nevertheless, in questions between fellow tenants it is a convenient procedure, as it does not involve the landlord, and it is an option too frequently overlooked; the mere threat of an action for nuisance is often very effective.

Obligations Under the Lease

Rent

The law concerning ways of enforcing the payment of rent is highly complex and technical. As the rent under long leases of the kind considered in this book is seldom more than nominal, this obligation is rarely of practical importance.

Occasionally a lease contains a provision treating insurance premiums or service charges as if they were rent, but this is not common in residential leases. If is does occur, and a tenant falls behind with these payments, the company should consult a solicitor.

Service Charges and Insurance Premiums

The obvious remedy against a tenant who has failed to pay a service charge or insurance premium is simply to sue for the money.

In most cases, however, the lease will provide that, if the tenant fails to comply with his obligations under the lease, the lease will be forfeited; and this generally provides a much more effective method of enforcement.

An ownership and management company can rely on a forfeiture in the same way as any other landlord; the decision to do this should be made in a director's meeting.

Once it is decided to forfeit the lease, the first step is to serve a notice on the tenant.[44] This must state what is the breach complained of; in this case, what instalment of the service charge or insurance premium is outstanding. It must require the money to be paid within a reasonable time. If this is not done, the company can sue the tenant for possession. At any time during this procedure, the tenant can apply to be relieved from forfeiture; the court then has a wide discretion to impose terms on the parties.

Other Breaches

Failure to repair and failure to obey house rules are different from the previous category, because the tenant's obligation is to do something other than paying money.

Once more, the company may sue the tenant for breach of his obligation. The court may then:

(i) award damages; or
(ii) grant an injunction; or
(iii) grant an order for specific performance.

The difference between these last two is this. An injunction is an order to refrain from doing something; for example, to refrain from holding noisy parties after midnight. An order for specific performance requires the tenant to do something positive, such as carry out repairs. The court will only grant these orders if damages alone are not sufficient to solve the problem. If the tenant disobeys the order, the court has the power to commit him to prison.

As with the previous category, it is more usual to proceed for forfeiture, provided that the lease allows it. Points to watch are these:

(a) Where the breach is one that can be put right (for example, failure to repair), the notice must require the tenant to do this.

[44] Law of Property Act 1925, s.146.

If it cannot be put right, the notice should ask for compensation only;

(b) There is a difference between continuing breaches (such as a failure to repair or to pay a sum of money) and breaches which are once for all (such as if the tenant sub-lets contrary to the terms of the lease). In the second case, the company must claim the forfeiture as soon as it knows of the breach. If it does anything which treats the lease as still existing, such as accepting rent, it has lost the opportunity to forfeit for that particular breach.[45]

Shareholder's Obligations

It should be noticed that, even once proceedings for forfeiture have been taken against a tenant, the tenant only loses his lease: he remains a shareholder in the company. For this reason, it is desirable to have a provision in the company's Articles that, if the lease is forfeited, the share is forfeited with it. An example of such a provision is included in the model Articles given on page 116.

The other possible situation is where the company issues shares at a premium "to be called for", and the shareholder fails to pay when a call is made. In this case, the company may sue for the premium. Alternatively, the Articles may allow the company to treat the shares in question as forfeited to the company. This does not of course enable the company to forfeit the lease as well.

In rare cases, where one shareholder is treated oppressively by others, he may petition the court to have the company wound up. This will almost never be appropriate in the case of an ownership and management company.

[45] *London & County (A. & D.)* v. *Wilfred Sportsman* [1971] Ch. 764.

PART FOUR: THE STORY OF A COMPANY

This Part contains the fictional history of the takeover of a house, the setting up an ownership and management company and the later vicissitudes in the life of the company. It takes the form of a complete company file, with all the documents set out in chronological order. The aim was to make a single consistent story rather than branching off into alternative possibilities, and at the same time to illustrate as many as possible of the situations described in the rest of the book. For this reason the company is shown issuing shares at a premium to finance the purchase of the freehold, and later borrowing more money from two of its members on debenture to pay for a new roof, issuing further shares at a premium to be called for as a means of repaying the loans; this illustrates three separate ways of raising money from the members: by issuing shares at a premium, by debenture and by calls. All the printed forms can be obtained from law stationers or Companies House.

999 Acacia Avenue is divided into six flats, owned by Anthony Absolute, Belinda Bott, Charles Crawford, Dahlia Dymond, Edward Extract and Felicity Fowler. They wish to acquire a shelf company called Grebecat Limited. As it is to be a small association, all six tenants wish to become directors. At present the only two issued shares (numbered, naturally enough, one and two) are held by Gregory Grebe and Caroline Cat, clerks in the employment of Reginald Registrations Limited; Gregory Grebe has been the director and Caroline Cat the secretary since the date of incorporation.

The package delivered by Reginald Registrations Limited will include an index book, called the Register of Members, showing Gregory Grebe and Caroline Cat, in their alphabetical places, as holders of one share each; share transfers signed by Gregory Grebe and Caroline Cat;[1] the share certificates of Gregory Grebe and Caroline Cat; a blank book full of share certificate forms; letters of resignation as director and secretary signed by Gregory Grebe and Caroline Cat; and, probably, a company seal. The share transfers will be "in blank": that is, the name of the transferee is left blank to be filled in later.

The Procedure in General

It is wrongly believed by many accountants that, once the share transfers in blank have been physically given to the tenants, they have

[1] For share transfer, see pp. 55–57.

immediately become full owners of the company and may proceed to allot shares and elect directors and secretary with no further problem. A moment's thought should show that this is not so. Directors can only be elected by existing shareholders;[2] conversely, to become a shareholder it is necessary to have the transfer of the shares registered by the existing secretary with the approval of the existing directors.[3] Thus where it is desired to change both shareholders and directors and secretary, there is no way in which both changes can properly be carried out by the new group of people, each change validating the other. Now, many companies, when they change hands, are in fact transferred by precisely this (defective) procedure. This may well cause no problems for years, as it is in no-one's interests to deny the validity of the transfer, and a court may well decide to take a benevolent view[4]

There are two options for effecting the changes properly. By the first route, the change of shareholders takes place first. Thus, Gregory Grebe and Caroline Cat, in their role as existing director and secretary, are asked to register the share transfers in such a way as to transfer their two shares to (say) Anthony Absolute and Felicity Fowler. They do this by noting the changes in the Register of Members[5] and issuing share certificates to the new shareholders:[6] they also insert the names of Anthony Absolute and Felicity Fowler in the blank spaces on the transfer forms. After that, Anthony Absolute and Felicity Fowler call a meeting (of themselves, as shareholders: this is an Extraordinary General Meeting) at which they accept the resignations of Gregory Grebe and Caroline Cat and elect all six flat-owners as directors. After that, the six of them meet (in a directors' meeting), accept office as directors and elect Felicity Fowler as secretary. They do this by filling in and signing a Form 288 in which each new director (or secretary) gives his name, address and occupation and expresses his willingness to serve[7] This must be sent to Companies House within 14 days. In the same meeting, they allot four more shares to Belinda Bott, Charles Crawford, Dahlia Dymond and Edward Extract. These allotments are recorded in the Register of Members, and share certificates are issued to the four of them.

By the second route, the same changes are effected in the opposite order. Gregory Grebe and Caroline Cat, as shareholders, are asked to

[2] See Companies Act 1985, s.292, and Arts. 78 and 79 of Table A (Appendix A).

[3] See Companies Act 1985, ss.22(2), 182(1)(*b*), 183 and 352, and Arts. 23–28 of Table A. Any act of "the company" must always be performed by its directors for the time being.

[4] For an example of the stricter rule, see *Morris* v. *Kansen* [1946] A.C. 459.

[5] Companies Act 1985, ss.183, 352.

[6] Companies Act 1985, s.185.

[7] Companies Act 1985, s.288(2). The form is prescribed with effect from October, 1990 by Companies (Forms Amendment No. 2 and Company's Type and Principle Business Activities) Regulations 1990 (S.I. 1990 No. 1707).

elect (in an Extraordinary General Meeting) the six flat-owners as directors and to tender their own resignations from these positions. The new directors fill in and sign Form 288; they then register the share transfers to Anthony Absolute and Felicity Fowler, appoint Felicity Fowler as secretary and issue four more shares to Belinda Bott, Charles Crawford, Dahlia Dymond and Edward Extract. The second route is slightly more convenient in practice.

Whichever route is chosen, it is necessary to hold an Extraordinary General Meeting, at which resolutions can be passed to change the name of the company from Grebecat Limited to 999 Acacia Avenue Limited, to change the registered office from the address of the company formation agent to that of the house, and to adopt new Articles appropriate to an ownership and management company. An Extraordinary General Meeting is called by the secretary, at the direction of the chairman, at 21 days' notice;[8] but if *all* the shareholders are already present (*e.g.*, in a directors' meeting, where all the shareholders are directors) they can treat their meeting as an E.G.M. without further formalities.[9]

The procedure in detail

Thus the order of events will be as follows:

(1) Gregory Grebe and Caroline Cat are asked, in their role as shareholders, to elect, in place of themselves, all six tenants as directors. They do this in an Extraordinary General Meeting (which none of the tenants need attend), and provide a minute of the meeting, containing the resolution electing the new directors. The resolution must also empower the new directors to allot shares at any time in the next five years[10] (or a shorter period may be chosen), unless this power is already contained in the Articles. There must be a separate resolution for each director appointed, unless there has first been a unanimous resolution to allow a joint appointment.[11]

(2) A meeting is arranged which all six tenants can attend. At that meeting, the following business is transacted:
  (a) All the tenants accept office as directors, and appoint Felicity Fowler as secretary. They fill in and sign Form 288 there and then. From then on, the meeting is a directors' meeting;
  (b) The new directors elect a chairman: let us assume that this is Anthony Absolute;

[8] Companies Act 1985, s.369(1). The reason for the longer notice period is that special resolutions will be passed at the meeting: *ibid.*, s.378(2).
[9] By passing a resolution to do so: Companies Act 1985, s.369(3).
[10] Companies Act 1985, s.80.
[11] Companies Act 1985, s.292.

(c) A resolution is passed to register the transfers of the two existing shares (numbered one and two) from Gregory Grebe and Caroline Cat to Anthony Absolute and Felicity Fowler (or any other two tenants; it does not matter which), and to allot four more shares (to be numbered three to six) to the other four tenants. The names of Anthony Absolute and Felicity Fowler respectively are entered in the blank "transferee" spaces in the two share transfer forms, and Felicity Fowler makes the relevant entries in the Register of Members there and then. She also issues six new share certificates to the tenants: these come from the front of the book of certificates supplied by the agent. Each certificate states the number, type, nominal values and serial numbers of the shares held by the person to whom it is issued, and is signed by two directors and the secretary: there is a counterfoil stating all the same details, and referring to the relevant page number of the Register of Members. The certificate itself has a serial number, which represents the page number in the book of certificates: it is unrelated to the serial numbers of the shares;

(d) A resolution is passed appointing the company's bankers; a form for this is provided in advance by the bank;

(e) A resolution is passed appointing auditors; already explained;

(f) A resolution is passed to change the company's accounting year, if this is desired.

(3) At this point, if all the tenants are present, the meeting can become an Extraordinary General Meeting of the company. (Otherwise, such a meeting must be called for a date in the future, with not less than 21 days' notice).[12] The following business is then transacted:

(g) A resolution is passed to change the name of the company and to adopt a new company seal;

(h) A resolution is passed to change the registered office from the address of the company registration agents to the address of the house (or one of the flats, where there are separate letter boxes);

(i) A Resolution is passed to change the Memorandum and Articles to the desired form. The company formation agents, or the company's accountant or solicitor (if any) will advise on a suitable form for these.

Resolutions (g) and (i) must be in the form of special resolutions: that is, the meeting must be called with at least 21

[12] Companies Act 1985, s.378(2).

days' notice, and the notice of the meeting must contain the exact wording of the proposed resolution. If all the shareholders (or shareholders holding at least 95 per cent. of the shares so far issued, by nominal value) are already present (*e.g.*, because the meeting follows on from the directors' meeting) they can dispense with the notice requirement by passing unanimously:

(j) A resolution to do so.[13] This is best done by having them all sign a document containing that consent. Alternatively, the resolutions themselves may be put into writing and signed by all the shareholders.[14]

(4) Proper minutes must be drafted and signed in respect of both the directors' meeting and the Extraordinary General Meeting, containing all the resolutions (b) and (j) above. Alternatively, the resolutions can be typed out in advance and signed by all present.
(The accountant will provide these on request.)

(5) Within 14 days of the meeting, Felicity Fowler as secretary sends the Form 288 and copies of all the resolutions to the Registrar of Companies, together with a fee of £50[15] for the change of name. A copy of the Form 288 should be kept and added to the Register of Directors and Secretaries. She also completes and sends in a form called a Return of Allotments (Form 88(2)),[16] recording the issue of the four new shares, and (if applicable) a Form 225(1),[17] showing the new accounting year.

(6) The Registrar of Companies sends a new Certificate of Incorporation, giving the company's new name.[18]

Specimens of these documents are given on pages 109 to 119 below.

Large Associations

In the case of a large association, where it is not desired to make all the shareholders directors, the same procedure is followed except what the Extraordinary General Meeting will not follow immediately upon the director's meeting, but will be a separate occasion, with proper notice

[13] Companies Act 1985, s.369(3).
[14] Companies Act 1985, s.381A, as inserted by Companies Act 1989, s.113.
[15] Companies Act 1985, s.708, and Companies (Fees) Regulations 1991 (S.I. 1991 No. 1206).
[16] Companies Act 1985, s.88(2). The current form is prescribed by Companies (Forms) (Amendments) Regulations 1988 (S.I. 1988 No. 1351) with effect from August 1, 1990.
[17] Prescribed by Companies (Forms) (Amendment) Regulations 1990 (S.I. 1990 No. 572) with effect from April 1, 1990.
[18] Companies Act 1985, s.28(6).

given to all the shareholders. Also, each tenant, before being issued with his share certificate, must be made to sign a form saying "I [name] apply to the directors of [company] for [x] shares to be allotted to me [at par/at a premium of £y]". The Form 288 and a copy of the resolution to allot shares will be sent to the Registrar of Companies within 14 days of the directors' meeting;[19] copies of the remaining resolutions will be sent within 15 days of the Extraordinary General Meeting.[20]

Another option is to ask the formation agents to carry out the changes of name, registered office, Memorandum and Articles, for an extra fee. In this case, these three resolutions will be passed by Gregory Grebe and Caroline Cat in an Extraordinary General Meeting at the same time as they appoint the tenants directors; minutes of these resolutions will then accompany the package delivered by the agents.

As stated, the accountant will guide the tenants through these processes and assist in drafting Articles and resolutions. However, it is important for the tenants to check independently that each of the steps described has been taken. Otherwise it is possible that whoever is advising will scamp or telescope some of these steps, or at best provide one of the tenants with a neatly typed series of resolutions to sign without calling any meeting at all; which, if one thinks about it, is an invitation to forgery.

Opening a Bank Account

The company then needs to open a bank account. During the formation or acquisition process, the secretary will have been in touch with the local bank manager, who will provide the necessary forms. These will include a bank mandate signed by all the directors, and a signature card for each. It needs to be decided who is empowered to sign cheques: the usual system is that they can be signed by the secretary and one other director; and in any case the secretary will have custody of the cheque book. In the case of a very large association, it may be worth while to appoint a treasurer distinct from the secretary.

A. Specimen Lease Not Providing For Residents' Association

THIS LEASE is made the Twenty seventh day of September One thousand nine hundred and sixty seven BETWEEN: TERENCE SEIGNIOR of 17 Manor Road Dale in the County of Barset (hereinafter called "the Lessor") of the first part and LETITIA MALAPROP OF 80 Queen Square Bath in the County of Somerset (hereinafter called "the Lessee") of the second part

[19] Companies Act 1985, s.288(2).
[20] Companies Act 1985, s.380(1).

WHEREAS:

(1) The Lessor is the owner of freehold land situate at and known as 999 Acacia Avenue in Dale in the County of Barset registered at H.M. Land Registry under the number ——— and hereinafter called "the Site"

(2) The Lessor has agreed for the consideration hereinafter appearing to demise to the Lessee (*inter alia*) one of the Flats on the terms hereinafter contained and have demised or will demise all the other Flats on similar terms and subject to similar covenants on the part of the lessee and conditions as are contained in this Lease (subject only to such variations as any special circumstances may require) to the intent that the lessee for the time being of each of the said Flats may be able to enforce against the lessee of every other of the said Flats any of the said covenants a breach of which adversely affects him.

NOW THIS DEED WITNESSETH as follows namely:

1. IN this Lease the following expressions have the following meanings namely:

(a) "The Plan" means the plan annexed hereto;

(b) "The Site" means the land shown edged red on the Plan together with the house erected on part thereof divided into six flats with communal entrance and stairway and known as 999 Acacia Avenue aforesaid;

(c) "The Block" means the block of flats in which the flat hereby demised is comprised;

(d) "The Flat" means the flat demised by this Lease;

(e) "The Flats" means the six flats comprising the Block, including the Flat hereby demised;

(f) "The Reserved Premises" means the Site (including the Reserved Services but except all the Flats);

(g) "The Reserved Services" means the sewers drains water pipes tanks gutters wires cable conduits and other like means of passage or disposal or storage of soil water gas electricity television and other services and of soil smoke rubbish and other material or other matter which are now or may within eighty years from the date of the commencement of the term created by this Lease (which said period of eighty years shall be the perpetuity period applicable to this lease) be in or under the Site or any part thereof (hereinafter together called "service installations") not being Leased Services or Excluded Services as hereinafter defined:

(i) "The Leased Services" means service installations used or intended for use exclusively for the benefit of the demised premises;

(ii) "The Excluded Services" means service installations used or intended exclusively for use by any other of the Flats and situate within the demised premises.

2. IN consideration of the sum of THREE THOUSAND TWO HUNDRED POUNDS (£3,200–0–0) now paid by the Lessee to the Lessor (the receipt whereof the Lessor hereby acknowledges) and of the rent and covenants on the part of the Lessee hereinafter reserved and contained the Lessor HEREBY DEMISES unto the Lessee ALL THAT Flat described in the first part of the First Schedule hereto (hereinafter called "the demised premises") TOGETHER WITH the rights described in the second part of that Schedule and EXCEPTING AND RESERVING the rights described in the third part of that Schedule TO HOLD the same unto the Lessees for the term of NINETY NINE YEARS calculated from the Twenty–fourth day of June One thousand nine hundred and sixty seven

YIELDING AND PAYING therefor in advance during the said term and proportionately for any fraction of a year the net yearly rent of FIVE POUNDS (£5–0–0) on the Twenty fourth day of June in each year without any deduction the first of such payments or a due proportion thereof to be made on the date of this Lease.

3. The Lessees (if more than one) hereby declare that they shall hold the demised premises upon trust to sell the same with power to postpone the sale thereof and shall hold the net proceeds of sale and the other money applicable as capital and the net rents and profits thereof until sale upon trust for themselves as joint tenants.

4. THE Lessee HEREBY COVENANTS (and if more than one jointly and severally) with the Lessor and with each of the other lessees for the time being of any of the Flats that the Lessee will observe and perform (a) the covenants on the part of the Lessee set out in the Second Schedule hereto and (b) the regulations set out in the Third Schedule hereto.

5. THE Lessor hereby covenants with the Lessee:

(1) That the Lessee paying the rents hereinbefore reserved and performing and observing the covenants conditions and agreements on the part of the Lessee hereinbefore contained shall peaceably hold and enjoy the demised premises for the term hereby granted without any interruption by the Lessor or any person lawfully claiming under or in trust for him;

(2) That the Lessor has not granted and will not hereafter grant a Lease of any of the Flats except to a lessee who has entered or will enter into similar covenants and undertake similar obligations to those on the part of the Lessee herein contained so far as applicable and that the Lessor will himself be under like obligations in respect of any of the Flats for the time being undemised;

(3) That the Lessor will upon request in writing of the Lessee enforce the covenants entered into or to be entered into by the lessee of any other of the Flats upon the Lessee agreeing by deed in such form as the Lessor may reasonably require to indemnify the Lessor against all costs and expenses;

(4) That the Lessor will perform and observe the covenants on the part of the Lessor set out in the Fourth Schedule hereto PROVIDED THAT the Lessor shall not be liable to any Lessee or any invitee or licensee of the Lessee for or in any way arising out of any breach or non-performance on his part of any of the said covenants unless such breach or non-performance shall have been specifically notified to the Lessor in writing and the Lessor shall have failed to remedy such breach or non-performance within reasonable time of receiving such notice.

6. PROVIDED ALWAYS that:

(i) If the said rent hereby reserved or any part thereof shall be unpaid for Twenty one days after becoming payable (whether the same shall have been formally demanded or not) or if any of the covenants on the part of the Lessee herein contained shall not be performed or observed then and in any such case it shall be lawful for the Lessor or any person or persons authorised by him in that behalf at any time thereafter to re-enter upon the demised premises or any part thereof in the name of the whole and thereupon this demise shall absolutely determine but without prejudice to any right of action or remedy of the Lessor in respect of any breach of the covenants by the Lessee hereinbefore contained;

(ii) All rights and obligations of the Lessor and Lessee respectively under these presents shall be incident to the reversion expectant on this Lease and the leasehold interest thereby created respectively and shall pass and devolve therewith on any alienation or devolution thereof

(iii) Any notice hereby required or authorised to be given to the Lessor the Lessee shall be in writing and may be given in any of the modes provided by Section 196 of the Law of Property Act 1925.

7. IT IS HEREBY CERTIFIED that the transaction hereby effected does not form part of a larger transaction or series of transactions in respect of which the amount or value or the aggregate amount or value of the consideration other than rent exceeds Five thousand five hundred pounds (£5,500).

IN WITNESS whereof the Lessor and the Lessee have hereunto set their hands and seals the day and year first above written.

THE FIRST SCHEDULE

FIRST ALL THAT Flat being Flat Number One in the basement of the Site (site of such Flat being shown coloured red on the Plan) including the Balcony (if any) and the joists or beams on which the floors of the Flat are laid and the interior faces and the glass in the windows of the exterior walls and the interior face and the locks of the entrance door but excluding: (i) Any other part of such external walls and entrance door; (ii) The joists or beams securing the ceilings of the Flat; (iii) all parts of the Site above such joists or beams; and; (iv) all parts of the Site below the joists or beams on which the floors of the Flat are laid TOGETHER WITH:

(1) The right of passage and running storage and disposal of gas, water, electricity, television and other services and of soil, smoke, rubbish and other material in and through and by means of the Reserved Services and the Leased Services and all necessary rights of entry for the purpose of inspecting maintaining and repairing and renewing the same subject to the person exercising such right making good all damage thereby caused but without compensation for any inconvenience PROVIDED that the right to the passage of water shall so far as the same relates to the supply of mains water (whether or not through any tank or cistern) to the demised premises be subject to the payment by the Lessee to the Lessor or to the Statutory Water Authority (as the case may require) of the water rate assessed in respect of the demised premises or (if and so far as the water rate is not separately assessed upon the demised premises or some part thereof) of a fair proportion of such assessment to be determined by the Lessor or his surveyor;

(2) The right at all reasonable times with or without workmen and others to enter upon any part of the Site and the Reserved Premises for the purpose of cleansing and executing repairs or alterations to the demised premises provided that the Lessee shall only exercise the rights of entering other parts of the Site at reasonable times during the hours of daylight and after giving reasonable notice of his intention to enter (except in the case of emergency) and upon the terms that the Lessee shall make good any damage thereby occasioned but so that the Lessee shall not be liable for any temporary interference with the convenience of the lessee or occupier of the premises so entered upon.

(3) All such rights of support and protection from the elements and (subject as hereinafter provided) light and air for the demised premises over and from other parts of the Site and the Reserved Premises as are now enjoyed or intended to be enjoyed by the demised premises provided that the Lessor or his tenant may at any time hereafter build upon the Site and rebuild or alter any of the parts of the Site notwithstanding any interference thereby occasioned to the access of light or air to any part of the demised premises.

(4) The right (in common with the Lessor and all persons deriving title under the Lessor and the lessees for the time being of all the other Flats) for the Lessee his servants agents and licensees and invitees to use in accordance with such reasonable regulations as the Lessor may from time to time impose the entrance way entrance hall staircases landings passages and other communal services of the Site and the roads, footpaths, drives and gardens and communal parking areas of the Site for all purposes connected with the benefical user of the demised premises

(5) The right in common with the Lessor and all persons authorised by the Lessor to use the communal dustbin area coloured orange on the Plan.

EXCEPTING AND RESERVING unto the Lessor and each lessee of every other of the Flats

(1) All such rights of support and protection from the elements and light and air from and over the demised premises for the other parts of the Site as are now enjoyed or intended to be enjoyed by such other parts.

(2) The right of passage and running storage and disposal of gas, water, electricity, television, radio and other services and of soil, smoke, rubbish and other materials in and through and by means of the Reserved Services and the Excluded Services and the right with or without workmen and others on reasonable prior notice in the daytime (except in case of emergency) to enter the demised premises or any part thereof for the purpose of inspection maintenance repair or renewal of the said services or any of them subject to the person exercising such right making good all damage thereby caused but without compensation for any temporary inconvenience.

(3) The right with or without workmen and others at all reasonable times on reasonable prior notice in the day time (except in the case of emergency) to enter into and upon the demised premises or any part thereof to inspect cleanse repair alter renew or improve any part of the Reserved Premises or of any other of the Flats the person exercising such rights making good all damage thereby caused but without compensation for any temporary inconvenience.

(4) The right for the Lessor to decorate or redecorate (to the exclusion of the Lessee whose obligations shall not extend thereto) the outside faces of the external walls and the entrance doors of the Flat.

THE SECOND SCHEDULE
COVENANTS BY THE LESSEE

(a) To pay the rent hereby reserved at the time and in the manner aforesaid without any deduction whatsoever

(b) To pay and discharge all existing and future rates taxes assessments and outgoings whether parliamentary local or otherwise now or hereafter imposed or charged upon the demised premises or any part thereof or on the Lessor or Lessee or occupier in respect thereof PROVIDED THAT where any such outgoings are charged upon or payable in respect of the Block as a whole the Lessee's liability shall be limited to a due proportion of such outgoings to be determined (failing agreement) by the Lessor or his surveyors.

(c) To do all such works or other things as shall under any statutory or any other authority be required to be done in respect of the demised premises whether by the owner or occupier thereof and to conform in all respects with the provisions of and regulations made under any general or local Act of Parliament which may be applicable to the demised premises or any part thereof AND to keep the Lessor fully indemnified in respect thereof

(d) From time to time and at all times during the said term to keep in good and substantial repair and condition the demised premises and the landlord's fixtures and fittings and the Leased Services therein

(e) To prepare and paint with two coats of best quality paint in a workmanlike manner all the wood iron and other parts of the interior of the demised premises usually painted in every seventh year of the said term and in the last year of the term as well and after every painting to redecorate in like manner all such parts as are usually so dealt with as at the date hereto and stop whiten and colour all such parts as are usually so dealt with and to repaper the parts usually papered with suitable paper of as good quality as that in use at the date hereof.

(f) To make good at the Lessee's expense to the satisfaction of the Lessor or his surveyor any damage occasioned by the exercise of the rights demised to the Lessee.

(g) To permit the Lessor and the lessee or occupier of any other of the Flats and their respective agents or workmen at any time or times during the said term at reasonable hours in the daytime upon giving reasonable notice (except in the case of emergency) to enter upon the demised premises for the purpose of inspecting cleansing and for executing repairs or alterations upon or to the Reserved Premises or any other of the Flats without unreasonable delay and making good to the Lessee all damage thereby occasioned but without compensation for any temporary damage or inconvenience.

(h) Not at any time during the said term to make any structural addition or alteration to the demised premises not to remove alter or resposition any partition wall or walls or make any openings in any of them without the previous written consent of the Lessor and not to carry out any operation constituting development within the meaning of the Town and Country Planning Acts or any statutory amendment or replacement thereof or any Building Regulation for the time being in force.

(i) Not to use or occupy or permit the Flat to be used or occupied for any purpose whatsoever other than as private residence in the occupation of a single family.

(j) To insure the Flat and keep it insured against loss or damage by fire storm impact or aircraft and such other risks as are included in a Flat Owner's Comprehensive Policy with such insurance company of repute as the Lessor may decide and through such agency as the Lessor may nominate to an amount equal to the full replacement value thereof plus Surveyor's and Architect's fees and to effect such other insurance of or in respect of property owner's liability or other risks as the Lessor shall consider reasonable and to make all payments necessary for these purposes within seven days after the same become payable and to produce the Lessor on demand the policies of such insurance and the

receipts for such payments. Such insurance shall be effected in the joint names of the Lessor and the Lessee with regard to the demised premises.
(k) Not to store petrol or other inflammable material on the demised premises.
(l) Not to do or permit any waste, spoil or destruction to or upon the demised premises not to do or permit any act or thing which shall or may be or become a nuisance, damage, annoyance or inconvenience to the Lessor or his tenant or the tenants or occupiers of adjoining premises and in particular of any other Flats or to the neighbourhood or whereby any insurance for the time being effected on the demised premises may be rendered void or voidable or whereby the rate of premium may be increased.
(m) From time to time during the said term to pay all costs charges and expenses incurred by the Lessor in abating a nuisance arising from any act default or neglect of the Lessee and executing all such works as may be necessary for abating a nuisance in obedience to a notice served by a Local Authority.
(n) (i) To permit the Lessor or his agents with or without workmen and others at all reasonable times upon giving reasonable notice (except in the case of emergency) during the said term at convenient hours in the daytime to enter the demised premises to view and examine the state and condition of the demised premises and all decays, defects and wants of repair as shall be then and there found for which the Lessee may be liable hereunder; (ii) to remedy repair and amend any such decays, defects and wants of repair within two calendar months next following the service of notice in writing by or on behalf of the Lessor requiring him so to do.
(o) That if the Lessee shall make default in any of the covenants hereinbefore contained for or relating to the repair or painting of the demised premises it shall be lawful for the Lessor to enter upon the demised premises and repair the same at the expense of the Lessee in accordance with the covenants and provisions of these presents and the expense of such repairs shall be repaid by the Lessee to the Lessor on demand with interest at five pounds per cent per annum from the date of demand;
(p) All the demised premises painted repaired and kept as aforesaid at the expiration or sooner determination of the said term quietly to yield up unto the Lessor TOGETHER with all additions and improvements made thereto in the meantime and all fixtures of every kind in or upon the demised premises except tenant's fixtures;
(q) (i) To pay the Lessor all costs, charges and expenses (including legal costs and fees payable to a Surveyor) which may be incurred by the Lessor incidental to the preparation and service of a notice under section 146 of the Law of Property Act 1925 (whether or not any right of re-entry or forfeiture has been waived by the Lessor or the Lessee has been relieved under the provisions of the said Act) in respect of the demised

premises whether incurred in or in contemplation of proceedings under Section 146 or 147 of that Act;

(ii) To pay the Lessor all expenses including Solicitors' costs and Surveyors' fees incurred by the Lessor of and incidental to the service of all notices and Schedules relating to wants of repair to the demised premises accrued not later than the expiration or sooner determination of the term hereby granted but whether such Notices and Schedules be served before or after such expiration or sooner determination;

(r) Not during the last seven years of the said term (except by Will) to assign or underlet or part with possession of the demised premises or any part thereof without the prior written consent of the Lessor;

(s) Within 21 days after every assignment devolution disposition charge underlease or agreement for tenancy of the demised premises or any part thereof whether by express deed or by operation or implication of law TO give to the Lessor's Solicitors notice in writing thereof specifying in such notice the name and address of the assignee or personal representative or other person in or to whom the term or any part thereof may have become vested or charged and (if called upon) to produce the assignment probate letters of administration charge, counterpart lease or agreement for tenancy or other evidence of devolution at the office of the said Solicitors for registration and to pay the said Solicitors a fee of two pounds and ten shillings in respect of each such registration;

(t) Duly to pay to the Lessor at the times and in the manner set out in the Fifth Schedule hereto all such sums as shall under the provisions of that Schedule be payable in respect of the demised premises.

THE THIRD SCHEDULE
REGULATIONS TO BE OBSERVED BY THE LESSEE

1. The floors of all rooms of the Flat (except bathroom kitchen and W.C.) shall be suitably carpeted and all reasonable precautions taken (including the placing of rubber or cork insulators) to deaden the sound of sewing machines dish washers washing machines or other household machines radios gramophones television sets pianos or other musical instruments;

2. No musical instrument wireless set television set loudspeaker or other mechanical instrument of any kind shall be played or used or household machines used or noise made between the hours of 12 midnight and eight o'clock in the morning or between such other times as the Lessor shall decide nor at any time so as to cause annoyance or disturbance to the occupier of any other Flat;

3. The communal parts of the Site shall not be encumbered with bicycles prams boxes or other objects and the entrance doors to Flats shall be kept closed;

4. No dirt rubbish rags or other refuse shall be thrown into sinks baths lavatories cisterns or waste or soil pipes in the Flat;

5. No name writing drawing signboard notice placard or advertisement of any kind shall be put on or in any windows or the exterior of the Flat (other than a notice to be approved by the Lessor indicating that a particular Flat is to be sold or let);
6. The communal parts of the Site shall be used as quietly as possible and in particular between the hours of 12 midnight and eight o'clock in the morning;
7. No children shall be allowed to play and no undue noise shall be made in the communal parts of the Site;
8. No external wireless or television aerials shall be erected by the Lessee on any part of the demised premises;
9. No clothes window boxes flower pots or other articles shall be hung or exposed and no mat or carpet shall be shaken at the windows of the flat;
10. No bird dog or other animal shall be kept on the demised premises without the previous written consent of the Lessor and should such permission be given then dogs should be kept on the lead in all parts of the Reserved Premises provided nevertheless that such consent may be revoked at any time if in the opinion of the Lessor the bird dog or animal shall become a nuisance to the owner of any other Flat.
11. Each lessee shall curtain and keep curtained all the windows of his Flat.

THE FOURTH SCHEDULE
COVENANTS BY THE LESSOR

1. At all times during the term hereby granted to maintain the Reserved Premises in good and substantial repair and condition (except as regards damage caused by or resulting from any act or default of the Lessee or any person deriving title under the Lessee) making all necessary renewals and replacements as may be required thereto.
2. To redecorate the interior communal parts of the Site in a proper and workmanlike manner at least once in every five years and to paint the exterior wood and iron and cement work of the Site and all additions thereto with two coats of exterior quality paint in a proper and workmanlike manner at least once in every three years of the term hereby granted.
3. To keep the entrance halls landings and staircases of the Site clean and suitably lighted and the services thereof in good working order and condition.
4. To maintain the Reserved Premises in good order and condition with the drives properly maintained and the gardens properly planted with shrubs in due season and free from weeds and clean and tidy and free from all obstruction and carefully to preserve the timber trees and all ornamental trees and replace such of the shrubs or trees as may die or require replacing.

5. To employ such staff or contractors as may be reasonably required to carry out all necessary works of maintenance cleaning and repairs and such other duties as are necessary for the proper running and management of the Reserved Premises.

THE FIFTH SCHEDULE
PROVISIONS GOVERNING MAINTENANCE CHARGES

1. The maintenance charge for the demised premises shall be a sum equal to one sixth (hereinafter called "the appropriate proportion") of the aggregate cost to the Lessor of (a) complying with the Lessor's covenants in this Lease and of the corresponding covenants in the leases of the other Flats; and (b) providing such reserves for future anticipated maintenance as the Lessor shall from time to time think desirable.
2. The cost to the Lessor of complying with his covenants shall be deemed (without prejudice to the generality of the foregoing words) to include:

(a) The costs of and incidental to compliance by the Lessor with every notice regulation or order of any competent local or other authority;
(b) All fees and charges and expenses payable to any solicitor accountant surveyor agent or architect employed or instructed in connection with any question arising on the maintenance or management of the Site and the curtilage or the Reserved Premises or the ascertainment of the maintenance charge;
(c) The cost of insuring against claims of third parties;
(d) The cost of purchasing or hiring any equipment used for the benefit of residents of the Flats;
(e) All administration accountancy legal and other costs of the Lessor in carrying on his business in relation to the Site.

3. (i) The Lessee shall on account of the maintenance charge pay to the Lessor on the signing hereof and thereafter on the Twenty fifth day of December and the Twenty fourth day of June in each year of the said term a sum (hereinafter called "the minimum payment") determined as hereinafter provided the second of such payments to be made on the twenty fifth day of December next;
(ii) The minimum payment shall be the sum of FORTY POUNDS (£40) or such greater sum as the Lessor may from time to time determine to be the appropriate proportion of the amount reasonably required to enable the Lessor to cover his outgoings in relation to the Site for the relevant year;
(iii) The Lessee shall also pay on account of the maintenance charge to the Lessor within fourteen days of written demand from the Lessor (but not oftener than once in any one year) the appropriate proportion of such a sum (additional to the minimum payment) as the Lessor may determine

in any year of the said term to be requisite to cover any actual or expected deficiency in the cash resources of the Lessor to meet the actual or expected outgoings of the Lessor in relation to the Site in such year.

4. As soon as practicable after the expiration of each year ending on the Twenty fourth day of June the Lessor shall ascertain and certify the amount of the actual maintenance charge for the preceding 12 months and the amount standing to the credit of the reserve fund and serve on the Lessee a copy of such certificate (which shall be binding and conclusive on the Lessor and the Lessee) and any balance remaining to be paid by the Lessee after giving credit for the interim payments made by the Lessee in respect of such year shall be paid by the Lessee within 14 days of the service of such certificate or (if there is a balance repayable to the Lessee) such balance shall be repaid by the Lessor within the like time provided that the Lessor may at his absolute discretion defer until three months after the twenty fourth day of June next following the date of demise of the last of the Flats to be demised the ascertainment and certification of the maintenance charge for any year of the said Term ending prior to such date

SIGNED SEALED AND DELIVERED BY)
the said TERENCE SEIGNIOR)
in the presence of:)

SIGNED SEALED AND DELIVERED BY)
the said LETITIA MALAPROP)
in the presence of:)

Specimen Preliminary Notice Under Section 27 of The Landlord and Tenant Act 1987

IN THE MATTER OF the Landlord and Tenant Act 1987.

AND IN THE MATTER OF the building known as 999 Acacia Avenue, Dale in the County of Barset ("the Building")
TO: TERENCE SEIGNIOR of 17 Manor Road Dale, Barsetshire, BS20 2DJ
TAKE NOTICE that

1. This Notice is served by ANTHONY JOHN ABSOLUTE and LYDIA LANGUISH of flat 1 of the Building, BELINDA BOTT of flat 2 of the Building, CHARLES IAN CRAWFORD of flat 3 of the Building and FELICITY ANN FOWLER of flat 6 of the Building (hereinafter referred to as "the Tenants"). All counter-notices and other communications arising

out of this Notice may be served on Lawrence Grabbit of Messrs Sue Grabbit & Runne, 2 Church Walk Dale BS1 3JK instead of on the Tenants.

2. The Tenants intend to make an application for an acquisition order to be made by the Court in respect of the Site as defined in a Lease dated September 27, 1967 between yourself of the first part and Letitia Malaprop of the second part, on which the Building is erected; but they will not make such an application if you comply with the requirement specified in paragraph 4 of this Notice within the time specified in that paragraph.

3. The grounds on which the court would be asked to make an acquisition order are that you are in breach of the obligations owed by you to the Tenants under their respective leases and relating to their repair and management of the Building. The particulars on which the Tenants rely are:

(1) The skylight of the Building has been leaking for one year prior to the date hereof and you have taken no steps to repair it as required in the Tenants' leases;

(2) The steps leading to the front entrance to the Building are broken and dangerous and you have taken no steps (*sic*) to repair them;

(3) The tenants of flat 5 of the Building have been running an escort agency therefrom and you have not enforced the covenant that all flats in the Building are to be used for residential purposes only.

4. You are required, within three months of the date hereof, to repair the skylight in such manner that it is waterproof, and to replace the front steps in York stone. You are further required, within the same period, to commence proceedings against the tenants of flat 5 of the Building for an injunction prohibiting non-residential use of that flat, alternatively to commence proceedings against those tenants for forfeiture of their lease.

Dated March 30, 1990.

B. Specimen Lease Providing for Residents' Association

Note: this specimen lease is given for comparison only, and does not form part of the imaginary history.

THIS LEASE is made the Twenty fifth day of March One thousand nine hundred and eighty BETWEEN: DOMINIC LANDLESS of 20 Oliphant Road, London N30 (hereinafter called "the Lessor") of the first part and 62 TURTLE STREET LIMITED (hereinafter called "the Association") of the second part and MARK ALEXANDER TENNANT and AMORET FORSYTE both of 3 Grub Street, Puddingdale in the County of Buckingham (hereinafter called "the Lessees") of the third part.

WHEREAS:

(1) The Lessor is the owner of freehold land situate at and known as 62 Turtle Street in the London Borough of Thistledown registered at H.M. Land Registry under the number —— and hereinafter called "the Site".

(2) The Lessor has agreed for the consideration hereinafter appearing to demise to the Lessees (*inter alia*) one of the Flats on the terms hereinafter contained and have demised or will demise all the other Flats on similar terms and subject to similar covenants on the part of the lessee and conditions as are contained in this Lease (subject only to such variations as any special circumstances may require) to the intent that the lessee for the time being of each of the said Flats may be able to enforce against the lessee of every other of the said Flats any of the said covenants a breach of which adversely affects him.

(3) Before the demise of any of the said Flats, the Lessor was the beneficial owner of the entire issued share capital of the Association namely 24 £1 ordinary shares.

(4) The Lessor has transferred one £1 ordinary share in the Association to the lessee of each of the Flats heretofore demised and intends to transfer one £1 ordinary share to the lessee of each of the Flats to be demised hereafter.

(5) The Lessor and the Lessees have agreed that one of the Lessees is to become a member of the Association by the transfer to him of one £1 ordinary share therein immediately after the execution of these presents.

(6) The Lessor intends after the demise of the last of the Flats to be demised to transfer three more £1 ordinary shares in the Association to the lessee of each of the Flats thus divesting himself of all his interest in the Association, and immediately thereafter to transfer his entire estate and interest in the Site to the Association for a consideration of Five pounds (£5).

NOW THIS DEED WITNESSETH as follows namely:

1. IN this Lease the following expressions have the following meanings namely:

- (a) "The Plan" means the plan annexed hereto;
- (b) "The Site" means the land shown edged red on the Plan together with the house erected on part thereof divided into six flats with communal entrance and stairway and known as 62 Turtle Street aforesaid;
- (c) "The Block" means the block of flats in which the flat hereby demised is comprised;
- (d) "The Flat" means the flat demised by this Lease;
- (e) "The Flats" means the six flats comprising the Block, including the Flat hereby demised;

(f) "The Reserved Premises" means the Site (including the Reserved Services but except all the Flats);

(g) "The Reserved Services" means the sewers drains water pipes tanks gutters wires cable conduits and other like means of passage or disposal or storage of soil water gas electricity television and other services and of soil smoke rubbish and other material or other matter which are now or may within eighty years from the date of the commencement of the term created by this Lease (which said period of eighty years shall be the perpetuity period applicable to this lease) be in or under the Site of any part thereof (hereinafter together called "service installation") not being Leased Services or Excluded Services as hereinafter defined;

   (i) "The Leased Services" means service installations used or intended for use exclusively for the benefit of the demised premises;

   (ii) "The Excluded Services" means service installations used or intended exclusively for use by any other of the Flats and situate within the demised premises.

2. In consideration of the sum of Twenty Four Thousand pounds (£24,000.00) now paid by the Lessees to the Lessor (the receipt whereof the Lessor hereby acknowledges) and of the rent and covenants on the part of the Lessee hereinafter reserved and contained the Lessor HEREBY DEMISES unto the Lessees ALL THAT Flat described in the first part of the First Schedule hereto (hereinafter called "the demised premises") TOGETHER WITH the rights described in the second part of that Schedule and EXCEPTING AND RESERVING the rights described in the third part of that Schedule TO HOLD the same unto the Lessees for the term of NINETY NINE YEARS calculated from the Twenty fifth day of December 1979 YIELDING AND PAYING therefor in advance during the said term and proportionately for any fraction of a year the net yearly rent of FIVE POUNDS (£5) on the Twenty fourth day of June in each year without any deduction the first of such payments or a due proportion thereof to be made on the date of this Lease.

3. The Lessees hereby declare that they shall hold the demised premises upon trust to sell the same with power to postpone the sale thereof and shall hold the net proceeds of sale and the other money applicable as capital and the net rents and profits thereof until sale upon trust for themselves as joint tenants.

4. The Lessees HEREBY COVENANT jointly and severally with the Lessor and as a separate covenant also with the Association and with each of the other lessees for the time being of any of the Flats that the Lessees will observe and perform (a) the covenants on the part of the Lessees set out in the Second Schedule hereto and (b) the regulations set out in the Third Schedule hereto.

5. THE Lessor hereby covenants with the Lessees:

(1) That the Lessees paying the rents hereinbefore reserved and performing and observing the covenants conditions and agreements on the part of the Lessees herein before contained shall peaceably hold and enjoy the demised premises for the term hereby granted without any interruption by the Lessor or any person lawfully claiming under or in trust for him.

(2) That the Lessor has not granted and will not hereafter grant a Lease of any of the Flats except to a lessee who has entered or will enter into similar covenants and undertake similar obligations to those on the part of the Lessees herein contained so far as applicable and that the Lessor will himself be under like obligations in respect of any of the Flats for the time being undemised.

6. THE Lessor hereby covenants with the Lessees that the Lessor will upon request in writing of the Lessees enforce the covenants entered into or to be entered into by the lessee of any other of the Flats upon the Lessees agreeing by deed in such form as the Lessor may reasonably require to indemnify the Lessor against all costs and expenses.

7. The Association hereby covenants with the Lessees to perform and observe the covenants on the part of the Association set out in the Fourth Schedule hereto PROVIDED THAT the Association shall not be liable to any Lessee or any invitee or licensee of the Lessees for or in any way arising out of any breach or non-performance of any of the said covenants unless such breach or non-performance shall have been specifically notified to the Association in writing and the Association shall have failed to remedy such breach or non-performance within reasonable time of receiving such notice

8. PROVIDED ALWAYS that:

(i) If the said rent hereby reserved or any part thereof shall be unpaid for 21 days after becoming payable (whether the same shall have been formally demanded or not) or if any of the covenants on the part of the Lessees herein contained shall not be performed or observed then and in any such case it shall be lawful for the Lessor or any person or persons authorised by him in that behalf at any time thereafter to re-enter upon the demised premises or any part thereof in the name of the whole; and thereupon this demise shall absolutely determine but without prejudice to any right of action or remedy of the Lessor in respect of any breach of the covenants by the Lessees hereinbefore contained;

(ii) All rights and obligations of the Lessor and Lessees respectively under these presents shall be incident to the reversion expectant on this Lease and the leasehold interest thereby created respectively and shall pass and devolve therewith on any alienation or devolution thereof;

(iii) The Lessor shall not be liable to the Lessees or any invitee or licensee of the Lessees for or in any way arising out of any defect or want of repair in the demised premises in any property owned or occupied by the Lessor other than the Site or in any part of the Reserved Premises and the Lessor's liability for or arising out of any defect or want of repair in any other of the Flats shall be limited to his duty to enforce the covenants entered into by the lessee of that Flat as contained in clause 6 hereof

(iv) Any notice hereby required or authorised to be given to the Lessor or the Lessees shall be in writing and may be given in any of the modes provided by Section 196 of the Law of Property Act 1925.

9. IT IS HEREBY CERTIFIED that the transaction hereby effected does not form part of a larger transaction or series of transactions in respect of which the amount or value or the aggregate amount or value of the consideration other than rent exceeds Twenty five thousand Pounds (£25,000).

IN WITNESS whereof the Lessor and the Lessees have hereunto set their hands and seals and the Association has caused its Common Seal to be hereunto affixed the day and year first above written.

THE FIRST SCHEDULE

FIRST ALL THAT Flat being Flat Number One in the basement of the Site (the site of such Flat being shown coloured red on the Plan) including the Balcony (if any) and the joists or beams on which the floors of the Flat are laid and the interior faces and the glass in the windows of the exterior walls and the interior face and the locks of the entrance door but excluding: (i) Any other part of such external walls and entrance door; (ii) The joists or beams securing the ceilings of the Flat; (iii) all parts of the Site above such joists or beams and; (iv) all parts of the Site below the joists or beams on which the floors of the Flat are laid TOGETHER WITH:

(1) The right of passage and running storage and disposal of gas water electricity television and other services and of soil, smoke, rubbish and other material in and through and by means of the Reserved Services and the Leased Services and all necessary rights of entry for the purpose of inspecting maintaining and repairing and renewing the same subject to the person exercising such right making good all damage thereby caused but without compensation for any inconvenience PROVIDED that the right to the passage of water shall so far as the same relates to the supply of main water (whether or not through any tank or cistern) to the demised premises be subject to the payment by the Lessees to the Lessor or to the Statutory Water Authority (as the case may require) of the water rate assessed in respect of the demised premises or (if and so far as the water rate is not separately assessed upon the demised premises or some part

thereof) of a fair proportion of such assessment to be determined by the Lessor or his surveyor.

(2) The right at all reasonable times with or without workmen and others to enter upon any part of the Site and the Reserved Premises for the purpose of cleansing and executing repairs or alterations to the demised premises PROVIDED that the Lessees shall only exercise the rights of entering other parts of the Site at reasonable times during the hours of daylight and after giving reasonable notice of their intention to enter (except in the case of emergency) and upon the terms that the Lessees shall make good any damage thereby occasioned but so that the Lessees shall not be liable for any temporary interference with the convenience of the lessee or occupier of the premises so entered upon

(3) All such rights of support and protection from the elements and (subject as hereinafter provided) light and air for the demised premises over and from other parts of the Site and the Reserved Premises as are now enjoyed or intended to be enjoyed by the demised premises PROVIDED THAT the Lessor or his tenants may at any time hereafter build upon the Site and rebuild or alter any of the parts of the Site notwithstanding any interference thereby occasioned to the access of light or air to any part of the demised premises.

(4) The right (in common with the Association and the Lessor and all persons deriving title under the Lessor and the lessees for the time being of all the other Flats) for the Lessees their servants agents and licensees and invitees to use in accordance with such reasonable regulations as the Association or the Lessor may from time to time impose the entrance way entrance hall staircases landings passages and other communal services of the Site and the roads footpaths drives gardens and communal parking areas of the Site for all purposes connected with the benefical user of the demised premises.

(5) The right in common with the Lessor and all persons authorised by the Lessor to use the communal dustbin area coloured orange on the Plan.

EXCEPTING AND RESERVING unto the Lessor and the Association and each lessee of every other of the Flats:

(1) All such rights of support and protection from the elements and light and air from and over the demised premises for the other parts of the Site as are now enjoyed or intended to be enjoyed by such other parts;

(2) The right of passage and running storage and disposal of gas water electricity television radio and other services and of soil smoke rubbish and other materials in and through and by means of the Reserved Services and the Excluded Services and the right with or without workmen and others on reasonable prior notice in the daytime (except in case of emergency) to enter the demised premises or any part thereof for the purpose of inspection maintenance repair or renewal of the said services or any of them subject to the person exercising such right making

good all damage thereby caused but without compensation for any temporary inconvenience;
(3) The right with or without workmen and others at all reasonable times on reasonable prior notice in the day time (except in the case of emergency) to enter into and upon the demised premises or any part thereof to inspect cleanse repair alter renew or improve any part of the Reserved Premises (including the Site) the person exercising such rights making good all damage thereby caused but without compensation for any temporary inconvenience;
(4) The right for the Association or the Lessor to decorate or redecorate (to the exclusion of the Lessees whose obligations shall not extend thereto) the outside faces of the external walls and the entrance doors of the Flat.

THE SECOND SCHEDULE
COVENANTS BY THE LESSEES

(a) To pay the rent hereby reserved at the time and in the manner aforesaid without any deduction whatsoever;
(b) To pay and discharge all existing and future rates taxes assessments and outgoings whether parliamentary local or otherwise now or hereafter imposed or charged upon the demised premises or any part thereof or on the Lessor or Lessees or occupier in respect thereof PROVIDED THAT where any such outgoings are charged upon or payable in respect of the Block as a whole the Lessees' liability shall be limited to a due proportion of such outgoings to be determined (failing agreement) by the Lessor or his surveyors;
(c) To do all such works or other things as shall under any statutory or any other authority be required to be done in respect of the demised premises whether by the owner or occupier thereof and to conform in all respects with the provisions of and regulations made under any general or local Act of Parliament which may be applicable to the demised premises or any part thereof AND to keep the Lessor and the Association fully indemnified in respect thereof;
(d) From time to time and at all times during the said term to keep in good and substantial repair and condition the demised premises and the landlord's fixtures and fittings and the Leased Services therein provided that if any event shall occur giving rise to a claim under the insurance policy or policies required to be effected by the Association under paragraph 1 of the Fourth Schedule hereto and the moneys recovered pursuant to such claim shall be applied in the repair or reinstatement of the demised premises the Lessees shall pro tanto be released from their liability to carry out repairs to the demised premises as a consequence of that event or to contribute to the cost of such repairs;
(e) To prepare and paint with two coats of best quality paint in a workmanlike manner all the wood iron and other parts of the interior of

the demised premises usually painted in every seventh year of the said term and in the last year of the term as well and after every painting to redecorate in like manner all such parts as are usually so dealt with as at the date hereto and stop whiten and colour all such parts as are usually so dealt with and to repaper the parts usually papered with suitable paper of as good quality as that in use at the date hereof;

(f) To make good at the Lessees' expense to the satisfaction of the Lessor or his surveyor any damage occasioned by the exercise of the rights demised to the Lessee;

(g) To permit the Lessor and the Association and the lessee or occupier of any other of the Flats and their respective agents or workmen at any time or times during the said term at reasonable hours in the daytime upon giving reasonable notice (except in the case of emergency) to enter upon the demised premises for the purpose of inspecting cleansing and for executing repairs or alterations upon or to the Reserved Premises or any other of the Flats without unreasonable delay and making good to the Lessees all damage thereby occasioned but without compensation for any temporary damage or inconvenience;

(h) Not at any time during the said term to make any structural addition or alteration to the demised premises not to remove alter or reposition any partition wall or walls or make any openings in any of them without the previous written consent of the Lessor and not to carry out any operation constituting development within the meaning of the Town and Country Planning Acts or any statutory amendment or replacement thereof or any Building Regulation for the time being in force;

(i) Not to use or occupy or permit the Flat to be used or occupied for any purpose whatsoever other than as a private residence in the occupation of a single family;

(j) To comply with and observe such amendments or additional regulations to those set forth in the Third Schedule hereto as the Association or the Lessor may (consistently with the provisions of this Lease) make to govern the use of the Site in the general interest of the residents;

(k) Not to store petrol or other inflammable material on the demised premises;

(l) Not to do or permit any waste spoil or destruction to or upon the demised premises not to do or permit any act or thing which shall or may be or become a nuisance damage annoyance or inconvenience to the Lessor or his tenant or occupiers of adjoining premises and in particular of any other Flats or to the neighbourhood or whereby any insurance for the time being effected on the demised premises may be rendered void or voidable or whereby the rate of premium may be increased;

(m) From time to time during the said term to pay all costs charges and expenses incurred by the Lessor or the Association in abating a nuisance arising from any act default or neglect of the Lessee and executing all such works as may be necessary for abating a nuisance in obedience to a notice served by a Local Authority;

(n) (i) To permit the Lessor or the Association or their agents with or without workmen and other at all reasonable times upon giving reasonable notice (except in the case of emergency) during the said term at convenient hours in the daytime to enter the demised premises to view and examine the state and condition of the demised premises and all decays defects and wants of repair as shall be then and there found for which the Lessees may be liable hereunder; (ii) to remedy repair and amend any such decays defects and wants of repair within two calendar months next following the service of notice in writing by or on behalf of the Lessor or the Association requiring them so to do;

(o) That if the Lessees shall make default in any of the covenants hereinbefore contained for or relating to the repair or painting of the demised premises it shall be lawful for the Lessor or the Association to enter upon the demised premises and repair the same at the expense of the Lessees in accordance with the covenants and provisions of these presents and the expense of such repairs shall be repaid by the Lessees to the Lessor or the Assocation on demand with interest at seven pounds per centum per annum from the date of demand;

(p) All the demised premises painted repaired and kept as aforesaid at the expiration or sooner determination of the said term quietly to yield up unto the Lessor together with all additions and improvements made thereto in the meantime and all fixtures of every kind in or upon the demised premises except tenant's fixtures;

(q) (i) To pay to the Lessor all costs charges and expenses (including legal costs and fees payable to a Surveyor) which may be incurred by the Lessor incidental to the preparation and service of a notice under Section 146 of the Law of Property Act 1925 (whether or not any right of re-entry of forfeiture has been waived by the Lessor or the Lessees have been relieved under the provisions of the said Act) in respect of the demised premises whether incurred in or in contemplation of proceedings under Section 146 or 147 of that Act;

(ii) To pay to the Lessor all expenses including Solicitors' costs and Surveyors' fees incurred by the Lessor of and incidental to the service of all Notices and Schedules relating to wants of repair to the demised premises accrued not later than the expiration or sooner determination of the term hereby granted but whether such Notice and Schedules be served before or after such expiration or sooner determination

(r) Not during the last seven years of the said term (except by Will) to assign or underlet or part with possession of the demised premises or any part thereof without prior written consent of the Lessor;

(s) Within 21 days after every assignment devolution disposition charge underlease or agreement for tenancy of the demised premises or any part thereof whether by express deed or by operation or implication of law to give to the Lessor's Solicitors notice in writing thereof specifying in such notice the name and address of the assignee or personal representative or other person in or to whom the term or any part thereof may have become vested or charged and (if called upon) to produce the assignment probate letters of adminstration charge counterpart lease or agreement for tenancy or other evidence of devolution at the office of the said Solicitors for registration and to pay the said Solicitors a fee of Five pounds and fifty pence (£5.50) plus VAT thereon in respect of each such registration; (ii) to become a member of the Association.

(t) Duly to pay to the Association at the times and in the manner set out in the Fifth Schedule hereto all sums as shall under the provisions of that Schedule be payable in respect of the demised premises.

THE THIRD SCHEDULE
REGULATIONS TO BE OBSERVED BY THE LESSEES

1. The floors of all the Flat (except bathroom kitchen and W.C.) shall be suitably carpeted and all reasonable precautions taken (including the placing of rubber or cork insulators) to deaden the sound of sewing machines dish washers washing machines or other household machines radios gramophones television sets pianos or other musical instruments;
2. No musical instrument wireless set television set loudspeaker or other mechanical instrument of any kind shall be played or used or household machines used or noise made between the hours of 12 midnight and eight o'clock in the morning or between such other times as the Association shall decide nor at any time so as to cause annoyance or disturbance to the occupier of any other Flat;
3. The communal parts of the Site shall not be encumbered with bicycles prams boxes or other objects and the entrance doors to Flats shall be kept closed;
4. No dirt rubbish rags or other refuse shall be thrown into sinks baths lavatories cisterns or waste or soil pipes in the Flat;
5. No name writing drawing signboard notice placard or advertisement of any kind shall be put on or in any windows or the exterior of the Flat (other than a notice to be approved by the Association indicating that a particular Flat is to be sold or let);
6. The communal parts of the Site shall be used as quietly as possible and in particular between the hours of 12 midnight and eight o'clock in the morning;
7. No children shall be allowed to play and no undue noise shall be made in the communal parts of the Site;
8. No external wireless or television aerials shall be erected by the Lessees on any part of the demised premises;
9. No clothes window boxes flower pots or other articles shall be hung or exposed and no mat or carpet shall be shaken at the windows of the flat;

10. No bird dog or other animal shall be kept on the demised premises without the previous written consent of the Association and should such permission be given then dogs should be kept on the lead in all parts of the Reserved Premises provided nevertheless that such consent may be revoked at any time if in the opinion of the Association the bird dog or animal shall become a nuisance to the owner or occupier of any other Flat;

11. Each lessee shall curtain and keep curtained all the windows of his Flat;

THE FOURTH SCHEDULE
COVENANTS BY THE ASSOCIATION

1. To insure the Block and keep it insured against loss or damage by fire storm impact or aircraft and such other risks as are included in a House Owner's Comprehensive Policy with such insurance company of repute as the Association may decide to an amount equal to the full replacement value thereof plus Surveyor's and Architect's fees and to effect such other insurance of or in respect of property owner's liability or other risks as the Association shall consider reasonable and to make all payments necessary for these purposes within seven days after the same become payable. Such insurance shall be effected in the joint names of the Association and the Lessees with regard to the demised premises and the premiums shall be recovered from the lessees of the Flats as part of the maintenance charges provided by the Fifth Schedule hereto. Any moneys recovered under such insurance shall be applied in the reinstatement of the Site and other expenses insured against and any excess shall be retained by the Association.

2. At all times during the term hereby granted to maintain the Reserved Premises in good and substantial repair and condition (except as regards damage caused by or resulting from any act or default of the Lessee or any person deriving title under the Lessee) making all such necessary renewals and replacements as may be required thereto.

3. To redecorate the interior communal parts of the Site in a proper and workmanlike manner at least once in every five years and to paint the exterior wood and iron and cement work of the Site and all additions thereto with two coats of exterior quality paint in a proper and workmanlike manner at least once in every three years of the term hereby granted.

4. To keep the entrance halls landings and staircases of the Site clean and suitably lighted and the services thereof in good working order and condition.

5. To maintain the Reserved Premises in good order and condition with the drives properly maintained and the gardens properly planted with shrubs in due season and free from weeds and clean and tidy and free from all obstruction and carefully to preserve the timber trees and all

ornamental trees and replace such of the shrubs or trees as may die or require replacing.

6. To employ such staff or contractors as may be reasonably required to carry out all necessary works of maintenance cleaning and repairs and such other duties as are necessary for the proper running and management of the Reserved Premises.

THE FIFTH SCHEDULE
PROVISIONS GOVERNING MAINTENANCE CHARGES

1. The maintenance charge for the demised premises shall be a sum equal to one sixth (hereinafter called "the appropriate proportion") of the aggregate cost to the Association of (a) complying with the Association's covenants in this Lease and of the corresponding covenants in the leases of the other Flats and (b) providing such reserves for future anticipated maintenance as the Association shall from time to time think desirable.

2. The cost to the Association of complying with its covenants shall be deemed (without prejudice to the generality of the foregoing words) to include:

(a) The costs of and incidental to compliance by the Association with every notice regulation or order of any competent local or other authority;

(b) All fees and charges and expenses payable to any Solicitor Accountant Surveyor Agent or Architect employed or instructed in connection with any question arising on the maintenance or management of the Site and the curtilage or the Reserved Premises or the ascertainment of the maintenance charge;

(c) The cost of the insurance required to be effected by paragraph 1 of the Fourth Schedule hereto and of insuring against claims of third parties;

(d) The cost of purchasing or hiring any equipment used for the benefit of residents of the Flats;

(e) All administration accountancy legal and other costs of the Association in carrying on its business in relation to the Site.

3. (i) The Lessees shall on account of the maintenance charge pay to the Association on the signing hereof and monthly thereafter throughout the said term a sum (hereinafter called "the minimum payment") determined as hereinafter provided;

(ii) The minimum payment shall be the sum of TWENTY POUNDS (£20) or such greater sum as the Association may from time to time by resolution of its directors determine to be the appropriate proportion of the amount reasonably required to enable the Association to cover its outgoings in relation to the Site for the relevant year;

(iii) The Lessees shall also pay on account of the maintenance charge to the Association within 14 days of written demand from the Association (but not oftener than once in any one year) the appropriate proportion of such a sum (additional to the minimum payment) as the Association may by resolution of its directors determine in any year of the said term to be requisite to cover any actual or expected deficiency in the cash resources of the Association to meet the actual or expected outgoings of the Association in relation to the Site in such year;

4. As soon as practicable after the expiration of each year ending on the twenty fourth day of June the Association shall ascertain and certify the amount of the actual maintenance charge for the preceding 12 months and the amount standing to the credit of the reserve fund and serve on the Lessees a copy of such certificate (which shall be binding and conclusive on the Association and the Lessees) and any balance remaining to be paid by the Lessees after giving credit for the interim payments made by the Lessees in respect of such year shall be paid by the Lessees within 14 days of the service of such certificate or (if there is a balance repayable to the Lessees) such balance shall be repaid by the Lessor within the like time Provided that the Association may at its absolute discretion defer until three months after the twenty fourth day of June next following the date of the demise of the last of the Flats to be demised the ascertainment and certification of the maintenance charge for any year of the said Term ending prior to such date.

SIGNED SEALED and DELIVERED)
by the said DOMINIC LANDLESS)
in the presence of:)

SIGNED SEALED AND DELIVERED BY)
the said MARK ALEXANDER TENNANT)
in the presence of:)

SIGNED SEALED AND DELIVERED)
by the said AMORET FORSYTE)
in the presence of:)

THE COMMON SEAL OF 62 TURTLE)
STREET LIMITED)
was hereunto affixed in the)
presence of:)

C. Formation of a Shelf Company by Registration Agents

Memorandum of Association

The Companies Act 1985
PRIVATE COMPANY LIMITED BY SHARES
MEMORANDUM OF ASSOCIATION
of
GREBECAT LIMITED

1. The company's name is Grebecat Limited.
2. The company's registered office is to be situated in England and Wales.
3. The company's objects are:

    (1) To carry on business as a property holding company;
    (2) To carry on any other business which may seem to the company capable of being conveniently carried on in connection with the objects specified in sub-clause (1) hereof.

4. The liability of the members is limited.
5. The company's share capital is £100 divided into 100 ordinary shares of £1 each.

We the subscribers to this memorandum of association wish to be formed into a company pursuant to this memorandum; and we agree to take the number of shares shown opposite our respective names.

	Names & addresses of subscribers	Number of shares taken by each subscriber
1.	Gregory Grebe, 20 Church Walk, Broxbourne, Herts	1
2.	Caroline Cat, 38 Bottleneck Way, Denham, Middx	1
Total Shares taken		2

Dated March 13, 1986
Witness to the above signatures
Luciano Samosata
Euphrates Drive
London N29

Articles of Association

THE COMPANIES ACT 1985
PRIVATE COMPANY LIMITED BY SHARES
ARTICLES OF ASSOCIATION
of
GREBECAT LIMITED

1. Subject as hereinafter provided the Regulations contained in Table A in the Schedule to the Companies (Tables A to F) Regulations 1985 shall apply to the company.
2. Regulation 64 of Table A shall not apply to the company, but the number of directors of the company shall not be less than one. If at any time there is only one director, he may act alone in exercising all the powers and authorities vested in the directors.
3. The directors are authorised pursuant to Section 80(i) of the Companies Act 1985 to allot unissued shares forming part of the share capital of the company to such persons on such terms and in such manner as they think fit at any time during the five years following the incorporation of the company; provided that this authority may be revoked at any earlier date by an ordinary resolution of the company

	Names & addresses of subscribers	Number of shares taken by each subscriber
1.	Gregory Grebe, 20 Church Walk, Broxbourne, Herts	1
2.	Caroline Cat, 38 Bottleneck Way, Denham, Middx	1
Total Shares taken		2

Dated March 13, 1986
Witness to the above signatures
Luciano Samosata
Euphrates Drive
London N29

Statement of First Directors and Secretary and Intended Situation of Registered Office

See Form 10 on pages 139–142.

Statement of Cash Contributed by Shareholders

This is an Inland Revenue form for the purpose of capital duty. As capital duty was abolished in 1988, this form will not be needed for company formations from then on: accordingly it is not reproduced here.

Statutory Declaration

See Form G12 on page 143.

Certificate of Incorporation

Not reproduced here.

Entries in the Register of Members

CAROLINE EMMA CAT of 38 Bottleneck Way, Denham, Middlesex became the holder of one £1 ordinary share numbered 2 on 20th October 1986 by subscribing therefor.
GREGORY CHRISTOPHER GREBE of 20 Church Walk, Broxbourne, Herts became the holder of one £1 ordinary share numbered 1 on the 20th October 1986 by subscribing therefor.

Share Certificates

See Share Certificates on page 144.

D. Acquisition of the Company

(a) *Letter of Resignation*

Welbeck Chambers
19 Duxbury Street
London WC3 7TD
February 1, 1991

Dear Mr Absolute

GREBECAT LIMITED

In connection with the proposed acquisition by you and your fellow leaseholders at 999 Acacia Avenue of the above company, we wish to inform you that we have tendered our resignations as director and secretary of the company. These resignations will take effect upon your acceptance of office as directors.

We enclose a copy of the minutes of the E.G.M. in which we elected you and your fellow leaseholders directors of the company and the share transfers to yourself and Miss Fowler.

Yours sincerely

G A Grebe

C E Cat

Share Transfers

See Stock Transfer Forms on pages 145–148.

Minutes of EGM (at Company Formation Agents)

GREBECAT LIMITED
MINUTES OF AN EXTRAORDINARY GENERAL MEETING
HELD ON JANUARY 28, 1991
AT 19 DUXBURY STREET LONDON WC3 7TD

Present at the meeting were Gregory Grebe, Chairman, and Caroline Cat, Secretary.

IT WAS RESOLVED unanimously as follows:

(1) The requirement of notice for this meeting is waived in accordance with section 378(3) of the Companies Act 1985.
(2) The authority of the directors to allot unissued shares pursuant to Section 80 of the Companies Act 1985, as conferred by Article 3 of the company's Articles, is extended for a further five years from the date of this resolution.
(3) (By special resolution) The directors, in exercising their authority under Resolution 2, shall have power to allot shares

in the company as if section 89(1) of the Companies Act 1985 did not apply to the allotment.

(4) The motion for the appointment as directors of the persons hereinafter named shall be made by a single resolution, notwithstanding the provisions of section 292(1) of the Companies Act 1985.

(5) The following persons are appointed directors of the Company in place of Gregory Grebe, who tenders his resignation conditionally upon acceptance of office as director by any one or more of them:

ANTHONY JOHN ABSOLUTE
BELINDA BOTT
CHARLES IAN DYMOND
DAHLIA LOUISA DYMOND
EDWARD EXTRACT
FELICITY ANN FOWLER

all of 999 Acacia Avenue, Dale, Barsetshire, BS20 5QR

G.C.Grebe
Chairman

Minutes of Directors' Meeting

GREBECAT LIMITED
MINUTES OF A MEETING OF THE DIRECTORS
HELD ON APRIL 3, 1991
AT FLAT 1, 999 ACACIA AVENUE, DALE
BARSETSHIRE, BS20 5QR

Present at the meeting were Anthony Absolute, Belinda Bott, Charles Crawford, Dahlia Dymond, Edward Extract and Felicity Fowler.

All present confirmed that they had accepted office as directors of the above company, having been elected thereto in an Extraordinary General Meeting dated January 28, 1991, and completed and signed Form 238.

The following resolutions were then passed:

(1) Anthony Absolute is appointed the chairman secretary;

(2) Felicity Fowler is appointed the company secretary;

(3) The transfers of share number 1 from Gregory Grebe to Anthony Absolute and of share number 2 from Caroline Cat to Felicity Fowler are approved;

(4) In exercise of the directors' powers under Regulation 3 of the Articles of Association, four more £1 ordinary shares, numbered 3 to 6, are allotted to Belinda Bott, Charles Crawford, Dahlia Dymond and Edward Extract respectively;
(5) Accordingly, all six persons present shall be registered as shareholders in the Register of Members, and the appropriate share certificates issued;
(6) Barcloyds Plc are appointed the company's bankers and the mandate in the form provided by the bank is approved and signed;
(7) Messrs Bouncer are appointed the company's auditors until the next Annual General Meeting;
(8) The company's accounting year shall start on the first day of September in each year and end on the last day of August in the following year;
(9) An Extraordinary General Meeting is called, to follow immediately after the conclusion of the present meeting.

A J Absolute
Chairman

Minutes of E G M (of Tenants)

GREBECAT LIMITED
MINUTES OF AN EXTRAORDINARY GENERAL MEETING
HELD ON APRIL 3, 1991
AT FLAT 1, 999 ACACIA AVENUE, DALE
BARSETSHIRE BS20 5QR

Present at the meeting were Anthony Absolute, Belinda Bott, Charles Crawford, Dahlia Dymond, Edward Extract and Felicity Fowler.
The following resolutions were passed unanimously:

(1) It is agreed to waive the requirement of notice for the present meeting and for any special resolutions passed therein, in accordance with section 378(3) of the Companies Act 1985
(2) The name of the company shall be changed from Grebecat Limited to 999 Acacia Avenue Limited;
(3) A new company seal shall be adopted, in the following form:

INSERT LOGO HERE

(4) The registered office of the company shall be changed to 999 Acacia Avenue, Dale, Barsetshire, BS20 5QR.

(5) For Clause 3(i) of the Memorandum of Association, there shall be substituted the following:

"3 (i) To carry on the business of a holding company in all its branches, and to acquire by purchase, lease, concession, grant, licence or otherwise such businesses, options, rights, privileges, lands, buildings, leases, underleases, stocks, shares, debentures, bonds, obligations, securities, reversionary interests, annuities, policies of assurance and other property and rights and interests in property as the Company shall deem fit and generally to hold, manage, develop, lease, sell or dispose of the same; and to vary any of the investments of the company, to act as trustees of any deeds constituting or securing any debentures, debenture stock or other securities or obligation; to enter into, assist or participate in financial, commercial, mercantile industrial and other transactions, undertakings and businesses of every description, and to establish, carry on, develop and extend the same or sell, dispose of or otherwise turn the same to account, and to co-ordinate the policy and administration of any companies of which this Company is a member or which are in any manner controlled by or connected with the Company, and to carry on all or any of the businesses of capitalists, trustees and financiers;

(ii) To carry on all or any of the businesses of proprietors of flats, maisonettes, dwellinghouses, shops, offices and clubs; to manage or let the same or any part thereof for any period, whether belonging to the Company or not and at such rent and on such conditions as the Company shall think fit; to collect rents and income and to supply to tenants and occupiers and others, light, heat, refreshments, garages, and other advantages which from time to time the Company shall consider desirable or to provide for such management, letting and advantages as aforesaid by employing any person, firm or company to carry out or supply the same on such terms as the Company may think fit;

(iii) To carry on all or any of the businesses of proprietors, builders, developers and civil engineering contractors for homes, commercial buildings, hotels, motels restaurants, clubs, bungalows, casinos, licensed premises, holiday accommodation, swimming pools, baths, property dealers and developers in any part of the world, proprietors of shops, stores, kiosks, baths, gaming rooms, dressing rooms, laundries, libraries, dance halls, concert halls and rooms for public or private use;

(iv) To purchase or by any other means acquire for investment purposes or otherwise, any freehold, leasehold, or other property for any estate whatever, and any ground rents, rights, privileges or easements over or in respect of any property; to develop and turn to account any land acquired by or in which the company is interested, and in particular by laying out and preparing the same for building purposes, constructing, altering, fitting up and improving buildings, and by planting, paving, draining, farming, cultivating, letting on building lease or building agreement, and by advancing money to and entering into contracts and arrangements of all kinds with builders, tenants and others."

(6) Sections 89 and 90 of the Companies Act 1985 shall apply to any allotment of shares made after the date hereof, but shall not apply to the allotment made in the directors' meeting that took place today.

(7) The Articles of Association shall be amended to the form hereto annexed.

A J Absolute
Chairman

Amended Articles of Association

THE COMPANIES ACT 1985
PRIVATE COMPANY LIMITED BY SHARES
ARTICLES OF ASSOCIATION
(adopted by a special resolution dated April 3, 1991)

1. Subject as hereinafter provided the Regulations contained in Table A in the Schedule to the Companies (Tables A to F) Regulations 1985 ("Table A"), as it stood at the time of registration of these regulations, shall apply to the company.

INTERPRETATION

2. The definitions in regulation 1 of Table A shall also apply in the interpretation of these regulations. In addition:

"these regulations" shall mean the text of the present document, not including Table A;
"the articles" shall mean the articles of the company, including both these regulations and Table A (where not excluded by these regulations);
any reference to a regulation by number shall mean the paragraph so numbered within these regulations unless otherwise stated;
"flat" shall mean any premises forming part of a building owned or managed by the company capable of forming a self-contained residential or commercial unit, and "the flats" shall be construed accordingly;
"qualifying interest" shall have the meaning given in regulation 5.

SHARES

3. The directors are authorised pursuant to section 80(*i*) to allot unissued shares forming part of the share capital of the company to such persons on such terms and in such manner as they think fit, subject to regulations 4 and 5, at any time during the five years following the date of registration of these regulations; provided that this authority may be revoked at any earlier date by an ordinary resolution of the company.
4. No share in the company may be held by more than one person.
5. (1) Unless authorised by special resolution of the company, no share may be held by any person other than the following:

(a) a person with a qualifying interest in one of the flats;
(b) subject to regulation 6, a person who has ceased to hold such an interest;
(c) (in a case where the articles provide for the purchase by the company of its own shares or the forfeiture of shares to the company) the company.

(2) A person has a qualifying interest in a flat if:

(a) he, alone or concurrently with others, has a legal estate or equitable interest in that flat which is granted for a term of not less than seven years and entitles him to immediate possession thereof or would so entitle him but for the existence of any interest granted for a term of less than seven years; or
(b) he is the mortgagee or chargee of a legal estate or equitable interest such as is mentioned in (a) above.

(3) Where a person has a qualifying interest in more than one flat, he shall be treated as a separate person in relation to each of his flats; accordingly, in the application of these regulations to shares held by him in right of his qualifying interest in any one flat, his interest in any other flat shall be disregarded.
(4) No more than one person at a time may hold shares in the company by virtue of a qualifying interest in the same flat. In a case where several persons have a qualifying interest in the same flat, the

decision of the directors as to which one of them may hold shares in the company shall be final.

6. If the holder of any share ceases to have a qualifying interest in the flat by virtue of which he holds that share, he shall immediately inform the directors of that fact. The directors may at any time after such cesser give him notice requiring him to transfer that share within 30 days of the notice to a person who has a qualifying interest in that flat. The notice shall state that if it is not complied with the share shall be liable to be forfeited; and regulations 19 to 22 of Table A shall apply in relation to such a notice in the same way as they do to a notice under regulation 18 of Table A.

7. Regulation 24 of Table A shall apply to the company, with the substitution of "one transferee" for "four transferees." In addition, the directors may decline to register any transfer of any share, unless:

(i) there is no rent, service charge or other sum owed or other obligation outstanding by or on the part of the transferor to the company by virtue of any lease or tenancy agreement; and

(ii) by reason of the creation or disposal of any interest in one of the flats, alone or in conjunction with other transactions, the transferor has ceased to have a qualifying interest in the flat and the proposed transferee has such an interest; and

(iii) (where there is more than one person having a qualifying interest in that flat) the directors have decided, in exercise of their powers under regulation 5(2), that the proposed transferee may hold shares in the company to the exclusion of the other eligible persons.

8. If a member's relevant interest in any of the flats shall become liable to be forfeited to the company under the terms of any lease or tenancy agreement or otherwise, the shares held by him shall also be liable to be forfeited, and regulations 20 to 22 of Table A shall apply to such forfeiture.

DIRECTORS

9. Regulation 64 of Table A shall not apply to the company. The number of directors of the company at any time shall not be less than one or more than six. If at any time there shall only be one director, he may act alone in exercising all the powers and authorities vested in the directors.

10. No person who is not a member of the company may be a director, and section 291 of the Act shall apply.

11. Regulations 73 to 79 of Table A shall not apply to the company.

12. At every Annual General Meeting:

(a) If the company has six members or fewer, and all of them are directors, they shall remain in office unless it is otherwise resolved;
(b) in any other case, all the directors shall retire from office and the meeting shall elect directors, not exceeding six in number.

13. If an elective resolution has been passed dispensing with the holding of annual general meetings, the directors shall remain in office from year to year unless the company revokes the elective resolution or a member requires an annual general meeting to be held in any year.
14. If a director ceases to hold a qualifying interest in any of the flats he shall forthwith cease to be a director whether or not he then ceases to be a member.
15. The company in general meeting may at any time appoint a person who is willing to act to be a director, either to fill a vacancy or as an additional director, provided that the appointment does not cause the number of directors to exceed six. The person so appointed shall continue to hold office until the office is vacated by virtue of the articles.
16. The directors may at any time appoint a person who is willing to act to be a director, either to fill a vacancy or as an additional director, provided that the appointment does not cause the number of directors exceed six. The person so appointed shall hold office only until the next annual general meeting, notwithstanding anything in regulation 12.
17. A director may, with the consent of the directors, appoint any other person who concurrently with him has a qualifying interest in any flat to be an alternate director, notwithstanding that the proposed alternate director is not a member of the company; and regulations 65 to 69 of Table A shall apply in relation to the person so appointed.
18. Regulation 82 of Table A shall not apply to the company, and directors shall accordingly not be entitled to remuneration.
19. If under the terms of any lease or tenancy agreement the company has the right to determine the amount of a service charge or other periodical payment due to the company, this power may be exercised by the directors from time to time. The company in general meeting may vary or revoke a previous determination by the directors by ordinary resolution, but such variation or revocation shall only have effect as concerns amounts payable after the date of the general meeting.

NOTICES

20. The directors may erect a house notice board conveniently near the entrance of any building owned or managed by the company, and notice placed on the board shall be conclusively presumed to have been given to all members resident or interested in any of the flats in that building.
21. A notice may be given to any member resident or interested in any flat by being placed in the normal place for incoming post to that flat, or by being sent to him at that flat by post in a prepaid envelope.

Election of Directors and the Secretary

See Form 288 on pages 149–160.

Return of Allotments

For the four shares allotted to Belinda Bott, Charles Crawford, Dahlia Dymond and Edward Extract

See Form 88(2) on pages 161–162.

Entries in Register of Members

Anthony John Absolute of 999 Acacia Avenue, Dale, Barsetshire BS20 5QR, acquired one £1 ordinary share numbered 1 by transfer from Gregory Grebe on April 3, 1991.

Belinda Bott of 999 Acacia Avenue, Dale, Barsetshire, BS20 5QR acquired one £1 ordinary share numbered 3 by virtue of the allotment of that share to her on April 3, 1991.

(After existing entry for Caroline Cat) On February 1, 1991 she transferred that share to Felicity Ann Fowler.

Charles Ian Crawford of 999 Acacia Avenue, Dale, Barsetshire, BS20 5QR acquired one £1 ordinary share numbered 4 by virtue of the allotment of that share to him on April 3, 1991.

Dahlia Louisa Dymond of 999 Acacia Avenue, Dale, Barsetshire BS20 5QR acquired one £1 ordinary share numbered 5 by virtue of the allotment of that share to her on April 3, 1991.

Edward Extract of 999 Acacia Avenue, Dale, Barsetshire BS20 5QR acquired one £1 ordinary share numbered 6 by virtue of the allotment of that share to him on April 3, 1991.

Felicity Ann Fowler of 999 Acacia Avenue, Dale, Barsetshire BS20 5QR acquired one £1 ordinary share numbered 2 by transfer from Caroline Cat on April 3, 1991

(After existing entry for Gregory Grebe) On February 1, 1991 he transferred that share to Anthony John Absolute.

Share certificates

See Share Certificate Forms on pages 163–165.

Bank mandate

These forms are supplied by the bank, and no example is included here for copyright reasons.

Notice of New Accounting Year

See Form G225(1) on page 166.

Change of Registered Office

See Form G287 on page 167.

New Certificate of Incorporation

E. Deed of Variation

THIS DEED OF VARIATION is made the First day of December One thousand nine hundred and ninety one between 999 ACACIA AVENUE LIMITED (hereinafter called "the Association") of the first part and ANTHONY JOHN ABSOLUTE and LYDIA LANGUISH both of 999 Acacia Avenue, Dale, Barsetshire BS20 5QR (hereinafter called "the Tenants") of the second part WHEREAS

(1) By a Lease dated 27th day of September 1967 between Terence Seignior and Letitia Malaprop ("hereinafter called "the Lease") premises known as Flat 1, 999 Acacia Avenue, Dale in the County of Barset and more particularly described therein were demised for a term of 99 years from the 29th day of June 1967.

(2) The Lessor's interest under the Lease is now vested in the Association and the Lessee's interest under the Lease is now vested in the Tenants.

(3) The Association and the Tenants wish to vary the terms of the Lease in the manner hereinafter set out.

(4) The Association and the tenants of all the other flats at 999 Acacia Avenue aforesaid intend to vary the terms of their respective leases in the same manner.

NOW THIS DEED WITNESSETH that the Association and the Tenants agree to vary the terms of the Lease as follows, all such variations to take effect from the First day of September One thousand nine hundred and ninety one.

1. In the Second Schedule, the following words to be inserted at the end of paragraph (d):

> "provided that if any event shall occur giving rise to a claim under the insurance policy or policies required to be effected by the Lessor under paragraph 1 of the Fourth Schedule hereto as inserted by a Deed of Variation dated the 1st day of December 1991 and the

moneys recovered pursuant to such claim shall be applied in the repair or reinstatement of the demised premises the Lessees shall pro tanto be released from their liability to carry out repairs to the demised premises as a consequence of that event or to contribute to the costs of such repairs."

2. In the Second Schedule, paragraph (j) to be deleted and the following substituted:

"(j) To comply with and observe such amendements or additional regulations to those set forth in the Third Schedule hereto as the Lessor may (consistently with the provisions of this Lease) make to govern the use to the Site in the general interest of the residents."

3. In the Fourth Schedule, the following paragraph to be inserted at the beginning and the existing paragraphs 1 to 5 to be renumbered as paragraphs 2 to 6:

"1. To insure the Site and keep it insured against loss or damage by fire storm impact or aircraft or such other risks as are included in a House Owner's Comprehensive Policy with an insurance company of repute and for such sum as the Lessor shall reasonably believe to represent full replacement value of the Site plus Surveyor's and Architect's fees and to make all payments necessary for these purposes within seven days after the same become payable and to produce the Lessee on demand the policies of such insurance and the receipts for such payments. Such insurance shall be effected in the joint names of the Lessor and the Lessee and the lessees for the time being of all of the Flats and the premiums shall be recovered from the lessees of the Flats as part of the maintenance charges provided for by the Fifth Schedule hereto. Any moneys recovered under such insurance shall be applied to the reinstatement of the Site and other expenses insured against and any excess shall be retained by the Lessor."

F. Raising the Price of the Freehold

Resolution to Raise the Price of the Freehold by Issuing Extra Shares

999 ACACIA AVENUE LIMITED
MINUTES OF A MEETING OF THE DIRECTORS
HELD ON SEPTEMBER 25, 1991
AT FLAT 1, 999 ACACIA AVENUE, DALE,
BARSETSHIRE, BS20 5QR

Present at the meeting were Anthony Absolute, Belinda Bott, Charles Crawford, Dahlia Dymond, Edward Extract and Felicity Fowler (the secretary).

The secretary reported that contracts had been exchanged with the landlord (Mr Seignior) for the sale of the freehold of 999 Acacia Avenue by him to the company for £1,600; it was estimated that legal and other expenses would amount to a further £200.

It was therefore resolved to allot one unissued £1 ordinary share to each member at a premium of £299.

A.J. Absolute
Chairman

Entry in Register of Members

[After existing entry for Anthony Absolute]

He acquired one £1 ordinary share numbered 7 by virtue of the allotment of that share to him on September 25, 1991.

(Other entries similarly)

Return of allotments

See Form G88(2) on pages 168–169.

G. Loan of Money by some of the Tenants to Pay for Major Repairs

In the following, it is necessary to raise £30,000 for the cost of a new roof, each tenant can contribute £1,000 immediately and Anthony Absolute and Belinda Bott are each willing to lend the company £12,000.

Resolution to Execute Debentures and Issue Extra Shares at a Premium

999 ACACIA AVENUE LIMITED

MINUTES OF A MEETING OF THE DIRECTORS
HELD ON APRIL 5, 1993
AT FLAT 1, 999 ACACIA AVENUE, DALE,
BARSETSHIRE BS20 5QR

Present at the meeting were Anthony Absolute, Belinda Bott, Charles Crawford, Dahlia Dymond and Felicity Fowler. Apologies for absence were received from Edward Extract, believed to be currently standing in the attic holding up the roof timbers.

1. It was resolved to accept the quotation of £30,000 from Messrs. Clatter and Bang for the replacement of the roof.

2. It was resolved to accept the offers of Anthony Absolute and Belinda Bott to lend £12,000 each to the company, and to authorise Charles Crawford and Dahlia Dymond as directors to sign the appropriate debentures on behalf of the company.

3. It was resolved to allot one £1 ordinary share to each member at a premium of £4,000, £999 to be paid on allotment and the rest when called for.

A.J. Absolute
Chairman

Debenture

999 ACACIA AVENUE

....

LIMITED

(Incorporated under the Companies Act 1985*)*

DEBENTURE

£ 12,000

1. 999 ACACIA AVENUE *LIMITED (hereinafter called "the Company" will, on the* FIFTH *day of* APRIL *19* 98, *or on such earlier day as the principal moneys hereby secured become payable in accordance with the Conditions endorsed hereon, pay to* ANTHONY JOHN ABSOLUTE *of* FLAT 1, 999 ACACIA AVENUE, DALE BARSETSHIRE BS20 5QR *or other the registered holder for the time being hereof, the sum of £* 12,000.

*2. The Company will, during the continuance of this security, pay to such registered holder interest on the said sum of £*12,000 *at the rate specified in the conditions attached by half-yearly payments on the* FIFTH *day of* APRIL *and the* FIFTH *day of* OCTOBER *in every year, the first of such half-yearly payments, or a proportionate part thereof, calculated from the date of the issue of this Debenture to be made on the* FIFTH *day of* OCTOBER *next.*

3. The Company hereby charges with such payments its undertaking and all its property and assets, both present and future, including its uncalled capital for the time being.

4. This Debenture is issued subject to and with the benefit of the Conditions endorsed hereon, which shall be deemed to be incorporated herewith.

Executed as the deed of 999 ACACIA AVENUE *LIMITED this* FIFTH *day of* APRIL *19* 93 *by*

CHARLES CRAWFORD..........................

DAHLIA DYMOND.............................. }

FELICITY FOWLER..............................

THE CONDITIONS WITHIN REFERRED TO

1. Every transfer of this Debenture must be in writing under the hand or hands of the holder or holders hereof or the personal representatives of a sole or only surviving holder. The transfer must be delivered at the registered office of the Company with [a fee of 15p and] such evidence of title or identity as the Company may reasonably require. The Company shall be entitled to retain the transfer. The Company shall not be bound by or take any account of any transfer not complying with this condition, and shall not recognise any equitable interest in this Debenture.

2. In the case of joint holders, the principal moneys and interest hereby secured shall be deemed to be owing to them upon a joint account.

3. In respect of each half year's instalment of interest on this Debenture, a warrant on the Company's bankers, payable to the order of the holder hereof, or the personal representatives of a sole or only surviving holder, or in the case of joint holders to the order of that one whose name stands first in the relevant instrument of transfer will be sent by first class post to the last known address of such holder, and the Company shall not be responsible for any loss in transmission, and the payment of the warrant shall be a good discharge to the Company for the same.

4. The principal moneys and interest hereby secured will be paid without regard to any equities between the Company and the original or any intermediate holder hereof or to any counter-claim or right of set-off, and the receipt of the holder hereof for the time being or the personal representatives of a sole or only surviving holder, or in the case of joint holders of that one whose name stands first in the relevant instrument of transfer as one of such joint holders, for such principal moneys and interest shall be a good discharge to the Company for the same.

5. The Company may at any time give notice in writing to the holder or holders hereof, or the personal representatives of a sole or only surviving holder, of its intention to redeem this Debenture, and upon the

expiration of [three] months from such notice being given, the principal moneys hereby secured shall become payable.

6. The principal moneys hereby secured shall become payable—

(A) If the Company makes default for a period of [two] months in the payment of any interest hereby secured;
(B) If an order is made or an effective resolution is passed for the winding up of the Company;
(C) If a distress or execution is levied or enforced upon or against any of the chattels or property of the Company, and is not paid out or discharged within five days;
(D) If a Receiver or Administrative Receiver (within the meaning of the Insolvency Act 1986) is appointed of the undertaking, property or assets of the Company or any part thereof:
(E) If the Company stops payment or ceases or threatens to cease to carry on its business;
(F) If a petition is presented applying for an administration order to be made in relation to the Company.

7. The principal moneys hereby secured will be paid at the Company's bankers, or at the registered office of the Company.

8. The holder or holders of this Debenture shall have power by writing under his or their hand or hands to sanction or agree to any modification or compromise of the rights of the holders of the Debenture against the Company or against its undertaking, property and assets (including the creation and issue of any mortgages, charges, Debentures or Debenture Stock ranking in priority to or *pari passu* with this Debenture or any variation of the rate of interest or extension of the time for payment of all or any part of the principal moneys or interest secured by such Debenture) or any modification of these Conditions or any arrangement which the Court would have jurisdiction to sanction under Section 425 of the Companies Act 1985, if the requisite majority at a meeting of such holders duly convened and held in accordance with that section or any modification or re-enactment thereof had agreed thereto, and any modification, compromise or arrangement so sanctioned or agreed to shall be binding on the holders of this Debenture and notice thereof shall be given to each holder, who shall be bound to produce this Debenture to the Company and to permit a note thereof to be endorsed thereon.

9. The registered holder or holders of this Debenture may, in accordance with the provisions of the Insolvency Act 1986, at any time after the principal moneys hereby secured shall have come payable, by writing under his or their hand or hands, appoint any person authorised to act as an insolvency practioner to be an Administrative Receiver of the undertaking, property and assets hereby charged. The said registered holder or holders may, so far as is permitted by law, also apply to the Court pursuant to Section 45 of the Insolvency Act 1986 for the removal

from office of any Administrative Receiver so appointed and may appoint another in his place in like manner as is provided above. Any Administrative Receiver as may be appointed shall, in accordance with Section 42 of the Insolvency Act 1986, have all the powers specified in Schedule 1 to that Act. For the avoidance of doubt and in addition thereto and without prejudice to the powers thereby conferred, it is stated that the powers of any such Administrative Receiver shall include:

(A) power to take possession of, collect and get in the undertaking, property and assets hereby charged and, for that purpose, to take such proceedings as may seem to him expedient;
(B) power to sell or otherwise dispose of all or any part of the undertaking, property and assets hereby charged by public auction or private contract:
(C) power to raise or borrow money and grant security therefor over the undertaking, property and assets hereby charged;
(D) power to manage and carry on the business of the Company;
(E) power to execute in the name and on behalf of the Company any deed, receipt or other document (for which purpose the Company hereby irrevocably appoints every such Administrative Receiver its attorney to do so in its name and on its behalf).

So far as is permitted by law, any such Administrative Receiver shall be deemed for all purposes to be the agent of the Company and none of the Debenture holders shall be under any liability for his remuneration or otherwise. All moneys received by any such Administrative Receiver shall, subject to the provisions of the Law of Property Act 1925 as to the application of insurance money, be applied by him as follows:—

(1) for his remuneration, and in satisfaction of all costs, charges and expenses incurred by him as Administrative Receiver, a commission at a rate fixed in accordance with the provisions of Section 109(6) of the Law of Property Act 1925; then
(2) in providing for the matters specified in the first three paragraphs of Section 109(8) of the Law of Property Act 1925 (excluding the payment of the commission provided for above); then
(3) in providing for the preferential debts specified in Sections 40, 175, 386, 387 and Schedule 6 of the Insolvency Act 1986; then
(4) in or towards satisfaction, *pari passu,* of the principal moneys and interest secured by the said Debentures.

and subject as aforesaid the balance remaining, if any, shall be held in trust for the Company. The foregoing provisions shall take effect by way of variation and extension of Sections 101 and 104 to 109 inclusive of the Law of Property Act 1925 and the provisions of those Sections as so varied and extended shall apply to any Administrative Receiver to the extent that the same are consistent with and permitted by the Insolvency Act 1986. Section 103 of the Law of Property Act 1925 shall not apply.

10. A notice may be served by the Company on the holder or holders of this Debenture, or on the personal representatives of a sole or only surviving holder, by sending it through the post in a prepaid first class letter or letters addressed to him or them at the last known address or addresses of such holder or holders, and any such notice served by post shall be deemed to have been served on the day following that on which it is posted, and in providing service of such notice it shall be sufficient to prove that the envelope containing the notice was properly addressed and stamped and put into the post office. In the case of a notice to the personal representatives of a deceased holder it shall not be necessary to specify their names.

11. The principal sum of £12,000 shall be repaid in five equal instalments, the first such instalment to be paid on 5th April 1994 and the remaining instalments to be paid on the successive anniversaries of that date.

12. Interest shall be paid at the rate of one per cent. more than the base rate of Barcloyds plc for the time being. It shall be deemed to accrue from day to day and be charged on so much of the principal as shall be for the time being outstanding.

999 ACACIA AVENUE

LIMITED

(Incorporated under the Companies Act 1985*)*

DEBENTURE £ 12,000

1. 999 ACACIA AVENUE *LIMITED (hereinafter called "the Company" will, on the* FIFTH *day of* APRIL *19* 98, *or on such earlier day as the principal moneys hereby secured become payable in accordance with the Conditions endorsed hereon, pay to* BELINDA BOTT *of* FLAT 2, 999 ACACIA AVENUE, DALE BARSETSHIRE BS20 5QR *or other the registered holder for the time being hereof, the sum of £* 12,000.

2. The Company will, during the continuance of this security, pay to such registered holder interest on the said sum of £12,000 *at the rate specified in the conditions attached by half-yearly payments on the* FIFTH *day of* APRIL *and the* FIFTH *day of* OCTOBER *in every year, the first of such half-yearly payments, or a proportionate part thereof, calculated from the date of the issue of this Debenture to be made on the* FIFTH *day of* OCTOBER *next.*

3. The Company hereby charges with such payments its undertaking and all its property and assets, both present and future, including its uncalled capital for the time being.

4. This Debenture is issued subject to and with the benefit of the Conditions endorsed hereon, which shall be deemed to be incorporated herewith.

Executed as the deed of 999 ACACIA AVENUE *Limited this* FIFTH *day of* APRIL *19* 93 *by*

CHARLES CRAWFORD ....
DAHLIA DYMOND .... }
FELICITY FOWLER ....

THE CONDITIONS WITHIN REFERRED TO

1. Every transfer of this Debenture must be in writing under the hand or hands of the holder or holders hereof or the personal representatives of a sole or only surviving holder. The transfer must be delivered at the registered office of the Company with [a fee of 15p and] such evidence of title or identity as the Company may reasonably require. The Company shall be entitled to retain the transfer. The Company shall not be bound by or take any account of any transfer not complying with this condition, and shall not recognise any equitable interest in this Debenture.

2. In the case of joint holders, the principal moneys and interest hereby secured shall be deemed to be owing to them upon a joint account.

3. In respect of each half year's instalment of interest on this Debenture, a warrant on the Company's bankers, payable to the order of the holder hereof, or the personal representatives of a sole or only surviving holder, or in the case of joint holders to the order of that one whose name stands first in the relevant instrument of transfer will be sent by first class post to the last known address of such holder, and the Company shall not be responsible for any loss in transmission, and the payment of the warrant shall be a good discharge to the Company for the same.

4. The principal moneys and interest hereby secured will be paid without regard to any equities between the Company and the original or any intermediate holder hereof or to any counter-claim or right of set-off, and the receipt of the holder hereof for the time being or the personal representatives of a sole or only surviving holder, or in the case of joint holders of that one whose name stands first in the relevant instrument of transfer as one of such joint holders, for such principal moneys and interest shall be a good discharge to the Company for the same.

5. The Company may at any time give notice in writing to the holder or holders hereof, or the personal representatives of a sole or only surviving holder, of its intention to redeem this Debenture, and upon the expiration of [three] months from such notice being given, the principal moneys hereby secured shall become payable.

6. The principal moneys hereby secured shall become payable—

(A) If the Company makes default for a period of [two] months in the payment of any interest hereby secured;
(B) If an order is made or an effective resolution is passed for the winding up of the Company;
(C) If a distress or execution is levied or enforced upon or against any of the chattels or property of the Company, and is not paid out or discharged within five days;
(D) If a Receiver or Administrative Receiver (within the meaning of the Insolvency Act 1986) is appointed of the undertaking, property or assets of the Company or any part thereof:
(E) If the Company stops payment or ceases or threatens to cease to carry on its business;
(F) If a petition is presented applying for an administration order to be made in relation to the Company.

7. The principal moneys hereby secured will be paid at the Company's bankers, or at the registered office of the Company.

8. The holder or holders of this Debenture shall have power by writing under his or their hand or hands to sanction or agree to any modification or compromise of the rights of the holders of the Debenture against the Company or against its undertaking, property and assets (including the creation and issue of any mortgages, charges, Debentures or Debenture Stock ranking in priority to or *pari passu* with this Debenture or any variation of the rate of interest or extension of the time for payment of all or any part of the principal moneys or interest secured by such Debenture) or any modification of these Conditions or any arrangement which the Court would have jurisdiction to sanction under Section 425 of the Companies Act 1985, if the requisite majority at a meeting of such holders duly convened and held in accordance with that section or any modification or re-enactment thereof had agreed thereto, and any modification, compromise or arrangement so sanctioned or agreed to shall be binding on the holders of this Debenture and notice thereof shall be given to each holder, who shall be bound to produce this Debenture to the Company and to permit a note thereof to be endorsed thereon.

9. The registered holder or holders of this Debenture may, in accordance with the provisions of the Insolvency Act 1986, at any time after the principal moneys hereby secured shall have come payable, by writing under his or their hand or hands, appoint any person authorised to act as an insolvency practioner to be an Administrative Receiver of the undertaking, property and assets hereby charged. The said registered holder or holders may, so far as is permitted by law, also apply to the Court pursuant to Section 45 of the Insolvency Act 1986 for the removal from office of any Administrative Receiver so appointed and may appoint another in his place in like manner as is provided above. Any Administrative Receiver as may be appointed shall, in accordance with

Section 42 of the Insolvency Act 1986, have all the powers specified in Schedule 1 to that Act. For the avoidance of doubt and in addition thereto and without prejudice to the powers thereby conferred, it is stated that the powers of any such Administrative Receiver shall include:

(A) power to take possession of, collect and get in the undertaking, property and assets hereby charged and, for that purpose, to take such proceedings as may seem to him expedient;
(B) power to sell or otherwise dispose of all or any part of the undertaking, property and assets hereby charged by public auction or private contract:
(C) power to raise or borrow money and grant security therefor over the undertaking, property and assets hereby charged;
(D) power to manage and carry on the business of the Company;
(E) power to execute in the name and on behalf of the Company any deed, receipt or other document (for which purpose the Company hereby irrevocably appoints every such Administrative Receiver its attorney to do so in its name and on its behalf).

So far as is permitted by law, any such Administrative Receiver shall be deemed for all purposes to be the agent of the Company and none of the Debenture holders shall be under any liability for his remuneration or otherwise. All moneys received by any such Administrative Receiver shall, subject to the provisions of the Law of Property Act 1925 as to the application of insurance money, be applied by him as follows:

(1) for his remuneration, and in satisfaction of all costs, charges and expenses incurred by him as Administrative Receiver, a commission at a rate fixed in accordance with the provisions of Section 109(6) of the Law of Property Act 1925; then
(2) in providing for the matters specified in the first three paragraphs of Section 109(8) of the Law of Property Act 1925 (excluding the payment of the commission provided for above); then
(3) in providing for the preferential debts specified in Sections 40, 175, 386, 387 and Schedule 6 of the Insolvency Act 1986; then
(4) in or towards satisfaction, *pari passu*, of the principal moneys and interest secured by the said Debentures.

and subject as aforesaid the balance remaining, if any, shall be held in trust for the Company. The foregoing provisions shall take effect by way of variation and extension of Sections 101 and 104 to 109 inclusive of the Law of Property Act 1925 and the provisions of those Sections as so varied and extended shall apply to any Administrative Receiver to the extent that the same are consistent with and permitted by the Insolvency Act 1986. Section 103 of the Law of Property Act 1925 shall not apply.

10. A notice may be served by the Company on the holder or holders of this Debenture, or on the personal representatives of a sole or only surviving holder, by sending it through the post in a prepaid first class letter or letters addressed to him or them at the last known address or addresses of such holder or holders, and any such notice served by post shall be deemed to have been served on the day following that on which it is posted, and in providing service of such notice it shall be sufficient to prove that the envelope containing the notice was properly addressed and stamped and put into the post office. In the case of a notice to the personal representatives of a deceased holder it shall not be necessary to specify their names.

11. The principal sum of £12,000 shall be repaid in five equal instalments, the first such instalment to be paid on 5th April 1994 and the remaining instalments to be paid on the successive anniversaries of that date.

12. Interest shall be paid at the rate of one per cent. more than the base rate of Barcloyds plc for the time being. It shall be deemed to accrue from day to day and be charged on so much of the principal as shall be for the time being outstanding.

Entries in Company's Register of Charges

Anthony Absolute on April 5, 1993 became the holder of one debenture in the sum of £12,000.

Belinda Bott on April 5, 1993 became the holder of one debenture in the sum of £12,000.

Particulars of Mortgage or Charge

See Form M395 on pages 170–173.

Entries in Companies House Register of Charges

See Form 401 on pages 174–176.

Entries in Register of Members

[after existing entries for Anthony Absolute]

He acquired one £1 ordinary share numbered 13 by virtue of the allotment of that share to him on April 5, 1993.

The entries for the other five members will be similar.

Return of allotments

See Form G88(2) on pages 177–178.

First Call

999 ACACIA AVENUE LIMITED
MINUTES OF A MEETING OF THE DIRECTORS
HELD ON MARCH 17, 1994
AT FLAT 1, 999 ACACIA AVENUE, DALE
BARSETSHIRE, BS20 5QR

Present at the meeting were Anthony Absolute, Belinda Bott, Sardanapalus Snooks, Dahlia Dymond, Edward Extract and Felicity Fowler (secretary).

It was resolved to call for £800 of the premium outstanding on each of the shares numbered from 13 to 18, the said sums to be paid not later than April 3, 1994.

A.J. Absolute
Chairman

(Thus, on April 3, each member ought to pay the company £800; the company should then pay £2,400 to Anthony Absolute and £2,400 to Belinda Bott under the debenture. In practice, of course, Sardanapalus Snooks, Dahlia Dymond, Edward Extract and Felicity Fowler will each pay £800 to the company and the company will pay £1,600 to Anthony Absolute and £1,600 to Belinda Bott.)

The calls for 1995, 1996, 1997 and 1998 will be similar

Entries in Companies House Register of Charges

See Form 401 on pages 179–181.

Entries in Company's Register of Charges

(under entry for Anthony Absolute)
£2,400 was repaid to him on April 3, 1994

Declarations of Satisfaction

See Form M403a on page 182.

H. Change of Ownership of Flat

Share transfer

See Stock Transfer Forms on pages 183–184.

Directors' Meeting

999 ACACIA AVENUE LIMITED
MINUTES OF A MEETING OF THE DIRECTORS
HELD ON SEPTEMBER 2, 1993
AT FLAT 2, 999 ACACIA AVENUE
DALE, BARSETSHIRE BS20 5QR

Present at the meeting were Anthony Absolute, Belinda Bott, Sardanapalus Snooks and Felicity Fowler. Apologies for absence were received from Dahlia Dymond and Edward Extract.

Felicity Fowler reported that Sardanapalus Snooks had purchased flat number 3 from Charles Crawford, and introduced him to those present. The following resolutions were then passed:

1. The transfer of the shares numbered 4, 9, and 15 from Charles Crawford to Sardanapalus Snooks is hereby approved.
2. Sardanapalus Snooks is elected a director of the company in place of Charles Crawford.
3. Sardanapalus Snooks is to be a signatory of the company's bank account in place of Charles Crawford, and the altered mandate form provided by Barcloyds Plc is hereby approved.

Anthony Absolute
Chairman

Entries in Register of Members

(Under entry for Charles Crawford).

On September 2, 1993 he transferred the three shares numbered 4, 9 and 15 to Sardanapalus Snooks of flat 3, 999 Acacia Avenue, Dale, Barsetshire BS20 5QR.

(Under letter S in the Register).

SARDANAPALUS SNOOKS of flat 3, 999 Acacia Avenue, Dale, Barsetshire BS20 5QR became the holder of three £1 ordinary shares numbered 4, 9 and 15 by transfer from Charles Ian Crawford on September 2, 1993.

Share Certificate

See Share Certificate on page 186.

Notice of Change of Director

See Form 288 on pages 187–188.

I. Annual Formalities

Letter to Accountants

Flat 6,
999 Acacia Avenue
Dale
Barsetshire
BS20 5QR

September 20, 1992

Dear Mr Byng

999 ACACIA AVENUE LIMITED

As agreed in our telephone conversation yesterday, you will be preparing and auditing acounts for the above company for the year ended August 31, 1992. I therefore enclose the last five quarterly bank statements and supporting invoices.

The balance of £4 as at September 1, 1991 represents the nominal values of shares 3 to 6, which were issued on April 3, 1991. The £1,800 paid in on September 28, 1991 represents the nominal values plus premiums of shares 7 to 12, which were issued on the 25th of that month. The same sum, paid out on October 1, 1991, represents £1,600 for the price of the freehold and £200 legal fees: see solicitor's completion statement enclosed herewith.

On December 5, 1991 we set a service charge of £50 per flat per month, backdated to September 1, 1991: the sums of £500 and £400 paid in during that month represent the first three months' service charges. Thereafter the charges were all paid every month, except that Dahlia Dymond did not pay the instalments for July and August 1992 until September 15, 1992.

The remaining bank entries should all be explained by the invoices enclosed, except that the invoice for £100 for the entryphone has not been paid, since this has not been working for the last three months and we are in dispute with the company.

I hope that this tells you all you need to know and that you will be able to provide draft accounts soon. Please let me know if there is any further help you need.

Yours sincerely

Felicity Fowler
(Company secretary)

Messrs. Bouncer & Co. (Accountants)
attn. Bertram Byng Esq.
Astaire Chambers
St. Vitus Road
Dale
Barsetshire BS20 8ZL

Letter From the Accountants

Bouncer & Co
Accountants
Astaire Chambers
St. Vitus Road
Dale
Barsetshire BS20 8ZL

October 1, 1992

Dear Miss Fowler

999 ACACIA AVENUE LIMITED

I enclose eight sets of accounts, with audit certificates still unsigned. When these have been approved in a directors' meeting, please ask your chairman or another director to sign at least two copies in the places marked, and send them back to me so that I can sign the audit certificates.

Yours sincerely

Bertie Byng

Miss Felicity Fowler
Secretary, 999 Acacia Avenue Ltd.
999 Acacia Avenue
Dale
Barsetshire BS20 5QR

The accounts enclosed are those set out on pages 51 to 52 on accounting concepts.

Minutes of Directors' Meeting

999 ACACIA AVENUE LIMITED
MINUTES OF A MEETING OF THE DIRECTORS
HELD ON OCTOBER 4, 1992
AT FLAT 6, 999 ACACIA AVENUE
DALE, BARSETSHIRE BS20 5QR

Present at the meeting were Anthony Absolute, Belinda Bott, Dahlia Dymond and Felicity Fowler. Apologies for absence were received from Charles Crawford and Edward Extract.

Felicity Fowler distributed and explained the draft accounts prepared by Messrs. Bouncer & Co. It was resolved that the draft accounts be approved as the accounts of the company for the year ended August 31, 1992, and that Anthony Absolute be instructed to sign the copies on behalf of the company.

It was further resolved that the annual general meeting of the company for 1992 be called for December 1, 1992.

A.J. Absolute
Chairman

Minutes of Annual General Meeting

999 ACACIA AVENUE LIMITED
ANNUAL GENERAL MEETING FOR 1992
HELD ON DECEMBER 1, 1992 AT
FLAT 6, 999 ACACIA AVENUE, DALE

BARSETSHIRE BS20 5QR

Present at the meeting were Anthony Absolute, Charles Crawford, Dahlia Dymond, Edward Extract and Felicity Fowler:

1. The annual accounts for the year ended August 31, 1992 were laid before the company; it was resolved that they be received and adopted;
2. No dividend was declared for the year;
3. It was resolved that Messrs. Bouncer be re-appointed as auditors to the company until the following annual general meeting;
4. It was resolved that all the existing directors be re-appointed.

Annual Return

See Form 363a on pages 189–197. The returns for subsequent years are on pages 198 to 214.

J. De-regulation of the Company

Elective Resolution

999 ACACIA AVENUE LIMITED
WRITTEN RESOLUTIONS
AGREED ON NOVEMBER 27, 1993

The following resolutions are agreed unanimously pursuant to section 381A of the Companies Act 1985:

(1) It is resolved that the company's auditors, Messrs. Bouncer & Co., shall from and after the date of this resolution remain in office from year to year without the need for re-appointment in general meeting, until such time as the company shall in general meeting resolve to terminate their appointment; and this resolution is declared to be an elective resolution passed under the power of section 386 of the Companies Act 1985.

(2) It is resolved that, from and after the date of this resolution, the directors shall be exempt from the obligation under section 241(1) of the Companies Act 1985 to lay accounts before the company in general meeting; and this resolution is declared to be an elective resolution passed under the power of section 252 of the Companies Act 1985.

(3) It is resolved that the company shall be exempt from the obligation under section 366 of the Companies Act 1985 to

hold an annual general meeting for the year 1994 or any subsequent year; and this resolution is declared to be an elective resolution passed under the power of section 366A of the Companies Act 1985.

Signed

A. J. Absolute
B. Bott
S. Snooks
D. L. Dymond
E. Extract
F. A. Proctor (Mrs.)

Envoi

"And so I conclude with [ownership and management companies], wishing that these may ever be a perfect union between them and their [members], that they may have a feeling of each others' wrongs and injuries; that their so little commonwealth, having all its members knitted together in complete order, may flourish to the end."

(adapted from *Coke's Complete Copyholder*, last paragraph).

OYEZ
CHA1

10

Statement of first directors and secretary and intended situation of registered office

This form should be completed in black.

CN | For official use

Company name *(in full)* GREBECAT LIMITED

Registered office of the company on incorporation.

RO c/o REGINALD REGISTRATIONS LTD.
WELBECK CHAMBERS, 19 DUXBURY STREET
Post town LONDON
County/Region
Postcode WC3 7TD

If the memorandum is delivered by an agent for the subscribers of the memorandum mark 'X' in the box opposite and give the agent's name and address.

Name
RA
Post town
County/Region
Postcode

Number of continuation sheets attached

To whom should Companies House direct any enquiries about the information shown in this form?

CAROLINE CAT
REGINALD REGISTRATIONS LTD
address as above Postcode
Telephone 071-446 1111 Extension 370

Company Secretary *(See notes 1 - 5)*

Name	*Style/Title	CS MISS
	Forenames	CAROLINE EMMA
	Surname	CAT
	*Honours etc	
	Previous forenames	
	Previous surname	
Address		AD 38 BOTTLENECK WAY
Usual residential address must be given. In the case of a corporation, give the registered or principal office address.		
	Post town	DENHAM
	County/Region	MIDDLESEX
	Postcode	Country

I consent to act as secretary of the company named on page 1

Consent signature Signed C. E. Cat Date 13·3·1985

Directors *(See notes 1 - 5)*
Please list directors in alphabetical order.

Name	*Style/Title	CD MR.
	Forenames	GREGORY CHRISTOPHER
	Surname	GREBE
	*Honours etc	
	Previous forenames	
	Previous surname	
Address		AD 20 CHURCH WALK
Usual residential address must be given. In the case of a corporation, give the registered or principal office address.		
	Post town	BROXBOURNE
	County/Region	HERTFORDSHIRE
	Postcode	Country
	Date of birth	DO — Nationality NA
	Business occupation	OC COMPANY FORMATION AGENT
	Other directorships	OD POCHARD LTD, MERGANSER LTD, GOLDENEYE LTD

* Voluntary details

I consent to act as director of the company named on page 1

Page 2 **Consent signature** Signed G. C. Grebe Date 13·3·1985

Directors (continued)
(See notes 1 - 5)

Name	*Style/Title	CD
	Forenames	
	Surname	
	*Honours etc	
	Previous forenames	
	Previous surname	
Address		AD
Usual residential address must be given. In the case of a corporation, give the registered or principal office address.		
	Post town	
	County/Region	
	Postcode	Country
	Date of birth	DO
	Nationality	NA
	Business occupation	OC
	Other directorships	OD
* Voluntary details		I consent to act as director of the company named on page 1
Consent signature	Signed	Date

Delete if the form is signed by the subscribers.

~~Signature of agent on behalf of all subscribers~~ Date

Delete if the form is signed by an agent on behalf of all the subscribers.

All the subscribers must sign either personally or by a person or persons authorised to sign for them.

Signed G. C. Grebe	Date 13·3·1986
Signed C. E. Cat	Date 13·3·1986
Signed	Date
Signed	Date
Signed	Date
Signed	Date

Page 3

Notes

1 Show for an individual the full forenames NOT INITIALS and surname together with any previous forenames or surname(s).

If the director or secretary is a corporation or Scottish firm - show the corporate or firm name on the surname line.

Give previous forenames or surname except that:

- for a married woman, the name by which she was known before marriage need not be given.
- names not used since the age of 18 or for at least 20 years need not be given.

In the case of a peer, or an individual usually known by a British title, you may state the title instead of or in addition to the forenames and surname and you need not give the name by which that person was known before he or she adopted the title or succeeded to it.

Address:

Give the usual residential address.

In the case of a corporation or Scottish firm give the registered or principal office.

2 Directors known by another description:

A director includes any person who occupies that position even if called by a different name, for example, governor, member of council. It also includes a shadow director.

3 Directors details:

Show for each individual director their date of birth, business occupation and nationality.
The date of birth must be given for every individual director.

4 Other directorships:

Give the name of every company of which the individual concerned is a director or has been a director at any time in the past 5 years. You may exclude a company which either is or at all times during the past 5 years when the person was a director was:

- dormant,
- a parent company which wholly owned the company making the return,
- a wholly owned subsidiary of the company making the return,
- another wholly owned subsidiary of the same parent company.

If there is insufficient space on the form for other directorships you may use a separate sheet of paper.

5 Use photocopies of page 2 to provide details of joint secretaries or additional directors and include the company's name and number.

6 The address for companies registered in England and Wales is:-

The Registrar of Companies
Companies House
Crown Way
Cardiff
CF4 3UZ

or, for companies registered in Scotland:-

The Registrar of Companies
Companies House
100-102 George Street
Edinburgh
EH2 3DJ

OYEZ The Solicitor's Law Stationery Society Ltd., Oyez House, 27 Crimscott Street, London SE1 5TS

1990 Edition
9.90 F17984
5017288

G

COMPANIES FORM No. 12

Statutory Declaration of compliance with requirements on application for registration of a company

12

Please do not write in this margin

Pursuant to section 12(3) of the Companies Act 1985

Please complete legibly, preferably in black type, or bold block lettering

To the Registrar of Companies

For official use | For official use

Name of company

* insert full name of Company

* GREBECAT LIMITED

I, GREGORY CHRISTOPHER GREBE

of 20 CHURCH WALK, BROXBOURNE, HERTS.

† delete as appropriate

do solemnly and sincerely declare that I am a [Solicitor engaged in the formation of the company]† [person named as director or secretary of the company in the statement delivered to the registrar under section 10(2)]† and that all the requirements of the above Act in respect of the registration of the above company and of matters precedent and incidental to it have been complied with,

And I make this solemn declaration conscientiously believing the same to be true and by virtue of the provisions of the Statutory Declarations Act 1835

Declared at 201 LINCOLNS INN FIELDS

LONDON WC2

the SEVENTEENTH day of MARCH

One thousand nine hundred and EIGHTY SIX

before me PETER FOGG

A Commissioner for Oaths or Notary Public or Justice of the Peace or Solicitor having the powers conferred on a Commissioner for Oaths.

Declarant to sign below

G.C. Grebe

[STAMP]

Presentor's name address and reference (if any):

G. C. GREBE
REGINALD REGISTRATIONS LTD.
WELBECK CHAMBERS
19 DUXBURY STREET
LONDON WC3 7TD
REF: GC 90007

For official Use

New Companies Section | Post room

No. 1 No. OF SHARES 1 Nos. 1 ISSUED TO GREGORY CHRISTOPHER GREBE OF 20 CHURCH WALK BROXBOURNE HERTS DATE 23rd OCTOBER 1986 ENTERED ON REGISTER	No. 1 GREBECAT LIMITED Incorporated under the Companies Act CAPITAL £100 DIVIDED INTO 100 SHARES OF £1 EACH THIS IS TO CERTIFY *that* GREGORY CHRISTOPHER GREBE *of* 20 CHURCH WALK, BROXBOURNE, HERTS. *is the holder of* ONE ORDINARY *Share paid of* £1 *each Numbered* 1 *to* — *issued in the above named Company subject to the memorandum and Articles of Association thereof* GIVEN *by the said Company* *The* 23rd *day of* OCTOBER 1986 *acting by* *Director* G. C. GREBE *Secretary* C. E. CAT NO TRANSFER OF THE WHOLE OR ANY PORTION OF THE ABOVE SHARES CAN BE REGISTERED WITHOUT THE PRODUCTION OF THIS CERTIFICATE

No. 2 No. OF SHARES 1 Nos. 2 ISSUED TO CAROLINE EMMA CAT OF 38 BOTTLENECK WAY, DENHAM, MIDDX. DATE 23rd OCTOBER 1986 ENTERED ON REGISTER	No. 2 GREBECAT LIMITED Incorporated under the Companies Act CAPITAL £100 DIVIDED INTO 100 SHARES OF £1 EACH THIS IS TO CERTIFY *that* CAROLINE EMMA CAT *of* 38 BOTTLENECK WAY, DENHAM, MIDDX. *is the holder of* ONE ORDINARY *Share paid of* £1 *each Numbered* 2 *to* — *issued in the above named Company subject to the memorandum and Articles of Association thereof* GIVEN *by the said Company* *The* 23rd *day of* OCTOBER 1986 *acting by* *Director* G. C. GREBE *Secretary* C. E. CAT NO TRANSFER OF THE WHOLE OR ANY PORTION OF THE ABOVE SHARES CAN BE REGISTERED WITHOUT THE PRODUCTION OF THIS CERTIFICATE

CON. 40 (1963)

STOCK TRANSFER FORM

(Above this line for Registrars only)

Consideration Money £ 1:00	Certificate lodged with the Registrar (For completion by the Registrar/Stock Exchange)

Name of Undertaking.	GREBECAT LIMITED	
Description of Security.	£1 ORDINARY SHARE	
Number or amount of Shares, Stock or other security and, in figures column only, number and denomination of units, if any.	Words ONE SHARE NUMBERED 1	Figures 1 (1 units of £1)
Name(s) of registered holder(s) should be given in full: the address should be given where there is only one holder. If the transfer is not made by the registered holder(s) insert also the name(s) and capacity (e.g., Executor(s)) of the person(s) making the transfer.	In the name(s) of GREGORY CHRISTOPHER GREBE c/o REGINALD REGISTRATIONS LTD. WELBECK CHAMBERS 19 DUXBURY STREET LONDON WC3 7TD	

I/We hereby transfer the above security out of the name(s) aforesaid to the person(s) named below. Signature(s) of transferor(s) 1. G. C. Grebe 2. .... 3. .... 4.	Stamp of Selling Broker(s) or, for transactions which are not stock exchange transactions, of Agent(s), if any, acting for the Transferor(s) Date 1st FEB. 1991

Full name(s) and full postal address(es) (including County or, if applicable, Postal District number) of the person(s) to whom the security is transferred. Please state title, if any, or whether Mr., Mrs., or Miss. Please complete in typewriting or in Block Capitals.	ANTHONY JOHN ABSOLUTE (MR.) FLAT 1, 999 ACACIA AVENUE DALE BARSETSHIRE BS20 5QR

I/We request that such entries be made in the register as are necessary to give effect to this transfer.

Stamp of Buying Broker(s) (if any)	Stamp or name and address of person lodging this form (if other than the Buying Broker(s))
	GREGORY GREBE address as above

FORM OF CERTIFICATE REQUIRED WHERE TRANSFER IS EXEMPT FROM STAMP DUTY

Instruments executed on or after 1st May 1987 effecting any transactions within the following categories are exempt from stamp duty:—

A. The vesting of property subject to a trust in the trustees of the trust on the appointment of a new trustee, or in the continuing trustees on the retirement of a trustee.

B. The conveyance or transfer of property the subject of a specific devise or legacy to the beneficiary named in the will (or his nominee). Transfers in satisfaction of a general legacy of money should not be included in this category (see category D below).

C. The conveyance or transfer of property which forms part of an intestate's estate to the person entitled on intestacy (or his nominee). Transfers in satisfaction of the transferees entitlement to cash in the estate of an intestate, where the total value of the residuary estate exceeds that sum, should not be included in this category (see category D below).

D. The appropriation of property within section 84(4) of the Finance Act 1985 (death: appropriation in satisfaction of a general legacy of money) or section 84(5) or (7) of that Act (death: appropriation in satisfaction of any interest of surviving spouse and in Scotland also of any interest of issue).

E. The conveyance or transfer of property which forms part of the residuary estate of a testator to a beneficiary (or his nominee) entitled solely by virtue of his entitlement under the will.

F. The conveyance or transfer of property out of a settlement in or towards satisfaction of a beneficiary's interest, not being an interest acquired for money or money's worth, being a conveyance or transfer constituting a distribution of property in accordance with the provisions of the settlement.

G. The conveyance or transfer of property on and in consideration only of marriage to a party to the marriage (or his nominee) or to trustees to be held on the terms of a settlement made in consideration only of the marriage. A transfer to a spouse after the date of marriage is not within this category, unless made pursuant to an ante-nuptial contract.

H. The conveyance or transfer of property within section 83(1) of the Finance Act 1985 (transfers in connection with divorce etc.).

I. The conveyance or transfer by the liquidator of property which formed part of the assets of the company in liquidation to a shareholder of that company (or his nominee) in or towards satisfaction of the shareholder's rights on a winding-up.

J. The grant in fee simple of an easement in or over land for no consideration in money or money's worth.

K. The grant of a servitude for no consideration in money or money's worth.

L. The conveyance or transfer of property operating as a voluntary disposition inter vivos for no consideration in money or money's worth nor any consideration referred to in section 57 of the Stamp Act 1891 (conveyance in consideration of a debt etc.).

M. The conveyance or transfer of property by an instrument within section 84(1) of the Finance Act 1985 (death: varying disposition).

(1) Delete as appropriate.
(2) Insert "(A)", "(B)" or appropriate category.
(3) Delete second sentence if the certificate is given by the transferor or his solicitor.

(1) I/We hereby certify that the transaction in respect of which this transfer is made is one which falls within the category(2) above. (1)I/We confirm that (1)I/We have been duly authorised by the transferor to sign this certificate and that the facts of the transaction are within (1)my/our knowledge (3)

Signature(s) *Description ("Transferor", "Solicitor", etc.)*

______________________ ______________________

______________________ ______________________

______________________ ______________________

______________________ ______________________

Date ______________ 19____ ______________________

NOTES

(1) If the above certificate has been completed, this transfer does not need to be submitted to the Controller of Stamps but should be sent directly to the Company or its Registrars.

(2) If the above certificate is not completed, this transfer must be submitted to the Controller of Stamps and duly stamped. (See below).

FORM OF CERTIFICATE REQUIRED WHERE TRANSFER IS NOT EXEMPT BUT IS NOT LIABLE TO *AD VALOREM* STAMP DUTY

Instruments of transfer, other than those in respect of which the above certificate has been completed, are liable to a fixed duty of 50p when the transaction falls within one of the following categories:—

(*a*) Transfer by way of security for a loan or re-transfer to the original transferor on repayment of a loan.

(*b*) Transfer, not on sale and not arising under any contract of sale and where no beneficial interest in the property passes: (i) to a person who is a mere nominee of, and is nominated only by, the transferor; (ii) from a mere nominee who has at all times held the property on behalf of the transferee; (iii) from one nominee to another nominee of the same beneficial owner where the first nominee has at all times held the property on behalf of that beneficial owner. (NOTE—This category does not include a transfer made in any of the following circumstances: (i) by a holder of stock, etc., following the grant of an option to purchase the stock, to the person entitled to the option or his nominee; (ii) to a nominee in contemplation of a contract for the sale of the stock, etc., then about to be entered into; (iii) from the nominee of a vendor, who has instructed the nominee orally or by some unstamped writing to hold stock, etc., in trust for a purchaser, to such purchaser.)

(1) Delete as appropriate.
(2) Insert "(a)", "(b)".
(3) Here set out concisely the facts explaining the transaction. Adjudication may be required.

(1) I/We hereby certify that the transaction in respect of which this transfer is made is one which falls within the category(2) above. (1)I/we confirm that (1)I/We have been duly authorised by the transferor to sign this certificate and the facts of the transaction are within (1)my/our knowledge.

(3) ....

....

....

....

Signature(s) *Description ("Transferor", "Solicitor", etc.)*

______________________ ______________________

______________________ ______________________

______________________ ______________________

______________________ ______________________

Date .... 19____ ______________________

Conveyancing 40

CON. 40 (1963)

STOCK TRANSFER FORM

(Above this line for Registrars only)

Consideration Money £1·00	Certificate lodged with the Registrar (For completion by the Registrar/Stock Exchange)

Name of Undertaking.	GREBECAT LIMITED	
Description of Security.	£1 ORDINARY SHARE	
Number or amount of Shares, Stock or other security and, in figures column only, number and denomination of units, if any.	Words ONE SHARE NUMBERED 2	Figures 1 (1 units of £1)
Name(s) of registered holder(s) should be given in full: the address should be given where there is only one holder. If the transfer is not made by the registered holder(s) insert also the name(s) and capacity (e.g., Executor(s)) of the person(s) making the transfer.	In the name(s) of CAROLINE EMMA CAT c/o REGINALD REGISTRATIONS LTD. WELBECK CHAMBERS 19 DUXBURY STREET LONDON WC3 7TD	

I/We hereby transfer the above security out of the name(s) aforesaid to the person(s) named below. Signature(s) of transferor(s) 1. C. E. Cat 2. .... 3. .... 4.	Stamp of Selling Broker(s) or, for transactions which are not stock exchange transactions, of Agent(s), if any, acting for the Transferor(s) Date..................

Full name(s) and full postal address(es) (including County or, if applicable, Postal District number) of the person(s) to whom the security is transferred. Please state title, if any, or whether Mr., Mrs., or Miss. Please complete in typewriting or in Block Capitals.	FELICITY ANN FOWLER (MISS) FLAT 6, 999 ACACIA AVENUE DALE BARSETSHIRE BS20 5QR

I/We request that such entries be made in the register as are necessary to give effect to this transfer.

Stamp of Buying Broker(s) (if any)	Stamp or name and address of person lodging this form (if other than the Buying Broker(s))
	CAROLINE CAT address as above

FORM OF CERTIFICATE REQUIRED WHERE TRANSFER IS EXEMPT FROM STAMP DUTY

Instruments executed on or after 1st May 1987 effecting any transactions within the following categories are exempt from stamp duty:—

A. The vesting of property subject to a trust in the trustees of the trust on the appointment of a new trustee, or in the continuing trustees on the retirement of a trustee.

B. The conveyance or transfer of property the subject of a specific devise or legacy to the beneficiary named in the will (or his nominee). Transfers in satisfaction of a general legacy of money should not be included in this category (see category D below).

C. The conveyance or transfer of property which forms part of an intestate's estate to the person entitled on intestacy (or his nominee). Transfers in satisfaction of the transferees entitlement to cash in the estate of an intestate, where the total value of the residuary estate exceeds that sum, should not be included in this category (see category D below).

D. The appropriation of property within section 84(4) of the Finance Act 1985 (death: appropriation in satisfaction of a general legacy of money) or section 84(5) or (7) of that Act (death: appropriation in satisfaction of any interest of surviving spouse and in Scotland also of any interest of issue).

E. The conveyance or transfer of property which forms part of the residuary estate of a testator to a beneficiary (or his nominee) entitled solely by virtue of his entitlement under the will.

F. The conveyance or transfer of property out of a settlement in or towards satisfaction of a beneficiary's interest, not being an interest acquired for money or money's worth, being a conveyance or transfer constituting a distribution of property in accordance with the provisions of the settlement.

G. The conveyance or transfer of property on and in consideration only of marriage to a party to the marriage (or his nominee) or to trustees to be held on the terms of a settlement made in consideration only of the marriage. A transfer to a spouse after the date of marriage is not within this category, unless made pursuant to an ante-nuptial contract.

H. The conveyance or transfer of property within section 83(1) of the Finance Act 1985 (transfers in connection with divorce etc.).

I. The conveyance or transfer by the liquidator of property which formed part of the assets of the company in liquidation to a shareholder of that company (or his nominee) in or towards satisfaction of the shareholder's rights on a winding-up.

J. The grant in fee simple of an easement in or over land for no consideration in money or money's worth.

K. The grant of a servitude for no consideration in money or money's worth.

L. The conveyance or transfer of property operating as a voluntary disposition inter vivos for no consideration in money or money's worth nor any consideration referred to in section 57 of the Stamp Act 1891 (conveyance in consideration of a debt etc.).

M. The conveyance or transfer of property by an instrument within section 84(1) of the Finance Act 1985 (death: varying disposition).

(1) Delete as appropriate.
(2) Insert "(A)", "(B)" or appropriate category.
(3) Delete second sentence if the certificate is given by the transferor or his solicitor.

(1) I/We hereby certify that the transaction in respect of which this transfer is made is one which falls within the category(2) above. (1)I/We confirm that (1)I/We have been duly authorised by the transferor to sign this certificate and that the facts of the transaction are within (1)my/our knowledge (3)

Signature(s) *Description ("Transferor", "Solicitor", etc.)*

______________________ ______________________

______________________ ______________________

______________________ ______________________

______________________ ______________________

Date ______________________ 19______ ______________________

NOTES

(1) If the above certificate has been completed, this transfer does not need to be submitted to the Controller of Stamps but should be sent directly to the Company or its Registrars.

(2) If the above certificate is not completed, this transfer must be submitted to the Controller of Stamps and duly stamped. (See below).

FORM OF CERTIFICATE REQUIRED WHERE TRANSFER IS NOT EXEMPT BUT IS NOT LIABLE TO *AD VALOREM* STAMP DUTY

Instruments of transfer, other than those in respect of which the above certificate has been completed, are liable to a fixed duty of 50p when the transaction falls within one of the following categories:—

(*a*) Transfer by way of security for a loan or re-transfer to the original transferor on repayment of a loan.

(*b*) Transfer, not on sale and not arising under any contract of sale and where no beneficial interest in the property passes: (i) to a person who is a mere nominee of, and is nominated only by, the transferor; (ii) from a mere nominee who has at all times held the property on behalf of the transferee; (iii) from one nominee to another nominee of the same beneficial owner where the first nominee has at all times held the property on behalf of that beneficial owner. (NOTE—This category does not include a transfer made in any of the following circumstances: (i) by a holder of stock, etc., following the grant of an option to purchase the stock, to the person entitled to the option or his nominee; (ii) to a nominee in contemplation of a contract for the sale of the stock, etc., then about to be entered into; (iii) from the nominee of a vendor, who has instructed the nominee orally or by some unstamped writing to hold stock, etc., in trust for a purchaser, to such purchaser.)

(1) Delete as appropriate.
(2) Insert "(a)", "(b)".
(3) Here set out concisely the facts explaining the transaction. Adjudication may be required.

(1) I/We hereby certify that the transaction in respect of which this transfer is made is one which falls within the category(2) above. (1)I/we confirm that (1)I/We have been duly authorised by the transferor to sign this certificate and the facts of the transaction are within (1)my/our knowledge.

(3) ....

....

....

....

Signature(s) *Description ("Transferor", "Solicitor", etc.)*

______________________ ______________________

______________________ ______________________

______________________ ______________________

______________________ ______________________

Date ....19........ ______________________

Conveyancing 40

OYEZ

CHA1

288

Change of director or secretary or change of particulars.

This form should be completed in black.

Company number: CN 12345678

Company name: 999 ACACIA AVENUE LIMITED (formerly GREBECAT LIMITED)

Appointment

(Turn over page for resignation and change of particulars).

Date of appointment (Day Month Year): DA 03 04 91

Appointment of director: CD ✓

Appointment of secretary: CS

Please mark the appropriate box. If appointment is as a director and secretary mark both boxes.

Name

*Style/title: MR.

Forenames: ANTHONY JOHN

Surname: ABSOLUTE

*Honours etc:

Previous forenames:

Previous surname:

Usual residential address: AD FLAT 1, 999 ACACIA AVENUE

Post town: DALE

County/region: BARSETSHIRE

Postcode: BS20 5QR Country: ENGLAND

Date of birth†: DO 03 08 59 Nationality†: NA U.K.

Business occupation†: OC INSURANCE BROKER

Other directorships†: NONE

I consent to act as director/secretary of the above-named company

Consent signature: Signed A. J. Absolute Date 3 APRIL 1991

A serving director etc must also sign the form overleaf.

NOTES

Show the full forenames, NOT INITIALS. If the director or secretary is a Corporation or Scottish firm, show the name on surname line and registered or principal office on the usual residential address line.

Give previous forenames or surname except:
- for a married woman the name before marriage need not be given.
- for names not used since the age of 18 or for at least 20 years.

A peer or individual known by a title may state the title instead of or in addition to the forenames and surname.

Other directorships.

Give the name of every company of which the person concerned is a director or has been a director at any time in the past 5 years. Exclude a company which either is, or at all times during the past 5 years when the person was a director, was
- dormant
- a parent company which wholly owned the company making the return
- a wholly owned subsidiary of the company making the return
- another wholly owned subsidiary of the same parent company.

*Voluntary details †Directors only

Resignation

(This includes any form of ceasing to hold office e.g. death or removal from office).

Date of resignation etc	DR 0 3 0 4 9 1
Resignation etc. as director	XD ✓
Resignation etc. as secretary	XS
	Please mark the appropriate box. If resignation etc is as a director and secretary mark both boxes.
Forenames	GREGORY CHRISTOPHER
Surname	GREBE
Date of birth *(directors only)*	DO 0 1 1 1 5 6
If cessation is other than resignation, please state reason *(eg death)*	

Change of particulars

Complete this section in all cases where particulars have changed and then the appropriate section below.

Date of change of particulars	DC
Change of particulars, as director	ZD
Change of particulars, as secretary	ZS
	Please mark the appropriate box. If change of particulars is as a director and secretary mark both boxes.
Forenames *(name previously notified to Companies House)*	
Surname	
Date of birth *(directors only)*	DO
Change of name *(enter new name)* Forenames	NN
Surname	
Change of usual residential address *(enter new address)*	AD
Post town	
County/region	
Postcode	Country
Other change *(please specify)*	

A serving director, secretary etc must sign the form below.

Signature

Signed Felicity Fowler Date 3rd APRIL 1991

(by a serving director/secretary/~~administrator/administrative receiver/receiver~~). *(Delete as appropriate)*

After signing please return the form to the Registrar of Companies at

Companies House, Crown Way, Cardiff CF4 3UZ
for companies registered in England and Wales

or

Companies House, 100-102 George Street, Edinburgh EH2 3DJ
for companies registered in Scotland.

To whom should Companies House direct any enquiries about the information on this form?

FELICITY FOWLER, FLAT 6,
999 ACACIA AVENUE, DALE, BARSET
BS20 5QR Tel: (0999) 332861

OYEZ The Solicitors' Law Stationery Society Ltd, Oyez House, 7 Spa Road, London SE16 3QQ

1990 Edition 3.93 F24298

5017301

Companies 288

OYEZ

CHA1

288

Change of director or secretary or change of particulars.

This form should be completed in black.

Company number	CN 12345678
Company name	999 ACACIA AVENUE LIMITED (formerly GREBECAT LIMITED)

Appointment

(Turn over page for resignation and change of particulars).

Date of appointment	DA (Day Month Year) 03 04 91
Appointment of director	CD ✓
Appointment of secretary	CS

Please mark the appropriate box. If appointment is as a director and secretary mark both boxes.

NOTES

Show the full forenames, NOT INITIALS. If the director or secretary is a Corporation or Scottish firm, show the name on surname line and registered or principal office on the usual residential address line.

Give previous forenames or surname except:

- for a married woman the name before marriage need not be given.
- for names not used since the age of 18 or for at least 20 years.

A peer or individual known by a title may state the title instead of or in addition to the forenames and surname.

Name *Style/title	MISS
Forenames	BELINDA
Surname	BOTT
*Honours etc	
Previous forenames	
Previous surname	
Usual residential address	AD FLAT 2, 999 ACACIA AVENUE
Post town	DALE
County/region	BARSETSHIRE
Postcode	BS20 5QR Country ENGLAND
Date of birth†	DO 22 04 58 Nationality† NA U.K.
Business occupation†	OC STUDENT
Other directorships†	NONE

Other directorships.

Give the name of every company of which the person concerned is a director or has been a director at any time in the past 5 years. Exclude a company which either is, or at all times during the past 5 years when the person was a director, was

- dormant
- a parent company which wholly owned the company making the return
- a wholly owned subsidiary of the company making the return
- another wholly owned subsidiary of the same parent company.

I consent to act as director/~~secretary~~ of the above-named company

Consent signature Signed B. Bott Date 03/04/91

*Voluntary details †Directors only

A serving director etc must also sign the form overleaf.

Resignation

(This includes any form of ceasing to hold office e.g. death or removal from office).

Date of resignation etc DR

Resignation etc, as director XD

Resignation etc, as secretary XS

Please mark the appropriate box. If resignation etc is as a director and secretary mark both boxes.

Forenames

Surname

Date of birth *(directors only)* DO

If cessation is other than resignation, please state reason *(eg death)*

Change of particulars

Complete this section in all cases where particulars have changed and then the appropriate section below.

Date of change of particulars DC

Change of particulars, as director ZD

Change of particulars, as secretary ZS

Please mark the appropriate box. If change of particulars is as a director and secretary mark both boxes.

Forenames / Surname *(name previously notified to Companies House)*

Date of birth *(directors only)* DO

Change of name *(enter new name)* Forenames NN

Surname

Change of usual residential address *(enter new address)* AD

Post town

County/region

Postcode Country

Other change *(please specify)*

A serving director, secretary etc must sign the form below.

Signature

Signed F. Fowler Date 3rd APRIL 1991

(by a serving director/secretary/~~administrator/administrative receiver/receiver~~). *(Delete as appropriate)*

After signing please return the form to the Registrar of Companies at

Companies House, Crown Way, Cardiff CF4 3UZ for companies registered in England and Wales

or **Companies House, 100-102 George Street, Edinburgh EH2 3DJ** for companies registered in Scotland.

To whom should Companies House direct any enquiries about the information on this form?

MISS F. FOWLER, 999 ACACIA AVENUE,
DALE, BARSETSHIRE
BS20 5QR Tel: (0999) 332861

OYEZ The Solicitors' Law Stationery Society Ltd, Oyez House, 7 Spa Road, London SE16 3QQ 1990 Edition 3.93 F24298

5017301

Companies 288

OYEZ

CHA1

288

Change of director or secretary or change of particulars.

This form should be completed in black.

Company number	CN 12345678
Company name	999 ACACIA AVENUE LIMITED (formerly GREBECAT LIMITED)

Appointment

(Turn over page for resignation and change of particulars).

	Day Month Year
Date of appointment	DA 03 04 91
Appointment of director	CD ✓
Appointment of secretary	CS

Please mark the appropriate box. If appointment is as a director and secretary mark both boxes.

NOTES

Show the full forenames, NOT INITIALS. If the director or secretary is a Corporation or Scottish firm, show the name on surname line and registered or principal office on the usual residential address line.

Give previous forenames or surname except:
- for a married woman the name before marriage need not be given.
- for names not used since the age of 18 or for at least 20 years.

A peer or individual known by a title may state the title instead of or in addition to the forenames and surname.

Name *Style/title	MR.
Forenames	CHARLES IAN
Surname	CRAWFORD
*Honours etc	
Previous forenames	
Previous surname	
Usual residential address	AD FLAT 3, 999 ACACIA AVENUE
Post town	DALE
County/region	BARSETSHIRE
Postcode	BS20 5QR Country ENGLAND
Date of birth†	DO 02 10 58 Nationality† NA U.K.
Business occupation†	OC ADVERTISING EXECUTIVE
Other directorships†	PUFF AND PUFF LIMITED

Other directorships.

Give the name of every company of which the person concerned is a director or has been a director at any time in the past 5 years. Exclude a company which either is, or at all times during the past 5 years when the person was a director, was
- dormant
- a parent company which wholly owned the company making the return
- a wholly owned subsidiary of the company making the return
- another wholly owned subsidiary of the same parent company.

I consent to act as director/~~secretary~~ of the above-named company

Consent signature Signed *Chas. Crawford* Date 3/4/1991

*Voluntary details †Directors only

A serving director etc must also sign the form overleaf.

Resignation

(This includes any form of ceasing to hold office e.g. death or removal from office).

Date of resignation etc	DR
Resignation etc. as director	XD
Resignation etc. as secretary	XS
Forenames	
Surname	
Date of birth *(directors only)*	DO
If cessation is other than resignation, please state reason *(eg death)*	

Please mark the appropriate box. If resignation etc is as a director and secretary mark both boxes.

Change of particulars

Complete this section in all cases where particulars have changed and then the appropriate section below.

Date of change of particulars	DC
Change of particulars, as director	ZD
Change of particulars, as secretary	ZS
Forenames *(name previously notified to Companies House)*	
Surname *(name previously notified to Companies House)*	
Date of birth *(directors only)*	DO
Change of name *(enter new name)* Forenames	NN
Surname	
Change of usual residential address *(enter new address)*	AD
Post town	
County/region	
Postcode	Country
Other change *(please specify)*	

Please mark the appropriate box. If change of particulars is as a director and secretary mark both boxes.

A serving director, secretary etc must sign the form below.

Signature

Signed F. Fowler Date 3rd APRIL 1991

(by a serving director/secretary/~~administrator/administrative receiver/receiver~~). *(Delete as appropriate)*

After signing please return the form to the Registrar of Companies at

Companies House, Crown Way, Cardiff CF4 3UZ
for companies registered in England and Wales

or

Companies House, 100-102 George Street, Edinburgh EH2 3DJ
for companies registered in Scotland.

To whom should Companies House direct any enquiries about the information on this form?

FELICITY FOWLER, 999 ACACIA AVENUE,
DALE, BARSETSHIRE
BS 20 5QR Tel: (0999) 332861

OYEZ The Solicitors' Law Stationery Society Ltd. Oyez House, 7 Spa Road, London SE16 3QQ 1990 Edition 3.93 F24296 15017301

Companies 288

OYEZ

CHA1

288

Change of director or secretary or change of particulars.

This form should be completed in black.

Company number	CN 12345678
Company name	999 ACACIA AVENUE LIMITED (formerly GREBECAT LIMITED)

Appointment

(Turn over page for resignation and change of particulars).

Date of appointment	DA (Day Month Year) 03 04 91
Appointment of director	CD ✓
Appointment of secretary	CS

Please mark the appropriate box. If appointment is as a director and secretary mark both boxes.

Name	
*Style/title	MS.
Forenames	DAHLIA LOUISA
Surname	DYMOND
*Honours etc	
Previous forenames	
Previous surname	
Usual residential address	AD FLAT 4, 999 ACACIA AVENUE
Post town	DALE
County/region	BARSETSHIRE
Postcode	BS20 5QR Country ENGLAND
Date of birth†	DO 15 02 54 Nationality† NA U.K.
Business occupation†	OC TELEVISION PRODUCER
Other directorships†	NONE

NOTES

Show the full forenames, NOT INITIALS. If the director or secretary is a Corporation or Scottish firm, show the name on surname line and registered or principal office on the usual residential address line.

Give previous forenames or surname except:
- for a married woman the name before marriage need not be given.
- for names not used since the age of 18 or for at least 20 years.

A peer or individual known by a title may state the title instead of or in addition to the forenames and surname.

Other directorships.

Give the name of every company of which the person concerned is a director or has been a director at any time in the past 5 years. Exclude a company which either is, or at all times during the past 5 years when the person was a director, was
- dormant
- a parent company which wholly owned the company making the return
- a wholly owned subsidiary of the company making the return
- another wholly owned subsidiary of the same parent company.

I consent to act as director/~~secretary~~ of the above-named company

Consent signature Signed *Dahlia Dymond* Date 3 APRIL 1991

*Voluntary details †Directors only

A serving director etc must also sign the form overleaf.

Resignation

(This includes any form of ceasing to hold office e.g. death or removal from office).

Date of resignation etc DR

Resignation etc. as director XD

Resignation etc. as secretary XS

Please mark the appropriate box. If resignation etc is as a director and secretary mark both boxes.

Forenames

Surname

Date of birth *(directors only)* DO

If cessation is other than resignation, please state reason *(eg death)*

Change of particulars

Complete this section in all cases where particulars have changed and then the appropriate section below.

Date of change of particulars DC

Change of particulars, as director ZD

Change of particulars, as secretary ZS

Please mark the appropriate box. If change of particulars is as a director and secretary mark both boxes.

Forenames, Surname *(name previously notified to Companies House)*

Date of birth *(directors only)* DO

Change of name *(enter new name)* Forenames NN

Surname

Change of usual residential address *(enter new address)* AD

Post town

County/region

Postcode Country

Other change *(please specify)*

A serving director, secretary etc must sign the form below.

Signature Signed F. Fowler Date 3rd APRIL 1991

(by a serving director/secretary/~~administrator/administrative receiver/receiver~~). *(Delete as appropriate)*

After signing please return the form to the Registrar of Companies at

Companies House, Crown Way, Cardiff CF4 3UZ for companies registered in England and Wales

or **Companies House, 100-102 George Street, Edinburgh EH2 3DJ** for companies registered in Scotland.

To whom should Companies House direct any enquiries about the information on this form?

FELICITY FOWLER, 999 ACACIA AVENUE

DALE, BARSETSHIRE

BS20 5GR Tel: (0999) 332861

OYEZ The Solicitors' Law Stationery Society Ltd, Oyez House, 7 Spa Road, London SE16 3QQ 1990 Edition 3.93 F24298 5017301

OYEZ

CHA1

288

Change of director or secretary or change of particulars.

This form should be completed in black.

Company number: CN 12345678

Company name: 999 ACACIA AVENUE LIMITED (formerly GREBECAT LIMITED)

Appointment

(Turn over page for resignation and change of particulars).

Date of appointment (Day Month Year): DA 03 04 91

Appointment of director: CD ✓

Appointment of secretary: CS

Please mark the appropriate box. If appointment is as a director and secretary mark both boxes.

Name

*Style/title: MR.

Forenames: EDWARD

Surname: EXTRACT

*Honours etc:

Previous forenames:

Previous surname:

Usual residential address: AD FLAT 5, 999 ACACIA AVENUE

Post town: DALE

County/region: BARSETSHIRE

Postcode: BS20 5QR Country: ENGLAND

Date of birth†: DO 28 09 54 Nationality†: NA U.K.

Business occupation†: OC CATERING MANAGER

Other directorships†: NONE

NOTES

Show the full forenames, NOT INITIALS. If the director or secretary is a Corporation or Scottish firm, show the name on surname line and registered or principal office on the usual residential address line.

Give previous forenames or surname except:
- for a married woman the name before marriage need not be given.
- for names not used since the age of 18 or for at least 20 years.

A peer or individual known by a title may state the title instead of or in addition to the forenames and surname.

Other directorships.

Give the name of every company of which the person concerned is a director or has been a director at any time in the past 5 years. Exclude a company which either is, or at all times during the past 5 years when the person was a director, was
- dormant
- a parent company which wholly owned the company making the return
- a wholly owned subsidiary of the company making the return
- another wholly owned subsidiary of the same parent company.

I consent to act as director/~~secretary~~ of the above-named company

Consent signature: Signed E. Extract Date 3 APRIL 1991

A serving director etc must also sign the form overleaf.

*Voluntary details †Directors only

Resignation

(This includes any form of ceasing to hold office e.g. death or removal from office).

Date of resignation etc | DR

Resignation etc. as director | XD

Resignation etc. as secretary | XS

Please mark the appropriate box. If resignation etc is as a director and secretary mark both boxes.

Forenames

Surname

Date of birth *(directors only)* | DO

If cessation is other than resignation, please state reason *(eg death)*

Change of particulars

Complete this section in all cases where particulars have changed and then the appropriate section below.

Date of change of particulars | DC

Change of particulars, as director | ZD

Change of particulars, as secretary | ZS

Please mark the appropriate box. If change of particulars is as a director and secretary mark both boxes.

Forenames / Surname *(name previously notified to Companies House)*

Date of birth *(directors only)* | DO

Change of name *(enter new name)* Forenames | NN

Surname

Change of usual residential address *(enter new address)* | AD

Post town

County/region

Postcode Country

Other change *(please specify)*

A serving director, secretary etc must sign the form below.

Signature

Signed F. Fowler Date 3rd APRIL 1991

(by a serving director/secretary/~~administrator/ administrative receiver/receiver~~). *(Delete as appropriate)*

After signing please return the form to the Registrar of Companies at

Companies House, Crown Way, Cardiff CF4 3UZ
for companies registered in England and Wales

or

Companies House, 100-102 George Street, Edinburgh EH2 3DJ
for companies registered in Scotland.

To whom should Companies House direct any enquiries about the information on this form?

FELICITY FOWLER, 999 ACACIA AVENUE,
DALE, BARSETSHIRE
BS20 5QR Tel: (0999) 332861

OYEZ The Solicitors' Law Stationery Society Ltd, Oyez House, 7 Spa Road, London SE16 3QQ 1990 Edition 3.93 F24296 5017301

Companies 288

OYEZ

CHA1

288

Change of director or secretary or change of particulars.

This form should be completed in black.

Company number	CN 12345678
Company name	999 ACACIA AVENUE LIMITED (formerly GREBECAT LIMITED)

Appointment

(Turn over page for resignation and change of particulars).

Date of appointment	DA Day 03 Month 04 Year 91
Appointment of director	CD ✓
Appointment of secretary	CS ✓

Please mark the appropriate box. If appointment is as a director and secretary mark both boxes.

NOTES

Show the full forenames, NOT INITIALS. If the director or secretary is a Corporation or Scottish firm, show the name on surname line and registered or principal office on the usual residential address line.

Give previous forenames or surname except:
- for a married woman the name before marriage need not be given.
- for names not used since the age of 18 or for at least 20 years.

A peer or individual known by a title may state the title instead of or in addition to the forenames and surname.

Name *Style/title	MISS
Forenames	FELICITY ANN
Surname	FOWLER
*Honours etc	
Previous forenames	
Previous surname	
Usual residential address	AD FLAT 6, 999 ACACIA AVENUE,
Post town	DALE
County/region	BARSETSHIRE
Postcode	BS20 5QR Country ENGLAND
Date of birth†	DO 08 01 62 Nationality† NA U.K.
Business occupation†	OC SOLICITOR
Other directorships†	NONE

Other directorships.

Give the name of every company of which the person concerned is a director or has been a director at any time in the past 5 years. Exclude a company which either is, or at all times during the past 5 years when the person was a director, was
- dormant
- a parent company which wholly owned the company making the return
- a wholly owned subsidiary of the company making the return
- another wholly owned subsidiary of the same parent company.

I consent to act as director/secretary of the above-named company and

Consent signature Signed F Fowler Date 3rd APRIL 1991

A serving director etc must also sign the form overleaf.

*Voluntary details †Directors only

Resignation

(This includes any form of ceasing to hold office e.g. death or removal from office).

Date of resignation etc **DR** 0 3 0 4 9 1

Resignation etc, as director **XD** ✓

Resignation etc, as secretary **XS** ✓

Please mark the appropriate box. If resignation etc is as a director and secretary mark both boxes.

Forenames CAROLINE EMMA

Surname CAT

Date of birth *(directors only)* **DO** 2 6 0 1 1 6 0

If cessation is other than resignation, please state reason *(eg death)*

Change of particulars

Complete this section in all cases where particulars have changed and then the appropriate section below.

Date of change of particulars **DC**

Change of particulars, as director **ZD**

Change of particulars, as secretary **ZS**

Please mark the appropriate box. If change of particulars is as a director and secretary mark both boxes.

Forenames
Surname
(name previously notified to Companies House)

Date of birth *(directors only)* **DO**

Change of name *(enter new name)* Forenames **NN**

Surname

Change of usual residential address *(enter new address)* **AD**

Post town

County/region

Postcode Country

Other change *(please specify)*

A serving director, secretary etc must sign the form below.

Signature

Signed F. Fowler Date 3rd APRIL 1991

(by a serving director/secretary/~~administrator/administrative receiver/receiver~~). *(Delete as appropriate)*

After signing please return the form to the Registrar of Companies at

Companies House, Crown Way, Cardiff CF4 3UZ
for companies registered in England and Wales

or

Companies House, 100-102 George Street, Edinburgh EH2 3DJ
for companies registered in Scotland.

To whom should Companies House direct any enquiries about the information on this form?

FELICITY FOWLER
address as above
Tel: (0999) 332861

OYEZ The Solicitors Law Stationery Society Ltd, Oyez House, 7 Spa Road, London SE16 3QQ

1990 Edition 3.93 F24298

5017301

G

COMPANIES FORM No. 88(2)(Rev 1988)

Return of allotments of shares

88(2)

(REVISED 1988)

This form replaces forms PUC2, PUC3 and 88(2)

Pursuant to section 88(2) of the Companies Act 1985 (the Act)

Please do not write in this margin

To the Registrar of Companies **(address overleaf)** (see note 1)

Please complete legibly, preferably in black type, or bold block lettering

Company number

12345678

1. Name of company

* insert full name of company

* 999 ACACIA AVENUE LIMITED

(formerly GREBECAT LIMITED)

2. This section must be completed for all allotments

† Distinguish between ordinary, preference, etc.

Description of shares†	ORDINARY		
A Number allotted	4		
B Nominal value of each	£ 1	£	£
C Total amount (if any) paid or due and payable on each share (including premium if any)	£ 1	£	£

§ Complete (a) or (b) as appropriate

Date(s) on which the shares were allotted

(a) [on 3rd APRIL 19 91]§, or

(b) [from ______ 19 ______ to ______ 19 ______]§

The names and addresses of the allottees and the number of shares allotted to each should be given overleaf

3. If the allotment is wholly or partly other than for cash the following information must be given **(see notes 2 & 3)**

D Extent to which each share is to be treated as paid up. Please use percentage.			
E Consideration for which the shares were allotted			

Notes

1. This form should be delivered to the Registrar of Companies within one month of the (first) date of allotment.
2. If the allotment is wholly or partly other than for cash, the company must deliver to the Registrar a return containing the information at D & E. The company may deliver this information by completing D & E and the delivery of the information must be accompanied by the duly stamped contract required by section 88(2)(b) of the Act or by the duly stamped prescribed particulars required by section 88(3) (Form No 88(3)).
3. Details of bonus issues should be included only in section 2.

Presentor's name, address, telephone number and reference (if any):

FELICITY FOWLER
999 ACACIA AVENUE
DALE
BARSETSHIRE BS20 5GR
(0999) 332861

For official use

Post room

4. Names and addresses of the allottees

Please do not write in the margin

Please complete legibly, preferably in black type, or bold block lettering

Names and Addresses	Number of shares allotted		
	Ordinary	Preference	Other
BELINDA BOTT	1		
CHARLES IAN CRAWFORD	1		
DAHLIA LOUISA DYMOND	1		
EDWARD EXTRACT	1		
All of 999 ACACIA AVENUE			
DALE			
BARSETSHIRE			
BS20 5QR			
Total			

Where the space given on this form is inadequate, continuation sheets should be used and the number of sheets attached should be indicated in the box opposite:

Signed E Fowler Designation‡ Secretary Date 3rd APRIL 1991

‡ Insert Director, Secretary, Administrator, Administrative Receiver, or Receiver (Scotland) as appropriate

Companies registered in England and Wales or Wales should deliver this form to:-

The Registrar of Companies
Companies House
Crown Way
Maindy
Cardiff
CF4 3UZ

Companies registered in Scotland should deliver this form to:-

The Registrar of Companies
Companies Registration Office
102 George Street
Edinburgh
EH2 3DJ

Page 2

OYEZ The Solicitors' Law Stationery Society Ltd, Oyez House, 7 Spa Road, London SE16 3QQ

Companies G88(2) (Revised 1988)

1988 Edition
10.91 F21109
5019476

No. 3 No. OF SHARES 1 Nos. 1 ISSUED TO ANTHONY JOHN ABSOLUTE OF 999 ACACIA AVENUE, DALE, BARSETSHIRE BS20 5QR DATE 3rd APRIL 1991 ENTERED ON REGISTER PAGE 1	No. 3 999 ACACIA AVENUE LIMITED Incorporated under the Companies Act CAPITAL £100 DIVIDED INTO 100 SHARES OF £1 EACH THIS IS TO CERTIFY *that* ANTHONY JOHN ABSOLUTE *of* FLAT 1, 999 ACACIA AVENUE, DALE, BARSETSHIRE BS20 5QR *is the holder of* ONE ORDINARY *Share paid of* £1 *each Numbered* 1 *to* —— *issued in the above named Company subject to the memorandum and Articles of Association thereof* GIVEN *by the said Company* *The* 3rd *day of* APRIL *19*91 *acting by* .... *Director* A. J. ABSOLUTE *Secretary* F. FOWLER NO TRANSFER OF THE WHOLE OR ANY PORTION OF THE ABOVE SHARES CAN BE REGISTERED WITHOUT THE PRODUCTION OF THIS CERTIFICATE

No. 4 No. OF SHARES 1 Nos. 3 ISSUED TO BELINDA BOTT OF 999 ACACIA AVENUE, DALE, BARSETSHIRE, BS20 5QR DATE 3rd APRIL 1991 ENTERED ON REGISTER PAGE 3	No. 4 999 ACACIA AVENUE LIMITED Incorporated under the Companies Act CAPITAL £100 DIVIDED INTO 100 SHARES OF £1 EACH THIS IS TO CERTIFY *that* BELINDA BOTT *of* FLAT 2, 999 ACACIA AVENUE, DALE, BARSETSHIRE, BS20 5QR *is the holder of* ONE ORDINARY *Share paid of* £1 *each Numbered* 3 *to* —— *issued in the above named Company subject to the memorandum and Articles of Association thereof* GIVEN *by the said Company* *The* 3rd *day of* APRIL *19*91 *acting by* .... *Director* A. J. ABSOLUTE *Secretary* F. FOWLER NO TRANSFER OF THE WHOLE OR ANY PORTION OF THE ABOVE SHARES CAN BE REGISTERED WITHOUT THE PRODUCTION OF THIS CERTIFICATE

No. 5
No. OF SHARES 1
Nos. 4
ISSUED TO CHARLES IAN CRAWFORD
OF 999 ACACIA AVENUE, DALE, BARSETSHIRE, BS20 5QR
DATE 3rd APRIL, 1991
ENTERED ON REGISTER PAGE 5

No. 5

999 ACACIA AVENUE LIMITED

Incorporated under the Companies Act

CAPITAL £ 100

DIVIDED INTO 100 SHARES OF £1 EACH

THIS IS TO CERTIFY that CHARLES IAN CRAWFORD of FLAT 3, 999 ACACIA AVENUE, DALE, BARSETSHIRE, BS20 5QR is the holder of ONE ORDINARY Share paid of £1 each Numbered 4 to — issued in the above named Company subject to the memorandum and Articles of Association thereof

GIVEN by the said Company

The 3rd day of APRIL 1991
acting by
Director A. J. ABSOLUTE
Secretary F. FOWLER

NO TRANSFER OF THE WHOLE OR ANY PORTION OF THE ABOVE SHARES CAN BE REGISTERED WITHOUT THE PRODUCTION OF THIS CERTIFICATE

No. 6
No. OF SHARES 1
Nos. 5
ISSUED TO DAHLIA LOUISA DYMOND
OF 999 ACACIA AVENUE, DALE, BARSETSHIRE, BS20 5QR
DATE 3rd APRIL, 1991
ENTERED ON REGISTER PAGE 7

No. 6

999 ACACIA AVENUE LIMITED

Incorporated under the Companies Act

CAPITAL £ 100

DIVIDED INTO 100 SHARES OF £1 EACH

THIS IS TO CERTIFY that DAHLIA LOUISA DYMOND of FLAT 4, 999 ACACIA AVENUE, DALE, BARSETSHIRE, BS20 5QR is the holder of ONE ORDINARY Share paid of £1 each Numbered 5 to — issued in the above named Company subject to the memorandum and Articles of Association thereof

GIVEN by the said Company

The 3rd day of APRIL 1991
acting by
Director A. J. ABSOLUTE
Secretary F. FOWLER

NO TRANSFER OF THE WHOLE OR ANY PORTION OF THE ABOVE SHARES CAN BE REGISTERED WITHOUT THE PRODUCTION OF THIS CERTIFICATE

No. 7
No. OF SHARES 1
Nos. 6
ISSUED TO EDWARD EXTRACT
OF 999 ACACIA AVENUE, DALE, BARSETSHIRE, BS20 5QR
DATE 3rd APRIL, 1991
ENTERED ON REGISTER PAGE 9

No. 7

999 ACACIA AVENUE LIMITED
Incorporated under the Companies Act

CAPITAL £100

DIVIDED INTO 100 SHARES OF £1 EACH

THIS IS TO CERTIFY *that* EDWARD EXTRACT
of FLAT 5, 999 ACACIA AVENUE, DALE, BARSETSHIRE, BS20 5QR
is the holder of ONE ORDINARY *Share paid of* £1 *each Numbered* 6 *to* — *issued in the above named Company subject to the memorandum and Articles of Association thereof*

GIVEN *by the said Company*

The 3rd *day of* APRIL 1991
acting by
Director A. J. ABSOLUTE
Secretary F. FOWLER

NO TRANSFER OF THE WHOLE OR ANY PORTION OF THE ABOVE SHARES CAN BE REGISTERED WITHOUT THE PRODUCTION OF THIS CERTIFICATE

No. 8
No. OF SHARES 1
Nos. 2
ISSUED TO FELICITY ANN FOWLER
OF 999 ACACIA AVENUE, DALE, BARSETSHIRE, BS20 5QR
DATE 3rd APRIL, 1991
ENTERED ON REGISTER PAGE 11

No. 8

999 ACACIA AVENUE LIMITED
Incorporated under the Companies Act

CAPITAL £100

DIVIDED INTO 100 SHARES OF £1 EACH

THIS IS TO CERTIFY *that* FELICITY ANN FOWLER
of FLAT 6, 999 ACACIA AVENUE, DALE, BARSETSHIRE, BS20 5QR
is the holder of ONE ORDINARY *Share paid of* £1 *each Numbered* 2 *to* — *issued in the above named Company subject to the memorandum and Articles of Association thereof*

GIVEN *by the said Company*

The 3rd *day of* APRIL 1991
acting by
Director A. J. ABSOLUTE
Secretary F. FOWLER

NO TRANSFER OF THE WHOLE OR ANY PORTION OF THE ABOVE SHARES CAN BE REGISTERED WITHOUT THE PRODUCTION OF THIS CERTIFICATE

G

COMPANIES FORM No. 225(1)

225(1)

Notice of new accounting reference date given during the course of an accounting reference period

Please do not write in this margin.

Pursuant to section 225(1) of the Companies Act 1985 as inserted by section 3 of the Companies Act 1989

Please complete legibly, preferably in black type, or bold block lettering.

1. To the Registrar of Companies (Address overleaf—Note 6)

Company number: 12345678

Name of company

*Insert full name of company.

* 999 ACACIA AVENUE LIMITED
(formerly GREBECAT LIMITED)

Note
Details of day and month in 2, 3 and 4 should be the same.
Please read notes 1 to 5 overleaf before completing this form.
†Delete as appropriate.

2. Gives notice that the company's new accounting reference date on which the current accounting reference period and each subsequent accounting reference period of the company is to be treated as coming, or as having come, to an end is

Day		Month	
3	1	0	8

3. The current accounting reference period of the company is to be treated as [shortened] ~~[extended]~~† and [is to be treated as having come to an end] [will come to an end]† on

Day		Month		Year			
3	1	0	8	1	9	9	1

4. If this notice states that the current accounting reference period of the company is to be extended, and reliance is being placed on the exception in paragraph (a) in the second part of section 225(4) of the Companies Act 1985, the following statement should be completed:
The company is a [subsidiary] [parent]† undertaking of __________

__________ company number __________

the accounting reference date of which is __________

5. If this notice is being given by a company which is subject to an administration order and this notice states that the current accounting reference period of the company is to be extended AND it is to be extended beyond 18 months OR reliance is not being placed on the second part of section 225(4) of the Companies Act 1985, the following statement should be completed:
An administration order was made in relation to the company on __________
and it is still in force.

‡Insert Director, Secretary, Receiver, Administrator, Administrative Receiver or Receiver (Scotland) as appropriate.

6. Signed Felicity Fowler Designation‡ Secretary Date 15th APRIL 1991

Presentor's name, address, telephone number and reference (if any):

FELICITY FOWLER
FLAT 6, 999 ACACIA AVENUE
DALE
BARSETSHIRE BS20 5GR
(0999) 332861

For official use
D.E.B.
Post room

G

COMPANIES FORM No. 287

Notice of change in situation of registered office

287

Please do not write in this margin

Pursuant to section 287 of the Companies Act 1985 as substituted by section 136 of the Companies Act 1989

Please complete legibly, preferably in black type, or bold block lettering

To the Registrar of Companies (Address overleaf)

Company number: 12345678

Name of Company

*Insert full name of company

. 999 ACACIA AVENUE LIMITED
(formerly GREBECAT LIMITED)

gives notice of a change in the situation of the registered office of the company to:

FLAT 6, 999 ACACIA AVENUE
DALE
BARSETSHIRE
Postcode BS20 5QR

†Insert Director, Secretary, Administrator, Administrative Receiver or Receiver (Scotland) as appropriate

Signed F. Fowler Designation† Secretary Date 15th APRIL 1991

Presentor's name, address, telephone number and reference (if any):

FELICITY FOWLER
address as above
(0999) 332861

For official use	
General Section	Post room

G

COMPANIES FORM No. 88(2)(Rev 1988)

88(2)

Return of allotments of shares

Pursuant to section 88(2) of the Companies Act 1985 (the Act)

(REVISED 1988)
This form replaces forms PUC2, PUC3 and 88(2)

Please do not write in this margin

To the Registrar of Companies **(address overleaf)**
(see note 1)

Please complete legibly, preferably in black type, or bold block lettering

Company number: 12345678

1. Name of company

* insert full name of company

* 999 ACACIA AVENUE LIMITED

2. This section must be completed for all allotments

† Distinguish between ordinary, preference, etc.

Description of shares†	ORDINARY		
A Number allotted	6		
B Nominal value of each	£ 1	£	£
C Total amount (if any) paid or due and payable on each share (including premium if any)	£ 300	£	£

Date(s) on which the shares were allotted

§ Complete (a) or (b) as appropriate

(a) [on 25th SEPTEMBER 19 91]§, or

(b) [from ________ 19 ____ to ________ 19 ____]§

The names and addresses of the allottees and the number of shares allotted to each should be given overleaf

3. If the allotment is wholly or partly other than for cash the following information must be given **(see notes 2 & 3)**

D Extent to which each share is to be treated as paid up. Please use percentage.			
E Consideration for which the shares were allotted			

Notes

1. This form should be delivered to the Registrar of Companies within one month of the (first) date of allotment.
2. If the allotment is wholly or partly other than for cash, the company must deliver to the Registrar a return containing the information at D & E. The company may deliver this information by completing D & E and the delivery of the information must be accompanied by the duly stamped contract required by section 88(2)(b) of the Act or by the duly stamped prescribed particulars required by section 88(3) (Form No 88(3)).
3. Details of bonus issues should be included only in section 2.

Presentor's name, address, telephone number and reference (if any):

For official use

Post room

Page 1

4. Names and addresses of the allottees

Please do not write in the margin

Please complete legibly, preferably in black type, or bold block lettering

Names and Addresses	Number of shares allotted		
	Ordinary	Preference	Other
ANTHONY JOHN ABSOLUTE	1		
BELINDA BOTT	1		
CHARLES IAN CRAWFORD	1		
DAHLIA LOUISA DYMOND	1		
EDWARD EXTRACT	1		
FELICITY ANN FOWLER	1		
Total			

Where the space given on this form is inadequate, continuation sheets should be used and the number of sheets attached should be indicated in the box opposite:

‡ Insert Director, Secretary, Administrator, Administrative Receiver, or Receiver (Scotland) as appropriate

Signed F. Fowler Designation‡ Secretary Date 25/9/1991

Companies registered in England and Wales or Wales should deliver this form to:-

The Registrar of Companies
Companies House
Crown Way
Maindy
Cardiff
CF4 3UZ

Companies registered in Scotland should deliver this form to:-

The Registrar of Companies
Companies Registration Office
102 George Street
Edinburgh
EH2 3DJ

Page 2

M

COMPANIES FORM No. 395

Particulars of a mortgage or charge

395

Pursuant to section 395 of the Companies Act 1985

Please do not write in this margin

Please complete legibly, preferably in black type or bold block lettering

To the Registrar of Companies

For official use

Company number: 12345678

Name of company

*insert full name of company

* 999 ACACIA AVENUE LIMITED

Date of creation of the charge

5th APRIL 1993

Description of the instrument (if any) creating or evidencing the charge (note 2)

DEBENTURE

Amount secured by the mortgage or charge

£12,000, REPAYABLE IN FIVE EQUAL INSTALMENTS OVER FIVE YEARS

Names and addresses of the mortgagees or persons entitled to the charge

ANTHONY JOHN ABSOLUTE, FLAT 1, 999 ACACIA AVENUE, DALE, BARSETSHIRE

Postcode BS20 5QR

Presentor's name, address and reference (if any):

FELICITY FOWLER
FLAT 6, 999 ACACIA AVENUE
As above

For official use
Mortgage section | Post room

Time critical reference

Short particulars of all the property mortgaged or charged

THE UNDERTAKING OF THE COMPANY AND ALL ITS PROPERTY AND ASSETS, BOTH PRESENT AND FUTURE, INCLUDING ITS UNCALLED CAPITAL FOR THE TIME BEING.

Please do not write in this margin

Please complete legibly, preferably in black type or bold block lettering

Particulars as to commission allowance or discount (note 3)

N/A

Signed Felicity Fowler Date 8th APRIL 1993

On behalf of [company] [~~mortgagee/chargee~~]*

*Delete as appropriate

Notes

1. The original instrument (if any) creating or evidencing the charge, together with these prescribed particulars correctly completed must be delivered to the Registrar of Companies within 21 days after the date of creation of the charge (section 395). If the property is situated and the charge was created outside the United Kingdom delivery to the Registrar must be effected within 21 days after the date on which the instrument could in due course of post, and if dispatched with due diligence, have been received in the United Kingdom (section 398). A copy of the instrument creating the charge will be accepted where the property charged is situated and the charge was created outside the United Kingdom (section 398) and in such cases the copy must be verified to be a correct copy either by the company or by the person who has delivered or sent the copy to the registrar. The verification must be signed by or on behalf of the person giving the verification and where this is given by a body corporate it must be signed by an officer of that body. A verified copy will also be accepted where section 398(4) applies (property situate in Scotland or Northern Ireland) and Form No. 398 is submitted.
2. A description of the instrument, eg "Trust Deed", "Debenture", "Mortgage" or "Legal charge", etc, as the case may be, should be given.
3. In this section there should be inserted the amount or rate per cent. of the commission, allowance or discount (if any) paid or made either directly or indirectly by the company to any person in consideration of his:
   (a) subscribing or agreeing to subscribe, whether absolutely or conditionally, or
   (b) procuring or agreeing to procure subscriptions, whether absolute or conditional, for any of the debentures included in this return. The rate of interest payable under the terms of the debentures should not be entered.
4. If any of the spaces in this form provide insufficient space the particulars must be entered on the prescribed continuation sheet.

Page 2

OYEZ The Solicitors' Law Stationery Society Ltd, Oyez House, 7 Spa Road, London SE16 3QQ

1985 Edition
1.92 F21702
5010503

Companies M395

M

Please do not write in this margin

COMPANIES FORM No. 395

395

Particulars of a mortgage or charge

Pursuant to section 395 of the Companies Act 1985

Please complete legibly, preferably in black type or bold block lettering

To the Registrar of Companies

For official use | Company number: 12345678

Name of company

*insert full name of company

*999 ACACIA AVENUE LIMITED

Date of creation of the charge

5TH APRIL 1993

Description of the instrument (if any) creating or evidencing the charge (note 2)

DEBENTURE

Amount secured by the mortgage or charge

£12,000, REPAYABLE IN FIVE EQUAL INSTALMENTS OVER FIVE YEARS.

Names and addresses of the mortgagees or persons entitled to the charge

BELINDA BOTT, FLAT 2, 999 ACACIA AVENUE, DALE, BARSETSHIRE

Postcode: BS20 5QR

Presentor's name, address and reference (if any):

FELICITY FOWLER
FLAT 6, 999 ACACIA AVENUE
As above

For official use
Mortgage section | Post room

Time critical reference

Short particulars of all the property mortgaged or charged

THE UNDERTAKING OF THE COMPANY AND ALL ITS PROPERTY AND ASSETS, BOTH PRESENT AND FUTURE, INCLUDING ITS UNCALLED CAPITAL FOR THE TIME BEING.

Please do not write in this margin

Please complete legibly, preferably in black type or bold block lettering

Particulars as to commission allowance or discount (note 3)

N/A

Signed Felicity Fowler Date 8th APRIL 1993

On behalf of [company] ~~[mortgagee/chargee]~~*

*Delete as appropriate

Notes

1. The original instrument (if any) creating or evidencing the charge, together with these prescribed particulars correctly completed must be delivered to the Registrar of Companies within 21 days after the date of creation of the charge (section 395). If the property is situated and the charge was created outside the United Kingdom delivery to the Registrar must be effected within 21 days after the date on which the instrument could in due course of post, and if dispatched with due diligence, have been received in the United Kingdom (section 398). A copy of the instrument creating the charge will be accepted where the property charged is situated and the charge was created outside the United Kingdom (section 398) and in such cases the copy must be verified to be a correct copy either by the company or by the person who has delivered or sent the copy to the registrar. The verification must be signed by or on behalf of the person giving the verification and where this is given by a body corporate it must be signed by an officer of that body. A verified copy will also be accepted where section 398(4) applies (property situate in Scotland or Northern Ireland) and Form No. 398 is submitted.

2. A description of the instrument, eg "Trust Deed", "Debenture", "Mortgage" or "Legal charge", etc, as the case may be, should be given.

3. In this section there should be inserted the amount or rate per cent. of the commission, allowance or discount (if any) paid or made either directly or indirectly by the company to any person in consideration of his;
   (a) subscribing or agreeing to subscribe, whether absolutely or conditionally, or
   (b) procuring or agreeing to procure subscriptions, whether absolute or conditional, for any of the debentures included in this return. The rate of interest payable under the terms of the debentures should not be entered.

4. If any of the spaces in this form provide insufficient space the particulars must be entered on the prescribed continuation sheet.

Page 2

OYEZ The Solicitors' Law Stationery Society Ltd, Oyez House, 7 Spa Road, London SE16 3QQ

1985 Edition
1.93 F21702
5010503

Companies M395

No. of Company 12345678 **Form No. 401**

N.B. Searchers may find it desirable to refer to the documents mentioned in column (2) for more detailed particulars

REGISTER

OF

Charges
Memoranda of Satisfaction

AND

Appointments and Cessations
of Receivers

OF

999 ACACIA AVENUE

____________________ Limited

N.B. Searchers may find it desirable to refer to the documents mentioned in column (2) for more detailed particulars

REGISTER of Charges, Memoranda of

999 ACACIA AVENUE

(1) Date of Registration	(2) Serial No. of Document on File	(3) Date of Creation of each Charge and Description of	(4) Date of the acquisition of the Property	(5) Amount secured by the Charge	(6) Short Particulars of the Property Charged	(7) Names of the Persons entitled to the Charge
				£		
7.4.93	1	5.4.93		12,000	COMPANY'S UNDERTAKING AND PROPERTY (FLOATING CHARGE)	ANTHONY JOHN ABSOLUTE
7.4.93	2	5.4.93		12,000	"	BELINDA BOTT

Satisfaction and Appointments etc. of Receivers

____ Limited

Particulars relating to the issues of Debentures of a series							(14) Amount or rate of per cent of the Commission Allowance or Discount	(15) Memoranda of Satisfaction		(16) Receiver or Manager	
(8) Total amount secured by a series of Debentures	(9) Dates and amounts of each issue of the series		(10) Dates of the resolutions authorising the issue of the series	(11) Date of the covering Deed	(12) General description of the property charged	(13) Names of the Trustees for the Debenture Holders					
	Date	Amount						Amount	Nature	Name and Date of Appointment	Date of ceasing to act
£		£						£			
←———			N/A		———→						

G

COMPANIES FORM No. 88(2)(Rev 1988)

Return of allotments of shares

88(2)

(REVISED 1988)
This form replaces forms PUC2, PUC3 and 88(2)

Pursuant to section 88(2) of the Companies Act 1985 (the Act)

Please do not write in this margin

To the Registrar of Companies **(address overleaf)**
(see note 1)

Please complete legibly, preferably in black type, or bold block lettering

Company number
12345678

1. Name of company

* insert full name of company

* 999 ACACIA AVENUE LIMITED

2. This section must be completed for all allotments

† Distinguish between ordinary, preference, etc.

Description of shares†	ORDINARY		
A Number allotted	6		
B Nominal value of each	£ 1	£	£
C Total amount (if any) paid or due and payable on each share (including premium if any)	£ 5,000	£	£

§ Complete (a) or (b) as appropriate

Date(s) on which the shares were allotted
(a) [on 5TH APRIL 19 93]§, or
(b) [from ______ 19 ____ to ______ 19 ____]§
The names and addresses of the allottees and the number of shares allotted to each should be given overleaf

3. If the allotment is wholly or partly other than for cash the following information must be given **(see notes 2 & 3)**

D Extent to which each share is to be treated as paid up. Please use percentage.			

E Consideration for which the shares were allotted ______

Notes
1. This form should be delivered to the Registrar of Companies within one month of the (first) date of allotment.
2. If the allotment is wholly or partly other than for cash, the company must deliver to the Registrar a return containing the information at D & E. The company may deliver this information by completing D & E and the delivery of the information must be accompanied by the duly stamped contract required by section 88(2)(b) of the Act or by the duly stamped prescribed particulars required by section 88(3) (Form No 88(3)).
3. Details of bonus issues should be included only in section 2.

Presentor's name, address, telephone number and reference (if any):
FELICITY FOWLER
999 ACACIA AVENUE
DALE, BARSETSHIRE
BS20 5QR
(0999) 332861

For official use

Post room

4. Names and addresses of the allottees

Please do not write in the margin

Names and Addresses	Number of shares allotted		
	Ordinary	Preference	Other
ANTHONY JOHN ABSOLUTE	1		
BELINDA BOTT	1		
CHARLES IAN CRAWFORD	1		
DAHLIA LOUISA DYMOND	1		
EDWARD EXTRACT	1		
FELICITY ANN FOWLER	1		
Total			

Please complete legibly, preferably in black type, or bold block lettering

Where the space given on this form is inadequate, continuation sheets should be used and the number of sheets attached should be indicated in the box opposite:

Signed Felicity Fowler Designation‡ Secretary Date 5th APRIL 1993

‡ Insert Director, Secretary, Administrator, Administrative Receiver, or Receiver (Scotland) as appropriate

Companies registered in England and Wales or Wales should deliver this form to:-

The Registrar of Companies
Companies House
Crown Way
Maindy
Cardiff
CF4 3UZ

Companies registered in Scotland should deliver this form to:-

The Registrar of Companies
Companies Registration Office
102 George Street
Edinburgh
EH2 3DJ

Page 2

OYEZ The Solicitors' Law Stationery Society Ltd. Oyez House, 7 Spa Road, London SE16 3QC

1988 Edition
10.91 F21109
5019476

Companies G88(2) (Revised 1988)

No. of Company 12345678 **Form No. 401**

N.B. Searchers may find it desirable to refer to the documents mentioned in column (2) for more detailed particulars

REGISTER

OF

Charges
Memoranda of Satisfaction

AND

Appointments and Cessations of Receivers

OF

999 ACACIA AVENUE

______________________ Limited

N.B. Searchers may find it desirable to refer to the documents mentioned in column (2) for more detailed particulars

REGISTER of Charges, Memoranda of
999 ACACIA AVENUE

(1) Date of Registration	(2) Serial No. of Document on File	(3) Date of Creation of each Charge and Description of it	(4) Date of the acquisition of the Property	(5) Amount secured by the Charge	(6) Short Particulars of the Property Charged	(7) Names of the Persons entitled to the Charge
				£		
7·4·93	1	5·4·93		12,000	COMPANY'S UNDERTAKING	ANTHONY
					AND PROPERTY	JOHN
					(FLOATING CHARGE)	ABSOLUTE
7·4·93	2	5·4·93		12,000	"	BELINDA
						BOTT

Satisfaction and Appointments etc. of Receivers

____ Limited

Particulars relating to the issues of Debentures of a series							(14)	(15)		(16)	
(8) Total amount secured by a series of Debentures	(9) Dates and amounts of each issue of the series		(10) Dates of the resolutions authorising the issue of the series	(11) Date of the covering Deed	(12) General description of the property charged	(13) Names of the Trustees for the Debenture Holders	Amount or rate of per cent of the Commission Allowance or Discount	Memoranda of Satisfaction		Receiver or Manager	
	Date	Amount						Amount	Nature	Name and Date of Appointment	Date of ceasing to act
£		£						£			
							/	2,400	PAID TO ANTHONY ABSOLUTE, 3RD APRIL, 1994		
←			N/A			→	/				
								2,400	PAID TO BELINDA BETT, 3RD APRIL, 1994		

M

COMPANIES FORM No. 403a

Declaration of satisfaction in full or in part of mortgage or charge

403a

Please do not write in this margin

Pursuant to section 403(1) of the Companies Act 1985

Please complete legibly, preferably in black type, or bold block lettering

To the Registrar of Companies

For official use

Company number 12345678

Name of company

* Insert full name of company

* 999 ACACIA AVENUE LIMITED

I, FELICITY ANN FOWLER

of 999 ACACIA AVENUE, DALE, BARSETSHIRE BS20 5QR

† Delete as appropriate

~~[a director]~~ [the secretary] ~~[the administrator]~~ ~~[the administrative receiver]~~† of the above company, do solemnly and sincerely declare that the debt for which the charge described below was given has been paid or satisfied in ~~[full]~~[part]†

‡ Insert a description of the instrument(s) creating or evidencing the charge, eg 'Mortgage', 'Charge', 'Debenture' etc.

Date and Description of charge‡ DEBENTURE DATED 5th APRIL 1993

§ The date of registration may be confirmed from the certificate

Date of Registration§ 7th APRIL 1993

Name and address of [chargee]~~[trustee for the debenture holders]~~ ANTHONY JOHN ABSOLUTE, 999 ACACIA AVENUE, ETC. AS ABOVE

ø Insert brief details of property

Short particulars of property chargedø THE WHOLE PROPERTY AND UNDERTAKING OF THE COMPANY

And I make this solemn declaration conscientiously believing the same to be true and by virtue of the provisions of the Statutory Declarations Act 1835.

Declared at 2 CHURCH WALK DALE, BARSETSHIRE BS1 3JK

the EIGHTH day of APRIL

one thousand nine hundred and NINETY FOUR

before me LAWRENCE GRABBIT

A Commissioner for Oaths or Notary Public or Justice of the Peace or Solicitor having the powers conferred on a Commissioner for Oaths

Declarant to sign below

Felicity Fowler

[stamp]

Presentor's name, address and reference (if any):

FELICITY FOWLER
ETC.
AS ABOVE

For official use
Mortgage section
Post room

OYEZ The Solicitors' Law Stationery Society Ltd, Oyez House, 7 Spa Road, London SE16 3QQ

1987 Edition
9.91 F20804
5010406

Companies M403a

M

COMPANIES FORM No. 403a

Declaration of satisfaction in full or in part of mortgage or charge

403a

Please do not write in this margin

Pursuant to section 403(1) of the Companies Act 1985

Please complete legibly, preferably in black type, or bold block lettering

To the Registrar of Companies

For official use | Company number 12345678

Name of company

* Insert full name of company

* 999 ACACIA AVENUE LIMITED

I, FELICITY ANN FOWLER

of 999 ACACIA AVENUE, DALE, BARSETSHIRE BS20 5QR

† Delete as appropriate

[a director] [the secretary] [the administrator] [the administrative receiver]† of the above company, do solemnly and sincerely declare that the debt for which the charge described below was given has been paid or satisfied in ~~[full]~~[part]†

‡ Insert a description of the instrument(s) creating or evidencing the charge, eg 'Mortgage', 'Charge', 'Debenture' etc.

Date and Description of charge‡ DEBENTURE DATED 5th APRIL 1993

§ The date of registration may be confirmed from the certificate

Date of Registration§ 7th APRIL 1993

Name and address of [chargee]~~[trustee for the debenture holders]~~ BELINDA BOTT, 999 ACACIA AVENUE, ETC, AS ABOVE

ø Insert brief details of property

Short particulars of property chargedø THE WHOLE PROPERTY AND UNDERTAKING OF THE COMPANY

And I make this solemn declaration conscientiously believing the same to be true and by virtue of the provisions of the Statutory Declarations Act 1835.

Declared at 2 CHURCH WALK
DALE, BARSETSHIRE BS1 3JK

the EIGHTH day of APRIL
one thousand nine hundred and NINETY FOUR
before me LAWRENCE GRABBIT

A Commissioner for Oaths or Notary Public or Justice of the Peace or Solicitor having the powers conferred on a Commissioner for Oaths

Declarant to sign below

Felicity Fowler

[stamp]

Presentor's name, address and reference (if any):

For official use
Mortgage section | Post room

OYEZ The Solicitors' Law Stationery Society Ltd., Oyez House, 7 Spa Road, London SE16 3QQ

1987 Edition
9.91 F20804
5010406

Companies M403a

CON 40 (1963)

STOCK TRANSFER FORM

(Above this line for Registrars only)

Consideration Money £ 5,301

Certificate lodged with the Registrar

(For completion by the Registrar/Stock Exchange)

Name of Undertaking.	999 ACACIA AVENUE LIMITED
Description of Security.	£1 ORDINARY SHARES
Number or amount of Shares, Stock or other security and, in figures column only, number and denomination of units, if any.	Words: THREE SHARES NUMBERED 4, 9 AND 15 — Figures: 3 (3 units of £1)
Name(s) of registered holder(s) should be given in full: the address should be given where there is only one holder. If the transfer is not made by the registered holder(s) insert also the name(s) and capacity (e.g., Executor(s)) of the person(s) making the transfer.	In the name(s) of CHARLES IAN CRAWFORD FLAT 3, 999 ACACIA AVENUE DALE BARSETSHIRE BS20 5QR

I/We hereby transfer the above security out of the name(s) aforesaid to the person(s) named below.

Signature(s) of transferor(s)

1. C. I. Crawford
2. ....
3. ....
4. ....

Stamp of Selling Broker(s) or, for transactions which are not stock exchange transactions, of Agent(s), if any, acting for the Transferor(s)

Date 26th AUGUST 1993

Full name(s) and full postal address(es) (including County or, if applicable, Postal District number) of the person(s) to whom the security is transferred. Please state title, if any, or whether Mr., Mrs., or Miss. Please complete in typewriting or in Block Capitals.	SARDANAPALUS SNOOKS (MR.) 38 NINEVEH CLOSE HUGGLESTOCK BARSETSHIRE SB3 1NN

I/We request that such entries be made in the register as are necessary to give effect to this transfer.

Stamp of Buying Broker(s) (if any)	Stamp or name and address of person lodging this form (if other than the Buying Broker(s))

FORM OF CERTIFICATE REQUIRED WHERE TRANSFER IS EXEMPT FROM STAMP DUTY

Instruments executed on or after 1st May 1987 effecting any transactions within the following categories are exempt from stamp duty:—

A. The vesting of property subject to a trust in the trustees of the trust on the appointment of a new trustee, or in the continuing trustees on the retirement of a trustee.

B. The conveyance or transfer of property the subject of a specific devise or legacy to the beneficiary named in the will (or his nominee). Transfers in satisfaction of a general legacy of money should not be included in this category (see category D below).

C. The conveyance or transfer of property which forms part of an intestate's estate to the person entitled on intestacy (or his nominee). Transfers in satisfaction of the transferees entitlement to cash in the estate of an intestate, where the total value of the residuary estate exceeds that sum, should not be included in this category (see category D below).

D. The appropriation of property within section 84(4) of the Finance Act 1985 (death: appropriation in satisfaction of a general legacy of money) or section 84(5) or (7) of that Act (death: appropriation in satisfaction of any interest of surviving spouse and in Scotland also of any interest of issue).

E. The conveyance or transfer of property which forms part of the residuary estate of a testator to a beneficiary (or his nominee) entitled solely by virtue of his entitlement under the will.

F. The conveyance or transfer of property out of a settlement in or towards satisfaction of a beneficiary's interest, not being an interest acquired for money or money's worth, being a conveyance or transfer constituting a distribution of property in accordance with the provisions of the settlement.

G. The conveyance or transfer of property on and in consideration only of marriage to a party to the marriage (or his nominee) or to trustees to be held on the terms of a settlement made in consideration only of the marriage. A transfer to a spouse after the date of marriage is not within this category, unless made pursuant to an ante-nuptial contract.

H. The conveyance or transfer of property within section 83(1) of the Finance Act 1985 (transfers in connection with divorce etc.).

I. The conveyance or transfer by the liquidator of property which formed part of the assets of the company in liquidation to a shareholder of that company (or his nominee) in or towards satisfaction of the shareholder's rights on a winding-up.

J. The grant in fee simple of an easement in or over land for no consideration in money or money's worth.

K. The grant of a servitude for no consideration in money or money's worth.

L. The conveyance or transfer of property operating as a voluntary disposition inter vivos for no consideration in money or money's worth nor any consideration referred to in section 57 of the Stamp Act 1891 (conveyance in consideration of a debt etc.).

M. The conveyance or transfer of property by an instrument within section 84(1) of the Finance Act 1985 (death: varying disposition).

(1) Delete as appropriate.
(2) Insert "(A)", "(B)" or appropriate category.
(3) Delete second sentence if the certificate is given by the transferor or his solicitor.

(1) I/We hereby certify that the transaction in respect of which this transfer is made is one which falls within the category(2) ________ above. (1)I/We confirm that (1)I/We have been duly authorised by the transferor to sign this certificate and that the facts of the transaction are within (1)my/our knowledge (3)

Signature(s) ________________ *Description ("Transferor", "Solicitor", etc.)* ________________

________________ ________________

________________ ________________

________________ ________________

Date ________________ 19____ ________________

NOTES
(1) If the above certificate has been completed, this transfer does not need to be submitted to the Controller of Stamps but should be sent directly to the Company or its Registrars.
(2) If the above certificate is not completed, this transfer must be submitted to the Controller of Stamps and duly stamped. (See below).

FORM OF CERTIFICATE REQUIRED WHERE TRANSFER IS NOT EXEMPT BUT IS NOT LIABLE TO *AD VALOREM* STAMP DUTY

Instruments of transfer, other than those in respect of which the above certificate has been completed, are liable to a fixed duty of 50p when the transaction falls within one of the following categories:—

(*a*) Transfer by way of security for a loan or re-transfer to the original transferor on repayment of a loan.

(*b*) Transfer, not on sale and not arising under any contract of sale and where no beneficial interest in the property passes: (i) to a person who is a mere nominee of, and is nominated only by, the transferor; (ii) from a mere nominee who has at all times held the property on behalf of the transferee; (iii) from one nominee to another nominee of the same beneficial owner where the first nominee has at all times held the property on behalf of that beneficial owner. (NOTE—This category does not include a transfer made in any of the following circumstances: (i) by a holder of stock, etc., following the grant of an option to purchase the stock, to the person entitled to the option or his nominee; (ii) to a nominee in contemplation of a contract for the sale of the stock, etc., then about to be entered into; (iii) from the nominee of a vendor, who has instructed the nominee orally or by some unstamped writing to hold stock, etc., in trust for a purchaser, to such purchaser.)

(1) Delete as appropriate.
(2) Insert "(a)", "(b)".
(3) Here set out concisely the facts explaining the transaction. Adjudication may be required.

(1) I/We hereby certify that the transaction in respect of which this transfer is made is one which falls within the category(2) ________ above. (1)I/we confirm that (1)I/We have been duly authorised by the transferor to sign this certificate and the facts of the transaction are within (1)my/our knowledge.

(3)..

....

....

....

Signature(s) .... *Description ("Transferor", "Solicitor", etc.)* ....

....

....

....

....

Date ....19........ ....

No. 21
No. OF SHARES 3
Nos. 4, 9 AND 15
ISSUED TO SARDANAPALUS SNOOKS

OF FLAT 3,
999 ACACIA AVENUE, DALE,
BARSETSHIRE,
BS20 5QR
DATE 2nd SEPTEMBER 1993
ENTERED ON REGISTER
PAGE 39

No. 21

999 ACACIA AVENUE LIMITED
Incorporated under the Companies Act

CAPITAL £100

DIVIDED INTO 100 SHARES OF £1 EACH

THIS IS TO CERTIFY *that* SARDANAPALUS SNOOKS
of FLAT 3, 999 ACACIA AVENUE, DALE, BARSETSHIRE, BS20 5QR
is the holder of THREE ORDINARY *Share paid of* £1 *each Numbered* 4, 9 AND 15 *issued in the above named Company subject to the memorandum and Articles of Association thereof*
GIVEN *by the said Company*

The 2nd *day of* SEPTEMBER *19* 93
acting by
Director A. J. ABSOLUTE
Secretary F. FOWLER

NO TRANSFER OF THE WHOLE OR ANY PORTION OF THE ABOVE SHARES CAN BE REGISTERED WITHOUT THE PRODUCTION OF THIS CERTIFICATE

OYEZ

CHA1

288

Change of director or secretary or change of particulars.

This form should be completed in black.

Company number	CN 12345678
Company name	999 ACACIA AVENUE LIMITED

Appointment

(Turn over page for resignation and change of particulars).

Date of appointment	Day Month Year DA 0 2 0 9 9 3
Appointment of director	CD ✓
Appointment of secretary	CS

Please mark the appropriate box. If appointment is as a director and secretary mark both boxes.

NOTES

Show the full forenames, NOT INITIALS. If the director or secretary is a Corporation or Scottish firm, show the name on surname line and registered or principal office on the usual residential address line.

Give previous forenames or surname except:
- for a married woman the name before marriage need not be given.
- for names not used since the age of 18 or for at least 20 years.

A peer or individual known by a title may state the title instead of or in addition to the forenames and surname.

Name *Style/title	MR.
Forenames	SARDANAPALUS
Surname	SNOOKS
*Honours etc	
Previous forenames	
Previous surname	
Usual residential address	AD FLAT 3, 999 ACACIA AVENUE
Post town	DALE
County/region	BARSETSHIRE
Postcode	BS20 5QR Country ENGLAND
Date of birth†	DO 0 6 0 5 6 1 Nationality† NA U.K.
Business occupation†	OC UNIVERSITY LECTURER
Other directorships†	

Other directorships.

Give the name of every company of which the person concerned is a director or has been a director at any time in the past 5 years. Exclude a company which either is, or at all times during the past 5 years when the person was a director, was
- dormant
- a parent company which wholly owned the company making the return
- a wholly owned subsidiary of the company making the return
- another wholly owned subsidiary of the same parent company.

I consent to act as director/~~secretary~~ of the above-named company

Consent signature Signed S. Snooks Date 2ND SEPT. 1993

*Voluntary details †Directors only

A serving director etc must also sign the form overleaf.

Resignation

(This includes any form of ceasing to hold office e.g. death or removal from office).

Date of resignation etc DR 2 9 0 8 9 3

Resignation etc, as director XD ✓

Resignation etc, as secretary XS

Please mark the appropriate box. If resignation etc is as a director and secretary mark both boxes.

Forenames CHARLES IAN

Surname CRAWFORD

Date of birth *(directors only)* DO 0 2 1 0 5 8

If cessation is other than resignation, please state reason *(eg death)* OFFICE VACATED UNDER ARTICLE 14

Change of particulars

Complete this section in all cases where particulars have changed and then the appropriate section below.

Date of change of particulars DC

Change of particulars, as director ZD

Change of particulars, as secretary ZS

Please mark the appropriate box. If change of particulars is as a director and secretary mark both boxes.

Forenames / Surname *(name previously notified to Companies House)*

Date of birth *(directors only)* DO

Change of name *(enter new name)* Forenames NN

Surname

Change of usual residential address *(enter new address)* AD

Post town

County/region

Postcode Country

Other change *(please specify)*

A serving director, secretary etc must sign the form below.

Signature Signed F. Fowler Date 2ND SEPT. 1993

(by a serving director/secretary/~~administrator/administrative receiver/receiver~~). *(Delete as appropriate)*

After signing please return the form to the Registrar of Companies at

Companies House, Crown Way, Cardiff CF4 3UZ for companies registered in England and Wales

or

Companies House, 100-102 George Street, Edinburgh EH2 3DJ for companies registered in Scotland.

To whom should Companies House direct any enquiries about the information on this form?

FELICITY FOWLER, FLAT 6,
999 ACACIA AVENUE, DALE, BARSETSHIRE
BS20 5QR Tel: (0999) 332861

OYEZ The Solicitors' Law Stationery Society Ltd, Oyez House, 7 Spa Road, London SE16 3QQ 1990 Edition 3.93 F24298 5017301

Companies 288

OYEZ

CHA1

363a
Annual Return

This form should be completed in black.

Company number — CN 12345678

Company name — 999 ACACIA AVENUE LIMITED

Date of this return *(See note 1)*
The information in this return is made up to

Day Month Year
DA 20 10 91
Show date

Date of next return *(See note 2)*
If you wish to make your next return to a date earlier than the anniversary of this return please show the date here. Companies House will then send a form at the appropriate time.

DB

Registered Office *(See note 3)*
Show here the address at the date of this return.

RO FLAT 6, 999 ACACIA AVENUE

Post town DALE

County/Region BARSETSHIRE

Postcode BS20 5QR

Any change of registered office must be notified on form 287.

Principal business activities
(See note 4)
Show trade classification code number(s) for principal activity or activities.

PA 9 6 0 0

If the code number cannot be determined, give a brief description of principal activity.

Register of members
(See note 5)
If the register of members is not kept at the registered office, state here where it is kept.

RM ______________________________

____

Post town ______________________________

County/Region ______________________________

Postcode ______________________________

Register of Debenture holders
(See note 6)
If there is a register of debenture holders and it is not kept at the registered office, state here where it is kept.

RD ______________________________

____

Post town ______________________________

County/Region ______________________________

Postcode ______________________________

Company type *(See note 7)*

Public limited company	T1	
Private company limited by shares	T2	✓
Private company limited by guarantee without share capital	T3	
Private company limited by shares exempt under section 30	T4	
Private company limited by guarantee exempt under section 30	T5	
Private unlimited company with share capital	T6	
Private unlimited company without share capital	T7	

Please mark the appropriate box.

Company Secretary *(See note 8)*
(Please photocopy this area to provide details of joint secretaries).

Details of a new company secretary must be notified on form 288.

Name

*Style/Title CS MISS

Forenames FELICITY ANN

Surname FOWLER

*Honours etc ______________________________

Previous forenames ______________________________

Previous surname ______________________________

Address AD FLAT 6, 999 ACACIA AVENUE

Usual residential address must be given. In the case of a corporation, give the registered or principal office address.

Post town DALE

County/Region BARSETSHIRE

Postcode BS20 5QR Country ENGLAND

* Voluntary details

Page 2

Directors *(See note 8)*
Please list directors in alphabetical order.

Details of new directors **must** be notified on form 288.

Name	*Style/Title	CD MR.
	Forenames	ANTHONY JOHN
	Surname	ABSOLUTE
	*Honours etc	
	Previous forenames	
	Previous surname	
Address		AD FLAT 1, 999 ACACIA AVENUE
Usual residential address must be given. In the case of a corporation, give the registered or principal office address.	Post town	DALE
	County/Region	BARSETSHIRE
	Postcode	BS20 5QR
	Country	ENGLAND
	Date of birth	DO 030859
	Nationality	NA U.K.
	Business occupation	OC INSURANCE BROKER
	Other directorships	OD NONE

Name	*Style/Title	CD MISS
	Forenames	BELINDA
	Surname	BOTT
	*Honours etc	
	Previous forenames	
	Previous surname	
Address		AD FLAT 2, 999 ACACIA AVENUE
Usual residential address must be given. In the case of a corporation, give the registered or principal office address.	Post town	DALE
	County/Region	BARSETSHIRE
	Postcode	BS20 5QR
	Country	ENGLAND
	Date of birth	DO 220458
	Nationality	NA U.K.
	Business occupation	OC STUDENT
	Other directorships	OD NONE

* Voluntary details

Directors (continued)

Name *Style/Title	CD MR.
Forenames	CHARLES IAN
Surname	CRAWFORD
*Honours etc	
Previous forenames	
Previous surname	
Address	AD FLAT 3, 999 ACACIA AVENUE
Usual residential address must be given. In the case of a corporation, give the registered or principal office address.	
	Post town DALE
	County/Region BARSETSHIRE
	Postcode BS20 5QR Country ENGLAND
Date of birth	DO 02 11 05 58 Nationality NA U.K.
Business occupation	OC ADVERTISING EXECUTIVE
Other directorships	OD PUFF AND PUFF LIMITED

Name *Style/Title	CD MS.
Forenames	DAHLIA LOUISA
Surname	DYMOND
*Honours etc	
Previous forenames	
Previous surname	
Address	AD FLAT 4, 999 ACACIA AVENUE
Usual residential address must be given. In the case of a corporation, give the registered or principal office address.	
	Post town DALE
	County/Region BARSETSHIRE
	Postcode BS20 5QR Country ENGLAND
Date of birth	DO 15 02 54 Nationality NA U.K.
Business occupation	OC TELEVISION PRODUCER
Other directorships	OD NONE

* Voluntary details

Directors (continued)

Name	*Style/Title	CD MR.
	Forenames	EDWARD
	Surname	EXTRACT
	*Honours etc	
	Previous forenames	
	Previous surname	
Address		AD FLAT 5, 999 ACACIA AVENUE
Usual residential address must be given. In the case of a corporation, give the registered or principal office address.		
		Post town DALE
		County/Region BARSETSHIRE
		Postcode BS20 5QR Country ENGLAND
	Date of birth	DO 28 09 54 Nationality NA U.K.
	Business occupation	OC CATERING MANAGER
	Other directorships	OD NONE

Name	*Style/Title	CD MISS
	Forenames	FELICITY ANN
	Surname	FOWLER
	*Honours etc	
	Previous forenames	
	Previous surname	
Address		AD FLAT 6, 999 ACACIA AVENUE
Usual residential address must be given. In the case of a corporation, give the registered or principal office address.		
		Post town DALE
		County/Region BARSETSHIRE
		Postcode BS20 5QR Country ENGLAND
	Date of birth	DO 08 01 62 Nationality NA U.K.
	Business occupation	OC SOLICITOR
	Other directorships	OD NONE

* Voluntary details

Issued share capital *(See note 9)*
Enter details of all the shares in issue at the date of this return.

Class	Number	Aggregate Nominal Value
£1 ORDINARY	12	£12
Totals	12	£12

List of past and present members
(Use attached schedule where appropriate)

A full list is required if one was not included with either of the last two returns.
(See note 10)

Please mark the appropriate box(es)

There were no changes in the period ☐

	on paper	not on paper
A list of changes is enclosed	✓	☐
A full list of members is enclosed	✓	☐

Elective resolutions *(See note 11)*
(Private companies only)

If an election is in force at the date of this return to dispense with annual general meetings, *mark this box* ☐

If an election is in force at the date of this return to dispense with laying accounts in general meetings, *mark this box* ☐

Certificate
I certify that the information given in this return is true to the best of my knowledge and belief.

Signed Felicity Fowler Secretary/Director*
(delete as appropriate)*

Date 25th OCTOBER 1991

This return includes 1 continuation sheets.
(enter number)

To whom should Companies House direct any enquiries about the information shown in this return?

FELICITY FOWLER
Address as above

Postcode

Telephone (0999) 332861 Extension

When you have signed the return send it with the fee to the Registrar of Companies at

Companies House, Crown Way, Cardiff CF4 3UZ
for companies registered in England and Wales
or
Companies House, 100-102 George Street, Edinburgh EH2 3DJ
for companies registered in Scotland.

Page 6

OYEZ The Solicitors' Law Stationery Society Ltd., Oyez House, 7 Spa Road, London SE16 3QQ

1992 Edition
11.92 F2353
5010448

Companies 363a (Schedule and Notes)

LIST OF PAST AND PRESENT MEMBERS | **SCHEDULE TO FORM 363**

Company Number:

Company Name:

Name and Address	Account of Shares: Number of shares or amount of stock held by existing members at date of this return.	Account of Shares: Particulars of shares transferred since the date of the last return, or, in the case of the first return, since the incorporation of the company, by (a) persons who are still members, and (b) persons who have ceased to be members. Number	Date of Registration of Transfer	Remarks
ANTHONY JOHN ABSOLUTE, FLAT 1, ACACIA AVENUE,	2			1 TRANSFERRED
DALE, BARSETSHIRE				FROM G. GREBE
BS20 5QR				1 ALLOTTED 25.9.91
BELINDA BOTT, FLAT 2, ACACIA AVENUE,	2			1 ALLOTTED 3.4.91
ETC.				1 ALLOTTED 25.9.91
CHARLES IAN CRAWFORD, FLAT 3, "	2			1 ALLOTTED 3.4.91
				1 ALLOTTED 25.9.91
DAHLIA LOUISA DYMOND, FLAT 4, "	2			1 ALLOTTED 3.4.91
				1 ALLOTTED 25.9.91
EDWARD EXTRACT, FLAT 5, "	2			1 ALLOTTED 3.4.91
				1 ALLOTTED 25.9.91
FELICITY ANN FOWLER, FLAT 6, "	2			1 TRANSFERRED FROM
				C. CAT
				1 ALLOTTED 25.9.91
CAROLINE EMMA CAT	/	1		TRANSFERRED TO
				F. FOWLER
GREGORY CHRISTOPHER GREBE	/	1		TRANSFERRED TO
				A. ABSOLUTE

Continued overleaf

NOTES FOR COMPLETION OF ANNUAL RETURN FORM 363a (to be retained)

Introduction

Every company MUST make an Annual Return to the Registrar of Companies.

The completed form must reach Companies House within 28 days from "the date of the return". Failure to comply is an offence.

Annual Returns are no longer tied to the date of the Annual General Meeting.

1. **Date of this return**

The date of the Annual Return must be within twelve months of:

- the date of the previous return, or
- in the case of a new company, the date of incorporation.

2. **Date of next return**

You may give, as the date of your next return, a date which is less than 12 months from the date of this return by entering the new date in the box shown. Companies House will then send your next return shortly before the date you give in this box. If no date is entered Companies House will send you the next annual return form shortly before the anniversary of this return.

3. **Registered office**

The registered office address you enter must be that currently registered at Companies House.

Any change in the registered office must be given on form 287 and it will only become effective when Companies House register it.

4. **Principal business activities**

Show the code or codes for the company's principal business activity or activities.

A list of codes based on the VAT trade classification is included with these notes. Use of these codes does not imply that the company is registered for VAT.

If you cannot determine the company's trade classification enter a brief description of the company's principal business activity or activities.

5. **Register of members**

You need only complete this section if you do not keep the register at the registered office.

6. **Register of debenture holders**

You need only complete this section if:

- the company has a register of debentures and
- you do not keep it (or a duplicate) at the registered office.

7. **Company type**

Please tick the appropriate box.

A company's type is determined by its Memorandum of Association.

Private companies limited by guarantee with a share capital should be shown under – "Private Company Limited by Shares".

Some private limited companies need not include the word "Limited" in their names (section 30 of the Companies Act 1985). Further details can be found in notes for guidance pamphlet, NG6, available from Companies House.

8. **Directors and secretaries**

Show for an individual the full forenames NOT THE INITIALS and surname together with any pervious forenames or surname. If the director or secretary is a corporation or Scottish firm – show the corporate or firm name on the surname line.

Give previous forenames or surname except that:

- for a married woman, the name by which she was known before marriage need not be given,
- names not used since the age of 18 or for at least 20 years need not be given.

In the case of a peer, or an individual usually known by a British title, you may state the title instead of or in addition to the forenames and surname and you need not give the name by which that person was known before he or she adopted the title or succeeded to it.

Address

Give the usual residential address. In the case of a corporation or Scottish firm give the registered or principal office.

Directors known by another description

A director includes any person who occupies that position even if called by a different name, for example, governor, member of council. It also includes a shadow director.

Directors details

Show for each individual director their date of birth (a new requirement), business occupation and nationality.

Other directorships

Give the name of every company of which the person concerned is a director or has been a director at any time in the past 5 years. You may exclude a company which, either is or at all times during the past 5 years when the person was a director was:

- dormant,
- a parent company which wholly owned the company making the return,
- a wholly owned subsidiary of the company making the return,
- another wholly owned subsidiary of the same parent company.

If there is insufficient space on the form for other directorships you may attach a list. This should include the company's name and number.

9. **Issued share capital**

This part does not apply to a company without share capital.

For each class of shares state:

- the nature of the class,
- the total number and aggregate nominal value of issued shares of that class as at the date of the return.

10. **List of past and present members**

Give names and addresses of all persons who hold shares or stock in the company at the date of this return and of all persons who have ceased to be members of the company since the date of the last return.

Show

- the number of shares or amount of stock held by present members together with their addresses,
- the number of shares of each class transferred since the date of the last return (or, if this is the first return, since the date of incorporation of the company) by current members or by persons who have ceased to be members. Also show the date of registration of these transfers.

If you do not show the list of members in alphabetical order please attach an index which will help to locate any member shown on the list.

If you have given full details on either of the last two returns you need only include details of persons, who since the date of the last return:

- have become members,
- have ceased to be members,
- are existing members whose holdings of stock or shares have changed.

Please mark "there were no changes in the period" if full details have been given on either of the last two returns and there have been no changes since.

Where the company has converted any of its shares into stock give the corresponding information in relation to that stock, stating the amount of stock instead of the number of nominal value of shares.

11. **Elective resolutions**

This part does not apply to a public company.

A private company may elect (by elective resolution):

- to dispense with the holding of annual general meetings,
- not to lay the accounts and reports before the company in general meeting.

You must send a copy of the resolution to the Registrar of Companies within 15 days of the passing of it.

The accounts of a company have to be delivered to Companies House even if the company has resolved that they need not be laid before it in general meeting. The accounts must normally be delivered to Companies House within 10 months after the end of the period to which they relate.

Completion of form

Please ensure the form is complete and is signed by a director or secretary. Do not forget to enclose the fee

[P.T.O.

Trade classification

This classification is based on the VAT trade classification but there are some additional codes (numbered from 9500).

Trade Code

PRIMARY INDUSTRIES

Group 01 - Agriculture, forestry and fishing

- 0011 Livestock farming (including pigs and poultry)
- 0012 Arable farming
- 0013 Dairying
- 0014 Mixed farming (no more than 60% in any of the above)
- 0015 Breeding of non-food producing animals (including horses)
- 0016 Agricultural contracting
- 0017 Market gardening and fruit farming
- 0018 Flower and seed growing
- 0020 Forestry
- 0030 Fishing

Group 02 - Mining and quarrying

- 1010 Coal mining other than opencast (heading 5030)
- 1020 Stone and slate quarrying and mining
- 1030 Chalk, clay, sand and gravel extraction
- 1040 Petroleum and natural gas
- 1090 Other mining and quarrying

MANUFACTURING INDUSTRIES

Group 03 - Food, drink and tobacco

- 2110 Grain milling
- 2120 Bread and flour confectionery (including retailing wholly or mainly of own production (see also code 8206)
- 2130 Biscuits
- 2140 Bacon-curing meat and fish products
- 2151 Milk and milk products (other than ice cream)
- 2152 Ice cream
- 2160 Sugar
- 2170 Cocoa, chocolate and sugar confectionery
- 2180 Fruit and vegetable products
- 2190 Animal and poultry foods
- 2210 Vegetable and animal oils and fats
- 2290 Food industries not elsewhere specified
- 2310 Brewing and malting
- 2320 Soft drinks
- 2391 Spirit distilling and compounding
- 2392 British wines cider and perry
- 2400 Tobacco

Group 04 - Coal and petroleum products

- 2610 Coke ovens and manufactured fuel
- 2620 Mineral oil refining
- 2630 Lubricating oils and greases

Group 05 - Chemicals and allied industries

- 2710 General chemicals (manufacture of chemical elements organic and inorganic compounds (except pharmaceuticals, dyestuffs and pesticides)
- 2720 Pharmaceutical chemicals and preparations
- 2730 Toilet preparations
- 2740 Paint
- 2750 Soap and detergents
- 2760 Synthetic resins, plastics materials and synthetic rubber
- 2770 Dyestuffs and pigments
- 2780 Fertilisers
- 2790 Other chemical industries (polishes, adhesives, explosives and fireworks, pesticides, printing ink, surgical bandages etc, photographic chemical materials)

Group 06 - Metal manufacture

- 3110 Iron and steel (general)
- 3120 Steel tubes
- 3130 Iron castings etc
- 3210 Aluminium and aluminium alloys
- 3220 Copper, brass and other copper alloys
- 3230 Other base metals

Group 07 - Mechanical engineering

- 3310 Agricultural machinery (except tractors)
- 3320 Metal working machine tools
- 3330 Pumps, valves and compressors
- 3340 Industrial engines
- 3350 Textile machinery and accessories
- 3360 Construction and earth moving equipment
- 3370 Mechanical handling equipment
- 3380 Office machinery
- 3390 Other machinery
- 3410 Industrial (including process) plant and steel work
- 3420 Ordnance and small arms
- 3490 Other mechanical engineering not elsewhere specified

Group 08 - Instrument engineering

- 3510 Photographic and document copying equipment
- 3520 Watches and clocks
- 3530 Surgical instruments and appliances
- 3540 Scientific and industrial instruments and systems

Group 09 - Electrical engineering

- 3610 Electrical machinery
- 3620 Insulated wires and cables
- 3630 Telegraph and telephone apparatus and equipment
- 3640 Radio and electronic components
- 3651 Gramophone records and tape recordings
- 3659 Other broadcast receiving and sound reproducing equipment
- 3660 Electronic computers
- 3670 Radio, radar and electronic capital goods
- 3680 Electric appliances primarily for domestic use
- 3690 Other electrical goods

Group 10 - Shipbuilding, boatbuilding and marine engineering

- 3700 Shipbuilding, boatbuilding and marine engineering

Group 11 - Vehicles

- 3800 Wheeled tractor manufacturing
- 3811 Motor vehicle manufacturing
- 3812 Caravan manufacturing
- 3820 Motor cycle, tricycle and pedal cycle manufacturing
- 3830 Aerospace equipment manufacturing and repairing
- 3840 Locomotives and railway track equipment
- 3850 Railway carriages, wagons and trams

Group 12 - Metal goods not elsewhere specified

- 3900 Engineers small tools and gauges
- 3910 Hand tools and implements
- 3920 Cutlery, spoons, forks, plated tableware etc
- 3930 Bolts, nuts, screws, rivets etc
- 3940 Wire and wire manufactures
- 3950 Cans and metal boxes
- 3961 Jewellery manufacturing
- 3962 Jewellery processing
- 3963 Precious metals and articles of precious metal (other than jewellery)
- 3990 Metal industries not elsewhere specified

Group 13 - Textiles

- 4110 Production of man-made fibres
- 4120 Spinning and doubling on the cotton and flax systems
- 4130 Weaving of cotton, linen and man-made fibres
- 4140 Woollen and worsted
- 4150 Jute
- 4160 Rope, twine and net
- 4170 Hosiery and other knitted goods
- 4180 Lace
- 4190 Carpets
- 4210 Narrow fabrics (not more than 30cm wide)
- 4220 Made up textiles
- 4230 Textile finishing
- 4290 Other textile industries

Group 14 - Leather, leather goods and fur

- 4310 Leather (tanning and dressing) and fellmongery
- 4321 Handbags (including handbags of plastic and imitation leather)
- 4322 Travel goods (including goods of plastic and imitation leather)
- 4329 Other leather goods (including imitation leather)
- 4331 Fur processing
- 4339 Other fur

Trade Code

PRIMARY INDUSTRIES

MANUFACTURING INDUSTRIES (Cont)

Group 15 - Clothing and footwear

- 4410 Weatherproof outerwear
- 4420 Men's and boy's tailored outerwear
- 4430 Women's and girl's tailored outerwear
- 4440 Overalls and men's shirts, underwear etc
- 4450 Dresses, lingerie, infants' wear etc
- 4460 Hats, caps and millinery
- 4490 Dress industries not elsewhere specified
- 4500 Footwear

Group 16 - Bricks, ceramics, glass, cement etc

- 4610 Bricks, fireclay and refractory goods
- 4620 Ceramics
- 4630 Glass
- 4640 Cement
- 4690 Abrasives and building materials not elsewhere specified

Group 17 - Timber, furniture etc

- 4710 Timber
- 4721 Upholstery
- 4722 Chair frames (other than of metal)
- 4729 Other furniture for home or office use
- 4730 Bedding etc
- 4740 Shop and office fitting
- 4750 Wooden containers and baskets
- 4791 Garden furniture
- 4799 Other miscellaneous wood and cork manufacturing

Group 18 - Paper, printing and publishing

- 4810 Paper and board
- 4820 Packaging products of paper, board and associated materials
- 4830 Manufactured stationery
- 4840 Manufacturers of paper and board not elsewhere specified
- 4850 Printing and publishing of newspapers
- 4860 Printing and publishing of periodicals
- 4891 Publishing of books
- 4892 Greeting cards
- 4893 Prints and reproductions
- 4894 Bookbinding
- 4899 Other printing

Group 19 - Other manufacturing industries

- 4910 Rubber
- 4920 Linoleum, plastics floor-coverings, leathercloth, etc
- 4930 Brushes and brooms
- 4940 Toys, games, children's carriages and sports equipment
- 4950 Miscellaneous stationers' goods
- 4960 Plastics products not elsewhere specified
- 4991 Musical instruments
- 4992 Imitation jewellery
- 4999 Other miscellaneous manufacturing industries

CONSTRUCTION

Group 20 - Construction

- 5001 General builders
- 5002 Building and civil engineering contractors
- 5003 Civil engineering contractors
- 5004 Plumbers
- 5005 Joiners and carpenters
- 5006 Painters and decorators
- 5007 Roofing contractors
- 5008 Plastering contractors
- 5009 Glazing contractors
- 5011 Demolition contractors
- 5012 Scaffolding specialists
- 5013 Reinforced concrete specialists
- 5014 Heating and ventilating engineers
- 5015 Electrical contractors
- 5016 Asphalt and tar spraying contractors
- 5017 Plant hirers
- 5018 Flooring contractors
- 5019 Constructional engineers
- 5021 Insulating specialists
- 5022 Suspended ceiling specialists
- 5023 Wall and floor tiling specialists
- 5029 Specialists not elsewhere specified
- 5030 Opencast coal mining

UTILITIES

Group 21 - Gas, electricity and water

- 6010 Gas
- 6020 Electricity
- 6030 Water

TRANSPORT AND COMMUNICATION

Group 22 - Transport and communication

- 7010 Railways
- 7021 Omnibus and tramway services
- 7022 Taxis and private hire cars
- 7030 Road haulage contracting for general hire or reward
- 7040 Other road haulage
- 7050 Sea transport
- 7060 Port and inland water transport
- 7070 Air transport
- 7080 Postal services and telecommunications
- 7091 Shipping agents and forwarding agents
- 7092 Travel agents
- 7093 Driving instruction
- 7094 Operation of car parks, toll roads and toll bridges
- 7099 Other miscellaneous transport services and storage

DISTRIBUTIVE TRADES

Group 23 - Wholesale distribution

(N.B. Wholesaling of motor vehicles (new and second hand), including motor cycles and caravans is allocated to heading 8941 and not to the headings within this group).

Wholesale distribution of:

- 8101 Fresh meat, fish, fruit and vegetables
- 8102 Alcoholic drink (including brewing)
- 8109 Other food and drink
- 8110 Petroleum products
- 8121 Chemists' sundries
- 8122 Clocks and watches
- 8123 Clothing
- 8124 Furs
- 8125 Textiles
- 8126 Footwear
- 8127 Electrical goods
- 8128 Radio, TV sets, tape recorders, tape recordings and gramophone records
- 8129 Jewellery
- 8131 Imitation jewellery
- 8132 Musical instruments
- 8133 Photographic goods
- 8134 Toys
- 8135 Travel and fancy goods (including shopping bags)
- 8136 Furniture and floor coverings
- 8137 China, glassware, hardware and ironmongery
- 8138 Paper and board products, including reading material
- 8139 Leasing and office furniture, vending machines, juke boxes and gaming machines
- 8149 Other goods

Trade Code

PRIMARY INDUSTRIES

Group 24 - Retail distribution

(N.B. Retailing of motor vehicles (new and second hand), including motor cycles and caravans is allocated to heading 8941 and not to the headings within this group).

- 8201 Grocers
- 8202 Dairymen
- 8204 Fishmongers and butchers
- 8205 Greengrocers and fruiterers
- 8206 Bread and flour confectioners selling wholly or mainly bought in goods (see also code 2120)
- 8207 Off licences
- 8211 Department stores
- 8212 Variety and other general stores
- 8213 General mail order houses
- 8214 Confectioners, tobacconists and newsagents
- 8215 Footwear shops
- 8216 Men's and boy's wear shops
- 8217 Women's and girl's wear, household textiles and general clothing shops
- 8218 Retail furriers
- 8219 Domestic furniture shops, floor coverings shops, furniture and upholstery repairers
- 8221 Antique dealers, second hand furniture shops, art dealers, picture framers and dealers in stamps and coins
- 8222 Radio and electrical goods shops (excluding radio and TV rental and relay shops)
- 8223 Radio and TV rental shops
- 8224 Hardware, china, wallpaper and paint shops
- 8225 Cycle and perambulator shops
- 8226 Booksellers and stationers
- 8227 Chemists and photographic shops
- 8228 Opticians
- 8229 Jewellery, watch and clock retailers and repairers
- 8231 Leather goods, sports goods, toys and fancy goods shops
- 8232 Music shops (including gramophone records)
- 8233 Florists, nurserymen and garden shops
- 8234 Pet and pet food shops
- 8239 Other non-food shops

Group 25 - Dealers

(N.B. Dealing in motor vehicles (new and second hand), including motor cycles and caravans, is allocated to heading 8941 and not to the headings within this group).

- 8311 Coal and oil merchants (not including bulk oil distributors or petrol filling stations)
- 8312 Builders' merchants
- 8313 Corn, seed and agricultural merchants, dealers in livestock
- 8321 Dealing in industrial materials
- 8322 Dealing in scrap and other waste metals
- 8323 Dealing in industrial and agricultural machinery
- 8324 Leasing industrial and office machinery

SERVICES

Group 26 - Insurance, banking, finance and business services

- 8600 Insurance
- 8610 Banking and bill discounting
- 8621 Stockbrokers
- 8622 Unit and investment trusts
- 8629 Other financial institutions
- 8630 Property owning and managing (see also 9600)
- 8640 Advertising and market research
- 8651 Industrial and commercial valuers, auctioneers and property agents
- 8652 Chartered or company secretaries (firms acting as)
- 8653 Computer services
- 8654 Contract cleaning
- 8655 Management consultants
- 8656 Staff bureaux and employment agencies
- 8657 Duplicating, addressing and typewriting agencies
- 8659 Other business services

Group 27 - Professional and scientific services

- 8710 Accountancy services
- 8720 Educational services
- 8730 Legal services
- 8741 Hospital and consultant services
- 8742 Local authority health services
- 8743 General medical services
- 8744 Dental services
- 8749 Other medical services
- 8750 Religious organisations
- 8760 Research and Development services
- 8791 Veterinary services
- 8792 Surveying (private sector)
- 8793 Architects (private practice)
- 8794 Draughtsmen (private practice)
- 8795 Consultant engineers
- 8796 Research chemists, analytical chemists, assayers, non-medical bacteriologists, metallurgists and geologists (private practice)
- 8797 Professional and scientific representative bodies
- 8798 Artists, sculptors, designers, authors, journalists (free-lance) and composers
- 8799 Other professional and scientific services
- 8811 Cinemas
- 8812 Theatres, music halls etc, radio and television services (excluding relay services), film and recording studios etc
- 8813 Performers and performing groups (drama, music, variety etc)
- 8814 Radio and television relay services
- 8821 Dance halls and dancing schools
- 8822 Sport
- 8829 Other recreations
- 8830 Betting and gaming
- 8841 Hotels and other residential establishments
- 8842 Holiday camps, camping and holiday caravan sites
- 8851 Restaurants, cafes, snack bars etc, selling food for consumption on the premises only
- 8852 Fish and chip shops, sandwich and snack bars and other establishments selling food partly or wholly for consumption off the premises
- 8860 Public houses
- 8870 Clubs (including sports clubs and gaming clubs)
- 8880 Catering contractors
- 8891 Men's hairdressing and manicure
- 8892 Women's hairdressing and manicure
- 8921 Launderettes
- 8922 Laundries
- 8923 Hire of towels, linen and industrial clothing
- 8930 Dry cleaning, job dyeing, carpet beating etc
- 8941 Distribution, repair and servicing of motor vehicles (including wholesaling, retailing and dealing in motor vehicles and caravans (new and second hand), tyres, motor accessories and spares)
- 8942 Petrol filling stations
- 8950 Repair of boots and shoes
- 8991 Funeral direction, cemeteries and crematoria
- 8992 Photography and photographic processing
- 8993 Welfare and charitable services
- 8994 Public museums, libraries and galleries
- 8995 Political parties and associations
- 8996 Service of Commonwealth and foreign governments
- 8997 Trade associations and unions
- 8999 Other services

Group 29 - Public administration and defence

- 9010 National government service
- 9020 Local government service

Other codes

- 9500 Holding company
- 9600 Residents' property management company
- 9999 Dormant company

OYEZ The Solicitors' Law Stationery Society Ltd., Oyez House, 7 Spa Road, London SE16 3QQ

(363a — Notes for guidance)

OYEZ

CHA1

This form should be completed in black.

363a
Annual Return

Company number	CN 12345678
Company name	999 ACACIA AVENUE LIMITED

Date of this return *(See note 1)*
The information in this return is made up to

Day Month Year
DA 20 | 10 | 92
Show date

Date of next return *(See note 2)*
If you wish to make your next return to a date earlier than the anniversary of this return please show the date here. Companies House will then send a form at the appropriate time.

DB

Registered Office *(See note 3)*
Show here the address at the date of this return.

RO FLAT 6, 999 ACACIA AVENUE

Any change of registered office must be notified on form 287.

Post town DALE

County/Region BARSETSHIRE

Postcode BS20 5QR

Principal business activities
(See note 4)
Show trade classification code number(s) for principal activity or activities.

PA 9600

If the code number cannot be determined, give a brief description of principal activity.

Register of members
(See note 5)
If the register of members is not kept at the registered office, state here where it is kept.

RM

Post town

County/Region

Postcode

Register of Debenture holders
(See note 6)
If there is a register of debenture holders and it is not kept at the registered office, state here where it is kept.

RD

Post town

County/Region

Postcode

Company type *(See note 7)*

Public limited company	T1	
Private company limited by shares	T2	✓
Private company limited by guarantee without share capital	T3	
Private company limited by shares exempt under section 30	T4	
Private company limited by guarantee exempt under section 30	T5	
Private unlimited company with share capital	T6	
Private unlimited company without share capital	T7	

Please mark the appropriate box.

Company Secretary *(See note 8)*
(Please photocopy this area to provide details of joint secretaries).

Details of a new company secretary must be notified on form 288.

Name

*Style/Title CS MISS

Forenames FELICITY ANN

Surname FOWLER

*Honours etc

Previous forenames

Previous surname

Address AD FLAT 6, 999 ACACIA AVENUE

Usual residential address must be given. In the case of a corporation, give the registered or principal office address.

Post town DALE

County/Region BARSETSHIRE

Postcode BS20 5QR Country ENGLAND

* Voluntary details

Directors *(See note 8)*
Please list directors in alphabetical order.

Details of new directors **must** be notified on form 288.

Name	*Style/Title	**CD** MR.
	Forenames	ANTHONY JOHN
	Surname	ABSOLUTE
	*Honours etc	
	Previous forenames	
	Previous surname	
Address		**AD** FLAT 1, 999 ACACIA AVENUE
Usual residential address must be given. In the case of a corporation, give the registered or principal office address.	Post town	DALE
	County/Region	BARSETSHIRE
	Postcode	BS20 5QR
	Country	ENGLAND
	Date of birth	**DO** 03 08 59
	Nationality	**NA** U.K.
	Business occupation	**OC** INSURANCE BROKER
	Other directorships	**OD** NONE

Name	*Style/Title	**CD** MISS
	Forenames	BELINDA
	Surname	BOTT
	*Honours etc	
	Previous forenames	
	Previous surname	
Address		**AD** FLAT 2, 999 ACACIA AVENUE
Usual residential address must be given. In the case of a corporation, give the registered or principal office address.	Post town	DALE
	County/Region	BARSETSHIRE
	Postcode	BS20 5QR
	Country	ENGLAND
	Date of birth	**DO** 22 04 58
	Nationality	**NA** U.K.
	Business occupation	**OC** LIBRARIAN
	Other directorships	**OD** NONE

* Voluntary details

Directors (continued)

Name	*Style/Title	CD MR.
	Forenames	CHARLES IAN
	Surname	CRAWFORD
	*Honours etc	
	Previous forenames	
	Previous surname	
Address		AD FLAT 3, 999 ACACIA AVENUE
Usual residential address must be given. In the case of a corporation, give the registered or principal office address.		
	Post town	DALE
	County/Region	BARSETSHIRE
	Postcode	BS20 5QR
	Country	ENGLAND
	Date of birth	DO 02110558
	Nationality	NA U.K.
	Business occupation	OC ADVERTISING EXECUTIVE
	Other directorships	OD PUFF AND PUFF LIMITED

Name	*Style/Title	CD MS.
	Forenames	DAHLIA LOUISA
	Surname	DYMOND
	*Honours etc	
	Previous forenames	
	Previous surname	
Address		AD FLAT 4, 999 ACACIA AVENUE
Usual residential address must be given. In the case of a corporation, give the registered or principal office address.		
	Post town	DALE
	County/Region	BARSETSHIRE
	Postcode	BS20 5QR.
	Country	ENGLAND
	Date of birth	DO 150254
	Nationality	NA U.K.
	Business occupation	OC TELEVISION PRODUCER
	Other directorships	OD NONE

* Voluntary details

Directors (continued)

Name	*Style/Title	CD MR.
	Forenames	EDWARD
	Surname	EXTRACT
	*Honours etc	
	Previous forenames	
	Previous surname	
Address		AD FLAT 5, 999 ACACIA AVENUE
Usual residential address must be given. In the case of a corporation, give the registered or principal office address.		
	Post town	DALE
	County/Region	BARSETSHIRE
	Postcode	BS20 5QR Country ENGLAND
	Date of birth	DO 28 01 9 54 Nationality NA U.K.
	Business occupation	OC CATERING MANAGER
	Other directorships	OD NONE

Name	*Style/Title	CD MISS
	Forenames	FELICITY ANN
	Surname	FOWLER
	*Honours etc	
	Previous forenames	
	Previous surname	
Address		AD FLAT 6, 999 ACACIA AVENUE
Usual residential address must be given. In the case of a corporation, give the registered or principal office address.		
	Post town	DALE
	County/Region	BARSETSHIRE
	Postcode	BS20 5QR Country ENGLAND
	Date of birth	DO 08 01 62 Nationality NA U.K.
	Business occupation	OC SOLICITOR
	Other directorships	OD NONE

* Voluntary details

Issued share capital *(See note 9)*
Enter details of all the shares in issue at the date of this return.

Class	Number	Aggregate Nominal Value
£1 ORDINARY	12	£12
Totals	12	£12

List of past and present members
(Use attached schedule where appropriate)

A full list is required if one was not included with either of the last two returns.
(See note 10)

Please mark the appropriate box(es)

There were no changes in the period ✓

	on paper	not on paper
A list of changes is enclosed		
A full list of members is enclosed		

Elective resolutions *(See note 11)*
(Private companies only)

If an election is in force at the date of this return to dispense with annual general meetings, *mark this box* ☐

If an election is in force at the date of this return to dispense with laying accounts in general meetings, *mark this box* ☐

Certificate
I certify that the information given in this return is true to the best of my knowledge and belief.

Signed Felicity Fowler Secretary/Director*
(delete as appropriate)*

Date 20TH OCTOBER 1992

This return includes 1 *(enter number)* continuation sheets.

To whom should Companies House direct any enquiries about the information shown in this return?

FELICITY FOWLER
Address as above

Postcode
Telephone (0999) 332861 Extension

When you have signed the return send it with the fee to the Registrar of Companies at

Companies House, Crown Way, Cardiff CF4 3UZ
for companies registered in England and Wales
or
Companies House, 100-102 George Street, Edinburgh EH2 3DJ
for companies registered in Scotland.

OYEZ The Solicitors' Law Stationery Society Ltd., Oyez House, 7 Spa Road, London SE16 3QQ
1992 Edition
11.92 F23531
5010448

Companies 363a (Schedule and Notes)

NOTES FOR COMPLETION OF ANNUAL RETURN FORM 363a (to be retained)

Introduction

Every company MUST make an Annual Return to the Registrar of Companies.

The completed form must reach Companies House within 28 days from "the date of the return". Failure to comply is an offence.

Annual Returns are no longer tied to the date of the Annual General Meeting.

1. Date of this return

The date of the Annual Return must be within twelve months of:

- the date of the previous return, or
- in the case of a new company, the date of incorporation.

2. Date of next return

You may give, as the date of your next return, a date which is less than 12 months from the date of this return by entering the new date in the box shown. Companies House will then send your next return shortly before the date you give in this box. If no date is entered Companies House will send you the next annual return form shortly before the anniversary of this return.

3. Registered office

The registered office address you enter must be that currently registered at Companies House.

Any change in the registered office must be given on form 287 and it will only become effective when Companies House register it.

4. Principal business activities

Show the code or codes for the company's principal business activity or activities.

A list of codes based on the VAT trade classification is included with these notes. Use of these codes does not imply that the company is registered for VAT.

If you cannot determine the company's trade classification enter a brief description of the company's principal business activity or activities.

5. Register of members

You need only complete this section if you do not keep the register at the registered office.

6. Register of debenture holders

You need only complete this section if:

- the company has a register of debentures and
- you do not keep it (or a duplicate) at the registered office.

7. Company type

Please tick the appropriate box.

A company's type is determined by its Memorandum of Association.

Private companies limited by guarantee with a share capital should be shown under – "Private Company Limited by Shares".

Some private limited companies need not include the word "Limited" in their names (section 30 of the Companies Act 1985). Further details can be found in notes for guidance pamphlet, NG6, available from Companies House.

8. Directors and secretaries

Show for an individual the full forenames NOT THE INITIALS and surname together with any pervious forenames or surname. If the director or secretary is a corporation or Scottish firm – show the corporate or firm name on the surname line.

Give previous forenames or surname except that:

- for a married woman, the name by which she was known before marriage need not be given,
- names not used since the age of 18 or for at least 20 years need not be given.

In the case of a peer, or an individual usually known by a British title, you may state the title instead of or in addition to the forenames and surname and you need not give the name by which that person was known before he or she adopted the title or succeeded to it.

Address

Give the usual residential address. In the case of a corporation or Scottish firm give the registered or principal office.

Directors known by another description

A director includes any person who occupies that position even if called by a different name, for example, governor, member of council. It also includes a shadow director.

Directors details

Show for each individual director their date of birth (a new requirement), business occupation and nationality.

Other directorships

Give the name of every company of which the person concerned is a director or has been a director at any time in the past 5 years. You may exclude a company which, either is or at all times during the past 5 years when the person was a director was:

- dormant,
- a parent company which wholly owned the company making the return,
- a wholly owned subsidiary of the company making the return,
- another wholly owned subsidiary of the same parent company.

If there is insufficient space on the form for other directorships you may attach a list. This should include the company's name and number.

9. Issued share capital

This part does not apply to a company without share capital.

For each class of shares state:

- the nature of the class,
- the total number and aggregate nominal value of issued shares of that class as at the date of the return.

10. List of past and present members

Give names and addresses of all persons who hold shares or stock in the company at the date of this return and of all persons who have ceased to be members of the company since the date of the last return.

Show

- the number of shares or amount of stock held by present members together with their addresses,
- the number of shares of each class transferred since the date of the last return (or, if this is the first return, since the date of incorporation of the company) by current members or by persons who have ceased to be members. Also show the date of registration of these transfers.

If you do not show the list of members in alphabetical order please attach an index which will help to locate any member shown on the list.

If you have given full details on either of the last two returns you need only include details of persons, who since the date of the last return:

- have become members,
- have ceased to be members,
- are existing members whose holdings of stock or shares have changed.

Please mark "there were no changes in the period" if full details have been given on either of the last two returns and there have been no changes since.

Where the company has converted any of its shares into stock give the corresponding information in relation to that stock, stating the amount of stock instead of the number of nominal value of shares.

11. Elective resolutions

This part does not apply to a public company.

A private company may elect (by elective resolution):

- to dispense with the holding of annual general meetings,
- not to lay the accounts and reports before the company in general meeting.

You must send a copy of the resolution to the Registrar of Companies within 15 days of the passing of it.

The accounts of a company have to be delivered to Companies House even if the company has resolved that they need not be laid before it in general meeting. The accounts must normally be delivered to Companies House within 10 months after the end of the period to which they relate.

Completion of form

Please ensure the form is complete and is signed by a director or secretary. Do not forget to enclose the fee

[P.T.O.

Trade classification

This classification is based on the VAT trade classification but there are some additional codes (numbered from 9500).

PRIMARY INDUSTRIES

Group 01 - Agriculture, forestry and fishing

Group 02 - Mining and quarrying

MANUFACTURING INDUSTRIES

Group 03 - Food, drink and tobacco

Group 04 - Coal and petroleum products

Group 05 - Chemicals and allied industries

Group 06 - Metal manufacture

Group 07 - Mechanical engineering

Group 08 - Instrument engineering

Group 09 - Electrical engineering

Group 10 - Shipbuilding, boatbuilding and marine engineering

Group 11 - Vehicles

Group 12 - Metal goods not elsewhere specified

Group 13 - Textiles

Group 14 - Leather, leather goods and fur

MANUFACTURING INDUSTRIES (Cont)

Group 15 - Clothing and footwear

Group 16 - Bricks, pottery, glass, cement etc

Group 17 - Timber, furniture etc

Group 18 - Paper, printing and publishing

Group 19 - Other manufacturing industries

CONSTRUCTION

Group 20 - Construction

UTILITIES

Group 21 - Gas, electricity and water

TRANSPORT AND COMMUNICATION

Group 22 - Transport and communication

DISTRIBUTIVE TRADES

Group 23 - Wholesale distribution

Group 24 - Retail distribution

Group 25 - Dealers

SERVICES

Group 26 - Insurance, banking, finance and business services

Group 27 - Professional and scientific services

Group 29 - Public administration and defence

Other codes

OYEZ

CHA1

363a
Annual Return

This form should be completed in black.

Company number	CN 12345678
Company name	999 ACACIA AVENUE LIMITED

Date of this return *(See note 1)*
The information in this return is made up to

Day	Month	Year
DA 20	10	93

Show date

Date of next return *(See note 2)*
If you wish to make your next return to a date earlier than the anniversary of this return please show the date here. Companies House will then send a form at the appropriate time.

DB

Registered Office *(See note 3)*
Show here the address at the date of this return.

Any change of registered office must be notified on form 287.

RO FLAT 6, 999 ACACIA AVENUE

Post town DALE

County/Region BARSETSHIRE

Postcode BS20 5QR

Principal business activities *(See note 4)*
Show trade classification code number(s) for principal activity or activities.

PA 9600

If the code number cannot be determined, give a brief description of principal activity.

Register of members
(See note 5)
If the register of members is not kept at the registered office, state here where it is kept.

RM

Post town

County/Region

Postcode

Register of Debenture holders
(See note 6)
If there is a register of debenture holders and it is not kept at the registered office, state here where it is kept.

RD

Post town

County/Region

Postcode

Company type *(See note 7)*

Public limited company	T1	
Private company limited by shares	T2	✓
Private company limited by guarantee without share capital	T3	
Private company limited by shares exempt under section 30	T4	
Private company limited by guarantee exempt under section 30	T5	
Private unlimited company with share capital	T6	
Private unlimited company without share capital	T7	

Please mark the appropriate box.

Company Secretary *(See note 8)*
(Please photocopy this area to provide details of joint secretaries).

Details of a new company secretary must be notified on form 288.

Name

*Style/Title: CS MRS

Forenames: FELICITY ANN

Surname: PROCTOR

*Honours etc

Previous forenames

Previous surname: FOWLER

Address

Usual residential address must be given. In the case of a corporation, give the registered or principal office address.

AD FLAT 6, 999 ACACIA AVENUE

Post town: DALE

County/Region: BARSETSHIRE

Postcode: BS20 5QR Country: ENGLAND

* Voluntary details

Directors *(See note 8)*
Please list directors in alphabetical order.

Details of new directors **must** be notified on form 288.

Name	*Style/Title	CD MR.
	Forenames	ANTHONY JOHN
	Surname	ABSOLUTE
	*Honours etc	
	Previous forenames	
	Previous surname	
Address		AD FLAT 1, 999 ACACIA AVENUE
Usual residential address must be given. In the case of a corporation, give the registered or principal office address.		
	Post town	DALE
	County/Region	BARSETSHIRE
	Postcode	BS20 5QR Country ENGLAND
	Date of birth	DO 03 08 59 Nationality NA U.K.
	Business occupation	OC INSURANCE BROKER
	Other directorships	OD NONE

Name	*Style/Title	CD MISS
	Forenames	BELINDA
	Surname	BOTT
	*Honours etc	
	Previous forenames	
	Previous surname	
Address		AD FLAT 2, 999 ACACIA AVENUE
Usual residential address must be given. In the case of a corporation, give the registered or principal office address.		
	Post town	DALE
	County/Region	BARSETSHIRE
	Postcode	BS20 5QR Country ENGLAND
	Date of birth	DO 22 04 58 Nationality NA U.K.
	Business occupation	OC UNEMPLOYED
	Other directorships	OD NONE

* Voluntary details

Directors (continued)

Name
*Style/Title — CD MS.
Forenames — DAHLIA LOUISA
Surname — DYMOND
*Honours etc —
Previous forenames —
Previous surname —

Address — AD FLAT 4, 999 ACACIA AVENUE

Usual residential address must be given. In the case of a corporation, give the registered or principal office address.

Post town — DALE
County/Region — BARSETSHIRE
Postcode — BS20 5QR Country — ENGLAND

Date of birth — DO 15 02 54 Nationality — NA U.K.
Business occupation — OC TELEVISION PRODUCER
Other directorships — OD NONE

Name
*Style/Title — CD MR.
Forenames — EDWARD
Surname — EXTRACT
*Honours etc —
Previous forenames —
Previous surname —

Address — AD FLAT 5, 999 ACACIA AVENUE

Usual residential address must be given. In the case of a corporation, give the registered or principal office address.

Post town — DALE
County/Region — BARSETSHIRE
Postcode — BS20 5QR Country — ENGLAND

Date of birth — DO 28 09 54 Nationality — NA U.K.
Business occupation — OC CATERING MANAGER
Other directorships — OD FREELODER & JUNKET LTD.

* Voluntary details

Directors (continued)

Name	*Style/Title	CD MRS.
	Forenames	FELICITY ANN
	Surname	PROCTOR
	*Honours etc	
	Previous forenames	
	Previous surname	FOWLER
Address		AD FLAT 6, 999 ACACIA AVENUE
Usual residential address must be given. In the case of a corporation, give the registered or principal office address.		
	Post town	DALE
	County/Region	BARSETSHIRE
	Postcode	BS20 5QR Country ENGLAND
	Date of birth	DO 0 8 0 1 6 2 Nationality NA U.K.
	Business occupation	OC SOLICITOR
	Other directorships	OD NONE

Name	*Style/Title	CD MR.
	Forenames	SARDANAPALUS
	Surname	SNOOKS
	*Honours etc	
	Previous forenames	
	Previous surname	
Address		AD FLAT 3, 999 ACACIA AVENUE
Usual residential address must be given. In the case of a corporation, give the registered or principal office address.		
	Post town	DALE
	County/Region	BARSETSHIRE
	Postcode	BS20 5QR Country ENGLAND
	Date of birth	DO 0 6 0 5 6 1 Nationality NA U.K.
	Business occupation	OC UNIVERSITY LECTURER
	Other directorships	OD

* Voluntary details

Issued share capital *(See note 9)*
Enter details of all the shares in issue at the date of this return.

Class	Number	Aggregate Nominal Value
ORDINARY	18	£18
Totals	18	£18

List of past and present members
(Use attached schedule where appropriate)

A full list is required if one was not included with either of the last two returns.
(See note 10)

Please mark the appropriate box(es)

There were no changes in the period [ ]

	on paper	not on paper
A list of changes is enclosed	[ ]	[ ]
A full list of members is enclosed	[✓]	[ ]

Elective resolutions *(See note 11)*
(Private companies only)

If an election is in force at the date of this return to dispense with annual general meetings, *mark this box* [ ]

If an election is in force at the date of this return to dispense with laying accounts in general meetings, *mark this box* [ ]

Certificate
I certify that the information given in this return is true to the best of my knowledge and belief.

Signed F. Proctor (Mrs.) Secretary/Director*
(*delete as appropriate)

Date 27th OCTOBER 1993

This return includes 1 continuation sheets.
(enter number)

To whom should Companies House direct any enquiries about the information shown in this return?

MRS. FELICITY PROCTOR
FLAT 6, 999 ACACIA AVENUE
DALE
BARSETSHIRE Postcode BS20 5QR
Telephone (0999) 332861 Extension

When you have signed the return send it with the fee to the Registrar of Companies at

Companies House, Crown Way, Cardiff CF4 3UZ
for companies registered in England and Wales
or
Companies House, 100-102 George Street, Edinburgh EH2 3DJ
for companies registered in Scotland.

OYEZ The Solicitors' Law Stationery Society Ltd., Oyez House, 7 Spa Road, London SE16 3QQ

1992 Edition
11.92 F23531
5010448

Companies 363a (Schedule and Notes)

(Please detach from notes for completion)

LIST OF PAST AND PRESENT MEMBERS **SCHEDULE TO FORM 363**

Company Number: 12345678

Company Name: 999 ACACIA AVENUE LIMITED

Name and Address	Number of shares or amount of stock held by existing members at date of this return	Account of Shares: Particulars of shares transferred since the date of the last return, or, in the case of the first return, since the incorporation of the company, by (a) persons who are still members, and (b) persons who have ceased to be members — Number	Date of Registration of Transfer	Remarks
ANTHONY JOHN ABSOLUTE, FLAT 1, 999 ACACIA AVENUE, DALE, BARSETSHIRE, BS20 5QR	3			1 SHARE ALLOTTED 5·4·93
BELINDA BUTT, FLAT 2, 999 ACACIA AVENUE, ETC	3			1 SHARE ALLOTTED 5·4·93
CHARLES IAN CRAWFORD, FLAT 3, 999 ACACIA AVENUE, ETC.	/	3	2·9·93	TRANSFERRED TO S. SNOOKS
DAHLIA LOUISA DYMOND, FLAT 4, "	3			1 SHARE ALLOTTED 5·4·93
EDWARD EXTRACT, FLAT 5, "	3			1 SHARE ALLOTTED 5·4·93
FELICITY ANN PROCTOR, FLAT 6, "	3			1 SHARE ALLOTTED 5·4·93
SARDANAPALUS SNOOKS, FLAT 3, "	3			TRANSFERRED FROM C. CRAWFORD

Continued overleaf

NOTES FOR COMPLETION OF ANNUAL RETURN FORM 363a (to be retained)

Introduction

Every company MUST make an Annual Return to the Registrar of Companies.

The completed form must reach Companies House within 28 days from "the date of the return". Failure to comply is an offence.

Annual Returns are no longer tied to the date of the Annual General Meeting.

1. Date of this return

The date of the Annual Return must be within twelve months of:

- the date of the previous return, or
- in the case of a new company, the date of incorporation.

2. Date of next return

You may give, as the date of your next return, a date which is less than 12 months from the date of this return by entering the new date in the box shown. Companies House will then send your next return shortly before the date you give in this box. If no date is entered Companies House will send you the next annual return form shortly before the anniversary of this return.

3. Registered office

The registered office address you enter must be that currently registered at Companies House.

Any change in the registered office must be given on form 287 and it will only become effective when Companies House register it.

4. Principal business activities

Show the code or codes for the company's principal business activity or activities.

A list of codes based on the VAT trade classification is included with these notes. Use of these codes does not imply that the company is registered for VAT.

If you cannot determine the company's trade classification enter a brief description of the company's principal business activity or activities.

5. Register of members

You need only complete this section if you do not keep the register at the registered office.

6. Register of debenture holders

You need only complete this section if:

- the company has a register of debentures and
- you do not keep it (or a duplicate) at the registered office.

7. Company type

Please tick the appropriate box.

A company's type is determined by its Memorandum of Association.

Private companies limited by guarantee with a share capital should be shown under – "Private Company Limited by Shares".

Some private limited companies need not include the word "Limited" in their names (section 30 of the Companies Act 1985). Further details can be found in notes for guidance pamphlet, NG6, available from Companies House.

8. Directors and secretaries

Show for an individual the full forenames NOT THE INITIALS and surname together with any pervious forenames or surname. If the director or secretary is a corporation or Scottish firm - show the corporate or firm name on the surname line.

Give previous forenames or surname except that:

- for a married women, the name by which she was known before marriage need not be given.
- names not used since the age of 18 or for at least 20 years need not be given.

In the case of a peer, or an individual usually known by a British title, you may state the title instead of or in addition to the forenames and surname and you need not give the name by which that person was known before he or she adopted the title or succeeded to it.

Address

Give the usual residential address. In the case of a corporation or Scottish firm give the registered or principal office.

Directors known by another description

A director includes any person who occupies that position even if called by a different name, for example, governor, member of council. It also includes a shadow director.

Directors details

Show for each individual director their date of birth (a new requirement), business occupation and nationality.

Other directorships

Give the name of every company of which the person concerned is a director or has been a director at any time in the past 5 years. You may exclude a company which, either is or at all times during the past 5 years when the person was a director was:

- dormant,
- a parent company which wholly owned the company making the return,
- a wholly owned subsidiary of the company making the return,
- another wholly owned subsidiary of the same parent company.

If there is insufficient space on the form for other directorships you may attach a list. This should include the company's name and number.

9. Issued share capital

This part does not apply to a company without share capital.

For each class of shares state:

- the nature of the class,
- the total number and aggregate nominal value of issued shares of that class as at the date of the return.

10. List of past and present members

Give names and addresses of all persons who hold shares or stock in the company at the date of this return and of all persons who have ceased to be members of the company since the date of the last return.

Show

- the number of shares or amount of stock held by present members together with their addresses,
- the number of shares of each class transferred since the date of the last return (or, if this is the first return, since the date of incorporation of the company) by current members or by persons who have ceased to be members. Also show the date of registration of these transfers.

If you do not show the list of members in alphabetical order please attach an index which will help to locate any member shown on the list.

If you have given full details on either of the last two returns you need only include details of persons, who since the date of the last return:

- have become members,
- have ceased to be members,
- are existing members whose holdings of stock or shares have changed.

Please mark "there were no changes in the period" if full details have been given on either of the last two returns and there have been no changes since.

Where the company has converted any of its shares into stock give the corresponding information in relation to that stock, stating the amount of stock instead of the number of nominal value of shares.

11. Elective resolutions

This part does not apply to a public company.

A private company may elect (by elective resolution):

- to dispense with the holding of annual general meetings,
- not to lay the accounts and reports before the company in general meeting.

You must send a copy of the resolution to the Registrar of Companies within 15 days of the passing of it.

The accounts of a company have to be delivered to Companies House even if the company has resolved that they need not be laid before it in general meeting. The accounts must normally be delivered to Companies House within 10 months after the end of the period to which they relate.

Completion of form

Please ensure the form is complete and is signed by a director or secretary. Do not forget to enclose the fee

[P.T.O.

Trade classification

This classification is based on the VAT trade classification but there are some additional codes (numbered from 9500).

Trade Code

PRIMARY INDUSTRIES

Group 01 - Agriculture, forestry and fishing

0011 Livestock farming including pigs and poultry
0012 Arable farming
0013 Dairying
0014 Mixed farming and more than 50% in any of the above
0015 Breeding of non-food producing animals including horses
0016 Agricultural contracting
0017 Market gardening and fruit farming
0018 Flower and seed growing
0020 Forestry
0030 Fishing

Group 02 - Mining and quarrying

1010 Coal mining other than opencast (heading 5030)
1020 Stone and slate quarrying and mining
1030 Chalk, clay, sand and gravel extraction
1040 Petroleum and natural gas
1090 Other mining and quarrying

MANUFACTURING INDUSTRIES

Group 03 - Food, drink and tobacco

2110 Grain milling
2120 Bread and flour confectionery including retailing wholly or mainly of own production (see also code 8206)
2130 Biscuits
2140 Bacon-curing meat and fish products
2151 Milk and milk products other than ice cream
2152 Ice cream
2160 Sugar
2170 Cocoa, chocolate and sugar confectionery
2180 [illegible]
2190 [illegible]
2210 [illegible]
2290 [illegible]
2310 [illegible]
2320 [illegible]
2391 [illegible]
2392 [illegible]
2400 [illegible]

Group 04 - [illegible]

2610 [illegible]
2620 [illegible]
2630 [illegible]

Group 05 - [illegible]

2710 [illegible]
2720 [illegible]
2730 [illegible]
2740 [illegible]
2750 [illegible]
2760 [illegible]
2770 [illegible]
2780 [illegible]
2790 [illegible]

Group 06 - [illegible]

3110 [illegible]
3120 [illegible]
3130 [illegible]
3210 [illegible]
3220 [illegible]
3230 [illegible]

Group 07 - [illegible]

3310 [illegible]
3320 [illegible]
3330 [illegible]
3340 [illegible]
3350 [illegible]
3360 [illegible]
3370 [illegible]
3380 [illegible]
3390 [illegible]
3410 [illegible]
3420 [illegible]
3480 [illegible]

Group 08 - [illegible]

3510 [illegible]
3520 [illegible]
3530 [illegible]
3540 [illegible]

Group 09 - [illegible]

3610 [illegible]
3620 [illegible]
3630 [illegible]
3640 [illegible]
3650 [illegible]
3651 [illegible]
3659 [illegible]
3660 [illegible]
3670 [illegible]
3680 [illegible]
3690 [illegible]

Group 10 - [illegible]

3700 [illegible]

Group 11 - [illegible]

3800 [illegible]
3811 [illegible]
3812 [illegible]
3820 [illegible]
3830 [illegible]
3840 [illegible]
3850 [illegible]

Group 12 - [illegible]

3900 [illegible]
3910 [illegible]
3920 [illegible]
3930 [illegible]
3940 [illegible]
3950 [illegible]
3961 [illegible]
3962 [illegible]
3963 [illegible]
3990 [illegible]

Group 13 - [illegible]

4110 [illegible]
4120 [illegible]
4130 [illegible]
4140 [illegible]
4150 [illegible]
4160 [illegible]
4170 [illegible]
4180 [illegible]
4190 [illegible]
4210 [illegible]
4220 [illegible]
4230 [illegible]
4290 [illegible]

Group 14 - [illegible]

4310 [illegible]
4321 [illegible]
4322 [illegible]
4329 [illegible]
4331 [illegible]
4339 [illegible]

Trade Code

PRIMARY INDUSTRIES

MANUFACTURING INDUSTRIES (Cont)

Group 15 - [illegible]

4410 [illegible]
4420 [illegible]
4430 [illegible]
4440 [illegible]
4450 [illegible]
4460 [illegible]
4490 [illegible]
4500 [illegible]

Group 16 - [illegible]

4610 [illegible]
4620 [illegible]
4630 [illegible]
4640 [illegible]
4680 [illegible]

Group 17 - [illegible]

4710 [illegible]
4721 [illegible]
4722 [illegible]
4729 [illegible]
4730 [illegible]
4740 [illegible]
4750 [illegible]
4791 [illegible]
4799 [illegible]

Group 18 - [illegible]

4810 [illegible]
4820 [illegible]
4830 [illegible]
4840 [illegible]
4850 [illegible]
4860 [illegible]
4891 [illegible]
4892 [illegible]
4893 [illegible]
4894 [illegible]
4899 [illegible]

Group 19 - [illegible]

4910 [illegible]
4920 [illegible]
4930 [illegible]
4940 [illegible]
4950 [illegible]
4960 [illegible]
4961 [illegible]
4962 [illegible]
4999 [illegible]

CONSTRUCTION

Group 20 - Construction

5001 [illegible]
5002 [illegible]
5003 [illegible]
5004 [illegible]
5005 [illegible]
5006 [illegible]
5007 [illegible]
5008 [illegible]
5009 [illegible]
5011 [illegible]
5012 [illegible]
5013 [illegible]
5014 [illegible]
5015 [illegible]
5016 [illegible]
5017 [illegible]
5018 [illegible]
5019 [illegible]
5021 [illegible]
5022 [illegible]
5023 [illegible]
5029 [illegible]
5030 [illegible]

UTILITIES

Group 21 - Gas, electricity and water

6010 Gas
6020 Electricity
6030 Water

TRANSPORT AND COMMUNICATION

Group 22 - [illegible]

7010 [illegible]
7021 [illegible]
7022 [illegible]
7030 [illegible]
7040 [illegible]
7050 [illegible]
7060 [illegible]
7070 [illegible]
7080 [illegible]
7081 [illegible]
7092 [illegible]
7093 [illegible]
7094 [illegible]
7099 [illegible]

DISTRIBUTIVE TRADES

Group 23 - [illegible]

N.B. [illegible]

[illegible]

8101 [illegible]
8102 [illegible]
8109 [illegible]
8110 [illegible]
8121 [illegible]
8122 [illegible]
8123 [illegible]
8124 [illegible]
8125 [illegible]
8126 [illegible]
8127 [illegible]
8128 [illegible]
8129 [illegible]
8131 [illegible]
8132 [illegible]
8133 [illegible]
8134 [illegible]
8135 [illegible]
8136 [illegible]
8137 [illegible]
8138 [illegible]
8139 [illegible]
8149 [illegible]

Trade Code

PRIMARY INDUSTRIES

Group 24 - [illegible]

N.B. [illegible]

8201 [illegible]
8202 [illegible]
8204 [illegible]
8205 [illegible]
8206 [illegible]
8207 [illegible]
8211 [illegible]
8212 [illegible]
8213 [illegible]
8214 [illegible]
8215 [illegible]
8216 [illegible]
8217 [illegible]
8218 [illegible]
8219 [illegible]
8221 [illegible]
8222 [illegible]
8223 [illegible]
8224 [illegible]
8225 [illegible]
8226 [illegible]
8227 [illegible]
8228 [illegible]
8229 [illegible]
8231 [illegible]
8232 [illegible]
8233 [illegible]
8234 [illegible]
8239 [illegible]

Group 25 - [illegible]

N.B. [illegible]

8311 [illegible]
8312 [illegible]
8313 [illegible]
8321 [illegible]
8322 [illegible]
8323 [illegible]
8324 [illegible]

SERVICES

Group 26 - [illegible]

8600 [illegible]
8610 [illegible]
8621 [illegible]
8622 [illegible]
8629 [illegible]
8630 [illegible]
8640 [illegible]
8651 [illegible]
8652 [illegible]
8653 [illegible]
8654 [illegible]
8655 [illegible]
8656 [illegible]
8657 [illegible]
8659 [illegible]

Group 27 - [illegible]

[illegible]

Group 28 - [illegible]

9010 [illegible]
9090 [illegible]

[illegible]

9500 [illegible]
9600 [illegible]
9999 [illegible]

OYEZ The Solicitors' Law Stationery Society Ltd., Oyez House, 7 Spa Road, London SE16 3QQ ©1992 F23532

(363a — Notes for guidance)

APPENDIX A

The Companies (Tables A-F) Regulations 1985 (S.I. 1985 No. 805)

TABLE A

REGULATIONS FOR MANAGEMENT OF A COMPANY LIMITED BY SHARES

INTERPRETATION

1. In these regulations—

"the Act" means the Companies Act 1985 including any statutory modification or re-enactment thereof for the time being in force.

"the articles" means the articles of the company.

"clear days" in relation to the period of a notice means that period excluding the day when the notice is given or deemed to be given and the day for which it is given or on which it is to take effect.

"executed" means any mode of execution.

"office" means the registered office of the company.

"the holder" in relation to shares means the member whose name is entered in the register of members as the holder of the shares.

"the seal" means the common seal of the company.

"secretary" means the secretary of the company or any other person appointed to perform the duties of the secretary of the company, including a joint, assistant or deputy secretary.

"the United Kingdom" means the United Kingdom of Great Britain and Northern Ireland.

Unless the context otherwise requires, words or expressions contained in these regulations bear the same meaning as in the Act but excluding any statutory modification thereof not in force when these regulations become binding on the company.

SHARE CAPITAL

2. Subject to the provisions of the Act and without prejudice to any rights attached to any existing shares, any share may be issued with such rights or restrictions as the company may by ordinary resolution determine.

3. Subject to the provisions of the Act, shares may be issued which are to be redeemed or are to be liable to be redeemed at the option of the company or the holder on such terms and in such manner as may be provided by the articles.

4. The company may exercise the powers of paying commissions conferred by the Act. Subject to the [provisions] of the Act, any such commission may be satisfied by the payment of cash or by the allotment of fully or partly paid shares partly in one way and partly in the other.

5. Except as required by law, no person shall be recognised by the company as holding any share upon any trust and (except as otherwise provided by the articles or by law) the company shall not be bound by or recognise any interests in any share except an absolute right to the entirety thereof in the holder.

AMENDMENTS

In para. 4 the word "provisions" is substituted by S.I. 1985 No. 1052.

SHARE CERTIFICATES

6. Every member, upon becoming the holder of any shares, shall be entitled without payment to one certificate for all the shares of each class held by him (and, upon transferring a part of his holding of shares of any class, to a certificate for the balance of such holding) or several certificates each for one or more of his shares upon payment for every certificate after the first of such reasonable sum as the directors may determine. Every certificate shall be sealed with the seal and shall specify the number, class and distinguishing numbers (if any) of the shares to which it relates and the amount or respective amounts paid up thereupon. The company shall not be bound to issue more than one certificate for shares held jointly by several persons and delivery of a certificate to one joint holder shall be a sufficient delivery to all of them.

7. If a share certificate is defaced, worn-out, lost or destroyed, it may be renewed on such terms (if any) as to evidence and indemnity and payment of the expenses reasonably incurred by the company investigating evidence as the directors may determine but otherwise free of charge, and (in the case of defacement or wearing-out) on delivery up of the old certificate.

LIEN

8. The company shall have the first and paramount lien on any share (not being fully paid share) for all moneys (whether presently payable or not) payable at a fixed time or called in respect of that share. The directors may at any time declare any share to be wholly or in part exempt from the provisions of this regulation. The company's lien on a share shall extend to any amount payable in respect of it.

9. The company may sell in such manner as the directors determine any share on which the company has lien of a sum in respect of which the lien exists presently payable and is not paid within fourteen clear days after notices has been given to the holder of the share or to the person entitled to it in consequence of the death or bankruptcy of the holder, demanding payment and stating that if the notice is not complied with the shares may be sold.

10. To give effect to a sale the directors may authorise some persons to execute an instrument of transfer of the shares sold to, or in accordance with the directions of, the purchaser. The title of the transferee of the shares shall not be affected by any irregularity in or invalidity of the proceedings in reference to the sale.

11. The net proceeds of the sale, after payment of the costs, shall be applied in payment of so much of the sum for which the lien exists as is presently payable, any residue shall (upon surrender to the company for cancellation of the certificate for the shares sold and subject to a like lien for any moneys not presently payable as existed upon the shares before the sale) be paid to the person entitled to the shares at the date of the sale.

CALLS ON SHARES AND FORFEITURE

12. Subject to the terms of allotment, the directors may make calls upon the members in respect of any moneys unpaid on their shares (whether in respect of nominal value or premium) and each member shall (subject to receiving at least 14 clear days' notice specifying when and where payment is to be made) pay the company as required by the notice the amount called on his shares. A call may be required to be paid by instalments. A call may, before receipt by the company of any sum due thereunder, be revoked in whole or part and payment of a call may be postponed in whole or part. A person upon whom a call is made shall remain liable for calls made upon him notwithstanding the subsequent transfer of the shares in respect whereof the call was made.

13. A call shall be deemed to have been made at the time when the resolution of the directors authorising the call was passed.

14. The joint holders of a share shall be jointly and severally liable to pay all calls in respect thereof.

15. If a call remains unpaid after it has become due and payable the person from whom it is due and payable shall pay interest on the amount unpaid from the day it became due and payable until it is paid at the rate fixed by the terms of allotment of the share or in the notice of the call or, if no rate is fixed, at the appropriate rate (as defined by the Act) but the directors may waive payment of the interest wholly or in part.

16. An amount payable in respect of a share on allotment or at any fixed rate, whether in respect of nominal value or premium or as an instalment of a call, shall be deemed to be a call and if it is not paid the provisions of the articles shall apply as if that amount had become due and payable by virtue of a call.

17. Subject to the terms of allotment, the directors may make arrangements on the issue of shares for a difference between the holders in the amounts and times of payment of calls on their shares.

18. If a call remains unpaid after it has become due and payable the directors may give to the person from whom it is due not less than fourteen clear days' notice requiring payment of the amount unpaid together with any interest which may have accrued. The notice shall name the place where payment is to be made and shall state that if the notice is not complied with the shares in respect of which the call was made will be liable to be forfeited.

19. If the notice is not complied with any share in respect of which it was given may, before the payment required by the notice has been made, be forfeited by a resolution of the directors and the forfeiture shall include all dividends or other moneys payable in respect of the forfeited shares and not paid before the forfeiture.

20. Subject to the provisions of the Act, a forfeited share may be sold, re-allotted or otherwise disposed of on such terms and in such manner as the directors determine either to the person who was before the forfeiture the holder or to any other person and at any time before sale, re-allotment or other disposition, the forfeiture may be cancelled on such terms as the directors think fit. Where for the purposes of its disposal a forfeited share is to be transferred to any person the directors may authorise some person to execute an instrument of transfer of the share to that person.

21. A person any of whose shares have been forfeited shall cease to be a member in respect of them and shall surrender to the company for cancellation the certificate for the shares forfeited but shall remain liable to the company for all moneys which at the date of forfeiture were presently payable by him to the company in respect of those shares with interest at the rate at which interest was payable on those moneys before the forfeiture or, if no interest was payable, at the appropriate rate (as defined in the Act) from the date of forfeiture until payment but the directors may waive payment wholly or in part or enforce payment without any allowance for the value of the shares at the time of forfeiture or for any consideration received on their disposal.

22. A statutory declaration by a director or the secretary that a share has been forfeited on a specified date shall be conclusive evidence of the facts stated in it as against all persons claiming to be entitled to the share and the declaration shall (subject to the execution of an instrument of transfer if necessary) constitute a good title to the share and the person to whom the share is disposed of shall not be bound to see to the application of the consideration, if any, nor shall his title to the share be affected by any irregularity of the proceedings in reference to the forfeiture or disposal of the share.

TRANSFER OF SHARES

23. The instrument of transfer of a share may be in the usual form or in any other form which the directors may approve and shall be executed by or on behalf of the transferor and, unless the share is fully paid, by or on behalf of the transferee.

24. The directors may refuse the transfer of a share which is not fully paid to a person of whom they do not approve and they may refuse to register the transfer of a share on which the company has a lien. They may also refuse to register the transfer of a share on which the company has lien. They may also refuse to register a transfer unless—

(*a*) it is lodged at the office or at such other place as the directors may appoint and is accompanied by the certificate for the shares to which it relates and such other evidence as the directors may reasonably require to show the right of the transferor to make the transfer;

(*b*) it is in respect of only one class of shares; and

(*c*) it is favour of not more than four transferees.

25. If the directors refuse to register a transfer of a share, they shall within two months after the date on which the transfer was lodged with the company send to the transferee notice of the refusal.

26. The registration of transfers of shares or of transfers of any class of shares may be suspended at such times and for such periods (not exceeding thirty days in any year) as the directors may determine.

27. No fee shall be charged for the registration of any instrument of transfer or other document relating to or affecting the title to any share.

28. The company shall be entitled to retain any instrument of transfer which is registered, but any instrument of transfer which the directors refuse to register shall be returned to the person lodging it when notice of the refusal is given.

TRANSMISSION OF SHARES

29. If a member dies the survivor or survivors where he was joint holder, and his personal representatives where he was a sole holder or only the survivor of joint holders, shall be the persons recognised by the company as having any title to his interest; but nothing herein contained shall release the estate of a deceased member from any liablity in respect of any share which had been jointly held by him.

30. A person becoming entitled to a share in consequence of the death or bankruptcy of a member may, upon such evidence being produced as the directors may properly require, elect either to become the holder of the share or to have some person nominated by him registered as the transferee. If he elects to become the holder he shall give notice to the company to that effect. If he elects to have another person registered he shall execute an instrument of transfer of the share to that person. All the articles relating to the transfer of shares shall apply to the notice or instrument of transfer as if it were an instrument of transfer executed by the member and the death or bankruptcy of the member had not occurred.

31. A person becoming entitled to a share in consequence of the death or bankruptcy of a member shall have the rights to which he would be entitled if he were the holder of the share, except that he shall not, before being registered as the holder of the share, be entitled in respect of it to attend or vote at any meeting of the company or at any separate meeting of the holders of any class of shares in the company.

ALTERATION OF SHARE CAPITAL

32. The company by ordinary resolution—

(*a*) increase its share capital by new shares of such amount as the resolution prescribes;

(*b*) consolidate and divide all or any of its share capital into shares of larger amount than its existing shares;

(*c*) subject to the provisions of the Act, sub-divide its shares, or any of them, into shares of smaller amount and the resolution may determine that, as between the shares resulting from the sub-division, any of them may have any preference or advantage as compared with the others; and

(*d*) cancel shares which, at the date of the passing of the resolution, have not been taken or agreed to be taken by any person and diminish the amount of its share capital by the amount of shares so cancelled.

33. Whenever as a result of a consolidation of shares any member would become entitled to fractions of a share, the directors may, on behalf of those members, sell the shares representating the fractions for the best price reasonably obtainable to any person (including, subject to the provisions of the Act, the company) and distribute the net proceeds of sale in due proportion among those members, and the directors may authorise some persons to execute an instrument of transfer of the shares to, or in accordance with the directions of, the purchaser. The transferee shall not be bound to see the application of the purchase money nor shall his title to the shares be affected by any irregularity in or invalidity of the proceedings in reference to the sale.

34. Subject to the provisions of the Act, the company may by special resolution reduce in share capital, any capital redemption reserve and any share premium account in any way.

PURCHASE OF OWN SHARES

35. Subject to the provisions of the Act, the company may purchase its own shares (including any redeemable shares) and, if it is a private company, make a payment in respect of the redemption or purchase of its own shares otherwise than out of distributable profits of the company or the proceeds of a fresh issue of shares.

GENERAL MEETINGS

36. All general meeings other than annual general meetings shall be called extraordinary general meetings.

37. The directors may call general meetings and, on the requisition of members pursuant to the provisions of the Act, shall forthwith proceed to convene an extraordinary general meeting for a date not later than eight weeks after receipt of the requisition. If there are not within the United Kingdom sufficient directors to call a general meeting, any director or any member of the company may call a general meeting.

NOTICE OF GENERAL MEETING

38. An annual general meeting and an extraordinary general meeting called for the passing of a special resolution or a resolution appointing a person as a director shall be called by at least 21 clear days' notice. All other extraordinary meetings shall be called by at least

14 clear days' notice but a general meeting may be called by shorter notice if it is so agreed—

(*a*) in the case of annual general meeting, by all the members entitled to attend and vote thereat; and
(*b*) in the case of any other meeting by a majority in number of the members having a right to attend and vote being a majority together holding not less than 95 per cent. in nominal value of the shares giving that right.

The notice shall specify the time and place of the meeting and the general nature of the business to be transacted and, in the case of an annual general meeting, shall specify the meeting as such.

Subject to the provisions of the articles and to any restrictions imposed on any shares, the notice shall be given to all the members, to all persons entitled to a share in consequence of the death or bankruptcy of a member and to the directors and auditors.

39. The accidental omission to give notice of a meeting to, or the non-receipt of notice of a meeting by, any person entitled to receive notice shall not invalidate the proceedings at that meeting.

PROCEEDINGS AT GENERAL MEETINGS

40. No business shall be transacted at any meeting unless a quorum is present. Two persons entitled to vote upon the business to be transacted, each being a member or a proxy for a member or a duly authorised representative of a corporation, shall be a quorum.

41. If such a quorum is not present within half an hour from the time appointed for the meeting, or if during a meeting such a quorum ceases to be present, the meeting shall stand adjourned to the same day in the next week at the same time and place or [to] such time and place as the directors may determine.

42. The chairman, if any, of the board of directors or in his absence some other director nominated by the directors shall preside as chairman of the meeting, but if neither the chairman nor such other director (if any) be present within fifteen minutes after the time appointed for holding the meeting and willing to act, the directorts present shall elect one of their number to be chairman and, if there is only one director present and willing to act, he shall be chairman.

43. If no director is willing to act as chairman, or if no director is present within fifteen minutes after the time appointed for holding the meeting, the members present and entitled to vote shall choose one of their number to be chairman.

44. A director shall, notwithstanding that he is not a member, be entitled to attend and speak at any general meeting and at any separate meeting of the holders of any class of shares in the company.

45. The chairman may, with the consent of a meeting at which a quorum is present (and shall if so directed by the meeting), adjourn the meeting from time to time and from place to place, but no business shall be transacted at the meeting had the adjournment not taken place. When a meeting is adjourned for fourteen days or more, at least seven clear days' notice shall be given specifying the time and place of the adjourned meeting and the general nature of the business to be transacted. Otherwise it shall not be necessary to give any such notice.

46. A resolution put to the vote of a meeting shall be decided on a show of hands unless before, or on the declaration of the result of, the show of hands a poll is duly demanded. Subject to the provisions of the Act, a poll may be demanded—

(*a*) by the chairman, or

(*b*) by at least two members having the right to vote at the meeting; or

(*c*) by a member or members representing not less than one-tenth of the total voting rights of all the members having the right to vote at the meeting or;

(*d*) by a member or members holding shares conferring a right to vote at the meeting being shares on which an aggregate sum has been paid up equal to not less than one-tenth of the total sum paid up on all the shares conferring that right;

and a demand by a person as proxy for a member shall be the same as a demand by the member.

47. Unless a poll is duly demanded a declaration by the chairman that a resolution has been carried or carried unanimously, or by a particular majority, or lost, or not carried by a particular majority and an entry to that effect in the minutes of the meeting shall be conclusive evidence of the fact without proof of the number or proportion of the votes recorded in favour of or against the resolution.

48. The demand for a poll may, before the poll is taken, be withdrawn but only with the consent of the chairman and a demand so withdrawn shall not be taken to have invalidated the result of a show of hands declared before the demand was made.

49. A poll shall be taken as the chairman directs and he may appoint scrutineers (who need not be members) and fix a time and place for declaring the result of the poll. The result of the poll shall be deemed to be the resoltuion of the meeting at which the poll was demanded.

50. In the case of an equality of votes, whether on a show of hands or on a poll, the chairman shall be entitled to a casting vote in addition to any other vote he may have.

51. A poll demanded on the election of a chairman or on a question of adjournment shall be taken forthwith. A poll demanded on any other question shall be taken either forthwith or at such time and place as the chairman directs not being more than thirty days after the poll is demanded. The demand for a poll shall not prevent the continuance of a meeting for the transaction of any business other than the question on which the poll was demanded. If a poll is demanded before the declaration of the result of a show of hands and the demand is duly withdrawn, the meeting shall continue as if the demand has not been made.

52. No notice need be given of a poll not taken forthwith if the time and place at which it is to be taken are announced at the meeting at which it is demanded. In any other case at least seven clear days' notice shall be given specifying the time and place at which the poll is to be taken.

53. A resolution in writing executed by or on behalf of each member who would have been entitled to vote upon it if it had been proposed at a general meeting at which he was present shall be as effectual as if it had been passed at a general meeting duly convened and held and may consist of several instruments in the like form each executed by or on behalf of one or more members.

AMENDMENTS

In para. 41 the word "to" is added by S.I. 1985 No. 1052.

VOTES OF MEMBERS

54. Subject to any rights or restrictions attached to any shares, on a show of hands every member who (being an individual) is present in person or (being a corporation) is present by a duly authorised representative, not being himself a member entitled to vote, shall have one vote on a poll every member shall have one vote for every share of which he is the holder.

55. In the case of joint holders the vote of the senior who tenders a vote, whether in person or by proxy, shall be accepted to the exclusion of the votes of the other joint holders; and seniority shall be determined by the order in which the names of the holders stand in the register of members.

56. A member in respect of whom an order has been made by any court having jurisdiction (whether in the United Kingdom or elsewhere) in matters concerning mental disorder may vote, whether on a show of hands or on a poll, by his receiver, curator bonis or other person authorised in that behalf appointed by that court, and any such receiver, curator bonis or other person may, on a poll, vote by proxy. Evidence to the satisfaction of the directors of the authority of the person claiming to exercise the right to vote shall be deposited at the office, or at such other place as is specified in accordance with the articles for the deposit of instruments of proxy, not less than 48 hours before the time appointed for holding the meeting or adjourned meeting at which the right to vote is to be exercised and in default the right to vote shall not be exercisable.

57. No member shall vote at any general meeting or at any separate meeting of the holders of any class of shares in the company, either in person or by proxy, in respect of any share held by him unless all moneys presently payable by him in respect of that share have been paid.

58. No objection shall be raised to the qualification of any voter except at the meeting or adjourned at which the vote objected to is tendered, and every vote not disallowed at the meeting shall be valid. Any objection made in due time shall be referred to the chairman whose decision shall be final and conclusive.

59. On a poll votes may be given either personally or by proxy. A member may appoint more than one proxy to attend on the same occasion.

60. An instrument appointing a proxy shall be in writing, executed by or on behalf of the appointor and shall be in the following form (or in a form as near thereto as circumstances allow or in any other form which is usual or which the directors may approve)—

" PLC/Limited

I/We, , of

, being a

member/members of the above-named company, hereby appoint

of

, or failing him,

of , as my/our proxy to vote in my/our name[s] and on my/our behalf at the annual/extraordinary general meeting of the company to be held on

19 , and any adjournment thereof.

Signed on 19 ."

61. Where it is desired to afford members an opportunity of instructing the proxy how he shall act the instrument appointing a proxy shall be in the following form (or in a form as near thereto as circumstances allow or in any other form which is usual or which the directors may approve)—

" PLC/Limited

I/We, , of

, being a

member/members of the above-named company, hereby appoint

of

, or failing him,

of , as my/our proxy to vote in my/our name[s] and on my/our behalf at the annual/extraordinary general meeting of the company to be held on
19 , and at any adjournment thereof.

This form is to be used in repsect of the resolutions mentioned below as follows:

Resolution No. 1 * for * against
Resolution No. 2 * for * against

*Strike out whichever is not desired.

Unless otherwise instructed, the proxy may vote as he thinks fit or abstain from voting.

Signed this day of 19 ."

62. The instrument appointing a proxy and any other authority under which it is executed or a copy of such authority certified notarially or in some other way approved by the directors may

(*a*) be deposited at the office or at such other place within the United Kingdom as is specified in the notice convening the meeting or in any instrument of proxy sent out by the company in relation to the meeting not less than 48 hours before the time for holding the meeting or adjourned meeting at which the person named in the instrument proposes to vote; or
(*b*) in the case of a poll taken more than 48 hours after it is demanded, be deposited as aforesaid after the poll has been demanded and not less than 24 hours before the time appointed for the taking of the poll; or
(*c*) where the poll is not taken forthwith but is taken not more than 48 hours after it was demanded, be delivered at the meeting at which the poll was demanded to the chairman or to the secretary or to any director;

and an instrument of proxy, which is not deposited or delivered on a manner so permitted shall be invalid.

63. A vote given or a poll demanded by proxy or by the duly authorised representative of a corporation shall be valid notwithstanding the previous determination of the authority of the person voting or demanding a poll unless notice of the determination was received by the company at the office or at such other place at which the instrument of proxy was duly deposited before the commencement of the meeting or adjourned meeting at which the vote is given or the poll demanded or (in the case of a poll taken otherwise than on the same day as the meeting or adjourned meeting) the time appointed for taking the poll.

NUMBER OF DIRECTORS

64. Unless otherwise determined by ordinary resolution, the number of directors (other than alternate directors) shall not be subject to any maximum but shall be not less than two.

ALTERNATIVE DIRECTORS

65. Any director (other than an alternate director) may appoint any other director, or any other person approved by resolution of the directors and willing to act, to be an alternate director and may remove from office an alternate director so appointed by him.

66. An alternate director shall be entitled to receive notice of all meetings of directors and of all meetings of committees of directors of which his appointor is a member, to attend and vote at any such meeting at which the director appointing him is not personally present, and generally to perform all the functions of his appointor as a director in his absence but shall not be entitled to receive any remuneration from the company for his services as an alternate director. But it shall not be necessary to give notice of such a meeting to an alternate director who is absent from the United Kingdom.

67. An alternate director shall cease to be an alternate director if his appointor ceases to be a director; but if a director retires by rotation or otherwise but is reappointed or deemed to have been reappointed at the meeting at which he retires, any appointment of an alternate director made by him which was in force immediately prior to his retirement shall continue after his reappointment.

68. Any appointment or removal of an alternate director shall be by notice to the company signed by the director making or revoking the appointment or in any other manner approved by the directors.

69. Save as otherwise provided in the articles, an alternate director shall be deemed for all purposes to be a director and shall alone be responsible for his own acts and defaults and he shall not be deemed to be the agent of the director appointing him.

POWERS OF DIRECTORS

70. Subject to the provisions of the Act, the memorandum and the articles and to any directions given by a special resolution, the business of the company shall be managed by the directotrs who may exercise all the powers of the company. No alteration of the memorandum or articles and no such direction shall invalidate any prior act of the directors which would have been valid if that alteration has not been made or that direction had not been given. The powers given by this regulation shall not be limited by any special power given to the directors by the articles and a meeting of directors at which a quorum is present may exercise all powers excisable by the directors.

71. The directors may, by power of attorney or otherwise, appoint any person to be the agent of the company for such purposes and on such conditions as they determine, including authority for the agent to delegate all or any of his powers.

DELEGATION OF DIRECTORS' POWERS

72. The directors may delegate any of their powers to any committee consisting of one or more directors. They may also delegate to any managing director or any director holding any other executive office such of their powers as they consider desirable to be exercised by him. Any such delegation may be made subject to any conditions the directors may impose, and either collaterally with or to the exclusion of their own powers and may be revoked or altered. Subject to any such conditions, the proceedings of a committee with two or more members shall be governed by the articles regulating the proceedings of directors so far as they are capable of applying.

APPOINTMENT AND RETIREMENT OF DIRECTORS

73. At the first annual general meeting all the directors shall retire from office, and at every subsequent annual general meeting one-third of the directors who are subject to retirement by rotation or, if their number is not three or a multiple of three, the number nearest one-third shall retire from office; but, if there is only one director who is subject to retirement by rotation, he shall retire.

74. Subject to the provisions of the Act, the directors to retire by rotation shall be those who have been longest in office since their last appointment or reappointment, but as between persons who became or were last reappointed directors on the same day those to retire shall (unless they otherwise agree among themselves) be determined by lot.

75. If the company, at the meeting at which a director retires by rotation, does not fill the vacancy the retiring director shall, if willing to act, be deemed to have been reappointed unless at the meeting it is resolved not to fill the vacancy or unless a resolution for the reappointment of the director is put to the meeting and lost.

76. No person other than a director retiring by rotation shall be appointed or reappointed a director at any general meeting unless—

(*a*) he is recommended by the directors; or

(*b*) not less than 14 nor more than 35 clear days before the date appointed for the meeting, notice executed by a member qualified to vote at the meeting has been given to the company of the intention to propose that person for appointment or reappointment stating the particulars which would, if he were so appointed or reappointed, be required to be included on the company's register of directors together with notice executed by that person of his willingness to be appointed or reappointed.

77. Not less than seven nor more than 28 clear days before the date appointed for holding a general meeting notice shall be given to all who are entitled to receive notice of the meeting of any person (other than a director retiring by rotation at the meeting) who is recommended by the directors for appointment or reappointment as a director at the meeting or in respect of whom notice has been duly given to the company of the intention to propose him at the meeting for appointment or reappointment as a director. The notice shall give the particulars of that person which would, if he were so appointed or reappointed, be required to be included in the company's register of directors.

78. Subject to aforesaid, the company may by ordinary resolution appoint a person who is willing to act to be a director either to fill a vacancy or as an additional director and may also determine the rotation in which any additional directors are to retire.

79. The directors may appoint a person who is willing to act to be a director, either to fill a vacancy or as an additional director, provided that the appointment does not cause the number of directors to exceed any number fixed by or in accordance with the articles as the maximum number of directors. A director so appointed shall hold office only until the next following annual general meeting and shall not be taken into account in determining the directors who are to retire by rotation at the meeting. If not reappointed at such annual general meeting, he shall vacate office at the conclusion thereof.

80. Subject as aforesaid, a director who retires at an annual general meeting may, if willing to act, be reappointed. If he is not reappointed, he shall retain office until the meeting appoints someone in his place, or if it does not do so, until the end of the meeting.

DISQUALIFICATION AND REMOVAL OF DIRECTORS

81. The office of a director shall be vacated if—

(*a*) he ceases to be a director by virtue of any provisions of the Act or he becomes prohibited by law from being a director; or

(*b*) he becomes bankrupt or makes any arrangement or composition with his creditors generally; or

(*c*) he is, or may be, suffering from mental disorder and either—
   (i) he is admitted to hospital in pursuance of an application for admission for treatment under the Mental Health Act 1983, or, in Scotland, an application for admission under the Mental Health (Scotland) Act 1960, or
   (ii) an order is made by a court having jurisdiction (whether in the United Kingdom or elsewhere) in matters concerning mental disorder for his detention or for the appointment of a receiver, curator bonis or other person to exercise powers with respect to his property or affairs; or

(*d*) he resigns his office by notice to the company; or

(*e*) he shall for more than six consecutive months have been absent without permission of the directors from the meetings of directors held during that period and the directors resolve that his office be vacated.

REMUNERATION OF DIRECTORS

82. The directors shall be entitled to such remuneration at the company may by ordinary resolution determine and, unless the resolution provides otherwise, the remuneration shall be deemed to accure from day to day.

DIRECTORS' EXPENSES

83. The directors may be paid all travelling, hotel, and other expenses properly incurred by them in connection with their attendance at meetings of directors or committees of directors or general meetings of directors or separate meetings of the holders of any class of shares or of debentures of the company or otherwise in connection with the discharge of their duties.

DIRECTORS' APPOINTMENTS AND INTERESTS

84. Subject to the provisions of the Act, the directors may appoint one or more of their number to the office of managing director or to any other executive office under the company and may enter into an agreement or arrangement with any director for his employment by the company or for the provisions by him of any service outside the scope of the ordinary duties of a director. Any such appointment, agreement or arrangement may be made upon such terms as the directors determine and they may remunerate any such director for his services as they think fit. Any appointment of a director to an executive office shall terminate if he ceases to be director but without prejudice to any claim to damages for breach of the contract of service between the director and the company. A managing director and a director holding another executive office shall not be subject to retirement by rotation.

85. Subject to the provisions of the Act, and provided that he has disclosed to the directors the nature and extent of any material interest of his, a director notwithstanding his office—

(*a*) may be a party to, or otherwise interested in, any transaction or arrangement with the company or in which the company is otherwise interested;

(*b*) may be a director or other officer of, or employed by, or a party to any transaction or arrangement with, or otherwise interested in, any body corporate promoted by the company or in which the company is otherwise interested; and

(*c*) shall not, by reason of his office, be accountable to the company for any benefit which he derives from any such office or employment or from any such transaction or arrangement or from any interest in any such body corporate and no such transaction or arrangement shall be liable to be avoided on the ground of any such interest or benefit.

86. For the purposes of regulation 85—

(*a*) a general notice given to the directors that a director is to be regarded as having an interest of the nature and extent specified in the notice in any transaction or arrangement in which a specified person or class of persons is interested shall be deemed to be a disclosure that the director has an interest in any such transaction of the nature and extent so specified; and

(*b*) and interest of which a director has no knowledge and of which it is unreasonable to expect him to have knowledge shall not be treated as an interest of his.

DIRECTORS' GRATUITIES AND PENSIONS

87. The directors may provide benefits, whether by the payment of gratuities or pensions or by insurance or otherwise, for any director who has held but no longer holds any executive office or employment with the company or with any body corporate which is or has been a subsidiary of the company or a predecessor in business of the company or of any such subsidiary, and for any member of his family (including as spouse and a former spouse) or any person who is or was dependent on him, and may (as well before as after he ceases to hold such office or employment) contribute to any fund and pay premiums for the purchase or provision of any such benefit.

PROCEEDINGS OF DIRECTORS

88. Subject to the provisions of the articles, the directors may regulate their proceedings as they think fit. A director may, and the secretary at the request of a director shall, call a meeting of the directors. It shall not be necessary to give notice of a meeting to a director who is absent from the United Kingdom. Questions arising at a meeting shall be decided by a majority of votes. In the case of an equality of votes, the chairman shall have a second or casting vote. A director who is also an alternate director shall be entitled in the absence of his appointor to a separate vote on behalf of his appointor in addition to his own vote.

89. The quorum for the transaction of the business of the directors may be fixed by the directors and unless so fixed at any other number shall be two. A person who holds office only as an alternate director shall, if his appointor is not present, be counted in the quorum.

90. The continuing directors or a sole continuing director may act notwithstanding any vacancies in their number, but, if the number of directors is less than the number fixed as the quorum, the continuing directors or director may act only for the purpose of filling vacancies or of calling a general meeting.

91. The directors may appoint one of their number to be the chairman of the board of directors and may at any time remove from that office. Unless he is unwilling to do so the director so appointed shall preside at every meeting of directors at which he is present. But if there is no director holding that office, or if the director holding it is unwilling to preside or is not present within five minutes after the time appointed for the meeting, the directors present may appoint one of their number to be the chairman of the meeting.

92. All acts done by a meeting of directors, or of a committee of directors, or by a person acting as a director shall, notwithstanding that it be afterwards discovered that there was a defect in the appointment of any director or that any of them were disqualified from holding office, or had vacated office, or were not entitled to vote, be as valid as if every such person had been duly appointed and was qualified and had continued to be a director and had been entitled to vote.

93. A resolution in writing signed by all the directors entitled to receive notice of a meeting of directors or of a committee of dirctors shall be as valid and effectual as if it had been passed at a meeting of directors or (as the case may be) a committee of directors duly convened and held and may consist of several documents in the like form each signed by one or more directors, but a resolution signed by an alternate director need not also be signed by his appointor and, if it is signed by a director who has appointed an alternate director, it need not be signed by the alternate director in that capacity.

94. Save as otherwise provided by the articles, a director shall not vote at a meeting of directors or of a committee of directors on any resolution concerning a matter in which he has, directly or indirectly, an interest or duty which is material and which conflicts or may conflict with the interests of the company unless his interests or duty arises only because the case falls within one or more of the following paragraphs—

(*a*) the resolution relates to the giving of a guarantee, security, or indemnity in respect of money let to, or an obligation incurred by him for the benefit of, the company or any of its subsidiaries;

(*b*) the resolution relates to the giving to a third party of a guarantee, security, or indemnity in respect of an obligation of the company or any of its subsidiaries for which the director has assumed responsibility in whole or part and whether alone or jointly with others under a guarantee or indemnity or by the giving of security;

(*c*) his interest arises by virtue of his subscribing or agreeing to subscribe for any shares, debentures or other securities of the company or any of its subsidiaries, or by virtue of his being, or intending to become, a participant in the underwriting or sub-underwriting of an offer of any such shares, debentures, or other securities by the company or any of its subsidiaries for subscription, purchase or exchange;

(*d*) the resolution relates in any way to a retirement benefits scheme which has been approved, or is conditional upon approval, by the Board of Inland Revenue for taxation purposes.

For the purpose of this regulation, an interest of a person who is, for any purpose the Act (excluding any statutory modification thereof not in force when this regulation becomes binding on the company), connected a director shall be treated as an interest of the director and, in relation to an alternate director, an interest of his appointor shall be treated as an interest of the alternate director without prejudice to any interest which the alternate director has otherwise.

95. A director not be counted in the quorum present at a meeting in relation to a resolution on which he is not entitled to vote.

96. The company may by ordinary resolution suspend or relax to extent, either generally or in respect of any particular matter, any provision of the articles prohibiting a director from voting at a meeting of directors or of a committee of directors.

97. Where proposals are under consideration concerning the appointment of two or more directors to offices or employment with the company or any body corporate in which the company is interested the proposals may be divided and considered in relation to each director separately and (provided he is not for another reason precluded from voting) each of the directors concerned shall be entitled to vote and be counted in the quorum in respect of each resolution except that concerning his own appointment.

98. If a question arises at a meeting of directors or of a committee of directors as to the right of a director to vote, the question may, before the conclusion of the meeting, be referred to the chairman of the meeting and his ruling in relation to any director other than himself shall be final and conclusive.

SECRETARY

99. Subject to the provisions of the Act, the secretary shall be appointed by the directors for such term, at such remuneration and upon such conditions as they may think fit; and any secretary so appointed may be removed by them.

MINUTES

100. The directors shall cause minutes to be made in books kept for the purpose—

(*a*) of all appointments of officers made by directors; and

(*b*) of all proceedings at meetings of the company, of the holders of any class of shares in the company, and of the directors, and of committees of directors, including the names of the directors present at each such meeting.

THE SEAL

101. The seal shall only be used by the authority of the directors or of a committee of directors authorised by the directors. The directors may determine who shall sign any instrument to which the seal is affixed and unless otherwise so determined it shall be signed by a director and by the secretary or by a second director.

DIVIDENDS

102. Subject to the provisions of the Act, the company may by ordinary resolution declare dividends in accordance with the respective rights of the members, but no dividend shall exceed the amount recommended by the directors.

103. Subject to the provisions of the Act, the directors may pay interim dividends if it appears to them that they are justified by the profits of the company available for distribution. If the share capital is divided into different classes, the directors may pay interim dividends on shares which confer deferred or non-preferred rights with regard to dividend as well as on shares which confer preferential rights with regard to dividend, but no interim dividend shall be paid on shares carrying deferred or non-preferred rights if, at the time of payment, any preferential dividend is in arrear. The directors may also pay at intervals settled by them any dividend payable at a fixed rate if it appears to them that the profits available for distribution justify the payment. Provided the directors act in good faith they shall not incur any liability to the holders of shares conferring preferred rights for any loss they may suffer by the lawful payment of an interim dividend on any shares having deferred or non-preferential rights.

104. Except as otherwise provided by the rights attached to shares, all dividends shall be declared and paid according to the amounts paid up on the shares on which the dividend is paid. All dividends shall be apportioned and paid proportionately to the amounts paid up on the shares during any portion or portions of the period in respect of which the dividend is paid; but, if any share is issued on terms providing that it shall rank for dividend as from a particular date, that share shall rank for dividend accordingly.

105. A general meeting declaring a dividend may, upon the recommendation of the directors, direct that it shall be satisfied wholly or partly by the distribution of assets and, where any difficulty arises in regard to the distribution, the directors may settle the same and in particular may issue fractional certificates and fix the value for distribution of any assets and may determine that cash shall be paid to any member upon the footing of the value so fixed in order to adjust the rights of members and may vest any assets in trustees.

106. Any dividend or other moneys payable in respect of a share may be paid by cheque sent by post to the registered address of the person entitled or, if two or more persons are the holders of the share or are joinly entitled to it by reason of the death or bankruptcy of the holder, to the registered address of that one of those persons who is first named in the register of members or to such person and to such address as the person or persons entitled may in writing direct. Every cheque shall be made payable to the order of the person or persons entitled or to such other person as the person or persons entitled may in writing direct and payment of the cheque shall be a good discharge to the company. Any joint holder or other person jointly entitled to a share as aforesaid may give receipts for any dividend or other moneys payable in respect of the share.

107. No dividend or other moneys payable in respect of a share shall bear interest against the company unless otherwise provided by the rights attached to the share.

108. Any dividend which has remained unclaimed for 12 years from the date when it became due for payment shall, if the directors so resolve, be forfeited and cease to remain owing by the company.

ACCOUNTS

109. No member shall (as such) have any right of inspecting any accounting records or other book or document of the company except as conferred by statute or authorised by the directors or by ordinary resolution of the company.

CAPITALISATION OF PROFITS

110. The directors may with the authority of an ordinary resolution of the company—

(*a*) subject as hereinafter provided, resolve to capitalise any undividend profits of the company not required for paying any preferential dividend (whether or not they are available for distribution) or any sum standing to the credit of the company's share premium account or capital redemption reserve;

(*b*) appropriate the sum resolved to be capitalised to the members who would have been entitled to it if it were distributed by way of dividend and in the same proportions and apply such sum on their behalf either in or towards paying up the amounts, if any, for the time being unpaid on any shares held by them respectively, or in paying up in full unissued shares or debentures of the company of a nominal amount equal to that sum, and allot the shares or debentures credited as fully paid to those members, or as they may direct, in those proportions, or partly in one way and partly in the other: but the share premium account, the capital redemption reserve, and any profits which are not available for distribution may, for the purposes of this regulation, only be applied in paying up unissued shares to be allotted to members credited as fully paid;

(*c*) make such provision by the issue of fractional certificates or by payment in cash or otherwise as they determine in the case of shares or debentures becoming distributable under this regulation in fractions; and

(*d*) authorise any person to enter on behalf of all the members concerned into an agreement with the company providing for the allotment to them respectively, credited as fully paid, of any shares or debentures to which they are entitled upon such capitalisation, any agreement made under such authority being binding in all such members.

NOTICES

111. Any notice to be given to or by any person pursuant to the articles shall be in writing except that a notice calling a meeting of the directors need not be in writing.

112. The company may give any notice to a member at his registered address or by leaving it at that address. In the case of joint holders of a share, all notices shall be given to the joint holder whose name stands first in the register of members in respect of the joint holding and notice so given shall be sufficient notice to all the joint holders. A member whose registered address is not within the United Kingdom and who gives to the company an address within the United Kingdom at which notices may be given to him shall be entitled to have notices given to him at that address, but otherwise no such member shall be entitled to receive any notice from the company.

113. A member present, either in person or by proxy, at any meeting of the company or of the holders of any class of shares in the company shall be deemed to have received notice of the meeting and, where requisite, of the purposes for which it was called.

114. Every person who becomes entitled to a share shall be bound by any notice in respect of that share which, before his name is entered in the register of members, has been duly given to a person from whom he derives his title.

115. Proof that an envelope containing a notice was properly addressed, prepaid and posted shall be conclusive evidence that the notice was given. A notice shall [. . .] be deemed to be given at the expiration of 48 hours after the envelope containing it was posted.

116. A notice may be given by the company to the persons entitled to a share in consequence of the death or bankruptcy of a member by sending or delivering it, in any manner authorised by the articles for the giving of notice to a member, addressed to them by name, or by the title of representatives of the deceased, or trustee of the bankrupt or by any like description at the address, if any, within the United Kingdom supplied for that purpose by the persons claiming to be so entitled. Until such an address has been supplied, a notice may be given in any manner in which it might have been given if the death or bankruptcy had not occurred.

AMENDMENT

In para. 115 words omitted are deleted by S.I. 1985 No. 1052.

WINDING UP

117. If the company is wound up, the liquidator may, with the sanction of an extraordinary resolution of the company and any other sanction required by the Act, divide among the members in specie the whole or any part of the assets of the company and may, for that purpose value any assets and determine how the division shall be carried out as between the members or different classes of members. The liquidator may, with the like sanction, vest the whole or any part of the assets in trustees upon such trusts for the benefit of the members as he with the like sanction determines, but no member shall be compelled to accept any assets upon which there is a liability.

INDEMNITY

118. Subject to the provisions of the Act but without prejudice to any indemnity to which a director may otherwise be entitled, every director or other officer or auditor of the company shall be indemnified out of the assets of the company against any liability incurred by him in defending any proceedings, whether civil or criminal, in which judgment is given in his favour or in which he is acquitted or in connection with any application in which relief is granted to him by the court from liability for negligence, default, breach of duty or breach of trust in relation to the affairs of the company.

APPENDIX B

Leasehold Reform, Housing and Urban Development Act 1993

PART I

LANDLORD AND TENANT

CHAPTER I

COLLECTIVE ENFRANCHISEMENT IN CASE OF TENANTS OF FLATS

Preliminary

1.—(1) This Chapter has effect for the purpose of conferring on qualifying tenants of flats contained in premises to which this Chapter applies on the relevant date the right, exercisable subject to and in accordance with this Chapter, to have the freehold of those premises acquired on their behalf—

(a) by a person or persons appointed by them for the purpose, and
(b) at a price determined in accordance with this Chapter;

and that right is referred to in this Chapter as "the right to collective enfranchisement".

(2) Where the right to collective enfranchisement is exercised in relation to any such premises ("the relevant premises")—

(a) the qualifying tenants by whom the right is exercised shall be entitled, subject to and in accordance with this Chapter, to have acquired, in like manner, the freehold of any property which is not comprised in the relevant premises but to which this paragraph applies by virtue of subsection (3); and

(b) section 2 has effect with respect to the acquisition of leasehold interests to which paragraph (a) or (b) of subsection (1) of that section applies.

(3) Subsection (2)(a) applies to any property if the freehold of it is owned by the person who owns the freehold of the relevant premises and at the relevant date either—

(a) it is appurtenant property which is demised by the lease held by a qualifying tenant of a flat contained in the relevant premises; or

(b) it is property which any such tenant is entitled under the terms of the lease of his flat to use in common with the occupiers of other premises (whether those premises are contained in the relevant premises or not).

(4) The right of acquisiton in respect of the freehold of any such property as is mentioned in subsection (3)(*b*) shall, however, be taken to be satisfied with respect to that property if, on the acquisition of the relevant premises in pursuance of this Chapter, either—

(a) there are granted by the freeholder—
    (i) over that property, or
    (ii) over any other property,
such permanent rights as will ensure that thereafter the occupier of the flat referred to in that provision has as nearly as may be the same rights as those enjoyed in relation to that property on the relevant date by the qualifying tenant under the terms of his lease; or

(b) there is acquired from the freeholder the freehold of any other property over which any such permanent rights may be granted.

(5) A claim by qualifying tenants to exercise the right to collective enfranchisement may be made in relation to any premises to which this Chapter applies despite the fact that those premises are less extensive than the entirety of the premises in relation to which those tenants are entitled to exercise that right.

(6) Any right or obligation under this Chapter to acquire any interest in property shall not extend to underlying minerals in which that interest subsists if—

(a) the owner of the interest requires the minerals to be excepted, and

(b) proper provision is made for the support of the property as it is enjoyed on the relevant date.

(7) In this section—

"appurtenant property", in relation to a flat, means any garage, outhouse, garden, yard or appurtenances belonging to, or usually enjoyed with, the flat;

"the freeholder" means the person who owns the freehold of the relevant premises;

"the relevant premises" means any such premises as are referred to in subsection (2).

(8) In this Chapter "the relevant date", in relation to any claim to exercise the right to collective enfranchisement, means the date on which notice of the claim is given under section 13.

2.—(1) Where the right to collective enfranchisement is exercised in relation to any premises to which this Chapter applies ("the relevant premises"), then, subject to and in accordance with this Chapter—

(a) there shall be acquired on behalf of the qualifying tenants by whom the right is exercised every interest to which this paragraph applies by virtue of subsection (2); and

(b) those tenants shall be entitled to have acquired on their behalf any interest to which this paragraph applies by virtue of subsection (3);

and any interest so acquired on behalf of those tenants shall be acquired in the manner mentioned in paragraphs (a) and (b) of section 1(1).

(2) Paragraph (a) of subsection (1) above applies to the interest of the tenant under any lease which is superior to the lease held by a qualifying tenant of a flat contained in the relevant premises.

(3) Paragraph (b) of subsection (1) above applies to the interest of the tenant under any lease (not falling within subsection (2) above) under which the demised premises consist of or include—

(a) any common parts of the relevant premises, or

(b) any property falling within section 1(2)(*a*) which is to be acquired by virtue of that provision,

where the acquisition of that interest is reasonably necessary for the proper management or maintenance of those common parts, or (as the case may be) that property, on behalf of the tenants by whom the right to collective enfranchisement is exercised.

(4) Where the demised premises under any lease falling within subsection (2) or (3) include any premises other than—

(a) a flat contained in the relevant premises which is held by a qualifying tenant,

(b) any common parts of those premises, or

(c) any such property as is mentioned in subsection (3)(*b*), the obligation or (as the case may be) right under subsection (1) above to acquire the interest of the tenant under the lease shall not extend to his interest under the lease in any such other premises.

(5) Where the qualifying tenant of a flat is a public sector landlord and the flat is let under a secure tenancy, then if—

(a) the condition specified in subsection (6) is satisfied, and
(b) the lease of the qualifying tenant is directly derived out of a lease under which the tenant is a public sector landlord,

the interest of that public sector landlord as tenant under that lease shall not be liable to be acquired by virtue of subsection (1) to the extent that it is an interest in the flat or in any appurtenant property; and the interest of a public sector landlord as tenant under any lease out of which the qualifying tenant's lease is indirectly derived shall, to the like extent, not be liable to be so acquired (so long as the tenant under every lease intermediate between that lease and the qualifying tenant's lease is a public sector landlord).

(6) The condition referred to in subsection (5)(*a*) is that either—

(a) the qualifying tenant is the immediate landlord under the secure tenancy, or
(b) he is the landlord under a lease which is superior to the secure tenancy and the tenant under that lease, and the tenant under every lease (if any) intermediate between it and the secure tenancy, is also a public sector landlord;

and in subsection (5) "appurtenant property" has the same meaning as in section 1.

(7) In this section "the relevant premises" means any such premises as are referred to in subsection (1).

3.—(1) Subject to section 4, this Chapter applies to any premises if—

(a) they consist of a self-contained building or part of a building and the freehold of the whole of the building or of that part of the building is owned by the same person;
(b) they contain two or more flats held by qualifying tenants; and
(c) the total number of flats held by such tenants is not less than two-thirds of the total number of flats contained in the premises.

(2) For the purposes of this section a building is a self-contained building if it is structurally detached, and a part of a building is a self-contained part of a building if—

(a) it constitutes a vertical division of the building and the structure of the building is such that that part could be redeveloped independently of the remainder of the building; and
(b) the relevant services provided for occupiers of that part either—

(i) are provided independently of the relevant services provided for occupiers of the remainder of the building, or

(ii) could be so provided without involving the carrying out of any works likely to result in a significant interruption in the provision of any such services for occupiers of the remainder of the building;

and for this purpose "relevant services" means services provided by means of pipes, cables or other fixed installations.

4.—(1) This Chapter does not apply to premises falling within section 3(1) if—

(a) any part or parts of the premises is or are neither—
  (i) occupied, or intended to be occupied, for residential purposes, nor
  (ii) comprised in any common parts of the premises; and

(b) the internal floor area of that part or of those parts (taken together) exceeds 10 per cent. of the internal floor area of the premises (taken as a whole).

(2) Where in the case of any such premises any part of the premises (such as, for example, a garage, parking space or storage area) is used, or intended for use, in conjunction with a particular dwelling contained in the premises (and accordingly is not comprised in any common parts of the premises), it shall be taken to be occupied, or intended to be occupied, for residential purposes.

(3) For the purpose of determining the internal floor area of a building or of any part of a building, the floor or floors of the building or part shall be taken to extend (without interruption) throughout the whole of the interior of the building or part, except that the area of any common parts of the building or part shall be disregarded.

(4) This Chapter does not apply to premises falling within section 3(1) if the premises are premises with a resident landlord and do not contain more than four units.

5.—(1) Subject to the following provisions of this section, a person is a qualifying tenant of a flat for the purposes of this Chapter if he is tenant of the flat under a long lease at a low rent.

(2) Subsection (1) does not apply where—

(a) the lease is a business lease; or

(b) the immediate landlord under the lease is a charitable housing trust and the flat forms part of the housing accommodation provided by it in the pursuit of its charitable purposes; or

(c) the lease was granted by sub-demise out of a superior lease other than a long lease at a low rent, the grant was made in breach of the terms of the superior lease, and there has been no waiver of the breach by the superior landlord;

and in paragraph (b) "charitable housing trust" means a housing trust within the meaning of the Housing Act 1985 which is a charity within the meaning of the Charities Act 1993.

(3) No flat shall have more than one qualifying tenant at any one time.

(4) Accordingly—

(a) where a flat is for the time being let under two or more leases to which subsection (1) applies, any tenant under any of those leases which is superior to that held by any other such tenant shall not be a qualifying tenant of the flat for the purposes of this Chapter; and

(b) where a flat is for the time being let to joint tenants under a lease to which subsection (1) applies, the joint tenants shall (subject to paragraph (a) and subsection (5)) be regarded for the purposes of this Chapter as jointly constituting the qualifying tenant of the flat.

(5) Where apart from this subsection—

(a) a person whould be regarded for the purposes of this Chapter as being (or as being among those constituting) the qualifying tenant of a flat contained in any particular premises consisting of the whole or part of a building, but

(b) that person would also be regarded for those purposes as being (or as being among those constituting) the qualifying tenant of each of two or more other flats contained in those premises,

then, whether that person is tenant of the flats referred to in paragraphs (a) and (b) under a single lease or otherwise, there shall be taken for those purposes to be no qualifying tenant of any of those flats.

(6) For the purposes of subsection (5) in its application to a body corporate any flat let to an associated company (whether alone or jointly with any other person or persons) shall be treated as if it were so let to that body; and for this purpose "associated company" means another body corporate which is (within the meaning of section 736 of the Companies Act 1985) that body's holding company, a subsidiary of that body or another subsidiary of that body's holding company.

6.—(1) For the purposes of this Chapter a qualifying tenant of a flat satisfies the residence condition at any time when the condition specified in subsection (2) is satisfied with respect to him.

(2) That condition is that the tenant has occupied the flat as his only or principal home—

(a) for the last 12 months, or

(b) for periods amounting to three years in the last ten years,

whether or not he has used it also for other purposes.

(3) For the purposes of subsection (2)—

(a) any reference to the tenant's flat includes a reference to part of it; and
(b) it is immaterial whether at any particular time the tenant's occupation was in right of the lease by virtue of which he is a qualifying tenant or in right of some other lease or otherwise;

but any occupation by a company or other artificial person, or (where the tenant is a corporation sole) by the corporator, shall not be regarded as occupation for the purposes of that subsection.

(4) In the case of a lease held by joint tenants—

(a) the condition specified in subsection (2) need only be satisfied with respect to one of the joint tenants; and
(b) subsection (3) shall apply accordingly (the reference to the lease by virtue of which the tenant is a qualifying tenant being read for this purpose as a reference to the lease by virtue of which the joint tenants are a qualifying tenant).

7.—(1) In this Chapter "long lease" means (subject to the following provisions of this section)—

(a) a lease granted for a term of years certain exceeding 21 years, whether or not it is (or may become) terminable before the end of that term by notice given by or to the tenant or by re-entry, forfeiture or otherwise;
(b) a lease for a term fixed by law under a grant with a covenant or obligation for perpetual renewal (other than a lease by sub-demise from one which is not a long lease) or a lease taking effect under section 149(6) of the Law of Property Act 1925 (leases terminable after a death or marriage);
(c) a lease granted in pursuance of the right to buy conferred by Part V of the Housing Act 1985 or in pursuance of the right to acquire on rent to mortgage terms conferred by that Part of that Act; or
(d) a shared ownership lease, whether granted in pursuance of that Part of that Act or otherwise, where the tenant's total share is 100 per cent.

(2) A lease terminable by notice after a death or marriage is not to be treated as a long lease for the purposes of this Chapter if—

(a) the notice is capable of being given at any time after the death or marriage of the tenant;
(b) the length of the notice is not more than three months; and
(c) the terms of the lease preclude both—
    (i) its assignment otherwise than by virtue of section 92 of the Housing Act 1985 (assignments by way of exchange), and

(ii) the sub-letting of the whole of the premises comprised in it.

(3) Where the tenant of any property under a long lease at a low rent, on the coming to an end of that lease, becomes or has become tenant of the property or part of it under any subsequent tenancy (whether by express grant or by implication of law), then that tenancy shall be deemed for the purposes of this Chapter (including any further application of this subsection) to be a long lease irrespective of its terms.

(4) Where—

(a) a lease is or has been granted for a term of years certain not exceeding 21 years, but with a covenant or obligation for renewal without payment of a premium (but not for perpetual renewal), and
(b) the lease is or has been renewed on one or more occasions so as to bring to more than 21 years the total of the terms granted (including any interval between the end of a lease and the grant of a renewal).

this Chapter shall apply as if the term originally granted had been one exceeding 21 years.

(5) References in this Chapter to a long lease include—

(a) any period during which the lease is or was continued under Part I of the Landlord and Tenant Act 1954 or under Schedule 10 to the Local Government and Housing Act 1989;
(b) any period during which the lease was continued under the Leasehold Property (Temporary Provisions) Act 1951.

(6) Where in the case of a flat there are at any time two or more separate leases, with the same landlord and the same tenant, and—

(a) the property comprised in one of those leases consists of either the flat or a part of it (in either case with or without any appurtenant property), and
(b) the property comprised in every other lease consists of either a part of the flat (with or without any appurtenant property) or appurtenant property only,

then in relation to the property comprised in such of those leases as are long leases, this Chapter shall apply as it would if at that time—

(i) there were a single lease of that property, and
(ii) that lease were a long lease;

but this subsection has effect subject to the operation of subsections (3) to (5) in relation to any of the separate leases.

(7) In this section—

"appurtenant property" has the same meaning as in section 1;
"shared ownership lease" means a lease—

(a) granted on payment of a premium calculated by reference to a percentage of the value of the demised premises or the cost of providing them, or

(b) under which the tenant (or his personal representatives) will or may be entitled to a sum calculated by reference, directly or indirectly, to the value of those premises; and

"total share", in relation to the interest of a tenant under a shared ownership lease, means his initial share plus any additional share or shares in the demised premises which he has acquired.

8.—(1) For the purposes of this Chapter a lease of a flat is a lease at a low rent if either no rent was payable under it in respect of the flat during the initial year or the aggregate amountof rent so payable during that year did not exceed the following amount, namely—

(a) where the lease was entered into before April 1, 1963, two-thirds of the letting value of the flat (on the same terms) on the date of the commencement of the lease;

(b) where—

(i) the lease was entered into either on or after April 1, 1963 but before April 1, 1990, or on or after April 1, 1990 in pursuance of a contract made before that date, and

(ii) the flat had a rateable value at the date of the commencement of the lease or else at any time before April 1, 1990,

two-thirds of the rateable value of the flat on the appropriate date; or

(c) in any other case, £1,000 if the flat is in Greater London or £250 if elsewhere.

(2) For the purposes of subsection (1)—

(a) "the initial year", in relation to any lease, means the period of one year beginning with the date of the commencement of the lease;

(b) "the appropriate date" means the date of the commencement of the lease or, if the flat in question did not have a rateable value on that date, the date on which the flat first had a rateable value;

(c) section 25(1), (2) and (4) of the Rent Act 1977 (rateable value etc.) shall apply, with any necessary modifications, for the purpose of determining the amount of the rateable value of a flat on a particular date;

(d) "rent" means rent reserved as such, and there shall be disregarded any part of the rent expressed to be payable in consideration of services to be provided, or of repairs, maintenance or insurance to be effected by the landlord, or to be payable in respect of the cost thereof to the landlord under the lease or a superior landlord; and

(e) there shall be disregarded any term of the lease providing for suspension or reduction of rent in the event of damage to property demised, or for any penal addition to the rent in the event of a contravention of or non-compliance with the terms of the lease or an agreement collateral thereto.

(3) In subsection (1)(*a*) above the reference to letting value shall be construed in like manner as, under the law of England and Wales, the reference to letting value is to be construed where it appears in the proviso to section 4(1) of the Leasehold Reform Act 1967 (meaning of "low rent").

(4) Accordingly, in determining the letting value of a flat at any time for the purposes of subsection (1)(*a*) above, regard shall be had to whether, and (if so) in what amount, a premium might then have been lawfully demanded as the whole or part of the consideration for the letting.

(5) Where, by virtue of section 7(4), a lease which has been renewed on one or more occasions is to be treated as a long lease for the purposes of this Chapter, then for the purpose of determining under this section whether it is for those purposes a long lease at a low rent—

(a) the lease shall be deemed to have been entered into on the date of the last renewal of the lease; and

(b) that date shall be deemed to be the date of the commencement of the lease.

(6) Subsection (2)(*a*) above shall have effect in relation to any shared ownership lease falling within section 7(1)(*d*) as if the reference to the date of commencement of the lease were a reference to the date on which the tenant's total share became 100 per cent; and section 7(7) shall apply for the interpretation of this subsection.

(7) In this section any reference to a flat let under a lease includes a reference to any appurtenant property (within the meaning of section 1) which on the relevant date is let with the flat to the tenant under the lease.

9.—(1) Where, in connection with any claim to exercise the right to collective enfranchisement in relation to any premises, it is now proposed to acquire any interests other than—

(a) the freehold of the premises, or

(b) any other interests of the person who owns the freehold of the premises,

that person shall be the reversioner in respect of the premises for the purposes of this Chapter.

(2) Where, in connection with any such claim, it is proposed to acquire interests of persons other than the person who owns the freehold of the premises to which the claim relates, then—

(a) the reversioner in respect of the premises shall for the purposes of this Chapter be the person identified as such by Part I of Schedule 1 to this Act; and

(b) the person who owns the freehold of the premises, and every person who owns any leasehold interest which it is proposed to acquire under or by virtue of section 2(1)(*a*) or (*b*), shall be a relevant landlord for those purposes.

(3) Subject to the provisions of Part II of Schedule 1, the reversioner in respect of any premises shall, in a case to which subsection (2) applies, conduct on behalf of all the relevant landlords all proceedings arising out of any notice given with respect to the premises under section 13 (whether the proceedings are for resisting or giving effect to the claim in question).

(4) Schedule 2 (which makes provision with respect to certain special categories of landlords) has effect for the purposes of this Chapter.

10.—(1) For the purposes of this Chapter any premises falling within section 3(1) are at any time premises with a resident landlord if—

(a) the premises are not, and do not form part of, a purpose-built block of flats; and

(b) the freeholder, or an adult member of the freeholder's family—

(i) at that time occupies a flat contained in the premises as his only or principal home, and

(ii) has so occupied such a flat throughout a period of not less than twelve months ending with that time.

(2) Where any premises falling within section 3(1) would at any time ("the relevant time") be premises with a resident landlord but for the fact that subsection (1)(*b*)(ii) above does not apply, the premises shall nevertheless be treated for the purposes of this Chapter as being at that time premises with a resident landlord if—

(a) immediately before the date when the freeholder acquired his interest in the premises the premises were (or, had this Chapter then been in force, would have been) such premises for the purposes of this Chapter; and

(b) the freeholder, or an adult member of the freeholder's family—

(i) entered into occupation of a flat contained in the premises within the period of 28 days beginning with that date, and

(ii) has occupied such a flat as his only or principal home throughout the period beginning with the time when he so entered into occupation and ending with the relevant time.

(3) In paragraph (b) of each of subsections (1) and (2) any reference to a flat includes a reference to a unit (other than a flat) which is used as a dwelling.

(4) Where the freehold interest in any premises is held on trust, subsections (1) and (2) shall apply as if, in paragraph (b) of each of those subsections, any reference to the freeholder were instead a reference to a person having an interest under the trust (whether or not also a trustee).

(5) For the purposes of this section a person is an adult member of another's family if that person is—

(a) the other's wife or husband; or
(b) a son or daughter or a son-in-law or daughter-in-law of the other, or of the other's wife or husband, who has attained the age of 18; or
(c) the father or mother of the other, or of the other's wife or husband;

and in paragraph (b) any reference to a person's son or daughter includes a reference to any stepson or stepdaughter of that person, and "son-in-law" and "daughter-in-law" shall be construed accordingly.

(6) In this section—

"the freeholder", in relation to any premises, means the person who owns the freehold of the premises;

"purpose-built block of flats" means a building which as constructed contained two or more flats.

Preliminary inquiries by tenants

11.—(1) A qualifying tenant of a flat may give—

(a) to his immediate landlord, or
(b) to any person receiving rent on behalf of his immediate landlord,

a notice requiring the recipient to give the tenant (so far as known to the recipient) the name and address of the person who owns the freehold of the relevant premises and the name and address of every other person who has an interest to which subsection (2) applies.

(2) In relation to a qualifying tenant of a flat, this subsection applies to the following interests, namely—

(a) the freehold of any property not contained in the relevant premises—
    (i) which is demised by the lease held by the tenant, or
    (ii) which the tenant is entitled under the terms of his lease to use in common with other persons; and
(b) any leasehold interest in the relevant premises or in such property which is superior to that of the tenant's immediate landlord.

(3) Any qualifying tenant of a flat may give to the person who owns the freehold of the relevant premises a notice requiring him to give the tenant (so far as known to him) the name and address of every person, apart from the tenant, who is—

- (a) a tenant of the whole of the relevant premises, or
- (b) a tenant or licensee of any separate set or sets of premises contained in the relevant premises, or
- (c) a tenant or licensee of the whole or any part of any common parts so contained or of any property not so contained—
  - (i) which is demised by the lease held by a qualifying tenant of a flat contained in the relevant premises, or
  - (ii) which any such qualifying tenant is entitled under the terms of his lease to use in common with other persons.

(4) Any such qualifying tenant may also give—

- (a) to the person who owns the freehold of the relevant premises, or
- (b) to any person falling within subsection (3)(*a*), (*b*) or (*c*),

a notice requiring him to give the tenant—

- (i) such information relating to his interest in the relevant premises or (as the case may be) in any such property as is mentioned in subsection (3)(*c*), or
- (ii) (so far as known to him) such information relating to any interest derived (whether directly or indirectly) out of that interest,

as is specified in the notice, where the information is reasonably required by the tenant in connection with the making of a claim to exercise the right to collective enfranchisement in relation to the whole or part of the relevant premises.

(5) Where a notice is given by a qualifying tenant under subsection (4), the following rights shall be exercisable by him in relation to the recipient of the notice, namely—

- (a) a right, on giving reasonable notice, to be provided with a list of documents to which subsection (6) applies;
- (b) a right to inspect, at any reasonable time and on giving reasonable notice, any documents to which that subsection applies; and
- (c) a right, on payment of a reasonable fee, to be provided with a copy of any document which are contained in any list provided under paragraph (a) or have been inspected under paragraph (b).

(6) This subsection applies to any document in the custody or under the control of the recipient of the notice under subsection (4)—

(a) sight of which is reasonably required by the qualifying tenant in connection with the making of such a claim as is mentioned in that subsection; and

(b) which, on a proposed sale by a willing seller to a willing buyer of the recipient's interest in the relevant premises or (as the case may be) in any such property as is mentioned in subsection (3)(c), the seller would be expected to make available to the buyer (whether at or before contract or completion).

(7) Any person who—

(a) is required by a notice under any of subsections (1) to (4) to give any information to a qualifying tenant, or

(b) is required by a qualifying tenant under subsection (5) to supply any list of documents, to permit the inspection of any documents or to supply a copy of any documents,

shall comply with that requirement within the period of 28 days beginning with the date of the giving of the notice referred to in paragraph (a) or (as the case may be) with the date of the making of the requirement referred to in paragraph (b).

(8) Where—

(a) a person has received a notice under subsection (4), and

(b) within the period of six months beginning with the date of receipt of the notice, he—

(i) disposes of any interest (whether legal or equitable) in the relevant premises otherwise than by the creation of an interest by way of security for a loan, or

(ii) acquires any such interest (otherwise than by way of security for a loan),

then (unless that disposal or acquision has already been notified to the qualifying tenant in accordance with subsection (7)) he shall notify the qualifying tenant of that disposal or acquisition within the period of 28 days beginning with the date when it occurred.

(9) In this section—

"document" has the same meaning as in Part I of the Civil Evidence Act 1968;

"the relevant premises", in relation to any qualifying tenant of a flat, means—

(a) if the person who owns the freehold interest in the flat owns the freehold of the whole of the building in which the flat is contained, that building, or

(b) if that person owns the freehold of part only of that building, that part of that building;

and any reference to an interest in the relevant premises includes an interest in part of those premises.

12.—(1) Any notice given by a qualifying tenant under section 11(4) shall, in addition to any other requirement imposed in accordance with that provision, require the recipient to give the tenant—

(a) the information specified in subsection (2) below; and
(b) (so far as known to the recipient) the information specified in subsection (3) below.

(2) The information referred to in subsection (1)(*a*) is—

(a) whether the recipient has received in respect of any premises containing the tenant's flat—
  (i) a notice under section 13 in the case of which the relevant claim is still current, or
  (ii) a copy of such a notice; and
(b) if so, the date on which the notice under section 13 was given and the name and address of the nominee purchaser for the time being appointed for the purposes of section 15 in relation to that claim.

(3) The information referred to in subsection (1)(*b*) is—

(a) whether the tenant's flat is comprised in any property in the case of which any of paragraphs (*a*) to (*d*) of section 31(2) is applicable; and
(b) if paragraph (*b*) or (*d*) of that provision is applicable, the date of the application in question.

(4) Where—

(a) within the period of six months beginning with the date of receipt of a notice given by a tenant under section 11(4), the recipient of the notice receives in respect of any premises containing the tenant's flat—
  (i) a notice under section 13, or
  (ii) a copy of such a notice, and
(b) the tenant is not one of the qualifying tenants by whom the notice under section 13 is given,

the recipient shall, within the period of 28 days beginning with the date of receipt of the notice under section 13 or (as the case may be) the copy, notify the tenant of the date on which the notice was given and of the name and address of the nominee purchaser for the time being appointed for the purposes of section 15 in relation to the relevant claim.

(5) Where—

(a) the recipient of a notice given by a tenant under section 11(4) has, in accordance with subsection (1) above, informed the tenant of any such application as is referred to in subsection (3)(b) above; and
(b) within the period of six months beginning with the date of receipt of the notice, the application is either granted or refused by the Commissioners of Inland Revenue or is withdrawn by the applicant,

the recipient shall, within the period of 28 days beginning with the date of the granting, refusal or withdrawal of the application, notify the tenant that it has been granted, refused or withdrawn.

(6) In this section "the relevant claim", in relation to a notice under section 13, means the claim in respect of which that notice is given; and for the purposes of subsection (2) above any such claim is current if—

(a) that notice continues in force in accordance with section 13(11), or
(b) a binding contract entered into in pursuance of that notice remains in force, or
(c) where an order has been made under section 24(4)(*a*) or (*b*) or 25(6)(*a*) or (*b*) with respect to any such premises as are referred to in subsection (2)(*a*) above, any interests which by virtue of the order fall to be vested in the nominee purchaser have yet to be so vested.

The initial notice

13.—(1) A claim to exercise the right to collective enfranchisement with respect to any premises is made by the giving of notice of the claim under this section.

(2) A notice given under this section ("the initial notice")—

(a) must be given to the reversioner in respect of those premises; and
(b) must be given by a number of qualifying tenant of flats contained in the premises as at the relevant date which—
    (i) is not less that two-thirds of the total number of such tenants, and
    (ii) is not less than one-half of the total number of flats so contained;

and not less than one-half of the qualifying tenants by whom the notice is given must satisfy the residence condition.

(3) The initial notice must—

(a) specify and be accompanied by a plan showing—

(i) the premises of which the freehold is proposed to be acquired by virtue of section 1(1),
(ii) any property of which the freehold is proposed to be acquired by virtue of section 1(2)(*a*), and
(iii) any property of the person who owns the freehold of the specified premises over which it is proposed the rights (specified in the notice) should be granted by him in connection with the acquisition of the freehold of the specified premises or of any such property so far as falling within section 1(3)(*a*);

(b) contain a statement of the grounds on which it is claimed that the specified premises are, on the relevant date, premises to which this Chapter applies;
(c) specify—
(i) any leasehold interest proposed to be acquired under or by virtue of section 2(1)(*a*) or (*b*), and
(ii) any flats or others units contained in the specified premises in relation to which it is considered that any of the requirements in Part II of Schedule 9 to this Act are applicable;
(d) specify the proposed purchase price for each of the following, namely—
(i) the freehold interest in the specified premises,
(ii) the freehold interest in any property specified under paragraph (*a*)(ii), and
(iii) any leasehold interest specified under paragraph (*c*)(i);
(e) state the full names of all the qualifying tenants of flats contained in the specified premises and the addresses of their flats, and contain the following particulars in relation to each of those tenants, namely—
(i) such particulars of his lease as are sufficient to identify it, including the date on which the lease was entered into, the term for which it was granted and the date of the commencement of the term,
(ii) such further particulars as are necessary to show that the lease is a lease at a low rent, and
(iii) if it is claimed that he satisfies the residence condition, particulars of the period or periods falling with the preceding ten years for which he has occupied the whole or part of his flat as his only or principal home;
(f) state the full name or names of the person or persons appointed as the nominee purchaser for the purposes of section 15, and an address in England and Wales at which notices may be given to that person or those persons under this Chapter; and
(g) specify the date by which the reversioner must respond to the notice by giving a counter-notice under section 21.

(4) In a case where the tenant's lease is held by joint tenants, subsection (3)(*e*)(iii) shall have effect as if any reference to the tenant were a reference to any joint tenant by virtue of whose occupation of the flat in question it is claimed that the residence condition is satisfied.

(5) The date specified in the initial notice in pursuance of subsection (3)(*g*) must be a date falling not less than two months after the relevant date.

(6) A notice shall not be given under this section with respect to any premises unless the qualifying tenants by whom it is given have obtained a valuation prepared by a qualified surveyor in respect of—

(a) the freehold interest in the specified premises,
(b) the freehold interest in any property specified under subsection (3)(*a*)(ii), and
(c) any leasehold interest specified under subsection (3)(*c*)(i),

and any such notice must contain a statement confirming that they have done so and state the name of the surveyor in question.

(7) For the purposes of subsection (6) a person is a qualified surveyor is—

(a) he is a fellow or professional associate of the Royal Institution of Chartered Surveyors or of the Incorporated Society of Valuers and Auctioneers or satisfies such other requirement or requirements as may be prescribed by regulations made by the Secretary of State; and
(b) he is reasonably believed by the qualifying tenants to have ability in, and experience of, the valuation of premises of the particular kind, and in the particular area, in question;

and any valuation prepared for the purposes of that subsection must be prepared in conformity with the provisions of Schedule 6 so far as relating to the determination of the price payable under this Chapter for the interest in question.

(8) Where any premises have been specified in a notice under this section, no subsequent notice which specifies the whole or part of those premises may be given under this section so long as the earlier notice continues in force.

(9) Where any premises have been specified in a notice under this section and—

(a) that notice has been withdrawn, or is deemed to have been withdrawn, under or by virtue of any provision of this Chapter or under section 74(3), or
(b) in response to that notice, an order has been applied for and obtained under section 23(1),

no subsequent notice which specifies the whole or part of those premises may be given under this section within the period of twelve months beginning with the date of the withdrawal or deemed withdrawal of the earlier notice or with the time when the order under section 23(1) becomes final (as the case may be).

(10) In subsection (8) and (9) any reference to a notice which specifies the whole or part of any premises includes a reference to a notice which specifies any premises which contain the whole or part of those premises; and in those subsections and this "specifies" means specifies under subsection (3)(*a*)(i).

(11) Where a notice is given in accordance with this section, then for the purposes of this Chapter the notice continues in force as from the relevant date—

- (a) until a binding contract is entered into in pursuance of the notice, or an order is made under section 24(4)(*a*) or (*b*) or 25(6)(a) or (b) providing for the vesting of interests in the nominee purchaser;
- (b) if the notice is withdrawn or deemed to have been withdrawn under or by virtue of any provision of this Chapter or under section 74(3), until the date of the withdrawal or deemed withdrawal, or
- (c) until such other time as the notice ceases to have effect by virtue of any provision of this Chapter.

(12) In this Chapter "the specified premises", in relation to a claim made under this Chapter, means—

- (a) the premises specified in the initial notice under subsection (3)(*a*)(i), or
- (b) if it is subsequently agreed or determined under this Chapter that any less extensive premises should be acquired in pursuance of the notice in satisfaction of the claim, those premises;

and similarly references to any property or interest specified in the initial notice under subsection (3)(*a*)(ii) or (*c*)(i) shall, if it is subsequently agreed or determined under this Chapter that any less extensive property or interest should be acquired in pursuance of the notice, be read as references to that property or interest.

(13) Schedule 3 to this Act (which contains restrictions on participating in the exercise of the right to collective enfranchisement, and makes further provision in connection with the giving of notice under this section) shall have effect.

Participating tenants and nominee purchaser

14.—(1) In relation to any claim to exercise the right to collective enfranchisement, the participating tenants are (subject to the provisions of this section and Part I of Schedule 3) the following persons, namely—

(a) in relation to the relevant date, the qualifying tenants by whom the initial notice is given; and
(b) in relation to any time falling after that date, such of those qualifying tenants as for the time being remain qualifying tenants of flats contained in the specified premises.

(2) Where the lease by virtue of which a participating tenants is a qualifying tenant of his flat is assigned to another person, the assignee of the lease shall, within the period of 14 days beginning with the date of the assignment, notify the nominee purchaser—

(a) of the assignment, and
(b) as to whether or not the assignee is electing to participate in the proposed acquisition.

(3) Where a qualifying tenant of a flat contained in the specified premises—

(a) is not one of the persons by whom the initial notice was given, and
(b) is not such an assignee of the lease of a participating tenant as is mentioned in subsection (2),

then (subject to paragraph 8 of Schedule 3) he may elect to participate in the proposed acquisition, but only with the agreement of all the persons who are for the time being participating tenants; and, if he does so elect, he shall notify the nominee purchaser forthwith of his election.

(4) Where a person notifies the nominee purchaser under subsection (2) or (3) of his election to participate in the proposed acquisition, he shall be regarded as a participating tenants for the purposes of this Chapter—

(a) as from the date of the assignment or agreement referred to in that subsection; and
(b) so long as he remains a qualifying tenant of a flat contained in the specified premiese.

(5) Where a participating tenants dies, his personal representatives shall, within the period of 56 days beginning with the date of death, notify the nominee purchaser—

(a) of the death of the tenant, and
(b) as to whether or not the personal representatives are electing to withdraw from participation in the proposed acquisition;

and, unless the personal representatives of a participating tenant so notify the nominee purchaser that they are electing to withdraw from participation in that acquisition, they shall be regarded as a participating tenant for the purposes of this Chapter—

(i) as from the date of the death of the tenant, and

(ii) so long as his lease remains vested in them.

(6) Where in accordance with subsection (4) or (5) any assignee or personal representatives of a participating tenant ("the tenant") is or are to be regarded as a participating tenant for the purposes of this Chapter, any arrangement made between the nominee purchaser and the participating tenants and having effect immediately before the date of the assignment or (as the case may be) the date of death shall have effect as from that date—

(a) with such modifications as are necessary for substituting the assignee or (as the case may be) the personal representatives as a party to the arrangements in the place of the tenant; or
(b) in the case of an assignment by a person who remains a qualifying tenant of a flat contained in the specified premises, with such modifications as are necessary for adding the assignee as a party to the arrangements.

(7) Where the nominee purchaser receives a notification under subsection (2), (3), or (5), he shall, within the period of 28 days beginning with the date of receipt of the notification—

(a) give a notice under subsection (8) to the reversioner in respect of the specified premises, and
(b) give a copy of that notice to every other relevant landlord.

(8) A notice under this subsection is a notice stating—

(a) in the case of a notification under subsection (2)—
    (i) the date of the assignment and the name and address of the assignee,
    (ii) that the assignee has or (as the case may be) has not become a participating tenant in accordance with subsection (4), and
    (iii) if he has become a participating tenant (otherwise than in a case to which subsection (6)(*b*) applies), that he has become such a tenant in place of his assignor;
(b) in the case of a notification under subsection (3), the name and address of the person who has become a participating tenant in accordance with subsection (4); and
(c) in the case of a notification under subsection (5)—
    (i) the date of death of the deceased tenant,
    (ii) the names and addresses of the personal representatives of the tenants, and
    (iii) that in accordance with that subsection those persons are or (as the case may be) are not to be regarded as a participating tenant.

(9) Every notice under subsection (8)—

(a) shall identify the flat with respect to which it is given; and
(b) if it states that any person or persons is or are to be regarded as a participating tenant, shall be signed by the person or persons in question.

(10) In this section references to assignment include an assent by personal representatives and assignment by operation of law, where the assignment is—

(a) to a trustee in bankruptcy, or
(b) to a mortgagee under section 89(2) of the Law of Property Act 1925 (foreclosure of leasehold mortgage),

and references to an assignee shall be construed accordingly.

(11) Nothing in this section has effect for requiring or authorising anything to be done at any time after a binding contract is entered into in pursuance of the initial notice.

15.—(1) The nominee purchaser shall conduct on behalf of the participating tenants all proceedings arising out of the initial notice, with a view to the eventual acquisition by him, on their behalf, of such freehold and other interests as fall to be so acquired under a contract entered into in pursuance of that notice.

(2) In relation to any claim to exercise the right to collective enfranchisement with respect to any premises, the nominee purchaser shall be such person or persons as may for the time being be appointed for the purposes of this section by the participating tenants; and in the first instance the nominee purchaser shall be the person or persons specified in the initial notice in pursuance of section 13(3)(*f*).

(3) The appointment of any person as the nominee purchaser, or as one of the persons constituting the nominee purchaser, may be terminated by the participating tenants by the giving of a notice stating that that person's appointment is to terminate on the date on which the notice is given.

(4) Any such notice must be given—

(a) to the person whose appointment is being terminated, and
(b) to the reversioner in respect of the specified premises.

(5) Any such notice must in addition either—

(a) specify the name or names of the person or persons constituting the nominee purchaser as from the date of the giving of the notice, and an address in England and Wales at which notices may be given to that person or those persons under this Chapter; or

(b) state that the following particulars will be contained in a further notice given to the reversioner within the period of 28 days beginning with that date, namely—

(i) the name of the person or persons for the time being constituting the nominee purchaser,

(ii) if falling after that date,the date of appointment of that

(iii) an address in England and Wales at which notices may be given to that person or those persons under this Chapter;

and the appointment of any person by way of replacement for the person whose appointment is being terminated shall not be valid unless his name is specified, or is one of those specified, under paragraph (a) or (b).

(6) Where the appointment of any person is terminated in accordance with this section, anything done by or in relation to the nominee purchaser before the date of termination of that person's appointment shall be treated, so far as necessary for the purpose of continuing its effect, as having been done by or in relation to the nominee purchaser as constituted on or after that date.

(7) Where the appointment of any person is so terminated, he shall not be liable under section 33 for any costs incurred in connection with the proposed acquisition under this Chapter at any time after the date of termination of his appointment; but if—

(a) at any such time he is requested by the nominee purchaser for the time being to supply to the nominee purchaser, at an address in England and Wales specified in the request, all or any documents in his custody or under his control that relate to that acquisition, and

(b) he fails without reasonable cause to comply with any such request or is guilty of any unreasonable delay in complying with it,

he shall be liable for any costs which are incurred by the nominee purchaser, or for which the nominee purchaser is liable under section 33, in consequence of the failure.

(8) Where—

(a) two or more persons together constitute the nominee purchaser, and

(b) the appointment of any (but not both or all) of them is terminated in accordance with this section without any person being appointed by way of immediate replacement,

the person or persons remaining shall for the time being constitute the nominee purchaser.

(9) Where—

(a) a notice given under subsection (3) contains such a statement as is mentioned in subsection (5)(*b*), and
(b) as a result of the termination of the appointment in question there is no nominee purchaser for the time being,

the running of any period which—

(i) is prescribed by or under this Part for the giving of any other notice or the making of any application, and
(ii) would otherwise expire during the period beginning with the date of the giving of the notice under subsection (3) and ending with the date when the particulars specified in subsection (5)(*b*) are notified to the reversioner,

shall (subject to subsection (10)) be suspended throughout the period mentioned in paragraph (ii).

(10) If—

(a) the circumstances are as mentioned in subsection (9)(*a*) and (*b*), but
(b) the particulars specified in subsection (5)(*b*) are not notified to the reversioner within the period of 28 days specified in that provision.

the initial notice shall be deemed to have been withdrawn at the end of that period.

(11) A copy of any notice given under subsection (3) or (5)(*b*) shall be given by the participating tenants to every relevant landlord (other than the reversioner) to whom the initial notice or copy of it was given in accordance with section 13 and Part II of Schedule 3; and, where a notice under subsection (3) terminates the appointment of a person who is one of two or more persons together constituting the nominee purchaser, a copy of the notice shall also be so given to every other person included among those persons.

(12) Nothing in this section applies in relation to the termination of the appointment of the nominee purchaser (or of any of the persons constituting the nominee purchaser) at any time after a binding contract is entered into in pursuance of the initial notice; and in this Chapter references to the nominee purchaser, so far as referring to anything done by or in relation to the nominee purchaser at any time falling after such a contract is so entered into, are references to the person or persons constituting the nominee purchaser at the time when the contract is entered into or such other person as is for the time being the purchaser under the contract.

16.—(1) The appointment of any person as the nominee purchaser, or as one of the persons constituting the nominee purchaser, may be terminated by that person by the giving of a notice stating that he is resigning his appointment with effect from 21 days after the date of the notice.

(2) Any such notice must be given—

(a) to each of the participating tenants; and
(b) to the reversioner in respect of the specified premises.

(3) Where the participating tenants have received any such notice, they shall, within the period of 56 days beginning with the date of the notice, give to the reversioner a notice informing him of the resignation and containing the following particulars, namely—

(a) the name or names of the person or persons for the time being constituting the nominee purchaser,
(b) if falling after that date, the date of appointment of that person or of each of those persons, and
(c) an address in England and Wales at which notices may be given to that person or those persons under this Chapter;

and the appointment of any person by way of replacement for the person resigning his appointment shall not be valid unless his name is specified, or is one of those specified, under paragraph (a).

(4) Subsections (6) to (8) of section 15 shall have effect in connection with a person's resignation of his appointment in accordance with this section as they have effect in connection with the termination of a person's appointment in accordance with that section.

(5) Where the person, or one of the persons, constituting the nominee purchaser dies, the participating tenants shall, within the period of 56 days beginning with the date of death, give to the reversioner a notice informing him of the death and containing the following particulars, namely—

(a) the name or names of the person or persons for the time being constituting the nominee purchaser,
(b) if falling after that date, the date of appointment of that person or of each of those persons, and
(c) an address in England and Wales at which notices may be given to that person or those persons under this Chapter;

and the appointment of any person by way of replacement for the person who has died shall not be valid unless his name is specified, or is one of those specified, under paragraph (a).

(6) Subsections (6) and (8) of section 15 shall have effect in connection with the death of any such person as they have effect in connection with the termination of a person's appointment in accordance with that section.

(7) If—

(a) the participating tenants are required to give a notice under subsection (3) or (5), and
(b) as a result of the resignation or death referred to in that subsection there is no nominee purchaser for the time being,

the running of any period which—

(i) is prescribed by or under this Part for the giving of any other notice or the making of any application, and
(ii) would otherwise expire during the period beginning with the relevant date and ending with the date when the particulars specified in that subsection are notified to the reversioner,

shall (subject to subsection (8)) be suspended throughout the period mentioned in paragraph (ii); and for this purpose "the relevant date" means the date of the notice of resignation under subsection (1) or the date of death (as the case may be).

(8) If—

(a) the circumstances are as mentioned in subsection (7)(*a*) and (*b*), but
(b) the participating tenants fail to give a notice under subsection (3) or (as the case may be) subsection (5) within the period of 56 days specified in that subsection,

the initial notice shall be deemed to have been withdrawn at the end of that period.

(9) Where a notice under subsection (1) is given by a person who is one of two or more persons together constituting the nominee purchaser, a copy of the notice shall be given by him to every other person included among those persons; and a copy of any notice given under subsection (3) or (5) shall be given by the participating tenants to every relevant landlord (other than the reversioner) to whom the initial notice or a copy of it was given in accordance with section 13 and Part II of Schedule 3.

(10) Nothing in this section applies in relation to the registration or death of the nominee purchaser (or any of the persons together constituting the nominee purchaser) at any time after a binding contract is entered into in pursuance of the initial notice.

Procedure following giving of initial notice

17.—(1) Once the initial notice or a copy of it has been given in accordance with section 13 or Part II of Schedule 3 to the reversioner or to any other relevant landlord, that person and any person authorised to act on his behalf shall, in the case of—

(a) any part of the specified premises, or

(b) any part of any property specified in the notice under section 13(3)(*a*)(ii),

in which he has a freehold or leasehold interest which is included in the proposed acquisition by the nominee purchaser, have a right of access thereto for the purpose of enabling him to obtain a valuation of that interest in connection with the notice.

(2) Once the initial notice has been given in accordance with section 13, the nominee purchaser and any person authorised to act on his behalf shall have a right of access to—

(a) any part of the specified premises, or
(b) any part of any property specified in the notice under section 13(3)(*a*)(ii),

where such access is reasonably required by the nominee purchaser in connection with any matter arising out of the notice.

(3) A right of access conferred by this section shall be exercisable at any reasonable time and on giving not less than 10 days' notice to the occupier of any premises to which access is sought (or, if those premises are unoccupied, to the person entitled to occupy them).

18.—(1) If at any time during the period beginning with the relevant date and ending with the valuation date for the purposes of Schedule 6—

(a) there subsists between the nominee purchaser and a person other than a participating tenant any agreement (of whatever nature) providing for the disposal of a relevant interest, or
(b) if the nominee purchaser is a company, any person other than a participating tenant holds any share in that company by virtue of which a relevant interest may be acquired,

the existence of that agreement or shareholding shall be notified to the reversioner by the nominee purchaser as soon as possible after the agreement or shareholding is made or established or, if in existence on the relevant date, as soon as possible after that date.

(2) If—

(a) the nominee purchaser is required to give any notification under subsection (1) but fails to do so before the price payable to the reversioner or any other relevant landlord in respect of the acquisition of any interest of his by the nominee purchaser is determined for the purposes of Schedule 6, and
(b) it may reasonably be assumed that, had the nominee purchaser given the notification, it would have resulted in the price so determined being increased by an amount referable to the existence of any agreement or shareholding falling within subsection (1)(*a*) or (*b*),

the nominee purchaser and the participating tenants shall be jointly and severally liable to pay the amount to the reversioner or (as the case may be) the other relevant landlord.

(3) In subsection (1) "relevant interest" means any interest in, or in any part of, the specified premises or any property specified in the initial notice under section 13(3)(*a*)(ii).

(4) Paragraph (a) of subsection (1) does not, however, apply to an agreement if the only disposal of such an interest for which it provides is one consisting in the creation of an interest by way of security for a loan.

19.—(1) Where the initial notice has been registered in accordance with section 97(1), then so long as it continues in force—

(a) the person who owns the freehold of the specified premises shall not—
  (i) make any disposal severing his interest in those premises or in any property specified in the notice under section 13(3)(*a*)(ii), or
  (ii) grant out of that interest any lease under which, if it had been granted before the relevant date, the interest of the tenant would to any extent have been liable on that date to acquisition by virtue of section 2(1)(*a*) or (*b*); and
(b) no other relevant landlord shall grant out of his interest in the specified premises or in any property so specified any such lease as is mentioned in paragraph (*a*)(ii);

and any transaction shall be void to the extent that it purports to effect any such disposal or any such grant of a lease as is mentioned in paragraph (*a*) or (*b*).

(2) Where the initial notice has been so registered and at any time when it continues in force—

(a) the person who owns the freehold of the specified premises disposes of his interest in those premises or in any property specified in the notice under section 13(3)(*a*)(ii), or
(b) any other relevant landlord disposes of any interest of his specified in the notice under section 13(3)(*c*)(i),

subsection (3) below shall apply in relation to that disposal.

(3) Where this subsection applies in relation to any such disposal as is mentioned in subsection (2)(*a*) or (*b*), all parties shall for the purposes of this Chapter be in the same position as if the person acquiring the interest under the disposal—

(a) had become its owner before the initial notice was given (and was accordingly a relevant landlord in place of the person making the disposal), and
(b) had been given any notice or copy of a notice given under this Chapter to that person, and

(c) had taken all steps which that person had taken;

and, if any subsequent disposal of that interest takes place at any time when the initial notice continues in force, this subsection shall apply in relation to that disposal as if any reference to the person making the disposal included any predecessor in title of his.

(4) Where immediately before the relevant date there is in force a binding contract relating to the disposal to any extent—

(a) by the person who owns the freehold of the specified premises, or

(b) by any other relevant landlord,

of any interest of his falling within subsection (2)(*a*) or (*b*), then, so long as the initial notice continues in force, the operation of the contract shall be suspended so far as it relates to any such disposal.

(5) Where—

(a) the operation of a contract has been suspended under subsection (4) ("the suspended contract"), and

(b) a binding contract is entered into in pursuance of the initial notice,

then (without prejudice to the general law as to the frustration of contracts) the person referred to in paragraph (*a*) or (*b*) of that subsection shall, together with all other persons, be discharged from the further performance of the suspended contract so far as it relates to any such disposal as is mentioned in subsection (4).

(6) In subsections (4) and (5) any reference to a contract (except in the context of such a contract as is mentioned in subsection (5)(*b*)) includes a contract made in pursuance of an order of any court; but those subsections do not apply to any contract providing for the eventuality of a notice being given under section 13 in relation to the whole or part of the property in which any such interest as is referred to in subsection (4) subsists.

20.—(1) The reversioner in respect of the specified premises may, within the period of 21 days beginning with the relevant date, give the nominee purchaser a notice requiring him, in the case of any person by whom the initial notice was given, to deduce the title of that person to the lease by virtue of which it is claimed that he is a qualifying tenant of a flat contained in the specified premises.

(2) The nominee purchaser shall comply with any such requirement within the period of 21 days beginning with the date of the giving of the notice.

(3) Where—

(a) the nominee purchaser fails to comply with a requirement under subsection (1) in the case of any person within the period mentioned in subsection (2), and

(b) the initial notice would not have been given in accordance with section 13(2)(*b*) if—
 (i) that person, and
 (ii) any other person in the case of whom a like failure by the nominee purchaser has occurred,

had been neither included among the persons who gave the notice nor included among the qualifying tenants of the flats referred to in that provision,

the initial notice shall be deemed to have been withdrawn at the end of that period.

21.—(1) The reversioner in respect of the specified premises shall give a counter-notice under this section to the nominee purchaser by the date specified in the initial notice in pursuance of section 13(3)(*g*).

(2) The counter-notice must comply with one of the following requirements, namely—

(a) state that the reversioner admits that the participating tenants were on the relevant date entitled to exercise the right to collective enfranchisement in relation to the specified premises;
(b) state that, for such reasons as are specified in the counter-notice, the reversioner does not admit that the participating tenants were so entitled;
(c) contain such a statement as is mentioned in paragraph (*a*) or (*b*) above but state that an application for an order under subsection (1) of section 23 is to be made by such appropriate landlord (within the meaning of that section) as is specified in the counter-notice, on the grounds that he intends to redevelop the whole or a substantial part of the specified premises.

(3) If the counter-notice complies with the requirement set out in subsection (2)(*a*), it must in addition—

(a) state which (if any) of the proposals contained in the initial notice are accepted by the reversioner and which (if any) of those proposals are not so accepted, and specify—
 (i) in relation to any proposal which is not so accepted, the reversioner's counter-proposal, and
 (ii) any additional leaseback proposals by the reversioner;
(b) if (in a case where any property specified in the initial notice under section 13(3)(*a*)(ii) is property falling within section 1(3)(*b*)) any such counter-proposal relates to the grant of rights or the disposal of any freehold interest in pursuance of section 1(4), specify—
 (i) the nature of those rights and the property over which it is proposed to grant them, or
 (ii) the property in respect of which it is proposed to dispose of any such interest,

as the case may be;

(c) state which interests (if any) the nominee purchaser is to be required to acquire in accordance with subsection (4) below;

(d) state which rights (if any) the person who owns the freehold of the specified premises, or any other relevant landlord, desires to retain—

(i) over any property in which he has any interest which is included in the proposed acquisition by the nominee purchaser, or

(ii) over any property in whcih he has any interest which the nominee purchaser is to be required to acquire in accordance with subsection (4) below,

on the grounds that the rights are necessary for the proper management or maintenance of property in which he is to retain a freehold or leasehold interest; and

(e) include a description of any provisions which the reversioner or any other relevant landlord considers should be included in any conveyance to the nominee purchaser in accordance with section 34 and Schedule 7.

(4) The nominee purchaser may be required to acquire on behalf of the participating tenants the interest in any property of the person who owns the freehold of the specified premises or of any other relevant landlord, if the property—

(a) would for all practical purposes cease to be of use and benefit to him or

(b) would cease to be capable of being reasonably managed or maintained by him,

in the event of his interest in the specified premises or (as the case may be) in any other property being acquired by the nominee purchaser under this Chapter.

(5) Where a counter-notice specifies any interest in pursuance of subsection (3)(*c*), the nominee purchaser or any person authorised to act on his behalf shall, in the case of any part of the property in which that interest subsists, have a right of access thereto for the purpose of enabling the nominee purchaser to obtain, in connection with the proposed acquisition by him, a valuation of that interest; and subsection (3) of section 17 shall apply in relation to the exercise of that right as it applies in relation to the exercise of a right of access conferred by that section.

(6) Every counter-notice must specify an address in England and Wales at which notices may be given to the reversioner under this Chapter.

(7) The reference in subsection (3)(*a*)(ii) to additional leaseback proposals is a reference to proposals which relate to the leasing back, in accordance with section 36 and Schedule 9, of flats or other units contained in the specified premises and which are made either—

(a) in respect of flats or other units in relation to which Part II of that Schedule is applicable but which were not specified in the initial notice under section 13(3)(*c*)(ii), or

(b) in respect of flats or other units in relation to which Part III of that Schedule is applicable.

(8) Schedule 4 (which imposes requirements as to the furnishing of information by the reversioner about the exercise of rights under Chapter II with respect to flats contained in the specified premises) shall have effect.

Applications to court or leasehold valuation tribunal

22.—(1) Where—

(a) the reversioner in respect of the specified premises has given the nominee purchaser a counter-notice under section 21 which (whether it complies with the requirement set out in subsection (2)(*b*) or (*c*) of that section) contains such a statement as is mentioned in subsection (2)(*b*) of that section, but

(b) the court is satisfied, on an application made by the nominee purchaser, that the participating tenants were on the relevant date entitled to exercise the right to collective enfranchisement in relation to the specified premises,

the court shall by order make a declaration to that effect.

(2) Any application for an order under subsection (1) must be made not later than the end of the period of two months beginning with the date of the giving of the counter-notice to the nominee purchaser.

(3) If on any such application the court makes an order under subsection (1), then (subject to subsection (4)) the court shall make an order—

(a) declaring that the reversioner's counter-notice shall be of no effect, and

(b) requiring the reversioner to give a further counter-notice to the nominee purchaser by such date as is specified in the order.

(4) Subsection (3) shall not apply if—

(a) the counter-notice complies with the requirement set out in section 21(2)(*c*), and

(b) either—

  (i) an application for an order under section 23(1) is pending, or

  (ii) the period specified in section 23(3) as the period for the making of such an application has not expired.

(5) Subsections (3) to (5) of section 21 shall apply to any further counter-notice required to be given by the reversioner under subsection

(3) above as if it were a counter-notice under that section complying with the requirement set out in subsection (2)(*a*) of that section.

(6) If an application by the nominee purchaser for an order under subsection (1) is dismissed by the court, the initial notice shall cease to have effect at the time when the order dismissing the application becomes final.

23.—(1) Where the reversioner in respect of the specified premises has given a counter-notice under section 21 which complies with the requirement set out in subsection (2)(*c*) of that section, the court may, on the application of any appropriate landlord, by order declare that the right to collective enfranchisement shall not be exercisable in relation to those premises by reason of that landlord's intention to redevelop the whole or a substantial part of the premises.

(2) The court shall not make an order under subsection (1) unless it is satisfied—

- (a) that not less than two-thirds of all the long leases on which flats contained in the specified premises are held are due to terminate within the period of five years beginning with the relevant date; and
- (b) that for the purposes of redevelopment the applicant intends, once the leases in question have so terminated—
  - (i) to demolish or reconstruct, or
  - (ii) to carry out substantial works of construction on,

  the whole or a substantial part of the specified premises; and
- (c) that he could not reasonably do so without obtaining possession of the flats demised by those leases.

(3) Any application for an order under subsection (1) must be made within the period of two months beginning with the date of the giving of the counter-notice to the nominee purchaser; but, where the counter-notice is one falling within section 22(1)(*a*), such an application shall not be proceeded with until such time (if any) as an order under section 22(1) becomes final.

(4) Where an order under subsection (1) is made by the court, the initial notice shall cease to have effect on the order becoming final.

(5) Where an application for an order under subsection (1) is dismissed by the court, the court shall make an order—

- (a) declaring that the reversioner's counter-notice shall be of no effect, and
- (b) requiring the reversioner to give a further counter-notice to the nominee purchaser by such date as is specified in the order.

(6) Where—

- (a) the reversioner has given such a counter-notice as is mentioned in subsection (1), but

(b) either—

(i) no application for an order under that subsection is made within the period referred to in subsection (3), or

(ii) such an application is so made but is subsequently withdrawn,

then (subject to subsection (8)), the reversioner shall give a further counter-notice to the nominee purchaser within the period of two months beginning with the appropriate date.

(7) In subsection (6) "the appropriate date" means—

(a) if subsection (6)(*b*)(i) applies, the date immediately following the end of the period referred to in subsection (3); and

(b) if subsection (6)(*b*)(ii) applies, the date of withdrawal of the application.

(8) Subsection (6) shall not apply if any application has been made by the nominee purchaser under section 22(1).

(9) Subsections (3) to (5) of section 21 shall apply to any further counter-notice required to be given by the reversioner under subsection (5) or (6) above as if it were a counter-notice under that section complying with the requirement set out in subsection (2)(*a*) of that section.

(10) In this section "appropriate landlord", in reltion to the specified premises, means—

(a) the reversioner or any other relevant landlord; or

(b) any two or more persons falling within paragraph (a) who are acting together.

24.—(1) Where the reversioner in respect of the specified premises has given the nominee purchaser—

(a) a counter-notice under section 21 complying with the requirement set out in subsection (2)(*a*) of that section, or

(b) a further counter-notice required by or by virtue of section 22(3) or section 23(5) or (6),

but any of the terms of acquisition remain in dispute at the end of the period of two months beginning with the date on which the counter-notice or further counter-notice was so given, a leasehold valuation tribunal may, on the application of either the nominee purchaser or the reversioner, determine the matters in dispute.

(2) Any application under subsection (1) must be made not later than the end of the period of six months beginning with the date on which the counter-notice or further counter-notice was given to the nominee purchaser.

(3) Where—

(a) the reversioner has given the nominee purchaser such a counter-notice or further counter-notice as is mentioned in subsection (1)(*a*) or (*b*), and
(b) all of the terms of acquisition have been either agreed between the parties or determined by a leasehold valuation tribunal under subsection (1),

but a binding contract incorporating those terms has not been entered into by the end of the appropriate period specified in subsection (6), the court may, on the application of either the nominee purchaser or the reversioner, make such order under subsection (4) as it thinks fit.

(4) The court may under this subsection make an order—

(a) providing for the interests to be acquired by the nominee purchaser to be vested in him on the terms referred to in subsection (3);
(b) providing for those interests to be vested in him on those terms, but subject to such modifications as—
    (i) may have been determined by a leasehold valuation tribunal, on the application of either the nominee purchaser or the reversioner, to be required by reason of any change in circumstances since the time when the terms were agreed or determined as mentioned in that subsection, and
    (ii) are specified in the order; or
(c) providing for the initial notice to be deemed to have been withdrawn at the end of the appropriate period specified in subsection (6);

and Schedule 5 shall have effect in relation to any such order as is mentioned in paragraph (*a*) or (*b*) above.

(5) Any application for an order under subsection (4) must be made not later than the end of the period of two months beginning immediately after the end of the appropriate period specified in subsection (6).

(6) For the purposes of this section the appropriate period is—

(a) where all of the terms of acquisition have been agreed between the parties, the period of two months beginning with the date when those terms were finally so agreed;
(b) where all or any of those terms have been determined by a leasehold valuation tribunal under subsection (1)—
    (i) the period of two months beginning with the date when the decision of the tribunal under that subsection becomes final, or
    (ii) such other period as may have been fixed by the tribunal when making its determination.

(7) In this section "the parties" means the nominee purchaser and the reversioner and any relevant landlord who has given to those persons a notice for the purposes of paragraph 7(1)(*a*) of Schedule 1.

(8) In this Chapter "the terms of acquisition", in relation to a claim made under this Chapter, means the terms of the proposed acquisition by the nominee purchaser, whether relating to—

(a) the interest to be acquired,
(b) the extent of the property to which those interests relate or the rights to be granted over any property,
(c) the amounts payable as the purchase price for such interests,
(d) the apportionment of conditions or other matters in connection with the severance of any reversionary interest, or
(e) the provisions to be contained in any conveyance, or

otherwise, and includes any such terms in respect of any interest to be acquired in pursuance of section 1(4) or 21(4).

25.—(1) Where the initial notice has been given in accordance with section 13 but—

(a) the reversioner has failed to give the nominee purchaser a counter-notice in accordance with section 21(1), or
(b) if required to give the nominee purchaser a further counter-notice by or by virtue of section 22(3) or section 23(5) or (6), the reversioner has failed to comply with that requirement,

the court may, on the application of the nominee purchaser, make an order determining the terms on which he is to acquire, in accordance with the proposals contained in the initial notice, such interests and rights as are specified in it under section 13(3).

(2) The terms determined by the court under subsection (1) shall, if Part II of Schedule 9 is applicable, include terms which provide for the leasing back, in accordance with section 36 and that Part of that Schedule, of flats or other units contained in the specified premises.

(3) The court shall not make any order on an application made by virtue of paragraph (a) of subsection (1) unless it is satisfied—

(a) that the participating tenants were on the relevant date entitled to exercise the right to collective enfranchisement in relation to the specified premises; and
(b) if applicable, that the requirements of Part II of Schedule 3 were complied with as respects the giving of copies of the initial notice.

(4) Any application for an order under subsection (1) must be made not later than the end of the period of six months beginning with the date by which the counter-notice or further counter-notice referred to in that subsection was to be given to the nominee purchaser.

(5) Where—

(a) the terms of acquisition have been determined by an order of the court under subsection (1), but

(b) a binding contract incorporating those terms has not been entered into by the end of the appropriate period specified in subsection (8),

the court may, on the application of either the nominee purchaser or the reversioner, make such order under subsection (6) as it thinks fit.

(6) The court may under this subsection make an order—

(a) providing for the interests to be acquired by the nominee purchaser to be vested in him on the terms referred to in subsection (5);

(b) providing for those interests to be vested in him on those terms, but subject to such modifications as—

(i) may have been determined by a leasehold valuation tribunal, on the application of either the nominee purchaser or the reversioner, to be required by reason of any change in circumstances since the time when the terms were determined as mentioned in that subsection, and

(ii) are specified in the order; or

(c) providing for the initial notice to be deemed to have been withdrawn at the end of the appropriate period specified in subsection (8);

and Schedule 5 shall have effect in relation to any such order as is mentioned in paragraph (*a*) or (*b*) above.

(7) Any application for an order under subsection (6) must be made not later than the end of the period of two months beginning immediately after the end of the appropriate period specified in subsection (8).

(8) For the purposes of this section the appropriate period is—

(a) the period of two months beginning with the date when the order of the court under subsection (1) becomes final, or

(b) such other period as may have been fixed by the court when making that order.

26.—(1) Where not less than two-thirds of the qualifying tenants of flats contained in any premises to which this Chapter applies desire to make a claim to exercise the right to collective enfranchisement in relation to those premises but—

(a) (in a case to which section 9(1) applies) the person who owns the freehold of the premises cannot be found or his identity cannot be ascertained, or

(b) (in a case to which section 9(2) applies) each of the relevant landlords is someone who cannot be found or whose identity cannot be ascertained, the court may, on the application of the qualifying tenants in question, make a vesting order under this subsection—

(i) with respect to any interests of that person (whether in those premises or in any other property) which are liable to acquisition on behalf of those tenants by virtue of section 1(1) or (2)(*a*) or section 2(1), or

(ii) with respect to any interests of those landlords which are so liable to acquisition by virtue of any of those provisions,

as the case may be.

(2) Where in a case to which section 9(2) applies—

(a) not less than two-thirds of the qualifying tenants of flats contained in any premises to which this Chapter applies desire to make a claim to exercise the right to collective enfranchisement in relation to those premises, and

(b) paragraph (*b*) of subsection (1) does not apply, but

(c) a notice of that claim or (as the case may be) a copy of such a notice cannot be given in accordance with section 13 or Part II of Schedule 3 to any person to whom it would otherwise be required to be so given because he cannot be found or his identity cannot be ascertained,

the court may, on the application of the qualifying tenants in question, make an order dispensing with the need to give such a notice or (as the case may be) a copy of such a notice to that person.

(3) If that person is the person who owns the freehold of the premises, then on the application of those tenants, the court may, in connection with an order under subsection (2), make an order appointing any other relevant landlord to be the reversioner in respect of the premises in place of that person; and if it does so references in this Chapter to the reversioner shall apply accordingly.

(4) The court shall not make an order on any application under subsection (1) or (2) unless it is satisfied—

(a) that on the date of the making of the application the premises to which the application relates were premises to which this Chapter applies; and

(b) that on that date the applicants would not have been precluded by any provision of this Chapter from giving a valid notice under section 13 with respect to those premises.

(5) Before making any such order the court may require the applicants to take such further steps by way of advertisement or otherwise as the court thinks proper for the purpose of tracing the person or persons in question; and if, after an application is made for a vesting order under subsection (1) and before any interest is vested in pursuance of the

application, the person or (as the case may be) any of the persons referred to in paragraph (*a*) or (*b*) of that subsection is traced, then no further proceedings shall be taken with a view to any interest being so vested, but (subject to subsection (6))—

(a) the rights and obligations of all parties shall be determined as if the applicants had, at the date of the application, duly given notice under section 13 of their claim to exercise the right to collective enfranchisement in relation to the premises to which the application relates; and
(b) the court may give such directions as the court thinks fit as to the steps to be taken for giving effect to those rights and obligations, including directions modifying or dispensing with any of the requirements of this Chapter or of regulations made under this Part.

(6) An application for a vesting order under subsection (1) may be withdrawn at any time before execution of a conveyance under section 27(3) and, after it is withdrawn, subsection (5)(*a*) above shall not apply; but where any step is taken (whether by the applicants or otherwise) for the purpose of giving effect to subsection (5)(*a*) in the case of any application, the application shall not afterwards be withdrawn except—

(a) with the consent of every person who is the owner of any interest the vesting of which is sought by the applicants, or
(b) by leave of the court,

and the court shall not give leave unless it appears to the court just to do so by reason of matters coming to the knowledge of the applicants in consequence of the tracing of any such person.

(7) Where an order has been made under subsection (2) dispensing with the need to give a notice under section 13, or a copy of such a notice, to a particular person with respect to any particular premises, then if—

(a) a notice is subsequently given under that section with respect to those premises, and
(b) in reliance on the order, the notice or a copy of the notice is not to be given to that person,

the notice must contain a statement of the effect of the order.

(8) Where a notice under section 13 contains such a statement in accordance with subsection (7) above, then in determining for the purposes of any provision of this Chapter whether the requirements of section 13 or Part II of Schedule 3 have been complied with in relation to the notice, those requirements shall be deemed to have been complied with so far as relating to the giving of the notice or a copy of it to the person referred to in subsection (7) above.

(9) Rules of court shall make provision—

(a) for requiring notice of any application under subsection (3) to be served by the persons making the application on any person who the applicants know or have reason to believe is a relevant landlord; and
(b) for enabling persons served with any such notice to be joined as parties to the proceedings.

27.—(1) A vesting order under section 26(1) is an order providing for the vesting of any such interests as are referred to in paragraph (i) or (ii) of that provision—

(a) in such person or persons as may be appointed for the purpose by the applicants for the order, and
(b) on such terms as may be determined by a leasehold valuation tribunal to be appropriate with a view to the interests being vested in that person or those persons in the like manner (so far as the circumstances permit) as if the applicants had, at the date of their application, given notice under section 13 of their claim to exercise the right to collective enfranchisement in relation to the premises with respect to which the order is made.

(2) If a leasehold valuation tribunal so determines in the case of a vesting order under section 26(1), the order shall have effect in relation to interests which are less extensive than those specified in the application on which the order was made.

(3) Where any interests are to be vested in any person or persons by virtue of a vesting order under section 26(1), then on his or their paying into court the appropriate sum in respect of each of those interests there shall be executed by such person as the court may designate a conveyance which—

(a) is in a form approved by a leasehold valuation tribunal, and
(b) contains such provisions as may be so approved for the purpose of giving effect so far as possible to the requirements of section 34 and Schedule 7;

and that conveyance shall be effective to vest in the person or persons to whom the conveyance is made the interests expressed to be conveyed, subject to and in accordance with the terms of the conveyance.

(4) In connection with the determination by a leasehold valuation tribunal of any question as to the interests to be conveyed by any such conveyance, or as to the rights with or subject to which they are to be conveyed, it shall be assumed (unless the contrary is shown) that any person whose interests are to be conveyed ("the transferor") has no interest in property other than those interests and for the purpose of excepting them from the conveyance, any minerals underlying the property in question.

(5) The appropriate sum which in accordance with subsection (3) is to be paid into court in respect of any interest is the aggregate of—

(a) such amount as may be determined by a leasehold valuation tribunal to be the price which would be payable in respect of that interest in accordance with Schedule 6 if the interest were being acquired in pursuance of such a notice as is mentioned in subsection (1)(*b*); and
(b) any amounts or estimated amounts determined by such a tribunal as being, at the time of execution of the conveyance, due to the transferor from any tenants of his of premises comprised in the premises in which that interest subsists (whether due under or in respect of their leases or under or in respect of agreements collateral thereto).

(6) Where any interest is vested in any person or persons in accordance with this section, the payment into court of the appropriate sum in respect of that interest shall be taken to have satisfied any claims against the applicants for the vesting order under section 26(1), their personal representatives or assigns in respect of the price payable under this Chapter for the acquisition of that interest.

(7) Where any interest is so vested in any person or persons, section 32(5) shall apply in relation to his or their acquisition of that interest as it applies in relation to the acquisition of any interest by a nominee purchaser.

Termination of acquistion procedures

28.—(1) At any time before a binding contract is entered into in pursuance of the initial notice, the participating tenants may withdraw that notice by the giving of a notice to that effect under this section ("a notice of withdrawal").

(2) A notice of withdrawal must be given—

(a) to the nominee purchaser;
(b) to the reversioner in respect of the specified premises; and
(c) to every other relevant landlord who is known or believed by the participating tenants to have given to the nominee purchaser a notice under paragraph 7(1) or (4) of Schedule 1;

and, if by virtue of paragraph (*c*) a notice of withdrawal fails to be given to any person falling within that paragraph, it shall state that he is a recipient of the notice.

(3) The nominee purchaser shall, on receiving a notice of withdrawal, give a copy of it to every relevant landlord who—

(a) has given to the nominee purchaser such a notice as is mentioned in subsection (2)(*c*); and

(b) is not stated in the notice of withdrawal to be a recipient of it.

(4) Where a notice of withdrawal is given by the participating tenants under subsection (1)—

(a) those persons, and
(b) (subject to subsection (5)) every other person who is not a participating tenant for the time being but has at any time been such a tenant,

shall be liable—

(i) to the reversioner, and
(ii) to every other relevant landlord,

for all relevant costs incurred by him in pursuance of the initial notice down to the time when the notice of withdrawal or a copy of it is given to him in accordance with subsection (2) or (3).

(5) A person falling within paragraph (*b*) of subsection (4) shall not be liable for any costs by virtue of that subsection if—

(a) the lease in respect of which was a participating tenant has been assigned to another person; and
(b) that other person has become a participating tenant in accordance with section 14(4);

and in paragraph (a) above the reference to an assignment shall be construed in accordance with section 14(10).

(6) Where any liability for costs arises under subsection (4)—

(a) it shall be a joint and several liability of the persons concerned; and
(b) the nominee purchaser shall not be liable for any costs under section 33.

(7) In subsection (4) "relevant costs", in relation to the reversioner or any other relevant landlord, means costs for which the nominee purchaser would (apart from subsection (6)) be liable to that person under section 33.

29.—(1) Where, in a case falling within paragraph (*a*) of subsection (1) of section 22—

(a) no application for an order under that subsection is made within the period specified in subsection (2) of that section, or
(b) such an application is so made but is subsequently withdrawn,

the initial notice shall be deemed to have been withdrawn—

(i) (if paragraph (*a*) applies) at the end of that period, or

(ii) (if paragraph (*b*) above applies) on the date of the withdrawal of the application.

(2) Where—

(a) in a case to which subsection (1) of section 24 applies, no application under that subsection is made within the period specified in subsection (2) of that section, or
(b) in a case to which subsection (3) of that section applies, no application for an order under subsection (4) of that section is made within the period specified in subsection (5) of that section,

the initial notice shall be deemed to have been withdrawn at the end of the period referred to in paragraph (*a*) or (*b*) above (as the case may be).

(3) Where, in a case falling within paragraph (*a*) or (*b*) of subsection (1) of section 25, no application for an order under that subsection is made within the period specified in subsection (4) of that section, the initial notice shall be deemed to have been withdrawn at the end of that period.

(4) Where, in a case to which subsection (5) of section 25 applies, no application for an order under subsection (6) of that section is made within the period specified in subsection (7) of that section, the initial notice shall be deemed to have been withdrawn at the end of that period.

(5) The following provisions, namely—

(a) section 15(10),
(b) section 16(8),
(c) section 20(3),
(d) section 24(4)(*c*), and
(e) section 25(6)(*c*),

also make provision for a notice under section 13 to be deemed to have been withdrawn at a particular time.

(6) Where the initial notice is deemed to have been withdrawn at any time by virtue of any provision of this Chapter, subsections (4) and (5) of section 28 shall apply for the purposes of this section in like manner as they apply where a notice of withdrawal is given under that section, but as if the reference in subsection (4) of that section to the time when a notice or copy is given as there mentioned were a reference to the time when the initial notice is so deemed to have been withdrawn.

(7) Where the initial notice is deemed to have been withdrawn by virtue of section 15(10) or 16(8)—

(a) the liability for costs arising by virtue of subsection (6) above shall be a joint and several liability of the persons concerned; and
(b) the nominee purchaser shall not be liable for any costs under section 33.

(8) In the provisions applied by subsection (6), "relevant costs", in relation to the reversioner or any other relevant landlord, means costs for which the nominee purchaser is, or would (apart from subsection (7)) be, liable to that person under section 33.

30.—(1) A notice given under section 13 shall be of no effect if on the relevant date—

(a) any acquiring authority has, with a view to the acquisition of the whole or part of the specified premises for any authorised purpose—
  (i) served notice to treat on any relevant person, or
  (ii) entered into a contract for the purchase of the interest of any such person in the premises or part of them, and
(b) the notice to treat or contract remains in force.

(2) In subsection (1) "relevant person", in relation to the specified premises, means—

(a) the person who owns the freehold of the premises; or
(b) any other person who owns any leasehold interest in the premises which is specified in the initial notice under section 13(3)(*c*)(i).

(3) A notice given under section 13 shall not specify under subsection (3)(*a*)(ii) or (*c*)(i) of that section any property or leasehold interest in property if on the relevant date—

(a) any acquiring authority has, with a view to the acquisition of the whole or part of the property for any authorised purpose—
  (i) served notice to treat on the person who owns the freehold of, or any such leasehold interest in, the property, or
  (ii) entered into a contract for the purchase of the interest of any such person in the property or part of it, and
(b) the notice to treat or contract remains in force.

(4) A notice given under section 13 shall cease to have effect if, before a binding contract is entered into in pursuance of the notice, any acquiring authority serves, with a view to the acquisition of the whole or part of the specified premises for any authorised purpose, notice to treat as mentioned in subsection (1)(*a*).

(5) Where any such authority so serves notice to treat at any time after a binding contract is entered into in pursuance of the notice given under section 13 but before completion of the acquisition by the nominee purchaser under this Chapter, then (without prejudice to the general law as to the frustration of contracts) the parties to the contract shall be discharged from the further performance of the contract.

(6) Where subsection (4) or (5) applies in relation to the initial notice or any contract entered into in pursuance of it, then on the occasion of

the compulsory acquisition in question the compensation payable in respect of any interest in the specified premises (whether or not the one to which the relevant notice to treat relates) shall be determined on the basis of the value of the interest—

(a) (if subsection (4) applies) subject to and with the benefit of the rights and obligations arising from the initial notice and affecting that interest; or
(b) (if subsection (5) applies) subject to and with the benefit of the rights and obligations arising from the contract and affecting that interest.

(7) In this section—

(a) "acquiring authority", in relation to the specified premises or any other property, means any person or body of persons who has or have been, or could be, authorised to acquire the whole or part of those premises or that property compulsorily for any purpose; and
(b) "authorised purpose", in relation to any acquiring authority, means any such purpose.

31.—(1) A notice given under section 13 shall be of no effect if on the relevant date the whole or any part of—

(a) the specified premises, or
(b) any property specified in the notice under section 13(3)(*a*)(ii), is qualifying property.

(2) For the purposes of this section the whole or any part of the specified premises, or of any property specified as mentioned in subsection (1), is qualifying property if—

(a) it has been designated under section 31(1)(*b*), (*c*) or (*d*) of the Inheritance Tax Act 1984 (designation and undertakings relating to conditionally exempt transfers), whether with or without any other property, and no chargeable event has subsequently occurred with respect to it; or
(b) an application to the Board for it to be so designated is pending; or
(c) it is the property of a body not established or conducted for profit and a direction has been given in relation to it under section 26 of that Act (gifts for public benefit), whether with or without any other property; or
(d) an application to the Board for a direction to be so given in relation to it is pending.

(3) For the purposes of subsection (2) an application is pending as from the time when it is made to tbe Board until such time as it is either granted or refused by the Board or withdrawn by the applicant; and for

this purpose an application shall not be regarded as made unless and until the applicant has submitted to the Board all such information in support of the application as is required by the Board.

(4) A notice given under section 13 shall cease to have effect if, before a binding contract is entered into in pursuance of the notice, the whole or any part of—

(a) the specified premises, or
(b) any property specified in the notice under section 13(3)(*a*)(ii), becomes qualifying property.

(5) Where a notice under section 13 ceases to have effect by virtue of subsection (4) above—

(a) the nominee purchaser shall not be liable for any costs under section 33; and
(b) the person who applied or is applying for designation or a direction shall be liable—
    (i) to the qualifying tenants by whom the notice was given for all reasonable costs incurred by them in the preparation and giving of the notice; and
    (ii) to the nominee purchaser for all reasonable costs incurred in pursuance of the notice by him or by any other person who has acted as the nominee purchaser.

(6) Where it is claimed that subsection (1) or (4) applies in relation to a notice under section 13, the person making the claim shall, at the time of making it, furnish the nominee purchaser with evidence in support of it; and if he fails to do so he shall be liable for any costs which are reasonably incurred by the nominee purchaser in consequence of the failure.

(7) In subsection (2)—

(a) paragraphs (*a*) and (*b*) apply to designation under section 34(1)(*a*), (*b*) or (*c*) of the Finance Act 1975 or section 77(1)(*b*), (*c*) or (*d*) of the Finance Act 1976 as they apply to designation under section 31(1)(*b*), (*c*) or (*d*) of the Inheritance Tax Act 1984; and
(b) paragraphs (*c*) and (*d*) apply to a direction under paragraph 13 of Schedule 6 to the Finance Act 1975 as they apply to a direction under section 26 of that Act 1984.

(8) In this section —

"the Board" means the Commissioners of Inland Revenue;
"chargeable event" means—
(a) any event which in accordance with any provision of Chapter II of Part II of the Inheritance Tax Act 1984 (exempt transfers) is a

chargeable event, including any such provision as applied by section 78(3) of that Act (conditionally exempt occasions); or

(b) any event which would have been a chargeable event in the circumstances mentioned in section 79(3) of that Act (exemption from ten-yearly charge).

Determination of price and costs of enfranchisement

32.—(1) Schedule 6 to this Act (which relates to the determination of the price payable by the nominee purchaser in respect of each of the freehold and other interests to be acquired by him in pursuance of this Chapter) shall have effect.

(2) The lien of the owner of any such interest (as vendor) on the specified premises, or (as the case may be) on any other property, for the price payable shall extend—

(a) to any amounts which, at the time of the conveyance of that interest, are due to him from any tenants of his of premises comprised in the premises in which that interest subsists (whether due under or in respect of their leases or under or in respect of agreements collateral thereto); and
(b) to any amount payable to him by virtue of section 18(2); and
(c) to any costs payable to him by virtue of section 33.

(3) Subsection (2)(*a*) does not apply in relation to amounts due to the owner of any such interest from tenants of any premises which are to be comprised in the premises demised by a lease granted in accordance with section 36 and Schedule 9.

(4) In subsection (2) the reference to the specified premises or any other property includes a reference to a part of those premises or that property.

(5) Despite the fact that in accordance with Schedule 6 no payment or only a nominal payment is payable by the nominee purchaser in respect of the acquisition by him of any interest he shall nevertheless be deemed for all purposes to be a purchaser of that interest for a valuable consideration in money or money's worth.

33.—(1) Where a notice is given under section 13, then (subject to the provisions of this section and sections 28(6), 29(7) and 31(5)) the nominee purchaser shall be liable, to the extent that they have been incurred in pursuance of the notice by the reversioner or by any other relevant landlord, for the reasonable costs of and incidental to any of the following matters, namely—

(a) any investigation reasonably undertaken—
  (i) of the question whether any interest in the specified premises or other property is liable to acquisition in pursuance of the initial notice, or
  (ii) of any other question arising out of that notice;

(b) deducing, evidencing and verifying the title to any such interest;
(c) making out and furnishing such abstracts and copies as the nominee purchaser may require;
(d) any valuation of any interest in the specified premises or other property;
(e) any conveyance of any such interest;

but this subsection shall not apply to any costs if on a sale made voluntarily a stipulation that they were to be borne by the purchaser would be void.

(2) For the purposes of subsection (1) any costs incurred by the reversioner or any other relevant landlord in respect of professional services rendered by any person shall only be regarded as reasonable if and to the extent that costs in respect of such services might reasonably be expected to have been incurred by him if the circumstances had been such that he was personally liable for all such costs.

(3) Where by virtue of any provision of this Chapter the initial notice ceases to have effect at any time, then (subject to subsection (4)) the nominee purchaser's liability under this section for costs incurred by any person shall be a liability for costs incurred by him down to that time.

(4) The nominee purchaser shall not be liable for any costs under this section if the initial notice ceases to have effect by virtue of section 23(4) or 30(4).

(5) The nominee purchaser shall not be liable under this section for any costs which a party to any proceedings under this Chapter before a leasehold valuation tribunal incurs in connection with the proceedings.

(6) In this section references to the nominee purchaser include references to any person whose appointment has terminated in accordance with section 15(3) or 16(1); but this section shall have effect in relation to such a person subject to section 15(7).

(7) Where by virtue of this section, or of this section and section 29(6) taken together, two or more persons are liable for any costs, they shall be jointly and severally liable for them.

Completion of acquisition

34.—(1) Any conveyance executed for the purposes of this Chapter, being a conveyance to the nominee purchaser of the freehold of the specified premises or of any other property, shall grant to the nominee purchaser an estate in fee simple absolute in those premises or that property, subject only to such incumbrances as may have been agreed or determined under this Chapter to be incumbrances subject to which that estate should be granted, having regard to the following provisions of this Chapter.

(2) Any such conveyance shall, where the nominee purchaser is to acquire any leasehold interest in the specified premises or (as the case

may be) in the other property to which the conveyance relates, provide for the disposal to the nominee purchaser of any such interest.

(3) Any conveyance executed for the purposes of this Chapter shall have effect under section 2(1) of the Law of Property Act 1925 (conveyances overreaching certain equitable interests etc.) to overreach any incumbrance capable of being overreached under section 2(1)—

(a) as if, where the interest conveyed is settled land for the purposes of the Settled Land Act 1925, the conveyance were made under the powers of that Act, and
(b) as if the requirements of section 2(1) as to the payment of the capital money allowed any part of the purchase price paid or applied in accordance with section 35 below or Schedule 8 to this Act to be so paid or applied.

(4) For the purposes of this section "incumbrances" includes—

(a) rentcharges, and
(b) (subject to subsection (5)) personal liabilities attaching in respect of the ownership of land or an interest in land though not charged on that land or interest.

(5) Burdens originating in tenure, and burdens in respect of the upkeep or regulation for the benefit of any locality of any land, building, structure, works, ways or watercourse shall not be treated as incumbrances for the purposes of this section; but any conveyance executed for the purposes of this Chapter shall be made subject to any such burdens.

(6) A conveyance executed for the purposes of this Chapter shall not be made subject to any incumbrance capable of being overreached by the conveyance, but shall be made subject (where they are not capable of being overreached) to—

(a) rentcharges redeemable under sections 8 to 10 of the Rentcharges Act 1977, and
(b) those falling within paragraphs (*c*) and (*d*) of section 2(3) of that Act (estate rentcharges and rentcharges imposed under certain enactments),

except as otherwise provided by subsections (7) and (8) below.

(7) Where any land is to be conveyed to the nominee purchaser by a conveyance executed for the purposes of this Chapter, subsection (6) shall not preclude the person who owns the freehold interest in the land from releasing, or procuring the release of, the land from any rentcharge.

(8) The conveyance of any such land ("the relevant land") may, with the agreement of the nominee purchaser (which shall not be unreasonably withheld), provide in accordance with section 190(1) of the Law of Property Act 1925 (charging of rentcharges on land without rent owner's consent) that a rentcharge—

(a) shall be charged exclusively on other land affected by it in exoneration of the relevant land, or
(b) shall be apportioned between other land affected by it and the relevant land.

(9) Except to the extent that any departure is agreed to by the nominee purchaser and the person whose interest is to be conveyed, any conveyance executed for the purposes of this Chapter shall—

(a) as respects the conveyance of any freehold interest, conform with the provisions of Schedule 7, and
(b) as respects the conveyance of any leasehold interest, conform with the provisions of paragraph 2 of that Schedule (any reference in that paragraph to the freeholder being read as a reference to the person whose leasehold interest is to be conveyed).

(10) Any such conveyance shall in addition contain a statement that it is a conveyance executed for the purposes of this Chapter; and any such statement shall comply with such requirements as may be prescribed by rules made in pursuance of section 144 of the Land Registration Act 1925 (power to make general rules).

35.—(1) Subject to the provisions of Schedule 8, where any interest is acquired by the nominee purchaser in pursuance of this Chapter, the conveyance by virtue of which it is so acquired shall, as regards any mortgage to which this section applies, be effective by virtue of this section—

(a) to discharge the interest from the mortgage, and from the operation of any order made by a court for the enforcement of the mortgage, and
(b) to extinguish any term of years created for the purposes of the mortgage,

and shall do so without the persons entitled to or interested in the mortgage or in any such order or term of years becoming parties to or executing the conveyance.

(2) Subject to subsections (3) and (4), this section applies to any mortgage of the interest so acquired (however created or arising) which—

(a) is a mortgage to secure the payment of money or the performance of any other obligation by the person from whom the interest is so acquired or any other person; and
(b) is not a mortgage which would be overreached apart from this section.

(3) This section shall not apply to any such mortgage if it has been agreed between the nominee purchaser and the reversioner or (as the case may be) any other relevant landlord that the interest in question should be acquired subject to the mortgage.

(4) In this section and Schedule 8 "mortgage" includes a charge or lien; but neither this section nor that Schedule applies to a rentcharge.

36.—(1) In connection with the acquisition by him of the freehold of the specified premises, the nominee purchaser shall grant to the person from whom the freehold is acquired such leases of flats or other units contained in those premises as are required to be so granted by virtue of Part II or III of Schedule 9.

(2) Any such lease shall be granted so as to take effect immediately after the acquisition by the nominee purchaser of the freehold of the specified premises.

(3) Where any flat or other unit demised under any such lease ("the relevant lease") is at the time of that acquisition subject to any existing lease, the relevant lease shall take effect as a lease of the freehold reversion in respect of the flat or other unit.

(4) Part IV of Schedule 9 has effect with respect to the terms of a lease granted in pursuance of Part II or III of that Schedule.

37. Schedule 10 to this Act (which makes provision with respect to the acquisition of interests from local authorities etc. in purusance of this Chapter) shall have effect.

Supplemental

38.—(1) In this Chapter (unless the context otherwise requires—

"conveyance" includes assignment, transfer and surrender, and related expressions shall be construed accordingly;

"the initial notice" means the notice given under section 13;

"the nominee purchaser" shall be construed in accordance with section 15;

"the participating tenants" shall be construed in accordance with section 14;

"premises with a resident landlord" shall be construed in accordance with section 10;

"public sector landlord" means any of the persons listed in section 171(2) of the Housing Act 1985;

"qualifying tenant" shall be construed in accordance with section 5;

"the relevant date" has the meaning given by section 1(8);

"relevant landlord" and "the reversioner" shall be construed in accordance with section 9;

"the right to collective enfranchisement" means the right specified in section 1(1);

"secure tenancy" has the meaning given by section 79 of the Housing Act 1985;

"the specified premises" shall be construed in accordance with section 13(12);

"the terms of acquisition" has the meaning given by section 24(8);
"unit" means—

(a) a flat;
(b) any other separate set of premises which is constructed or adapted for use for the purposes of a dwelling; or
(c) a separate set of premises let, or intended for letting, on a business lease.

(2) Any reference in this Chapter (however expressed) to the acqusition or proposed acquisition by the nominee purchaser is a reference to the acquisition or proposed acquisition by the nominee purchaser, on behalf of the participating tenants, of such freehold and other interests as fall to be so acquired under a contract entered into in pursuance of the initial notice.

(3) Any reference in this Chapter to the interest of a relevant landlord in the specified premises is a reference to the interest in those premises by virtue of which he is, in accordance with section 9(2)(*b*), a relevant landlord.

(4) Any reference in this Chapter to agreement in reltion to all or any of the terms of acqusition is a reference to agreement subject to contract.

CHAPTER II

INDIVIDUAL RIGHT OF TENANT OF FLAT TO ACQUIRE NEW LEASE

Preliminary

39.—(1) This Chapter has effect for the purpose of conferring on a tenant of a flat, in the circumstances mentioned in subsection (2), the right, exercisable subject to and in accordance with this Chapter, to acquire a new lease of the flat on payment of a premium determined in accordance with this Chapter.

(2) Those circumstances are that on the relevant date for the purposes of this Chapter—

(a) the tenant is a qualifying tenant of the flat; and
(b) the tenant has occupied the flat as his only or principal home—
    (i) for the last three years, or
    (ii) for periods amounting to three years in the last ten years,

whether or not he has used it also for other purposes.

(3) The following provisions, namely—

(a) section 5 (with the omission of subsections (5) and (6)),
(b) section 7, and
(c) section 8,

shall apply for the purposes of this Chapter as they apply for the purposes of Chapter I; and references in this Chapter to a qualifying tenant of a flat shall accordingly be construed by reference to those provisions.

(4) For the purposes of this Chapter a person can be (or be among those constituting) the qualifying tenant of each of two or more flats at the same time, whether he is tenant of those flats under one lease or under two or more separate leases.

(5) For the purposes of subsection (2)(*b*) above—

(a) any reference to the tenant's flat includes a reference to part of it; and
(b) it is immaterial whether at any particular time the tenant's occupation was in right of the lease by virtue of which he is a qualifying tenant or in right of some other lease or otherwise;

but any occupation by a company or other artificial person, or (where the tenant is a corporation sole) by the corporator, shall not be regarded as occupation for the purposes of that provision.

(6) In the case of a lease held by joint tenants—

(a) the condition in subsection (2)(*b*) need only be satisfied with respect to one of the joint tenants; and
(b) subsection (5) shall apply accordingly (the reference to the lease by virtue of which the tenant is a qualifying tenant being read for this purpose as a reference to the lease by virtue of which the joint tenants are a qualifying tenant).

(7) The right conferred by this Chapter on a tenant to acquire a new lease shall not extend to underlying minerals comprised in his existing lease if—

(a) the landlord requires the minerals to be excepted, and
(b) proper provision is made for the support of the premises demised by that existing lease as they are enjoyed on the relevant date.

(8) In this Chapter "the relevant date", in relation to a claim by a tenant under this Chapter, means the date on which notice of the claim is given to the landlord under section 42.

40.—(1) In this Chapter "the landlord", in relation to the lease held by a qualifying tenant of a flat, means the person who is the owner of that interest in the flat which for the time being fulfils the following conditions, namely—

(a) it is an interest in reversion expectant (whether immediately or not) on the termination of the tenant's lease, and
(b) it is either a freehold interest or a leasehold interest whose duration is such as to enable that person to grant a new lease of that flat in accordance with this Chapter,

and is not itself expectant (whether immediately or not) on an interest which fulfils those conditions.

(2) Where in accordance with subsection (1) the immediate landlord under the lease of a qualifying tenant of a flat is not the landlord in relation to that lease for the purposes of this Chapter, the person who for those purposes is the landlord in relation to it shall conduct on behalf of all the other landlords all proceedings arising out of any notice given by the tenant with respect to the flat under section 42 (whether the proceedings are for resisting or giving effect to the claim in question).

(3) Subsection (2) has effect subject to the provisions of Schedule 11 to this Act (which makes provision in relation to the operation of this Chapter in cases to which that subsection applies).

(4) In this section and that Schedule—

(a) "the tenant" means any such qualifying tenant as is referred to in subsection (2) and "the tenant's lease" means the lease by virtue of which he is a qualifying tenant;
(b) "the competent landlord" means the person who, in relation to the tenant's lease, is the landlord (as defined by subsection (1)) for the purposes of this Chapter;
(c) "other landlord" means any person (other than the tenant or a trustee for him) in whom there is vested a concurrent tenancy intermediate between the interest of the competent landlord and the tenant's lease.

(5) Schedule 2 (which makes provision with respect to certain special categories of landlords) has effect for the purposes of this Chapter.

Preliminary inquiries by qualifying tenant

41.—(1) A qualifying tenant of a flat may give—

(a) to his immediate landlord, or
(b) to any person receiving rent on behalf of his immediate landlord,

a notice requiring the recipient to state whether the immediate landlord is the owner of the freehold interest in the flat and, if not, to give the tenant such information as is mentioned in subsection (2) (so far as known to the recipient).

(2) That information is—

(a) the name and address of the person who owns the freehold interest in the flat;
(b) the duration of the leasehold interest in the flat of the tenant's immediate landlord and the extent of the premises in which it subsists; and
(c) the name and address of every person who has a leasehold interest in the flat which is superior to that of the tenant's

immediate landlord, the duration of any such interest and the extent of the premises in which is subsists.

(3) If the immediate landlord of any such qualifying tenant is not the owner of the freehold interest in the flat, the tenant may also—

(a) give to the person who is the owner of that interest a notice requiring him to give the tenant such information as is mentioned in paragraph (*c*) of subsection (2) (so far as known to that person);
(b) give to any person falling within that paragraph a notice requiring him to give the tenant—
  (i) particulars of the duration of his leasehold interest in the flat and the extent of the premises in which it subsists, and
  (ii) (so far as known to him) such information as is mentioned in paragraph (*a*) of that subsection and, as regards any other person falling within paragraph (*c*) of that subsection, such information as is mentioned in that paragraph.

(4) Any notice given by a qualifying tenant under this section shall, in addition to any other requirement imposed in accordance with subsections (1) to (3), require the recipient to state—

(a) whether he has received in respect of any premises containing the tenant's flat—
  (i) a notice under section 13 in the case of which the relevant claim under Chapter I is still current, or
  (ii) a copy of such a notice; and
(b) if so, the date on which the notice under section 13 was given and the name and address of the nominee purchaser for the time being appointed for the purposes of section 15 in relation to that claim.

(5) For the purposes of subsection (4)—

(a) "the relevant claim under Chapter I", in relation to a notice under section 13, means the claim in respect of which that notice is given; and
(b) any such claim is current if—
  (i) that notice continues in force in accordance with section 13(11), or
  (ii) a binding contract entered into in pursuance of that notice remains in force, or
  (iii) where an order has been made under section 24(4)(*a*) or (b) or 25(6)(*a*) or (*b*) with respect to any such premises as are referred to in subsection (4)(*a*) above, any interests which by virtue of the order fall to be vested in

the nominee purchaser for the purposes of Chapter I have yet to be so vested.

(6) Any person who is required to give any information by virtue of a notice under this section shall give that information to the qualifying tenant within the period of 28 days beginning with the date of the giving of the notice.

The tenant's notice

42.—(1) A claim by a qualifying tenant of a flat to exercise the right to acquire a new lease of the flat is made by the giving of notice of the claim under this section.

(2) A notice given by a tenant under this section ("the tenant's notice") must be given—

(a) to the landlord, and
(b) to any third party to the tenant's lease.

(3) The tenant's notice must—

(a) state the full name of the tenant and the address of the flat in respect of which he claims a new lease under this Chapter;
(b) contain the following particulars, namely—
  (i) sufficient particulars of that flat to identify the property to which the claim extends,
  (ii) such particulars of the tenant's lease as are sufficient to identify it, including the date on which the lease was entered into, the term for which it was granted and the date of the commencement of the term,
  (iii) such further particulars as are necessary to show that the tenant's lease is, in accordance with section 8 (as that section applies in accordance with section 39(3)), a lease at a low rent, and
  (iv) particulars of the period or periods falling within the preceding ten years for which the tenant has occupied the whole or part of the flat as his only or principal home;
(c) specify the premium which the tenant proposes to pay in respect of the grant of a new lease under this Chapter and, where any other amount will be payable by him in accordance with any provision of Schedule 13, the amount which he proposes to pay in accordance with that provision;
(d) specify the terms which the tenant proposes should be contained in any such lease;
(e) state the name of the person (if any) appointed by the tenant to act for him in connection with his claim, and an address in

England and Wales at which notices may be given to any such person under this Chapter; and

(f) specify the date by which the landlord must respond to the notice by giving a counter-notice under section 45.

(4) If the tenant's lease is held by joint tenants, the reference to the tenant in subsection (3)(*b*)(iv) shall be read as a reference to any joint tenants with respect to whom it is claimed that the condition in section 39(2)(*b*) is satisfied.

(5) The date specified in the tenant's notice in pursuance of subsection (3)(*f*) must be a date falling not less than two months after the date of the giving of the notice.

(6) Where a notice under this section has been given with respect to any flat, no subsequent notice may be given under this section with respect to the flat so long as the earlier notice continues in force.

(7) Where a notice under this section has been given with respect to a flat and—

(a) that notice has been withdrawn, or is deemed to have been withdrawn, under or by virtue of any provision of this Chapter, or

(b) in response to that notice, an order has been applied for and obtained under section 47(1),

no subsequent notice may be given under this section with respect to the flat within the period of twelve months beginning with the date of the withdrawal or deemed withdrawal of the earlier notice or with the time when the order under section 47(1) becomes final (as the case may be).

(8) Where a notice is given in accordance with this section, then for the purposes of this Chapter the notice continues in force as from the relevant date—

(a) until a new lease is granted in pursuance of the notice;

(b) if the notice is withdrawn, or is deemed to have been withdrawn, under or by virtue of any provision of this Chapter, until the date of the withdrawal or deemed withdrawal; or

(c) until such other time as the notice ceases to have effect by virtue of any provision of this Chapter;

but this subsection has effect subject to section 54.

(9) Schedule 12 (which contains restrictions on terminating a tenant's lease where he has given a notice under this section and makes other provision in connection with the giving of notices under this section) shall have effect.

43.—(1) Where a notice has been given under section 42 with respect to any flat, the rights and obligations of the landlord and the tenant arising from the notice shall enure for the benefit of and be enforceable against them, their personal representatives and assigns to the like extent (but no further) as rights and obligations arising under a contract for leasing freely entered into between the landlord and the tenant.

(2) Accordingly, in relation to matters arising out of any such notice, references in this Chapter to the landlord and the tenant shall, in so far as the context permits, include their respective personal representatives and assigns.

(3) Notwithstanding anything in subsection (1), the rights and obligations of the tenant shall be assignable with, but shall not be capable of subsisting apart from, the lease of the entire flat; and, if the tenant's lease is assigned without the benefit of the notice, the notice shall accordingly be deemed to have been withdrawn by the tenant as at the date of the assignment.

(4) In the event of any default by the landlord or the tenant in carrying out the obligations arising from the tenant's notice, the other of them shall have the like rights and remedies as in the case of a contract freely entered into.

(5) In a case to which section 40(2) applies, the rights and obligations of the landlord arising out of the tenant's notice shall, so far as their interest are affected, be rights and obligations respectively of the competent landlord and of each of the other landlords, and references to the landlord in subsections (1) and (2) above shall apply accordingly.

(6) In subsection (5) "competent landlord" and "other landlord" have the meaning given by section 40(4); and subsection (5) has effect without prejudice to the operation of section 40(2) or Schedule 11.

Procedure following giving of tenant's notice

44.—(1) Once the tenant's notice or a copy of it has been given in accordance with section 42 or Part I of Schedule 11—

(a) to the landlord for the purposes of this Chapter, or
(b) to any other landlord (as defined by section 40(4)),

that landlord and any person authorised to act on his behalf shall have a right of access to the flat to which the notice relates for the purpose of enabling that landlord to obtain, in connection with the notice, a valuation of his interest in the flat.

(2) That right shall be exercisable at any reasonable time and on giving not less than 3 days' notice to the tenant.

45.—(1) The landlord shall give a counter-notice under this section to the tenant by the date specified in the tenant's notice in pursuance of section 42(3)(f).

(2) The counter-notice must comply with one of the following requirements—

(a) state that the landlord admits that the tenants had on the relevant date the right to acquire a new lease of his flat;

(b) state that, for such reasons as are specified in the counter-notice, the landlord does not admit that the tenant had such a right on that date;

(c) contain such a statement as is mentioned in paragraph (*a*) or (*b*) above but state that the landlord intends to make an application for an order under section 47(1) on the grounds that he intends to redevelop any premises in which the flat is contained.

(3) If the counter-notice complies with the requirement set out in subsection (2)(*a*), it must in addition—

(a) state which (if any) of the proposals contained in the tenant's notice are accepted by the landlord and which (if any) of those proposals are not so accepted; and

(b) specify, in relation to each proposal which is not accepted, the landlord's counter-proposal.

(4) The counter-notice must specify an address in England and Wales at which notice may be given to the landlord under this Chapter.

(5) Where the counter-notice admits the tenant's right to acquire a new lease of his flat, the admission shall be binding on the landlord as to the matters mentioned in section 39(2)(*a*) and (*b*), unless the landlord shows that he was induced to make the admission by misrepresentation or the concealment of material facts; but the admission shall not conclude any question whether the particulars of the flat stated in the tenant's notice in pursuance of section 42(3)(*b*)(i) are correct.

Applications to court or leasehold valuation tribunal

46.—(1) Where—

(a) the landlord has given the tenant a counter-notice under section 45 which (whether it complies with the requirement set out in subsection (2)(*b*) or (*c*) of that section) contains such a statement as is mentioned in subsection (2)(*b*) of that section, and

(b) the court is satisfied, on an application made by the landlord, that on the relevant date the tenant had no right under this Chapter to acquire a new lease of his flat,

the court shall by order made a declaration to that effect.

(2) Any application for an order under subsection (1) must be made not later than the end of the period of two months beginning with the date of the giving of the counter-notice to the tenant; and if, in a case falling wihin paragraph (*a*) of that subsection, either—

(a) no application for such an order is made by the landlord with that period, or

(b) such an application is so made but is subsequently withdrawn,

section 49 shall apply as if the landlord had not given the counter-notice.

(3) If on any such application the court makes such a declaration as is mentioned in subsection (1), the tenant's notice shall cease to have effect on the order becoming final.

(4) If, however, any such application is dismissed by the court, then (subject to subsection (5)) the court shall make an order—

(a) declaring that the landlord's counter-notice shall be of no effect, and
(b) requiring the landlord to give a further counter-notice to the tenant by such date as is specified in the order.

(5) Subsection (4) shall not apply if—

(a) the counter-notice complies with the requirement set out in section 45(2)(*c*), and
(b) either—
 (i) an application for an order under section 47(1) is pending, or
 (ii) the period specified in section 47(3) as the period for the making of such an application has not expired.

(6) Subsection (3) of section 45 shall apply to any further counter-notice required to be given by the landlord under subsection (4) above as if it were a counter-notice under that section complying with the requirement set out in subsection (2)(*a*) of that section.

47.—(1) Where the landlord has given the tenant a counter-notice under section 45 which complies with the requirement set out in subsection (2)(*c*) of that section, the court may, on the application of the landlord, by order declare that the right to acquire a new lease shall not be exerciseable by the tenant by reason of the landlord's intention to redevelop any premises in which the tenant's flat is contained; and on such an order becoming final the tenant's notice shall cease to have effect.

(2) The court shall not make an order under subsection (1) unless it is satisfied—

(a) that the tenant's lease of his flat is due to terminate within the period of five years beginning with the relevant date; and
(b) that for the purposes of redevelopment the landlord intends, once the lease has so terminated
 (i) to demolish or reconstruct, or
 (ii) to carry out substantial works of construction on,
 the whole or a substantial part of any premises in which the flat is contained; and
(c) that he could not reasonably do so without obtaining possession of the flat.

(3) Any application for an order under subsection (1) must be made within the period of two months beginning with the date of the giving of

the counter-notice to the tenant; but where the counter-notice is one falling within section 46(1)(*a*), such an application shall not be proceeded with until such time (if any) as any order dismissing an application under section 46(1) becomes final.

(4) Where an application for an order under subsection (1) is dismissed by the court, the court shall make an order—

(a) declaring that the landlord's counter-notice shall be of no effect, and
(b) requiring the landlord to give a further counter-notice to the tenants by such date as is specified in the order.

(5) Where—

(a) the landlord has given such a counter-notice as is mentioned in subsection (1), but
(b) either—
    (i) no application for an order under that subsection is made within the period referred to in subsection (3), or
    (ii) such an application is so made but is subsequently withdrawn,

then (subject to subsection (7)), the landlord shall give a further counter-notice to the tenant within the period of two months beginning with the appropriate date.

(6) In subsection (5) "the appropriate date" means—

(a) if subsection (5)(*b*)(i) applies, the date immediately following the end of the period referred to in subsection (3); and
(b) if subsection (5)(*b*)(ii) applies, the date of withdrawal of the application.

(7) Subsection (5) shall not apply if any application has been made by the landlord for an order under section 46(1).

(8) Subsection (3) of section 45 shall to any further counter-notice required to be given by the landlord under subsection (4) or (5) above as if it were a counter-notice under that section complying with the requirement set out in subsection (2)(*a*) of that section.

48.—(1) Where the landlord has given the tenant—

(a) a counter-notice under section 45 which complies with the requirement set out in subsection (2)(*a*) of that section, or
(b) a further counter-notice required by or by virtue of section 46(4) or section 47(4) or (5),

but any of the terms of acquisition remain in dispute at the end of the period of two months beginning with the date when the counter-notice or further counter-notice was so given, a leasehold valuation tribunal may, on the application of either tenant or the landlord, determine the matters in dispute.

(2) Any application under subsection (1) must be made not later than the end of the period of six months beginning with the date on which the counter-notice or further counter-notice was given to the tenant.

(3) Where—

(a) the landlord has given the tenant such a counter-notice or further counter-notice as is mentioned in subsection (1)(*a*) or (b), and

(b) all the terms of acquisition have been either agreed between those persons or determined by a leasehold valuation tribunal under subsection (1),

but a new lease has not been entered into in pursuance of the tenant's notice by the end of the appropriate period specified in subsection (6), the court may, on the application of either the tenant or the landlord, make such order as it thinks fit with respect to the performance or discharge of any obligations arising out of that notice.

(4) Any such order may provide for the tenant's notice to be deemed to have been withdrawn at the end of the appropriate period specified in subsection (6).

(5) Any application for an order under subsection (3) must be made not later than the end of the period of two months beginning immediately after the end of the appropriate period specified in subsection (6).

(6) For the purposes of this section the appropriate period is—

(a) where all of the terms of acquisition have been agreed between the tenant and the landlord, the period of two months beginning with the date when those terms were finally so agreed; or

(b) where all or any of those terms have been determined by a leasehold valuation tribunal under subsection (1)—

(i) the period of two months beginning with the date when the decision of the tribunal under subsection (1) becomes final, or

(ii) such other period as may have been fixed by the tribunal when making its determination.

In this Chapter "the terms of acquisition", in relation to a claim by a tenant under this Chapter, means the terms on which the tenant is to acquire a new lease of his flat, whether they relate to the terms to be contained in the lease or to the premium or any other amount payable by virtue of Schedule 13 in connection with the grant of the lease, or otherwise.

49.—(1) Where the tenant's notice has been given in accordance with section 42 but—

(a) the landlord has failed to give the tenant a counter-notice in accordance with section 45(1), or

(b) if required to give a further counter-notice to the tenant by or by virtue of section 46(4) or section 47(4) or (5), the landlord has failed to comply with that requirement,

the court may, on the application of the tenant, make an order determining, in accordance with the proposals contained in the tenant's notice, the terms of acquisition.

(2) The court shall not make such an order on an application made by virtue of paragraph (a) of subsection (1) unless it is satisfied—

(a) that on the relevant date the tenant had the right to acquire a new lease of his flat; and
(b) if applicable, that the requirements of Part I of Schedule 11 were complied with as respects the giving of copies of the tenant's notice.

(3) Any application for an order under subsection (1) must be made not later than the end of the period of six months beginning with the date by which the counter-notice or further counter-notice referred to in that subsection was required to be given.

(4) Where—

(a) the terms of acquisition have been determined by an order of the court under this section, but
(b) a new lease has not been entered into in pursuance of the tenant's notice by the end of the appropriate period specified in subsection (7),

the court may, on the application of either the tenant or the landlord, make such order as it thinks fit with respect to the performance or discharge of any obligations arising out of that notice.

(5) Any such order may provide for the tenant's notice to be deemed to have been withdrawn at the end of the appropriate period specified in subsection (7).

(6) Any application for an order under subsection (4) must be make not later than the end of the period of two months beginning immediately after the end of the appropriate period specified in subsection (7).

(7) For the purposes of this section the appropriate period is—

(a) the period of two months beginning with the date when the order of the court under subsection (1) becomes final, or
(b) such other period as may have been fixed by the court when making that order.

50.—(1) Where—

(a) a qualifying tenant of a flat desires to make a claim to exercise the right to acquire a new lease of his flat, but

(b) the landlord cannot be found or his identity cannot be ascertained,

the court may, on the application of the tenant, make a vesting order under this subsection.

(2) Where—

(a) a qualifying tenant of a flat desires to make such a claim as is mentioned in subsection (1), and
(b) paragraph (*b*) of that subsection does not apply, but
(c) a copy of a notice of that claim cannot be given in accordance with Part I of Schedule 11 to any person to whom it would otherwise be required to be so given because that person cannot be found or his identity cannot be ascertained,

the court may, on the application of the tenant, make an order dispensing with the need to give a copy of such a notice to that person.

(3) The court shall not make an order on any application under subsection (1) or (2) unless it is satisfied—

(a) that on the date of the making of the application the tenant had the right to acquire a new lease of his flat; and
(b) that on that date he would not have been precluded by any provision of this Chapter from giving a valid notice under section 42 with respect to his flat.

(4) Before making any such order the court may require the tenant to take such further steps by way of advertisement or otherwise as the court thinks proper for the purpose of tracing the person in question; and if, after an application is make for a vesting order under subsection (1) and before any lease is executed in pursuance of the application, the landlord is traced, then no further proceedings shall be taken with a view to a lease being so executed, but (subject to subsection (5))—

(a) the rights and obligations of all parties shall be determined as if the tenant had, at the date of the application, duly given notice under section 42 of his claim to exercise the right to acquire a new lease of his flat; and
(b) the court may give such directions as the court thinks fit as to the steps to be taken for giving effect to those rights and obligations, including directions modifying or dispensing with any of the requirements of this Chapter or of regulations made under this Part.

(5) An application for a vesting order under subsection (1) may be withdrawn at any time before execution of a lease under section 51(3) and, after it is withdrawn, subsection (4)(*a*) above shall not apply; but where any step is taken (whether by the landlord or the tenant) for the purpose of giving effect to subsection (4)(*a*) in the case of any application, the application shall not afterwards be withdrawn except—

(a) with the consent of the landlord, or
(b) by leave of the court,

and the court shall not give unless it appears to the court just to do so by reason of matters coming to the knowledge of the tenant in consequence of the tracing of the landlord.

(6) Where an order has been made under subsection (2) dispensing with the need to give a copy of a notice under section 42 to a particular person with respect to any flat, then if—

(a) a notice is subsequently given under that section with respect to that flat, and
(b) in reliance on the order, a copy of the notice is not to be given to that person,

the notice must contain a statement of the effect of the order.

(7) Where a notice under section 42 contains such a statement in accordance with subsection (6) above, then in determining for the purposes of any provision of this Chapter whether the requirements of Part I of Schedule 11 have been complied with in relation to the notice, those requirements shall be deemed to have been complied with so far as relating to the giving of a copy of the notice to the person referred to in subsection (6) above.

51.—(1) A vesting order under section 50(1) is an order providing for the surrender of the tenant's lease of his flat and for the granting to him of a new lease of it on such terms as may be determined by a leasehold valuation tribunal to be appropriate with a view to the lease being granted to him in like manner (so far as the circumstances permit) as if he had, at the date of his application, given notice under section 42 of his claim to exercise the right to acquire a new lease of his flat.

(2) If a leasehold valuation tribunal so determines in the case of a vesting order under section 50(1), the order shall have effect in relation to property which is less extensive than that specified in the application on which the order was made.

(3) Where any lease is to be granted to a tenant by virtue of a vesting order under section 50(1), then on his paying into court the appropriate sum there shall be executed by such person as the court may designate a lease which—

(a) is in a form approved by a leasehold valuation tribunal, and
(b) contains such provision as may be so approved for the purpose of giving effect so far as possible to section 56(1) and section 57 (as that section applies in accordance with subsection (7) and (8) below);

and that lease shall be effective to vest in the person to whom it is granted the property expressed to be demised by it, subject to and in accordance with the terms of the lease.

(4) In connection with the determination by a leasehold valuation tribunal of any question as to the property to be demised by any such lease, or as to the rights with or subject to which it is to be demised, it shall be assumed (unless the contrary is shown) that the landlord has no interest in property other than the property to be demised and, for the purpose of excepting them from the lease, any minerals underlying that property.

(5) The appropriate sum to be paid into court in accordance with subsection (3) is the aggregate of—

- (a) such amount as may be determined by a leasehold valuation tribunal to be the premium which is payable under Schedule 13 in respect of the grant of the new lease;
- (b) such other amount or amounts (if any) as may be determined by such a tribunal to be payable by virtue of that Schedule in connection with the grant of that lease; and
- (c) any amounts or estimated amounts determined by such a tribunal as being, at the time of execution of that lease, due to the landlord from the tenant (whether due under or in respect of the tenant's lease of his flat or under or in respect of any agreement collateral thereto).

(6) Where any lease is granted to a person in accordance with this section, the payment into court of the appropriate sum shall be taken to have satisfied any claims against the tenant, his personal representatives or assigns in respect of the premium and any other amounts payable as mentioned in subsection (5)(*a*) and (*b*).

(7) Subject to subsection (8), the following provisions, namely—

- (a) sections 57 to 59, and
- (b) section 61 and Schedule 14,

shall, so far as capable of applying to a lease granted in accordance with this section, apply to such a lease as they apply to a lease granted under section 56; and subsections (6) and (7) of that section shall apply in relation to a lease granted in accordance with this section as they apply in relation to a lease granted under that section.

(8) In its application to a lease granted in accordance with this section—

- (a) section 57 shall have effect as if—
  - (i) any reference to the relevant date were a reference to the date of the application under section 50(1) in pursuance of which the vesting order under that provision was made, and
  - (ii) in subsection (5) the reference to section 56(3)(*a*) were a reference to subsection (5)(*c*) above; and

(b) section 58 shall have effect as if—
  (i) in subsection (3) the second reference to the landlord were a reference to the person designated under subsection (3) above, and
  (ii) subsections (6)(*a*) and (7) were omitted.

Termination or suspension of acquisition procedures

52.—(1) At any time before a new lease is entered into in pursuance of the tenant's notice, the tenant may withdraw that notice by the giving of a notice to that effect under this section ("a notice of withdrawal").

(2) A notice of withdrawal must be given—

(a) to the landlord for the purposes of this Chapter;
(b) to every other landlord (as defined by section 40(4)); and
(c) to any third party to the tenant's lease.

(3) Where a notice of withdrawal is given by the tenant to any person in accordance with subsection (2), the tenant's liability under section 60 for costs incurred by that person shall be a liability for costs incurred by him down to the time when the notice is given to him.

53.—(1) Where—

(a) in a case to which subsection (1) of section 48 applies, no application under that subsection is made within the period specified in subsection (2) of that section, or
(b) in a case to which subsection (3) of that section applies, no application for an order under that subsection is made within the period specified in subsection (5) of that section.

the tenant's notice shall be deemed to have been withdrawn at the end of the period referred to in paragraph (*a*) or (*b*) above (as the case may be).

(2) Where, in a case falling within paragraph (*a*) or (*b*) of subsection (1) of section 49, no application for an order under that subsection is made within the period specified in subsection (3) of that section, the tenant's notice shall be deemed to have been withdrawn at the end of that period.

(3) Where, in a case to which subsection (4) of section 49 applies, no application for an order under that subsection is made within the period specified in subsection (6) of that section, the tenant's notice shall be deemed to have been withdrawn at the end of that period.

(4) The following provisions, namely—

(a) section 43(3),
(b) section 48(4), and
(c) section 49(5),

also make provision for a notice under section 42 to be deemed to have been withdrawn at a particular time.

54.—(1) If, at the time when the tenant's notice is given—

(a) a notice has been given under section 13 with respect to any premises containing the tenant's flat, and
(b) the relevant claim under Chapter I is still current,

the operation of the tenant's notice shall be suspended during the currency of that claim; and so long as it is so suspended no further notice shall be given, and no application shall be made, under this Chapter with a view to resisting or giving effect to the tenant's claim.

(2) If, at any time when the tenant's notice continues in force, a notice is given under section 13 with respect to any premises containing the tenant's flat, then, as from the date which is the relevant date for the purposes of Chapter I in relation to that notice under section 13, the operation of the tenant's notice shall be suspended during the currency of the relevant claim under Chapter I; and so long as it is so suspended no further notice shall be given, and no application shall be made or proceeded with, under this Chapter with a view to resisting or giving effect to the tenant's claim.

(3) Where the operation of the tenant's notice is suspended by virtue of subsection (1) or (2), the landlord shall give the tenant a notice informing him of its suspension—

(a) (if it is suspended by virtue of subsection (1)) not later than the date specified in the tenant's notice in pursuance of section 42(3)(*f*); or
(b) (if it is suspended by virtue of subsection (2)) as soon as possible after the date referred to in that subsection;

and any such notice shall in addition inform the tenant of the date on which the notice under section 13 was given and of the name and address of the nominee purchaser for the time being appointed for the purposes of section 15 in relation to the relevant claim under Chapter I.

(4) Where—

(a) the operation of the tenant's notice is suspended by virtue of subsection (1), and
(b) as a result of the relevant claim under Chapter I ceasing to be current, the operation of the tenant's notice subsequently ceases to be so suspended and the tenant's notice thereupon continues in force in accordance with section 42(8),

then, as from the date when that claim ceases to be current ("the termination date"), this Chapter shall apply as if there were substituted for the date specified in the tenant's notice in pursuance of section 42(3)(*f*) such date as results in the period of time intervening between the termination date and that date being equal to the period of time intervening between the relevant date and the date originally so specified.

(5) Where—

(a) the operation of the tenant's notice is suspended by virtue of subsection (2), and
(b) its suspension began in circumstances falling within subsection (6), and
(c) as a result of the relevant claim under Chapter I ceasing to be current, the operation of the tenant's notice subsequently ceases to be so suspended and the tenant's notice thereupon continues in force in accordance with section 42(8),

any relevant period shall be deemed to have begun on the date when that claim ceases to be current.

(6) The circumstances referred to in subsection (5)(*b*) are that the suspension of the operation of the tenant's notice began—

(a) before the date specified in the tenant's notice in pursuance of section 42(3)(*f*) and before the landlord had given the tenant a counter-notice under section 45; or
(b) after the landlord had given the tenant a counter-notice under section 45 complying with the requirement set out in subsection (2)(*b*) or (*c*) of that section but—
    (i) before any application had been made for an order under section 46(1) or 47(1), and
    (ii) before the period for making any such application had expired; or
(c) after an order had been made under section 46(4) or 47(4) but—
    (i) before the landlord had given the tenant a further counter-notice in accordance with the order, and
    (ii) before the period for giving any such counter-notice had expired.

(7) Where—

(a) the operation of the tenant's notice is suspended by virtue of subsection (2), and
(b) its suspension began otherwise than in circumstances falling within subsection (6), and
(c) as a result of the relevant claim under Chapter I ceasing to be current, the operation of the tenant's notice subsequently ceases to be so suspended and the tenant's notice thereupon continues in force in accordance with section 42(8),

any relevant period shall be deemed to have begun on the date on which the tenant is given a notice under subsection (8) below or, if earlier, the date on which the tenant gives the landlord a notice informing him of the circumstances by virtue of which the operation of the tenant's notice has ceased to be suspended.

(8) Where subsection (4), (5) or (7) applies, the landlord shall, as soon as possible after becoming aware of the circumstances by virtue of which the operation of the tenant's notice has ceased to be suspended as mentioned in that subsection, give the tenant a notice informing him that, as from the date when the relevant claim under Chapter I ceased to be current, the operation of his notice is no longer suspended.

(9) Subsection (8) shall not, however, require the landlord to give any such notice if he has received a notice from the tenant under subsection (7).

(10) In subsection (5) and (7) "relevant period" means any period which—

- (a) is prescribed by or under this Part for the giving of any notice, or the making of any application, in connection with the tenant's notice; and
- (b) was current at the time when the suspension of the operation of the tenant's notice began.

(11) For the purposes of this section—

- (a) "the relevant claim under Chapter I", in relation to a notice under section 13, means the claim in respect of which that notice is given; and
- (b) any such claim is current if—
  - (i) that notice continues in force in accordance with section 13(11), or
  - (ii) a binding contract entered into in pursuance of that notice remain in force, or
  - (iii) where an order has been made under section 24(4)(*a*) or (*b*) or 25(6)(*a*) or (*b*) with respect to any such premises as are referred to in subsection (1) or (2) above (as the case may be), any interest which by virtue of the order fall to be vested in the nominee purchaser for the purposes of Chapter I have yet to be so vested.

55.—(1) A notice given by a tenant under section 42 shall be of no effect if on the relevant date—

- (a) any person or body of person who has or have been, or could be, authorised to acquire the whole or part of the tenant's flat compulsorily for any purpose has or have, with a view to its acquisition for that purpose—
  - (i) served notice to treat on the landlord or the tenant, or
  - (ii) entered into a contract for the purchase of the interest of either of them in the flat or part of it, and
- (b) the notice to treat or contract remains in force.

(2) A notice given by a tenant under section 42 shall cease to have effect if, before a new lease is entered into in pursuance of it, any such

person or body of persons as is mentioned in subsection (1) serves or serve notice to treat as mentioned in that subsection.

(3) Where subsection (2) applies in relation to a notice given by a tenant under section 42, then on the occasion of the compulsory acquisition in question the compensation payable in respect of any interest in the tenant's flat (whether or not the one to which the relevant notice to treat relates) shall be determined on the basis of the value of the interest subject to and with the benefit of the rights and obligations arising from the tenant's notice and affecting that interest.

Grant of new lease

56.—(1) Where a qualifying tenant of a flat has under this Chapter a right to acquire a new lease of the flat and gives notice of his claim in accordance with section 42, then except as provided by this Chapter the landlord shall be bound to grant to the tenant, and the tenant shall be bound to accept—

(a) in substitution for the existing lease, and
(b) on payment of the premium payable under Schedule 13 in respect of the grant,

a new lease of the flat at a peppercorn rent for a term expiring 90 years after the term date of the existing lease.

(2) In addition to any such premium there shall be payable by the tenant in connection with the grant of any such new lease such amounts to the owners of any intermediate leasehold interests (within the meaning of Schedule 13) as are so payable by virtue of that Schedule.

(3) A tenant shall not be entitled to require the execution of any such new lease otherwise than on tendering to the landlord, in addition to the amount of any such premium and any other amounts payable by virtue of Schedule 13, the amount so far as ascertained—

(a) of any sums payable by him by way of rent or recoverable from him as rent in respect of the flat up to the date of tender;
(b) of any sums for which at that date the tenant is liable under section 60 in respect of costs incurred by any relevant person (within the meaning of that section); and
(c) of any other sums due and payable by him to any such person under or in respect of the existing lease;

and, if the amount of any such sums is not or may not be fully ascertained, on offering reasonable security for the payment of such amount as may afterwards be found to be payable in respect of them.

(4) To the extent that any amount tendered to the landlord in accordance with subsection (3) is an amount due to a person other than the landlord, that amount shall be payable to that person by the landlord; and that subsection has effect subject to paragraph 7(2) of Schedule 11.

(5) No provision of any lease prohibiting, restricting or otherwise relating to a sub-demise by the tenant under the lease shall have effect with reference to the granting of any lease under this section.

(6) It is hereby declared that nothing in any of the provision specified in paragraph 1(2) of Schedule 10 (which impose requirements as to consent or consultation or other restrictions in relation to disposals falling within those provisions) applies to the granting of any lease under this section.

(7) For the purposes of subsection (6), paragraph 1(2) of Schedule 10 has effect as if the reference to section 79(2) of the Housing Act 1988 (which is not relevant in the context of subsection (6)) were omitted.

57.—(1) Subject to the provision of this Chapter (and in particular to the provisions as to rent and duration contained in section 56(1)), the new lease to be granted to a tenant under section 56 shall be a lease on the same terms as those of the existing lease, as they apply on the relevant date, but with such modifications as may be required or appropriate to take account—

- (a) of the omission from the new lease of property included in the existing lease but not comprised in the flat;
- (b) of alterations made to the property demised since the grant of the existing lease; or
- (c) in a case where the existing lease derives (in accordance with section 7(6) as it applies in accordance with section 39(3)) from more than one separate leases, of their combined effect and of the differences (if any) in their terms.

(2) Where during the continuance of the new lease the landlord will be under any obligation for the provision of services, or for repairs, maintenance or insurance—

- (a) the new lease may require payments to be made by the tenant (whether as rent or otherwise) in consideration of those matters or in respect of the cost thereof to the landlord; and
- (b) (if the terms of the existing lease do not include any provision for the making of any such payments by the tenant or include provision only for the payment of a fixed amount) the terms of the new lease shall make, as from the term date of the existing lease, such provision as may be just—
  - (i) for the making by the tenant of payments related to the cost from time to time to the landlord, and
  - (ii) for the tenant's liability to make those payments to be enforceable by distress, re-entry or otherwise in like manner as if it were a liability for payment of rent.

(3) Subject to subsection (4), provision shall be made by the terms of the new lease or by an agreement collateral thereto for the continuance,

with any suitable adaptations, of any agreement collateral to the existing lease.

(4) For the purposes of subsection (1) and (3) there shall be excluded from the new lease any term of the existing lease or of any agreement collateral thereto in so far as that term—

- (a) provides for or relates to the renewal of the lease,
- (b) confers any option to purchase or right of pre-emption in relation to the flat demised by the existing lease, or
- (c) provides for the termination of the existing lease before its term date otherwise than in the event of a breach of its terms;

and there shall be made in the terms of the new lease or any agreement collateral thereto such modifications as may be required or appropriate to take account of the exclusion of any such term.

(5) Where the new lease is granted after the term date of the existing lease, then on the grant of the new lease there shall be payable by the tenant to the landlord, as an addition to the rent payable under the existing lease, any amount by which, for the period since the term date or the relevant date (whichever is the later), the sums payable to the landlord in respect of the flat (after making any necessary apportionment) for the matters referred to in subsection (2) fall short in total of the sums that would have been payable for such matters under the new lease if it had been granted on that date, and section 56(3)(*a*) shall apply accordingly.

(6) Subsection (1) to (5) shall have effect subject to any agreement between the landlord and tenant as to the terms of the new lease or any agreement collateral thereto; and either of them may require that for the purposes of the new lease any term of the existing lease shall be excluded or modified in so far as—

- (a) it is necessary to do so in order to remedy a defect in the existing lease; or
- (b) it would be unreasonable in the circumstances to include, or include without modification, the term in question in view of changes occurring since the date of commencement of the existing lease which affect the suitability on the relevant date of the provisions of that lease.

(7) The terms of the new lease shall—

- (a) make provision in accordance with section 59(3); and
- (b) reserve to the person who is for the time being the tenant's immediate landlord the right to obtain possession of the flat in question in accordance with section 61.

(8) In granting the new lease the landlord shall not be bound to enter into any covenant for title beyond that implied from the grant, and a person entering into any covenant required of him as landlord shall be

entitled to limit his personal liability to breaches of that covenant for which he is responsible.

(9) Where any person—

(a) is a third party to the existing lease, or
(b) (not being the landlord or tenant) is a party to any agreement collateral thereto,

then (subject to any agreement between him and the landlord and the tenant) he shall be made a party to the new lease (as the case may be) to an agreement collateral thereto, and shall accordingly join in its execution; but nothing in this section has effect so as to require the new lease or (as the case may be) any such collateral agreement to provide for his to discharge any function at any time after the term date of the existing lease.

(10) Where—

(a) any such person ("the third party") is in accordance with subsection (9) to discharge any function down to the term date of the existing lease, but
(b) it is necessary or expedient in connection with the proper enjoyment by the tenant of the property demised by the new lease for provision to be made for the continued discharge of that function after that date,

the new lease or an agreement collateral thereto shall make provision for that function to be discharged after that date (whether by the third party or by some other person).

(11) The new lease shall contain a statement that it is a lease granted under section 56; and any such statement shall comply with such requirements as may be prescribed by rules made in pursuance of section 144 of the Land Registration Act 1925 (power to make general rules).

58.—(1) Subject to subsection (2), a qualifying tenant shall be entitled to be granted a new lease under section 56 despite the fact that the grant of the existing lease was subsequent to the creation of a mortgage on the landlord's interest and not authorised as against the persons interested in the mortgage; and a lease granted under that section—

(a) shall be deemed to be authorised as against the person interested in any mortgage on the landlord's interest (however created or arising), and
(b) shall be binding on those persons.

(2) A lease granted under section 56 shall not, by virtue of subsection (1) above, be binding on the persons interested in any such mortgage if the existing lease—

(a) is granted after the commencement of this Chapter, and

(b) being granted subsequent to the creation of the mortgage, would not, apart from that subsection, be binding on the persons interested in the mortgage.

(3) Where—

(a) a lease is granted under section 56, and
(b) any person having a mortgage on the landlord's interest is thereby entitled to possession of the documents of title relating to that interest,

the landlord shall, within one month of the execution of the lease, deliver to that person a counterpart of it duly executed by the tenant.

(4) Where the existing lease is, immediately before its surrender on the grant of a lease under section 56, subject to any mortgage, the new lease shall take effect subject to the mortgage in substitution for the existing lease; and the terms of the mortgage, as set out in the instrument creating or evidencing it, shall accordingly apply in relation to the new lease in like manner as they applied in relation to the existing lease.

(5) Where—

(a) a lease granted under section 56 takes effect subject to any such subsisting mortgage on the existing lease, and
(b) at the time of execution of the new lease the person having the mortgage is thereby entitled to possession of the documents of title relating to the existing lease,

he shall be similarly entitled to possession of the documents of title relating to the new lease; and the tenants shall deliver the new lease to him within one month of the date on which the lease is received from Her Majesty's Land Registry following its registration.

(6) Where—

(a) the landlord fails to deliver a counterpart of the new lease in accordance with subsection (3), or
(b) the tenant fails to deliver the new lease in accordance with subsection (5),

the instrument creating or evidencing the mortgage in question shall apply as if the obligation to deliver a counterpart or (as the case may be) deliver the lease were included in the terms of the mortgage as set out in that instrument.

(7) A landlord granting a lease under section 56 shall be bound to take such steps as may be necessary to secure that the lease is not liable in accordance with subsection (2) to be defeated by persons interested in a mortgage on his interest; but a landlord is not obliged, in order to grant a lease for the purposes of that section, to acquire a better title than he has or could require to be vested in him.

59.—(1) The right to acquire a new lease under this Chapter may be exercised in relation to a lease of a flat despite the fact that the lease is itself a lease granted under section 56; and the provisions of this Chapter shall, with any necessary modifications, apply for the purposes of or in connection with any claim to exercise that right in relation to a lease so granted as they apply for the purposes of or in connection with any claim to exercise that right in relation to a lease which has not been so granted.

(2) Where a lease has been granted under section 56—

- (a) none of the statutory provisions relating to security of tenure for tenants shall apply to the lease;
- (b) after the term of the lease none of the following provisions, namely—
  - (i) section 1 of the Landlord and Tenant Act 1954 or Schedule 10 to the Local Government and Housing Act 1989 (which make provision for security of tenure on the ending of long residential tenancies), or
  - (ii) Part II of that Act of 1954 (business tenancies), shall apply to any sub-lease directly derived out of the lease; and
- (c) after that date no person shall be entitled by virtue or any such sub-lease to retain possession under—
  - (i) Part VII of the Rent Act 1977 (security of tenure for protected tenancies etc.) or any enactment applying or extending that Part of that Act,
  - (ii) the Rent (Agriculture) Act 1976, or
  - (iii) Part I of the Housing Act 1988 (assured tenancies etc.).

(3) Where a lease has been granted under section 56, no long lease created immediately or derivatively by way of sub-demise under the lease shall confer on the sub-tenant, as against the tenant's landlord, any right under this Chapter to acquire a new lease (and for this purpose "long lease" shall be construed in accordance with section 7).

(4) Any person who—

- (a) grants a sub-lease to which subsection (2)(*b*) and (*c*) will apply, or
- (b) negotiates with a view to the grant of such a sub-lease by him or by a person for whom he is acting as agent,

shall inform the other party that the sub-lease is to be derived out of a lease granted under section 56, unless either he knows that the other party is aware of it or he himself is unaware of it.

(5) Where any lease contains a statement to the effect that it is a lease granted under section 56, the statement shall be conclusive for the purposes of subsections (2) to (4) in favour of any person who is not a party to the lease, unless the statement appears from the lease to be untrue.

Costs incurred in connection with new lease

60.—(1) Where a notice is given under section 42, then (subject to the provision of this section) the tenant by whom it is given shall be liable, to the extent that they have been incurred by any relevant person in pursuance of the notice, for the reasonable costs of and incidental to any of the following matters, namely—

(a) any investigation reasonably undertaken of the tenant's right to a new lease;
(b) any valuation of the tenant's flat obtained for the purpose of fixing the premium or any other amount payable by virtue of Schedule 13 in connection with the grant of a new lease under section 56;
(b) the grant of a new lease under that section;

but this subsection shall not apply to any costs if on a sale made voluntarily a stipulation that they were to be borne by the purchaser would be void.

(2) For the purposes of subsection (1) any costs incurred by a relevant person in respect of professional services rendered by any person shall only be regarded as reasonable if and to the extent that costs in respect of such services might reasonably be expected to have been incurred by him if the circumstances had been such that he was personally liable for all such costs.

(3) Where by virtue of any provision of this Chapter the tenant's notice ceases to have effect, or is deemed to have been withdrawn, at any time, then (subject to subsection (4)) the tenant's liability under this section for costs incurred by any person shall be a liability for costs incurred by him down to that time.

(4) A tenant shall not be liable for any costs under this section if the tenant's notice ceases to have effect by virtue of section 47(1) or 55 (2).

(5) A tenant shall not be liable under this section for any costs which a party to any proceedings under this Chapter before a leasehold valuation tribunal incurs in connection with the proceedings.

(6) In this section "relevant person", in relation to a claim by a tenant under this Chapter, means the landlord for the purposes of this Chapter, any other landlord (as defined by section 40(4)) or any third party to the tenant's lease.

Landlord's right to terminate new lease

61.—(1) Where a lease of a flat ("the new lease") has been granted under section 56 but the court is satisfied, on an application made by the landlord—

(a) that for the purposes of redevelopment the landlord intends—
    (i) to demolish or reconstruct, or

(ii) to carry out substantial works of construction on,
the whole or a substantial part of any premises in which the flat is contained, and

(b) that he could not reasonably do so without obtaining possession of the flat,

the court shall by order declare that the landlord is entitled as against the tenant to obtain possession of the flat and the tenant is entitled to be paid compensation by the landlord for the loss of the flat.

(2) An application for an order under this section may be made—

(a) at any time during the period fo 12 months ending with the term date of the lease in relation to which the right to acquire a new lease was exercised; and
(b) at any time during the period of five years ending with the term date of the new lease.

(3) Where the new lease is not the first lease to be granted under section 56 in respect of a flat, subsection (2) shall apply as if paragraph (b) included a reference to the term date of any previous lease granted under that section in respect of the flat, but paragraph (a) shall be taken to be referring to the term date of the lease in relation to which the right to acquire a new lease was first exercised.

(4) Where an order is made under this section, the new lease shall determine, and compensation shall become payable, in accordance with Schedule 14 to this Act; and the provisons of that Schedule shall have effect as regards the measure of compensation payable by virtue of any such order and the effects of any such order where there are sub-leases, and as regards other matters relating to orders and applications under this section.

(5) Except in subsection (1)(*a*) or (*b*), any reference in this section to the flat held by the tenant under the new lease includes any premises let with the flat under that lease.

Supplemental

62.—(1) In this Chapter—

"the existing lease", in relation to a claim by a tenant under this Chapter, means the lease in relation to which the claim is made;
"the landlord", in relation to such a claim, has the meaning given by section 40(1);
"mortgage" includes a charge or lien;
"qualifying tenant" shall be construed in accordance with section 39(3);
"the relevant date" (unless the context otherwise requires) has the meaning given by section 39(8);
"the tenant's notice" means the notice given under section 42;

"the terms of acquisition" shall be construed in accordance with section 48(7);

"third party", in relation to a lease, means any person who is a party to the lease apart from the tenant under the lease and his immediate landlord.

(2) Subject to subsection (3), references in this Chapter to a flat, in relation to a claim by a tenant under this Chapter, include any garage, outhouse, garden, yard and appurtenances belonging to, or usually enjoyed with, the flat and let to the tenant with the flat on the relevant date (or, in a case where an application is made under section 50(1), on the date of the making of the application).

(3) Subsection (2) does not apply—

(a) to any reference to a flat in section 47 or 55(1); or

(b) to any reference to a flat (not falling within paragraph (*a*) above) which occurs in the context of a reference to any premises containing the flat.

(4) In the application of section 8 for the purposes of this Chapter (in accordance with section 39(3)) references to a flat shall be construed in accordance with subsection (2) above, instead of in accordance with subsection (7) of section 8.

CHAPTER III

ENFRANCHISEMENT UNDER LEASEHOLD REFORM ACT 1967

Extension of right to enfranchise

63. After section 1 of the Leasehold Reform Act 1967 there shall be inserted—

1A—(1) Where subsection (1) of section 1 above would apply in the case of the tenant of a house but for the fact that the applicable financial limit specified in subsection (1)(*a*)(i) or (ii) or (as the case may be) subsection (5) or (6) of that section is exceeded, this Part of this Act shall have effect to confer on the tenant the same right to acquire the freehold of the house and premises as would be conferred by subsection (1) of that section if that limit were not exceeded.

(2) Where a tenancy of any property is not a tenancy at a low rent in accordance with section 4(1) below but is a tenancy falling within section 4A(1) below, the tenancy shall nevertheless be treated as a tenancy at a low rent for the purposes of this Part of this Act so far as it has effect for conferring on any person a right to acquire the freehold of a house and premises."

64.—(1) The following section shall be inserted in the Leasehold Reform Act 1967 after the section 1A inserted by section 63 above—

IB. Where a tenancy granted so as to become terminable by notice after a death or marriage—

(a) is (apart from this section) a long tenancy in accordance with section 3(1) below, but
(b) was granted before April 18, 1980 or in pursuance of a contract entered into before that date,

then (notwithstanding section 3(1)) the tenancy shall be a long tenancy for the purposes of this Part of the Act only so far as this Part has effect for conferring on any person a right to acquire the freehold of a house and premises."

(2) In section 3(1) of that Act (meaning of "long tenancy")—

(a) after "and includes" there shall be inserted "both a tenancy taking effect under section 149(6) of the Law of Property Act 1925 (leases terminable after a death or marriage) and"; and
(b) in the proviso (which prevents certain categories of tenancies terminable after death or marriage being long tenancies), for the words from "if either" onwards there shall be substituted "if—
    (a) the notice is capable of being given at any time after the death or marriage of the tenant;
    (b) the length of the notice is not more than three months; and
    (c) the terms of the tenancy preclude both—
(i) its assignment otherwise than by virtue of section 92 of the Housing Act 1985 (assignments by way of exchange), and
(ii) the sub-letting of the whole of the premises comprised in it."

65. After section 4 of the Leasehold Reform Act 1967 there shall be inserted—

4A.—(1) For the purposes of section 1A(2) above a tenancy of any property falls within this subsection if either no rent was payable under it in respect of the property during the initial year or the aggregate amount of rent so payable during that year did not exceed the following amount, namely—

(a) where the tenancy was entered into before April 1, 1963, two-thirds of the letting value of the property (on the same terms) on the date of the commencement of the tenancy;
(b) where—
    (i) the tenancy was entered into either on or after April 1, 1963 but before April 1, 1990, or on or after April 1, 1990 in pursuance of a contract made before that date, and
    (ii) the property had a rateable value at the date of the commencement of the tenancy or else at any time before April 1, 1990,

two-thirds of the rateable value of the property on the relevant date; or

(c) in any other case, £1,000 if the property is in Greater London or £250 if elsewhere.

(2) For the purposes of subsection (1) above—

(a) "the initial year", in relation to any tenancy, means the period of one year beginning with the date of the commencement of the tenancy;

(b) "the relevant date" means the date of the commencement of the tenancy or, if the property did not have a rateable value on that date, the date on which it first had a rateable value; and

(c) paragraphs (*b*) and (*c*) of section 4(1) above shall apply as they apply for the purposes of section 4(1);

and it is hereby declared that in subsection (1) above the reference to the letting value of any property is to be construed in like manner as the reference in similar terms which appears in the proviso to section 4(1) above.

(3) Section 1(7) above applies to any amount referred to in subsection (1)(*c*) above as it applies to the amount referred to in subsection (1)(*a*)(ii) of that section."

66.—(1) In section 9 of the Leasehold Reform Act 1967 (purchase price and costs of enfranchisement, etc.), after subsection (1B) there shall be inserted—

"(1C) Notwithstanding subsection (1) above, the price payable for a house and premises where the right to acquire the freehold arises by virtue of any one or more of the provisions of sections 1A and 1B above shall be determined in accordance with subsection (1A) above; but in any such case—

(a) if in determining the price so payable there falls to be taken into account any marriage value arising by virtue of the coalescence of the freehold and leasehold interests, the share of the marriage value to which the tenant is to be regarded as being entitled shall not exceed one-half of it; and

(b) section 9A below has effect for determining whether any additional amount is payable by way of compensation under that section;

and in a case where the provision (or one of the provisions) by virtue of which the right to acquire the freehold arises is section 1A(1) above, subsection (1A) above shall apply with the omission of the assumption set out in paragraph (*b*) of that subsection."

(2) Section 9 of that Act, as amended by this section and with the omission of repealed provisions, is set out in Schedule 15 to this Act.

(3) After section 9 of that Act there shall be inserted—

9A.—(1) If, in a case where the right to acquire the freehold of a house and premises arises by virtue of any one or more of the provisions of sections 1A and 1B above, the landlord will suffer any loss or dmaage to which this section applies, there shall be payable to him such amount as is reasonable to compensate him for that loss or damage.

(2) This section applies to—

(a) any diminution in value of any interest of the landlord in other property resulting from the acquisition of his interest in the house and premises; and

(b) any other loss or damage which results therefrom to the extent that it is referable to his ownership of any interest in other property.

(3) Without prejudice to the generality of paragraph (*b*) of subsection (2) above, the kinds of loss falling within that paragraph include loss of development value in relation to the house and premises to the extent that it is referable as mentioned in that paragraph.

(4) In subsection (3) above "development value", in relation to the house and premises, means any increase in the value of the landlord's interest in the house and premises which is attributable to the possibility of demolishing, reconstructing, or carrying out substantial works of construction on, the whole or a substantial part of the house and premises.

(5) In relation to any case falling within subsection (1) above—

(a) any reference (however expressed)—

(i) in section 8 or 9(3) or (5) above, or

(ii) in any of the following provisions of this Act,

to the price payable under section 9 above shall be construed as including a reference to any amount payable to the landlord under this section; and

(b) for the purpose of determining any such separate price as is mentioned in paragraph 7(1)(*b*) of Schedule 1 to this Act, this section shall accordingly apply (with any necessary modifications) to each of the superior interests in question."

Exceptions to right to enfranchise

67.—(1) Section 1 of the Leasehold Reform Act 1967 (tenants entitled to enfranchisement or extension) shall be amended as follows.

(2) In subsection (3) (expected cases) there shall be added at the end—

"or, in the case of any right to which subsection (3A) below applies, at any time when the tenant's immediate landlord is a charitable housing trust and the house forms part of the housing accommodation provided by the trust in the pursuit of its charitable purposes."

(3) After subsection (3) there shall be inserted—

"(3A) For the purposes of subsection (3) above this subsection applies as follows—

(a) where the tenancy was created after commencement of Chapter III of Part I of the Leasehold Reform, Housing and Urban Development Act 1993, this subsection applies to any right to acquire the freehold of the house and premises; but
(b) where the tenancy was created before that commencement, this subsection applies only to any such right exercisable by virtue of any one or more of the provisions of sections 1A and 1B below;

and in that subsection "charitable housing trust" means a housing trust within the meaning of the Housing Act 1985 which is a charity within the meaning of the Charities Act 1993."

68. After section 32 of the Leasehold Reform Act 1967 there shall be inserted—

32A.—(1) A notice of a person's desire to have the freehold of a house and premises under this Part shall be of no effect if at the relevant time the whole or any part of the house and premises is qualifying property and either—

(a) the tenancy was created after the commencement of Chapter III of Part I of the Leasehold Reform, Housing and Urban Development Act 1993; or
(b) (where the tenancy was created before that commencement) the tenant would not be entitled to have the freehold if either or both of sections 1A and 1B above were not in force.

(2) For the purposes of this section the whole or any part of the house and premises is qualifying property if—

(a) it has been designated under section 31(1)(*b*), (*c*) or (*d*) of the Inheritance Tax Act 1984 (designation and undertakings relating to conditionally exempt transfers), whether with or without any other property, and no chargeable event has subsequently occurred with respect to it; or
(b) an application to the Board for it to be so designated is pending; or
(c) it is the property of a body not established or conducted for profit and a direction has been given in relation to it under section 26 of that Act (gifts for public benefit), whether with or without any other property; or
(d) an application to the Board for a direction to be so given in realtion to it is pending.

(3) For the purposes of subsection (2) above an application is pending as from the time when it is made to the Board until such time as it is either granted or refused by the Board or withdrawn by the applicant; and for this purpose an application shall not be regarded as made unless and until the applicant has submitted to the Board all such information in support of the application as is required by the Board.

(4) A notice of a person's desire to have the freehold of a house and premises under this Part shall cease to have effect if—

(a) before completion of the conveyance in pursuance of the tenant's notice, the whole or any part of the house and premises becomes qualifying property; and

(b) the condition set out in subsection (1)(*a*) or (as the case may be) subsection (1)(*b*) above is satisfied.

(5) Where a tenant's notice ceases to have effect by virtue of subsection (4) above—

(a) section 9(4) above shall not apply to require the tenant to make any payment to the landlord in respect of costs incurred by reason of the notice; and

(b) the person who applied or is applying for designation or a direction shall be liable to the tenant for all reasonable costs incurred by the tenant in connection with his claim to acquire the freehold of the house and premises.

(6) Where it is claimed that subsection (1) or (4) above applies in relation to a tenant's ntoice, the person making the claim shall, at the time of making it, furnish the tenant with evidence in support of it; and if he fails to do so he shall be liable for any costs which are reasonably incurred by the tenant in consequence of the failure.

(7) In subsection (2) above—

(a) paragraphs (*a*) and (*b*) apply to designation under section 34(1)(*a*), (*b*) or (*c*) of the Finance Act 1975 or section 77(1)(*b*), (*c*) or (*d*) of the Finance Act 1976 as they apply to designation under section 31(1)(*b*), (*c*) or (*d*) of the Inheritance Tax Act 1984; and

(b) paragraphs (*c*) and (*d*) apply to a direction under paragraph 13 of Schedule 6 to the Finance Act 1975 as they apply to a direction under section 26 of that Act of 1984.

(8) In this section—

"the Board" means the Commissioners of Inland Revenue;

"chargeable event" means—

(a) any event which in accordance with any provision of Chapter II of Part II of the Inheritance Tax Act 1984 (exempt transfers) is a chargeable event, including any such provision as applied by section 78(3) of that Act (conditionally exempt occasions); or

(b) any event which would have been a chargeable event in the circumstances mentioned in section 79(3) of that Act (exemption from ten-yearly charge)."

CHAPTER IV

ESTATE MANAGEMENT SCHEMES IN CONNECTION WITH ENFRANCHISEMENT

69.—(1) For the purposes of this Chapter an estate management scheme is a scheme which (subject to sections 71 and 73) is approved by a leasehold valuation tribunal under section 70 for an area occupied directly or indirectly under leases held from one landlord (apart from property occupied by him or his licensees or for the time being unoccupied) and which is designed to secure that in the event of tenants—

(a) acquiring the landlord's interest in their house and premises ("the house") under Part I of the Leasehold Reform Act 1967 by virtue of any one or more of the provisions of sections 1A and 1B of that Act (as inserted by sections 63 and 64 above), or

(b) acquiring the landlord's interest in any premises ("the premises") in accordance with Chapter I of this Part of this Act, the landlord will—

(i) retain powers of management in respect of the house or premises and,

(ii) have rights against the house or premises in respect of the benefits arising from the exercise elsewhere of his powers of management.

(2) An estate management scheme may make different provision for different parts of the area of the scheme, and shall include provision for terminating or varying all or any of the provisions of the scheme, or excluding part of the area, if a change of circumstances makes it appropriate, or for enabling it to be done by or with the approval of a leasehold valuation tribunal.

(3) Without prejudice to any other provision of this section, an estate management scheme may provide for all or any of the following matters—

(a) for regulating the redevelopment, use or appearance of property in which tenants have acquired the landlord's interest as mentioned in subsection (*a*) or (*b*);

(b) for empowering the landlord for the time being to carry out works of maintenance, repair, renewal or replacement in relation to any such property or carry out work to remedy a failure in respect of any such property to comply with the scheme, or for making the operation of any provisions of the scheme conditional on his doing so or on the provision or maintenance by him of services, facilities or amenities of any description;

(c) for imposing on persons from time to time occupying or interested in any such property obligations in respect of the carrying out of works of maintenance, repair, renewal or replacement in relation to the property or property used or enjoyed by them in common with others, or in respect of costs incurred by the landlord for the time being on any matter referred to in this paragraph (*b*) above;

(d) for the inspection from time to time of any such property on behalf of the landlord for the time being, and for the recovery by him of sums due to him under the scheme in respect of any such property by means of a charge on the property.

and the landlord for the time being shall have, for the enforcement of any charge imposed under the scheme, the same powers and remedies under the Law of Property Act 1925 and otherwise as if he were a mortgagee by deed having powers of sale and leasing and of appointing a receiver.

(4) Except as provided by the scheme, the operation of an estate management scheme shall not be affected by any disposition or devolution of the landlord's interest in the property within the area of the scheme or in parts of that property; but the scheme—

(a) shall include provision for identifying the person who is for the purposes of the scheme to be treated as the landlord for the time being; and

(b) shall also include provision for transferring, or allowing the landlord for the time being to transfer, all or any of the powers and rights conferred by the scheme on the landlord for the time being to a local authority or other body, including a body constituted for the purpose.

(5) Without prejudice to the generality of paragraph (*b*) of subsection (4), an estate management scheme may provide for the operation of any provision for transfer included in the scheme in accordance with that paragraph to be dependent—

(a) on a determination of a leasehold valuation tribunal effecting or approving the transfer;

(b) on such other circumstances as the scheme may provide.

(6) An estate management scheme may extend to property in which the landlord's interest is disposed of otherwise than as mentioned in subsection (1)(*a*) or (*b*) (whether residential property or not), so as to make that property, or allow it to be made, subject to any such provision

as is or might be made by the scheme for property in which tenants acquire the landlord's interest as mentioned in either of those provisions.

(7) In this Chapter references to the landlord for the time being shall have effect, in relation to powers and rights transferred to a local authority or other body as contemplated by subsection (4)(*b*) above, as references to that authority or body.

70.—(1) A leasehold valuation tribunal may, on an application made by a landlord for the approval of a scheme submitted by him to the tribunal, approve the scheme as an estate management scheme for such area falling within section 69(1) as is specified in the scheme; but any such application must (subject to section 72) be made within the period of two years beginning with the date of the coming into force of this section.

(2) A leasehold valuation tribunal shall not approve a scheme as an estate management scheme for any area unless it is satisfied that, in order to maintain adequate standards of appearance and amenity and regulate redevelopment within the area in the event of tenants acquiring the interest of the landlord in any property as mentioned in section 69(1)(*a*) or (*b*), it is in the general interest that the landlord should retain such powers of management and have such rights falling within section 69(1)(i) and (ii) as are conferred by the scheme.

(3) In considering whether to approve a scheme as an estate management scheme for any area, a leasehold valuation tribunal shall have regard primarily to—

- (a) the benefit likely to result from the scheme to the area as a whole (including houses or premises likely to be acquired from the landlord as mentioned in section 69(1)(*a*) or (*b*)); and
- (b) the extent to which it is reasonable to impose, for the benefit of the area, obligations on tenants so acquiring the interest of their landlord;

but the tribunal shall also have regard to the past development and present character of the area and to architectural or historical considerations, to neighbouring areas and to the circumstances generally.

(4) A leasehold valuation tribunal shall not consider any application for it to approve a scheme unless it is satisfied that the applicant has, by advertisement or otherwise, given adequate notice to persons interested—

- (a) informing them of the application for approval of the scheme and the provision intended to be made by the scheme, and
- (b) inviting them to make representations to the tribunal about the application within a time which appears to the tribunal to be reasonable.

(5) In subsection (4) "persons interested" includes, in particular, in relation to any application for the approval of a scheme for any area ("the scheme area") within a conservation area—

(a) each local planning authority within whose area any part of the scheme area falls, and
(b) if the whole of the scheme area is in England, the Historic Buildings and Monuments Commission for England.

(6) Where representations about an application are made under subsection (4)(*b*), the tribunal shall afford to the persons making those representations an opportunity to appear and be heard by the tribunal at the time when the application is considered by it.

(7) Subject to the preceding provisions of this section, a leasehold valuation tribunal shall, after considering the application, approve the scheme in question either—

(a) as originally submitted, or
(b) with any relevant modifications proposed or agreed to by the applicant,

if the scheme (with those modifications, if any) appears to the tribunal—

(i) to be fair and practicable, and
(ii) not to give the landlord a degree of control out of proportion to that previously exercised by him or to that required for the purposes of the scheme.

(8) In subsection (7) "relevant modifications" means modifications relating to the extent of the area to which the scheme is to apply or to the provisions contained in it.

(9) If, having regard to—

(a) the matters mentioned in subsection (3), and
(b) the provision which it is practicable to make by a scheme,

the tribunal thinks it proper to do so, the tribunal may declare that no scheme can be approved for the area in question in pursuance of the application.

(10) A leasehold valuation tribunal shall not dismiss an application for the approval of a scheme unless—

(a) it makes such a declaration as is mentioned in subsection (9); or
(b) in the opinion of the tribunal the applicant is unwilling to agree to a suitable scheme or is not proceeding in the matter with due despatch.

(11) A scheme approved under this section as an estate management scheme for an area shall be a local land charge, notwithstanding section 2(*a*) or (*b*) of the Local Land Charges Act 1975 (matters which are not local land charges), and for the purposes of that Act the landlord for that

area shall be treated as the originating authority as respects any such charge.

(12) Where such a scheme is registered in the appropriate local land charges register—

(a) the provisions of the scheme relating to property of any description shall so far as they respectively affect the persons from time to time occupying or interested in that property be enforceable by the landlord for the time being against them, as if each of them had covenanted with the landlord for the time being to be bound by the scheme; and

(b) in relation to any acquisition such as is mentioned in section 69(1)(*a*) above, section 10 of the Leasehold Reform Act 1967 (rights to be conveyed on enfranchisement) shall have effect subject to the provisions of the scheme, and the price payable under section 9 of that Act shall be adjusted so far as is appropriate (if at all); and

(c) in relation to any acquisition such as is mentioned in section 69(1)(*b*) above, section 34 of, and Schedule 7 to, this Act shall have effect subject to the provisions of the scheme, and any price payable under Schedule 6 to this Act shall be adjusted so far as is appropriate (if at all).

(13) Section 10 of the Local Land Charges Act 1975 (compensation for non-registration etc.) shall not apply to schemes which, by virtue of subsection (11) above, are local land charges.

(14) In this section and in section 73 "conservation area" and "local planning authority" have the same meaning as in the Planning (Listed Buildings and Conservation Areas) Act 1990; and in connection with the latter expression—

(a) the expression "the planning Acts" in the Town and Country Planning Act 1990 shall be treated as including this Act; and

(b) paragraphs 4 and 5 of Schedule 4 to the Planning (Listed Buildings and Conservation Areas) Act 1990 (further provisions as to exercise of functions by different authorities) shall apply in relation to functions under or by virtue of this section or section 73 of this Act as they apply in relation to functions under section 69 of that Act.

71.—(1) Where, on a joint application made by two or more persons as landlords of neighbouring areas, it appears to a leasehold valuation tribunal—

(a) that a scheme could in accordance with subsections (1) and (2) of section 70 be approved as an estate management scheme for those areas, treated as a unit, if the interests of those persons were held by a single person, and

(b) that the applicants are willing to be bound by the scheme to co-operate in the management of their property in those areas and in the administration of the scheme,

the tribunal may (subject to the provisions of section 70 and subsection (2) below) approve the scheme under that section as an estate management scheme for those areas as a whole.

(2) Any such scheme shall be made subject to conditions (enforceable in such manner as may be provided by the scheme) for securing that the landlords and their successors co-operate as mentioned in subsection (1)(*b*) above.

(3) Where it appears to a leasehold valuation tribunal—

(a) that a scheme could, on the application of any landlord or landlords, be approved under section 70 as an estate management scheme for any area or areas, and

(b) that any body of persons—

(i) is so constituted as to be capable of representing for the purposes of the scheme the persons occupying or interested in property in the area or areas (other than the landlord or landlords or his or their licensees), or such of them as are or may become entitled to acquire their landlord's interest as mentioned in section 69(1)(*a*) or (*b*), and

(ii) is otherwise suitable,

an application for the approval of the scheme under section 70 may be made to the tribunal by the representative body alone or by the landlord or landlords alone or by both jointly and, by leave of the tribunal, may be proceeded with by the representative body or by the landlord or landlords despite the fact that the body or landlord or landlords in question did not make the application.

(4) Without prejudice to section 69(4)(*b*), any such scheme may with the consent of the landlord or landlords, or on such terms as to compensation or otherwise as appear to the tribunal to be just—

(a) confer on the representative body any such rights or powers under the scheme as might be conferred on the landlord or landlords for the time being, or

(b) enable the representative body to participate in the administration of the scheme or in the management by the landlord or landlords of his or their property in the area or areas.

(5) Where any such scheme confers any rights or powers on the representative body in accordance with subsection (4) above, section 70(11) and (12)(*a*) shall have effect with such modifications (if any) as are provided for in the scheme.

72.—(1) An application for the approval of a scheme for an area under section 70 (including an application in accordance with section 71(1) or (3)) may be made after the expiry of the period mentioned in subsection (1) of that section if the Secretary of State has, not more than six months previously, consented to the making of such an application for that area or for an area within which that area falls.

(2) The Secretary of State may give consent under subsection (1) to the making of an application ("the proposed application") only where he is satisfied—

(a) that either or both of the conditions mentioned in subsection (3) apply; and
(b) that adequate notice has been given to persons interested informing them of the request for consent and the purpose of the request.

(3) The conditions referred to in subsection (2)(*a*) are—

(a) that the proposed application could not have been made before the expiry of the period mentioned in section 70(1); and
(b) that—
   (i) any application for the approval under section 70 of a scheme for the area, or part of the area, to which the proposed application relates would probably have been dismissed under section 70(10)(a) had it been made before the expiry of that period; but
   (ii) because of a change in any of the circumstances required to be considered under section 70(3) the proposed application would, if made following the giving of consent by the Secretary of State, probably be granted.

(4) A request for consent under subsection (1) must be in writing and must comply with such requirements (if any) as to the form of, or the particulars to be contained in, any such request as the Secretary of State may by regulations prescribe.

(5) The procedure for considering a request for consent under subsection (1) shall be such as may be prescribed by regulations made by the Secretary of State.

73.—(1) Where it appears to a leasehold valuation tribunal after the expiry of the period mentioned in section 70(1) that a scheme could, on the application of any landlord or landlords within that period, have been approved under section 70 as an estate management scheme for any area or areas within a conservation area, an application for the approval of the scheme under that section may, subject to subsections (2) and (3) below, be made to the tribunal by one or more bodies constituting the relevant authority for the purposes of this section.

(2) An application under subsection (1) may only be made if—

(a) no scheme has been approved under section 70 for the whole or any part of the area or areas to which the application relates ("the scheme area"); and
(b) any application which has been made in accordance with section 70(1), 71(1) or 71(3) for the approval of a scheme for the whole or any part of the scheme area has been withdrawn or dismissed; and
(c) no request for consent under section 72(1) which relates to the whole or any part of the scheme area is pending or has been granted within the last six months.

(3) An application under subsection (1) above must be made within the period of six months beginning—

(a) with the date on which the period mentioned in section 70(1) expires, or
(b) if any application has been made as mentioned in subsection (2)(*b*) above, with the date (or, as the case may be, the latest date) on which any such application is withdrawn or dismissed,

whichever is the later; but if at any time during that period of six months a request of a kind mentioned in subsection (2)(*c*) above is pending or granted, an application under subsection (1) above may, subject to subsection (2) above, be made within the period of—

(i) six months beginning with the date on which the request is withdrawn or refused, or
(ii) twelve months beginning with the date on which the request is granted,

as the case may be.

(4) A scheme approved on an application under subsection (1) may confer on the applicant or applicants any such rights or powers under the scheme as might have been conferred on the landlord or landlords for the time being.

(5) For the purposes of this section the relevant authority for the scheme area is—

(a) where that area falls wholly within the area of a local planning authority—
    (i) that authority; or
    (ii) subject to subsection (6), that authority acting jointly with the Historic Buildings and Monuments Commission for England ("the Commission"); or
    (iii) subject to subsection (6), the Commission; or
(b) in any other case—
    (i) all of the local planning authorities within each of whose areas any part of the scheme area falls, acting jointly; or

(ii) subject to subsection (6), one or more of those authorities acting jointly with the Commission; or
(iii) subject to subsection (6), the Commission.

(6) The Commission may make, or join in the making of, an application under subsection (1) only if—

(a) the whole of the scheme area is in England; and
(b) they have consulted any local planning authority wihin whose area the whole or any part or the scheme area falls.

(7) Where a scheme is approved on an application under subsection (1) by two or more bodies acting jointly, the scheme shall, if the tribunal considers it appropriate, be made subject to conditions (enforceable in such manner as may be provided by the scheme) for securing that those bodies co-operate in the administration of the scheme.

(8) Where a scheme is approved on an application under subsection (1)—

(a) section 70(11) and (12)(*a*) shall (subject to subsection (9) below) have effect as if any reference to the landlord, or the landlord for the time being, for the area for which an estate management scheme has been approved were a reference to the applicant or applicants; and
(b) section 70(12)(*b*) and (*c*) shall each have effect with the omission of so much of that provision as relates to the adjustment of any such price as is there mentioned.

(9) A scheme so approved shall not be enforceable by a local planning authority in relation to any property falling outside the authority's area; and in the case of a scheme approved on a joint application made by one or more local planning authorities and the Commission, the scheme may provide for any of its provisions to be enforceable in relation to property falling within the area of a local planning authority either by the authority alone, or by the Commission alone, or by the authority and the Commission acting jointly, as the scheme may provide.

(10) For the purposes of—

(a) section 9(1A) of the Leasehold Reform Act 1967 (purchase price on enfranchisement) as it applies in relation to any acquisition such as is mentioned in section 69(1)(*a*) above, and
(b) paragraph 3 of Schedule 6 to this Act as it applies in relation to any acquisition such as is mentioned in section 69(1)(*b*) above (including that paragraph as it applies by virtue of paragraph 7 or 11 of that Schedule),

it shall be assumed that any scheme approved under subsection (1) and relating to the property in question had not been so approved, and accordingly any application for such an application being made, shall be disregarded.

(11) Section 70(14) applies for the purposes of this section.

74.—(1) Subject to subsections (5) and (6), this subsection applies where—

(a) an application ("the scheme application") is made for the approval of a scheme as an estate management scheme for any area or a request ("the request for consent") is made for consent under section 72(1) in relation to any area, and

(b) whether before or after the making of the application or request—

(i) the tenant of a house in that area gives notice of his desire to have the freehold under Part I of the Leasehold Reform Act 1967, being entitled to do so by virtue only of either or both of the sections of that Act referred to in section 69(1)(*a*) above, or

(ii) a notice is given under section 13 above in respect of any premises in the area.

(2) Where subsection (1) applies by virtue of paragraph (*b*)(i) of that subsection, then—

(a) no further steps need be taken towards the execution of a conveyance to give effect to section 10 of the 1967 Act beyond those which appear to the landlord to be reasonable in the circumstances; and

(b) if the notice referred to in subsection (1)(*b*)(i) ("the tenant's notice") was given before the making of the scheme application or the request for consent, that notice may be withdrawn by a further notice given by the tenant to the landlord.

(3) Where subsection (1) applies by virtue of paragraph (*b*)(ii) of that subsection, then—

(a) if the notice referred to in that provision ("the initial notice") was given before the making of the scheme application or the request for consent, the notice may be withdrawn by a further notice given by the nominee purchaser to the reversioner;

(b) unless the initial notice is so withdrawn, the reversioner shall, if he has not already given the nominee purchaser a counter-notice under section 21, give him by the date referred to in subsection (1) of that section a counter-notice which complies with one of the requirements set out in subsection (2) of that section (but in relation to which subsection (3) of that section need not be complied with); and

(c) no proceedings shall be brought under Chapter I in pursuance of the initial notice otherwise than under section 22 or 23, and, if the court in either of those sections makes an order requiring the reversioner to give a further counter-notice to the nominee purchaser, the date by which it is to be given shall be such date as falls two months after subsection (1) above ceases to apply;

but no other counter-notice need to given under Chapter I, and (subject to the preceding provisions of this subsection) no further steps need to be taken towards the final determination (whether by agreement or otherwise) of the terms of the proposed acquisition by the nominee purchaser beyond those which appear to the reversioner to be reasonable in the circumstances.

(4) If the tenant's notice or the initial notice is withdrawn in accordance with subsection (2) or (3) above, section 9(4) of the 1967 Act or (as the case may be) section 33 above shall not have effect to require the payment of any costs incurred in pursuance of that notice.

(5) Where the scheme application is withdrawn or dismissed, subsection (1) does not apply at any time falling after—

(a) the date of the withdrawal of the application, or
(b) the date when the decision of the tribunal dismissing the application becomes final,

as the case may be; and subsection (1) does not apply at any time falling after the date on which a scheme is approved for the area referred to in that subsection, or for any part of it, in pursuance of the scheme application.

(6) Where the request for consent is withdrawn or refused, subsection (1) does not apply at any time falling after the date on which the request is withdrawn or refused, as the case may be; and where the request is granted, subsection (1) does not apply at any time falling more than six months after the date on which it is granted (unless that subsection applies by virtue of an application made in reliance on the consent).

(7) Where, in accordance with subsection (5) or (6), subsection (1) ceases to apply as from a particular date, it shall do so without prejudice to—

(a) the effect of anything done before that date in pursuance of subsection (2) or (3); or
(b) the operation of any provision of this Part, or of regulations made under it, in relation to anything so done.

(8) If, however, no notice of withdrawal has been given in accordance with subsection (3) before the date when subsection (1) so ceases to apply and before that date either—

(a) the reversioner has given the nominee purchaser a counter-notice under section 21 complying with the requirement set out in subsection (2)(*a*) of that section, or

(b) section 23(6) would (but for subsection (3) above) have applied to require the reversioner to give a further counter-notice to the nominee purchaser,

the reversioner shall give a further counter-notice to the nominee purchaser within the period of two months beginning with the date when subsection (1) ceases to apply.

(9) Subsections (3) to (5) of section 21 shall apply to any further counter-notice required to be given by the reversioner under subsection (8) above as if it were a counter-notice under that section complying with the requirement set out in subsection (2)(*a*) of that section; and sections 24 and 25 shall apply in relation to any such counter-notice as they apply in relation to one required by section 22(3).

(10) In this section—

"the 1967 Act" means the Leasehold Reform Act 1967; and
"the nominee purchaser" and "the reversioner" have the same meaning as in Chapter I of this Part of this Act;

and references to the approval of a scheme for any area include references to the approval of a scheme for two or more areas in accordance with section 71 or 73 above.

75.—(1) Where a scheme under section 19 of the Leasehold Reform Act 1967 (estate management schemes in connection with enfranchisement under that Act) includes, in pursuance of subsection (6) of that section, provision for enabling the termination or variation of the scheme, or the exclusion of part of the area of the scheme, by or with the approval of the High Court, that provision shall have effect—

(a) as if any reference to the High Court were a reference to a leasehold valuation tribunal, and
(b) with such modifications (if any) as are necessary in consequence of paragraph (*a*).

(2) A scheme under that section may be varied by or with the approval of a leasehold valuation tribunal for the purpose of, or in connection with, extending the scheme to property within the area of the scheme in which the landlord's interest may be acquired as mentioned in section 69(1)(*a*) above.

(3) Where any such scheme has been varied in accordance with subsection (2) above, section 19 of that Act shall apply as if the variation has been effected under provisions included in the scheme in pursuance of subsection (6) of that section (and accordingly the scheme may be further varied under provisions so included).

(4) Any application made under or by virtue of this section to a leasehold valuation tribunal shall comply with such requirements (if any) as to the form of, or the particulars to be contained in, any such application as the Secretary of State may by regulations prescribe.

(5) In this section any reference to a leasehold valuation tribunal is a refernce to such a rent assessment committee as is mentioned in section 142(2) of the Housing Act 1980 (leasehold valuation tribunals).

CHAPTER V

TENANT'S RIGHT TO MANAGEMENT AUDIT

76.—(1) This Chapter has effect to confer on two or more qualifying tenants of dwellings held on leases from the same landlord the right, exerciseable subject to and in accordance with this Chapter, to have an audit carried out on their behalf which relates to the management of the relevant premises and any appurtenant property by or on behalf of the landlord.

(2) That right shall be exercisable—

(a) where the relevant premises consist of or include two dwellings let to qualifying tenants of the same landlord, by either or both of those tenants; and

(b) where the relevant premises consist of or include three or more dwellings let to qualifying tenants of the same landlord, by not less than two-thirds of those tenants;

and in this Chapter the dwellings let to those qualifying tenants are referred to as "the constituent dwellings".

(3) In relation to an audit on behalf of two or more qualifying tenants—

(a) "the relevant premises" means so much of—

(i) the building or buildings containing the dwellings let to those tenants, and

(ii) any other building or buildings,

as constitutes premises in relation to which management functions are discharged in respect of the costs of which common service charge contributions are payable under the leases of those qualifying tenants; and

(b) "appurtenant property" means so much of any property not contained in the relevant premises as constitutes property in relation to which any such management functions are discharged.

(4) This Chapter also has effect to confer on a single qualifying tenant of a dwelling the right, exerciseable subject to and in accordance with this Chapter, to have an audit carried out on his behalf which relates to the management of the relevant premises and any appurtenant property by or on behalf of the landlord.

(5) That right shall be exercisable by a single qualifying tenant of a dwelling where the relevant premises contain no other dwelling let to a qualifying tenant apart from that let to him.

(6) In relation to an audit on behalf of a single qualifying tenant—

(a) "the relevant premises" means so much of—
  (i) the building containing the dwelling let to him, and
  (ii) any other building or buildings,

as constitutes premises in relation to which management functions are discharged in respect of the costs of which a service charge is payable under his lease (whether as a common service charge contribution or otherwise); and

(b) "appurtenant property" means so much of any property not contained in the relevant premises as constitutes property in relation to which any such management functions are discharged.

(7) The provisions of sections 78 to 83 shall, with any necessary modifications, have effect in relation to an audit on behalf of a single qualifying tenant as they have effect in relation to an audit on behalf of two or more qualifying tenants.

(8) For the purposes of this section common service charge contributions are payable by two or more persons under their leases if they may be required under the terms of those leases to contribute to the same costs by the payment of service charges.

77.—(1) Subject to the following provisions of this section, a tenant is a qualifying tenant of a dwelling for the purposes of this Chapter if—

(a) he is a tenant of the dwelling under a long lease other than a business lease; and
(b) any service charge is payable under the lease.

(2) For the purposes of subsection (1) a lease is a long lease if—

(a) it is a lease falling within any of paragraphs (*a*) to (*c*) of subsection (1) of section 7; or
(b) it is a shared ownership lease (within the meaning of that section), whether granted in pursuance of Part V of the Housing Act 1985 or otherwise and whatever the share of the tenant under it.

(3) No dwelling shall have more than one qualifying tenant at any one time.

(4) Accordingly—

(a) where a dwelling is for the time being let under two or more leases falling within subsection (1), any tenant under any of those leases which is superior to that held by any other such tenant shall not be a qualifying tenant of the dwelling for the purposes of this Chapter; and

(b) where a dwelling is for the time being let to joint tenants under a lease falling within subsection (1), the joint tenants shall (subject to paragraph (*a*)) be regarded for the purposes of this Chapter as jointly constituting the qualifying tenant of the dwelling.

(5) A person can, however, be (or be among those constituting) the qualifying tenant of each of two or more dwellings at the same time, whether he is tenant of those dwellings under one lease or under two or more separate leases.

(6) Where two or more persons constitute the qualifying tenant of a dwelling in accordance with subsection (4)(*b*), any one or more of those persons may sign a notice under section 80 on behalf of both or all of them.

78.—(1) The audit referred to in section 76(1) is an audit carried out for the purpose of ascertaining—

(a) the extent to which the obligations of the landlord which—
   (i) are owed to the qualifying tenants of the constituent dwellings, and
   (ii) involve the discharge of management functions in relation to the relevant premises or any appurtenant property,

are being discharged in an efficient and effective manner; and

(b) the extent to which sums payable by those tenants by way of service charges are being applied in an efficient and effective manner;

and in this Chapter any such audit is referred to as a "management audit".

(2) In determining whether any such obligations as are mentioned in subsection (1)(*a*) are being discharged in an efficient and effective manner, regard shall be had to any applicable provisions of any code of practice for the time being approved by the Secretary of State under section 87.

(3) A management audit shall be carried out by a person who—

(a) is qualified for appointment by virtue of subsection (4); and
(b) is appointed—
   (i) in the circumstances mentioned in section 76(2)(*a*), by either or both of the qualifying tenants of the constituent dwellings, or
   (ii) in the circumstances mentioned in section 76(2)(*b*), by not less than two-thirds of the qualifying tenants of the constituent dwellings;

and in this Chapter any such person is referred to as "the auditor".

(4) A person is qualified for appointment for the purposes of subsection (3) above if—

(a) he has the necessary qualification (within the meaning of subsection (1) of section 28 of the 1985 Act (meaning of "qualified accountant")) or is a qualified surveyor;
(b) he is not qualified from acting (within the meaning of that subsection); and
(c) he is not a tenant of any premises contained in the relevant premises.

(5) For the purposes of subsection (4)(*a*) above a person is a qualified surveyor if he is a fellow or professional associate of the Royal Institution of Chartered Surveyors or of the Incorporated Society of Valuers and Auctioneers or satisfies such other requirement or requirements as may be prescribed by regulations made by the Secretary of State.

(6) The auditor may appoint such persons to assist him in carrying out the audit as he thinks fit.

79.—(1) Where the qualifying tenants of any dwellings exercise under section 80 their right to have a management audit carried out on their behalf, the rights conferred on the auditor by subsection (2) below shall be exercisable by him in connection with the audit.

(2) The rights conferred on the auditor by this subsection are—

(a) a right to require the landlord—
    (i) to supply him with such a summary as is referred to in section 21(1) of the 1985 Act (request for summary of relevant costs) in connection with any service charge payable by the qualifying tenants of the constituent dwellings, and
    (ii) to afford him reasonable facilities for inspecting, or taking copies of or extracts from, the accounts, receipts and other documents supporting any such summary;
(b) a right to require the landlord or any relevant person to afford him reasonable facilities for inspecting any other documents sight of which is reasonably required by him for the purpose of carrying out the audit; and
(c) a right to require the landlord or any relevant person to afford him reasonable facilities for taking copies of or extracts fromany documents falling within paragraph (*b*).

(3) The rights conferred on the auditor by subsection (2) shall be exercisable by him—

(a) in relation to the landlord, by means of a notice under section 80; and

(b) in relation to any relevant person, by means of a notice given to that person at (so far as is reasonably practicable) the same time as a notice under section 80 is given to the landlord;

and, where a notice is given to any relevant person in accordance with paragraph (b) above, a copy of that notice shall be given to the landlord by the auditor.

(4) The auditor shall also be entitled, on giving notice in accordance with section 80, to carry out an inspection of any common parts comprised in the relevant premises or any appurtenant property.

(5) The landlord or (as the case may be) any relevant person shall—

(a) where facilities for the inspection of any documents are required under subsection (2)(*a*)(ii) or (*b*), make those facilities available free of charge;

(b) where any documents are required to be supplied under subsection (2)(*a*)(i) or facilities for the taking of copies or extracts are required under subsection (2)(*a*)(ii) or (*c*), be entitled to supply those documents or (as the case may be) make those facilities available on payment of such reasonable charge as he may determine.

(6) The requirement imposed on the landlord by subsection (5)(a) to make any facilities available free of charge shall not be construed as precluding the landlord from treating as part of his costs of management any costs incurred by him in connection with making those facilities so available.

(7) In this Chapter "relevant person" means a person (other than the landlord) who—

(a) is charged with responsibility—
  (i) for the discharge of any such obligations as are mentioned in section 78(1)(*a*), or
  (ii) for the application of any such service charges as are mentioned in section 78(1)(*b*); or

(b) has a right to enforce payment of any such service charges.

(8) In this Chapter references to the auditor in the context of—

(a) being afforded any such facilities as are mentioned in subsection (2), or

(b) the carrying out of any inspection under subsection (4),

shall be read as including a person appointed by the auditor under section 78(6).

80.—(1) The right of any qualifying tenants to have a management audit carried out on their behalf shall be exercisable by the giving of a notice under this section.

(2) A notice given under this section—

(a) must be given to the landlord by the auditor, and
(b) must be signed by each of the tenants on whose behalf it is given.

(3) Any such notice must—

(a) state the full name of each of those tenants and the address of the dwelling of which he is a qualifying tenant;
(b) state the name and address of the auditor;
(c) specify any documents or description of documents—
 (i) which the landlord is required to supply to the auditor under section 79(2)(*a*)(i), or
 (ii) in respect of which he is required to afford the auditor facilities for inspection or for taking copies or extracts under any other provision of section 79(2); and
(d) if the auditor proposes to carry out an inspection under section 79(4), state the date on which he proposes to carry out the inspection.

(4) The date specified under subsection (3)(*d*) must be a date falling not less than one month nor more than two months after the date of the giving of the notice.

(5) A notice is duly given under this section to the landlord of any qualifying tenants if it is given to a person who receives on behalf of the landlord the rent payable by any such tenants; and a person to whom such a notice is so given shall forward it as soon as may be to the landlord.

81.—(1) Where the landlord is given a notice under section 80, then within the period of one month beginning with the date of the giving of the notice, he shall—

(a) supply the auditor with any document specified under subsection (3)(*c*)(i) of that section, and afford him, in respect of any document falling within section 79(2)(*a*)(ii), any facilities specified in relation to it under subsection (3)(*c*)(ii) of section 80;
(b) in the case of every other document or description of documents specified in the notice under subsection (3)(c)(ii) of that section, either—
 (i) afford the auditor facilities for inspection or (as the case may be) taking copies or extracts in respect of that document or those documents, or
 (ii) give the auditor a notice stating that he objects to doing so for such reasons as are specified in the notice; and
(c) if a date specified in the notice under subsection (3)(*d*) of that section, either approve the date or propose another date for the carrying out of an inspection under section 79(4).

(2) Any date proposed by the landlord under subsection (1)(*c*) must be a date falling not later than the end of the period of two months beginning with the date of the giving of the notice under section 80.

(3) Where a relevant person is given a notice under section 79 requiring him to afford the auditor facilities for inspection or taking copies or extracts in respect of any documents or description of documents specified in the notice, then within the period of one month beginning with the date of the giving of the notice, he shall, in the case of every such document or description of documents, either—

(a) afford the auditor the facilities required by him; or
(b) give the auditor a notice stating that he objects to doing so for such reasons as are specified in the notice.

(4) If by the end of the period of two months beginning with—

(a) the date of the giving of the notice under section 80, or
(b) the date of the giving of such a notice under section 79 as is mentioned in subsection (3) above,

the landlord or (as the case may be) a relevant person has failed to comply with any requirement of the notice, the court may, on the application of the auditor, make an order requiring the landlord or (as the case may be) the relevant person to comply with that requirement within such period as is specified in the order.

(5) The court shall not make an order under subsection (4) in respect of any document or documents unless it is satisfied that the document or documents falls or fall within paragraph (*a*) or (*b*) of section 79(2).

(6) If by the end of the period of two months specified in subsection (2) no inspection under section 79(4) has been carried out by the auditor, the court may, on the application of the auditor, make an order providing for such an inspection to be carried out on such date as is specified in the order.

(7) Any application for an order under subsection (4) or (6) must be made before the end of the period of four months beginning with—

(a) in the case of an application made in connection with a notice given under section 80, the date of the giving of that notice; or
(b) in the case of an application made in connection with such a notice under section 79 as is mentioned in subsection (3) above, the date of the giving of that notice.

82.—(1) Where the landlord is required by a notice under section 80 to supply any summary falling within section 79(2)(*a*), and any information necessary for complying with the notice so far as relating to any such summary is in the possession of a superior landlord—

(a) the landlord shall make a written request for the relevant information to the person who is his landlord (and so on, if that person is himself not the superior landlord);

(b) the superior landlord shall comply with that request within the period of one month beginning with the date of the making of the request; and

(c) the landlord who received the notice shall then comply with it so far as relating to any such summary within the time allowed by section 81(1) or such further time, if any, as is reasonable.

(2) Where—

(a) the landlord is required by a notice under section 80 to afford the auditor facilities for inspection or taking copies or extracts in respect of any documents or description of documents specified in the notice, and

(b) any of the documents in question is in the custody or under the control of a superior landlord,

the landlord shall on receiving the notice inform the auditor as soon as may be of that fact and of the name and address of the superior landlord, and the auditor may then give the superior landlord a notice requiring him to afford the facilities in question in respect of the document.

(3) Subsections (3) to (5) and (7) of section 81 shall, with any necessary modifications, have effect in relation to a notice given to a superior landlord under subsection (2) above as they have effect in relation to any such notice given to a relevant person as is mentioned in subsection (3) of that section.

83.—(1) Where—

(a) a notice has been given to a landlord under section 80, and

(b) at a time when any obligations arising out of the notice remain to be discharged by him—

  (i) he disposes of the whole or part of his interest as landlord of the qualifying tenants of the constituent dwellings, and

  (ii) the person acquiring any such interest of the landlord is in a position to discharge any of those obligations to any extent,

that person shall be responsible for discharging those obligations to that extent, as if he had been given the notice under that section.

(2) If the landlord is, despite any such disposal, still in a position to discharge those obligations to the extent referred to in subsection (1), he shall remain responsible for so discharging them; but otherwise the person referred to in that subsection shall be responsible for so discharging them to the exclusion of the landlord.

(3) Where a person is so responsible for discharging any such obligations (whether with the landlord or otherwise)—

(a) references to the landlord in section 81 shall be read as including, or as, references to that person to such extent as is appropriate to reflect his responsibility for discharging those obligations; but

(b) in connection with the discharge of any such obligations by that person, that section shall apply as if any reference to the date of the giving of the notice under section 80 were a reference to the date of the disposal referred to in subsection (1).

(4) Where—

(a) a notice has been given to a relevant person under section 79, and

(b) at a time when any obligations arising out of the notice remain to be discharged by him, he ceases to be a relevant person, but

(c) he is, despite ceasing to be a relevant person, still in a position to discharge those obligations to any extent,

he shall nevertheless remain responsible for discharging those obligations to that extent; and section 81 shall accordingly continue to apply to him as if he were still a relevant person.

(5) Where—

(a) a notice has been given to a landlord under section 80, or

(b) a notice has been given to a relevant person under section 79,

then during the period of twelve months beginning with the date of that notice, no subsequent such notice may be given to the landlord or (as the case may be) that person on behalf of any persons who, in relation to the earlier notice, were qualifying tenants of the constituent dwellings.

84. In this Chapter—

"the 1985 Act" means the Landlord and Tenant Act 1985;

"appurtenant property" shall be construed in accordance with section 76(3) or (6);

"the auditor", in relation to a management audit, means such a person as is mentioned in section 78(3);

"the constituent dwellings" means the dwellings referred to in section 76(2)(*a*) or (*b*) (as the case may be);

"landlord" means immediate landlord;

"management audit" means such an audit as is mentioned in section 78(1);

"management functions" includes functions with respect to the provisions of services or the repair, maintenance or insurance of property;

"relevant person" has the meaning given by section 79(7);

"the relevant premises" shall be construed in accordance with section 76(3) or (6);

"service charge" has the meaning given by section 18(1) of the 1985 Act.

CHAPTER VI

MISCELLANEOUS

Compulsory acquisition of landlord's interest

85.—(1) Part III of the Landlord and Tenant Act 1987 (compulsory acquisition by tenants of their landlord's interest) shall be amended as follows.

(2) In section 25 (compulsory acquisition of landlord's interest by qualifying tenants)—

(a) for subsection (2)(*c*) there shall be substituted—

"(c) the total number of flats held by such tenants is not less than two-thirds of the total number of flats contained in the premises."; and

(b) subsection (3) shall be omitted.

(3) In section 27(4) (meaning of requisite majority in relation to qualifying tenants), for "more than 50 per cent." there shall be substituted "not less than two-thirds".

(4) In section 29(2) (conditions for making acquisition orders), the words from "and (*c*)" onwards shall be omitted.

Variation of leases

86. In section 35(4) of the Landlord and Tenant Act 1987 (variation of lease on grounds that it fails to make satisfactory provision with respect to the computation of a service charge), in paragraph (*c*), for "exceed" there shall be substituted "either exceed or be less than".

Codes of practice

87.—(1) The Secretary of State may, if he considers it appropriate to do so, by order—

(a) approve any code of practice—
  (i) which appears to him to be designed to promote desirable practices in relation to any matter or matters directly or indirectly concerned with the management of residential property by relevant persons; and
  (ii) which has been submitted to him for his approval;

(b) approve any modifications of any such code which have been so submitted; or

(c) withdraw his approval for any such code or modifications.

(2) The Secretary of State shall not approve any such code or any modifications of any such code unless he is satisfied that arrangements

have been made for the text of the code or the modifications to be published in such manner as he considers appropriate for bringing the provisions of the code or the modifications to the notice of those likely to be affected by them (which, in the case of modifications of a code, may include publications of a text of the code incorporating the modifications).

(3) The power of the Secretary of State under this section to approve a code of practice which has been submitted to him for his approval includes power to approve a part of any such code; and references in this section to a code of practice may accordingly be read as including a reference to a part of a code of practice.

(4) At any one time there may be two or more codes of practice for the time being approved under this section.

(5) A code of practice approved under this section may make different provision with respect to different cases or descriptions of cases, including different provision for different areas.

(6) Without prejudice to the generality of subsections (1) and (5)—

(a) a code of practice approved under this section may, in relation to any such matter as is referred to in subsection (1), make provision in respect of relevant persons who are under an obligation to discharge any function in connection with that matter as well as in respect of relevant persons who are not under such an obligation; and

(b) any such code may make provision with respect to—

(i) the resolution of disputes with respect to residential property between relevant persons and the tenants of such property;

(ii) competitive tendering for works in connection with such property; and

(iii) the administration of trusts in respect of amounts paid by tenants by way of service charges.

(7) A failure on the part of any person to comply with any provision of a code of practice for the time being approved under this section shall not of itself render him liable to any proceedings; but in any proceedings before a court or tribunal—

(a) any code of practice approved under this section shall be admissible in evidence; and

(b) any provision of any such code which appears to the court or tribunal to be relevant to any question arising in the proceedings shall be taken into account in determining that question.

(8) For the purposes of this section—

(a) "relevant person" means any landlord of residential property or any person who discharges management functions in respect of such property, and for this purpose "management functions" includes functions with respect to the provision of services or the repair, maintenance or insurance of such property;

(b) "residential property" means any building or part of a building which consists of one or more dwellings let on leases, but references to residential property include—
   (i) any garage, outhouse, garden, yard and appurtenances belonging to or usually enjoyed with such dwellings,
   (ii) any common parts of any such building or part, and
   (iii) any common facilities which are not within any such building or part; and

(c) "service charge" means an amount payable by a tenant of a dwelling as part of or in addition to the rent—
   (i) which is payable, directly or indirectly, for services, repairs, maintenance or insurance or any relevant person's costs of management, and
   (ii) the whole or part of which varies or may vary according to the costs or estimated costs incurred or to be incurred by any relevant person in connection with the matters mentioned in sub-paragraph (i).

(9) This section applies in relation to dwellings let on licences to occupy as it applies in relation to dwellings let on leases, and references in this section to landlords and tenants of residential property accordingly include references to licensors and licensees of such property.

Jurisdiction of leasehold valuation tribunals in relation to enfranchisement etc. of Crown land

88.—(1) This section applies where any tenant under a lease from the Crown is proceeding with a view to acquiring the freehold or an extended lease of a house and premises in circumstances in which, but for the existence of any Crown interest in the land subject to the lease, he would be entitled to acquire the freehold or such an extended lease under Part I of the leasehold Reform Act 1967.

(2) Where—

(a) this section applies in accordance with subsection (1), and
(b) any question arises in connection with the acquisition of the freehold or an extended lease of the house and premises which is such that, if the tenant were proceeding as mentioned in that subsection in pursuance of a claim made under Part I of that Act, a leasehold valuation tribunal constituted for the purposes of that Part of that Act would have jurisdiction to determine it in proceedings under that Part, and

(c) it is agreed between—
    (i) the appropriate authority and the tenant, and
    (ii) all other persons (if any) whose interests would fall to be represented in proceedings brought under that Part for the determination of that question by such a tribunal,

that that question should be determined by such a tribunal,

a rent assessment committee constituted for the purposes of this section shall have jurisdiction to determine that question.

(3) A rent assessment committee shall, when constituted for the purposes of this section, be known as a leasehold valuation tribunal.

(4) Paragraphs 1 to 3 of Schedule 22 to the Housing Act 1980 (provisions relating to leasehold valuation tribunals constituted for the purposes of Part I of the Leasehold Reform Act 1967) shall apply to a leasehold valuation tribunal constituted for the purposes of this section.

(5) Any application made to such a leasehold valuation tribunal must comply with such requirements (if any) as to the form of, or the particulars to be contained in, any such application as the Secretary of State may by regualtions prescribe.

(6) For the purposes of this section "lease from the Crown" means a lease of land in which there is, or has during the subsistence of the lease been, a Crown interest superior to the lease; and "Crown interest" and "the appropriate authority" in relation to a Crown interest mean respectively—

(a) an interest comprised in the Crown Estate, and the Crown Estate Commissioners;
(b) an interest belonging to Her Majesty in right of the Duchy of Lancaster, and the Chancellor of the Duchy;
(c) an interest belonging to the Duchy of Cornwall, and such person as the Duke of Cornwall or the possessor for the time being of the Duchy appoints;
(d) any other interest belonging to a government department or held on behalf of Her Majesty for the purposes of a government department, and the Minister in charge of that department.

(7) In this section any reference to a leasehold valuation tribunal constituted for the purposes of Part I of the Leasehold Reform Act 1967 is a reference to such a rent assessment committee as is mentioned in section 142(2) of the Housing Act 1980 (leasehold valuation tribunals).

Provision of accommodation for persons with mental disorders

89.—(1) Any agreement relating to a lease of any property which comprises or includes a dwelling (whether contained in the instrument creating the lease or not and whether made before the creation of the lease or not) shall be void in so far as it would otherwise have the effect of prohibiting or imposing any restriction on—

(a) the occupation of the dwelling, or of any part of the dwelling, by persons with mental disorders (within the meaning of the Mental Health Act 1983), or

(b) the provision of accommodation within the dwelling for such persons.

(2) Subsection (1) applies to any agreement made after the coming into force of this section.

CHAPTER VII

GENERAL

90.—(1) Any jurisdiction expressed to be conferred on the court by this Part shall be exercised by a county court.

(2) There shall also be brought in a county court any proceedings for determining any question arising under or by virtue of any provision of Chapter I or II or this Chapter which is not a question falling within its jurisdiction by virtue of subsection (1) or one falling within the jurisdiction of a leasehold valuation tribunal by virtue of section 91.

(3) Where, however, there are brought in the High Court any proceedings which, apart from this subsection, are proceedings within the jurisdiction of the High Court, the High Court shall have jurisdiction to hear and determine any proceedings joined with those proceedings which are proceedings within the jurisdiction of a county court by virtue of subsection (1) or (2).

(4) Where any proceedings are brought in a county court by virtue of subsection (1) or (2), the court shall have jurisdiction to hear and determine any other proceedings joined with those proceedings, despite the fact that, apart from this subsection, those other proceedings would be outside the court's jurisdiction.

91.—(1) Any jurisdiction expressed to be conferred on a leasehold valuation tribunal by the provisions of this part (except section 75 or 88) shall be exercised by a rent assessment committee constituted for the purposes of this section; and any question arising in relation to any of the matters specified in subsection (2) shall, in default of agreement, be determined by such a rent assessment committee.

(2) Those matters are—

(a) the terms of acquisition relating to—

  (i) any interest which is to be acquired by a nominee purchaser in pursuance of Chapter I, or

  (ii) any new lease which is to be granted to a tenant in pursuance of Chapter II,

including in particular any matter which needs to be determined for the purposes of any provision of Schedule 6 or 13;

(b) the terms of any lease which is to be granted in accordance with section 36 and Schedule 9;
(c) the amount of any payment falling to be made by virtue of section 18(2);
(d) the amount of any costs payable by any person or persons by virtue of any provision of Chapter I or II and, in the case of costs to which section 33(1) or 60(1) applies, the liability of any person or persons by virtue of any such provision to pay any such costs; and
(e) the apportionment between two or more persons of any amount (whether of costs or otherwise) payable by virtue of any such provision.

(3) A rent assessment committee shall, when constituted for the purposes of this section, be known as a leasehold valuation tribunal; and in the following provisions of this section references to a leasehold valuation tribunal are (unless the context otherwise requires) references to such a committee.

(4) Where in any proceedings before a court there falls for determination any question falling within the jurisdiction of a leasehold valuation tribunal by virtue of Chapter I or II or this section, the court—

(a) shall by order transfer to such a tribunal so much of the proceedings as relate to the determination of that question; and
(b) may then dispose of all or any remaining proceedings, or adjourn the disposal of all or any such proceedings pending the determination of that question by the tribunal, as it thinks fit;

and accordingly once that question has been so determined the court shall, if it is a question relating to any matter falling to be determined by the court, give effect to the determination in an order of the court.

(5) Without prejudice to the generality of any other statutory provision—

(a) the power to make regulations under section 74(1)(*b*) of the Rent Act 1977 (procedure of rent assessment committees) shall extend to prescribing the procedure to be followed consequent on a transfer under subsection (4) above; and
(b) rules of court may prescribe the procedure to be followed in connection with such a transfer.

(6) Any application made to a leasehold valuation tribunal under or by virtue of this Part must comply with such requirements (if any) as to the form of, or the particulars to be contained in, any such application as the Secretary of State may by regulations prescribe.

(7) In any proceedings before a leasehold valuation tribunal which relate to any claim made under Chapter I, the interests of the participating tenants shall be represented by the nominee purchaser, and

accordingly the parties to any such proceedings shall not include those tenants.

(8) No costs which a party to any proceedings under or by virtue of this Part before a leasehold valuation tribunal incurs in connection with the proceedings shall be recoverable by order of any court (whether in consequence of a transfer under subsection (4) or otherwise).

(9) A leasehold valuation tribunal may, when determining the property in which any interest is to be acquired in pursuance of a notice under section 13 or 42, specify in its determination property which is less extensive than that specified in that notice.

(10) Paragraphs 1 to 3 and 7 of Schedule 22 to the Housing Act 1980 (provisions relating to leasehold valuation tribunals constituted for the purposes of Part I of the Leasehold Reform Act 1967) shall apply to a leasehold valuation tribunal constituted for the purposes of this section but—

(a) in relation to any proceedings which relate to a claim made under Chapter I of this Part of this Act, paragraph 7 of that Schedule shall apply as if the nominee purchaser were included among the persons on whom a notice is authorised to be served under that paragraph; and

(b) in relation to any proceedings on an application for a scheme to be approved by a tribunal under section 70, paragraph 2(*a*) of that Schedule shall apply as if any person appearing before the tribunal in accordance with subsection (6) of that section were a party to the proceedings.

(11) In this section—

"the nominee purchaser" and "the participating tenants" have the same meaning as in Chapter I;

"the terms of acquisition" shall be construed in accordance with section 24(8) or section 48(7), as appropriate;

and the reference in subsection (10) to a leasehold valuation tribunal constituted for the purposes of Part I of the Leasehold Reform Act 1967 shall be construed in accordance with section 88(7) above.

92.—(1) The court may, on the application of any person interested make an order requiring any person who has failed to comply with any requirement imposed on him under or by virtue of any provision of Chapter I or II to make good the default within such time as is specified in the order.

(2) An application shall not be made under subsection (1) unless—

(a) a notice has been previously given to the person in question requiring him to make good the default, and

(b) more than 14 days have elapsed since the date of the giving of that notice without his having done so.

93.—(1) Except as provided by this section, any agreement relating to a lease (whether contained in the instrument creating the lease or not and whether made before the creation of the lease or not) shall be void in so far as it—

(a) purports to exclude or modify—
 (i) any entitlement to participate in the making of a claim to exercise the right to collective enfranchisement under Chapter I,
 (ii) any right to acquire a new lease under Chapter II, or
 (iii) any right to compensation under section 61; or
(b) provides for the termination or surrender of the lease in the event of the tenant becoming a participating tenant for the purposes of Chapter I or giving a notice under section 42; or
(c) provides for the imposition of any penalty or disability on the tenant in that event.

(2) Subsection (1) shall not be taken to preclude a tenant from surrendering his lease, and shall not—

(a) invalidate any agreement for the acquisition on behalf of a tenant of an interest superior to his lease, or for the acquisition by a tenant of a new lease, on terms different from those provided by Chapters I and II; or
(b) where a tenant has become a participating tenant for the purposes of Chapter I or has given a notice under section 42, invalidate—
 (i) any agreement that the notice given under section 13 or (as the case may be) section 42 shall cease to have effect, or
 (ii) any provision of such an agreement excluding or restricting for a period not exceeding three years any such entitlement or right as is mentioned in subsection (1)(*a*)(i) or (ii); or
(c) where a tenant's right to compensation under section 61 has accrued, invalidate any agreement as to the amount of the compensation.

(3) Where—

(a) a tenant having the right to acquire a new lease under Chapter II—
 (i) has entered into an agreement for the surrender of his lease without the prior approval of the court, or
 (ii) has entered into an agreement for the grant of a new lease without any of the terms of acquisition (within the meaning of that Chapter) having been determined by a leasehold valuation tribunal under that Chapter, or

(b) a tenant has been granted a new lease undr Chapter II or by virtue of subsection (4) below and, on his landlord claiming possession for the purposes of redevelopment, enters into an agreement without the prior approval of the court for the surrender of the lease,

then on the application of the tenant a county court, or any court in which proceedings are brought on the agreement, may, if in its opinion the tenant is not adequately recompensed under the agreement for his rights under Chapter II, set aside or vary the agreement and give such other relief as appears to it to be just having regard to the situation and conduct of the parties.

(4) Where a tenant has the right to acquire a new lease under Chapter II, there may with the approval of the court be granted to him in satisfaction of that right a new lease on such terms as may be approved by the court, which may include terms excluding or modifying—

(a) any entitlement to participate in the making of a claim to exercise the right to collective enfranchisement under Chapter I, or
(b) any right to acquire a further lease under Chapter II.

(5) Subject to the provisions specified in subsection (6) and to subsection (7), a lease may be granted by virtue of subsection (4), and shall if so granted be binding on persons entitled to any interest in or charge on the landlord's estate—

(a) despite the fact that, apart from this subsection, it would not be authorised against any such persons, and
(b) despite any statutory or other restrictions on the landlord's powers of leasing.

(6) The provisions referred to in subsection (5) are—

(a) section 36 of the Charities Act 1993 (restrictions on disposition of charity land); and
(b) paragraph 8(2)(*c*) of Schedule 2 to this Act.

(7) Where the existing lease of the tenant is granted after the commencement of Chapter II and, the grant being subsequent to the creation of a charge on the landlord's estate, the existing lease is not binding on the persons interested in the charge, a lease granted by virtue of subsection (4) shall not be binding on those persons.

(8) Where a lease is granted by virtue of subsection (4), then except in so far as provision is made to the contrary by the terms of the lease, the following provisions shall apply in relation to the lease as they apply in relation to a lease granted under section 56, namely—

(a) section 58(3), (5) and (6);
(b) section 59(2) to (5); and

(c) section 61 and Schedule 14;

and subsections (5) to (7) of section 56 shall apply in relation to the lease as they apply in relation to a lease granted under that section.

94.—(1) Subject to subsection (2), Chapters I and II shall apply to a lease from the Crown if (and only if) there has ceased to be a Crown interest in the land subject to it.

(2) Where a tenant under a lease from the Crown would, but for the existence of any Crown interest, be entitled to acquire a new lease under Chapter II, then if—

(a) that Crown interest is superior to the interest of the person who for the purposes of Chapter II is the landlord in relation to the lease, and
(b) either—
  (i) that landlord is entitled to grant such a new lease without the concurrence of the appropriate authority, or
  (ii) the appropriate authority notifies that landlord that, as regards any Crown interest affected, the authority will concur in granting such a new lease,

subsection (1) shall apply as if there had ceased to be any Crown interest in the land subject to the lease and Chapter II shall apply accordingly.

(3) The restriction imposed by section 3(2) of the Crown Estate Act 1961 (general provisions as to management) on the term for which a lease may be granted by the Crown Estate Commissioners shall not apply where—

(a) the lease is granted by way of renewal of a long lease at a low rent, and
(b) it appears to the Crown Estate Commissioners that, but for the existence of any Crown interest, there would be a right to acquire a new lease under Chaper II of this Part of this Act.

(4) Where, in the case of land belonging—

(a) to Her Majesty in right of the Duchy of Lancaster, or
(b) to the Duchy of Cornwall,

it appears to the appropriate authoirty that a tenant under a long lease at a low rent would, but for the existence of any Crown interest, be entitled to acquire a new lease under Chapter II, then a lease corresponding to that to which the tenant would be so entitled may be granted to take effect wholly or partly out of the Crown interest by the same person and with the same formalities as in the case of any other lease of such land.

(5) In the case of land belonging to the Duchy of Cornwall, the purposes authorised by section 8 of the Duchy of Cornwall Management Act 1863 for the advancement of parts of such gross sums as are there mentioned shall include the payment to tenants under leases from the Crown of sums corresponding to those which, but for the existence of

any Crown interest, would be payable by way of compensation under section 61 above.

(6) The appropriate authority in relation to any area occupied under leases from the Crown may make an application for the approval under section 70 of a scheme for that area which is designed to secure that, in the event of tenants under those leases acquiring freehold interests in such circumstances as are mentioned in subsection (7) below, the authoirty will—

(a) retain powers of management in respect of the premises in which any such freehold interests are acquired, and
(b) have rights against any such premises in respect of the benefits arising from the exercise elsewhere of the authority's powers of management.

(7) The circumstances mentioned in subsection (6) are circumstances in which, but for the existence of any Crown interest, the tenants acquiring any such freehold interests would be entitled to acquire them as mentioned in section 69(1)(*a*) or (*b*).

(8) Subject to any necessary modifications—

(a) subsections (2) to (7) of section 69 shall apply in relation to any such scheme as is mentioned in subsection (6) above as they apply in relation to an estate management scheme; and
(b) section 70 shall apply in relation to the approval of such a scheme as it applies in relation to the approval of a scheme as an estate management scheme.

(9) Subsection (10) applies where—

(a) any tenants under leases from the Crown are proceeding with a view to acquiring the freehold of any premises in circumstances in which, but for the existence of any Crown interest, they would be entitled to acquire the freehold under Chapter I, or
(b) any tenant under a lease from the Crown is proceeding with a view to acquiring a new lease of his flat in circumstances in which, but for the existence of any Crown interest, he would be entitled to acquire such a lease under Chapter II.

(10) Where—

(a) this subsection applies in accordance with subsection (9), and
(b) any question arises in connection with the acquisition of the freehold of those premises or any such new lease which is such that, if the tenants or tenant were proceeding as mentioned in that subsection in pursuance of a claim made under Chapter I or (as the case may be) Chapter II, a leasehold valuation tribunal would have jurisdiction to determine it in proceedings under that Chapter, and

(c) it is agreed between—
  (i) the appropriate authority and the tenants or tenant, and
  (ii) all other persons (if any) whose interests would fall to be represented in proceedings brought under that Chapter for the determination of that question by a leasehold valuation tribunal

that that question should be determined by such a tribunal,

a leasehold valuation tribunal shall have jurisdiction to determine that question; and references in this subsection to a leasehold valuation tribunal are to such a tribunal constituted for the purposes of section 91.

(11) For the purposes of this section "lease from the Crown" means a lease of land in which there is, or has during the subsistence of the lease been, a Crown interest superior to the lease; and "Crown interest" and "the appropriate authority" in relation to a Crown interest mean respectively—

(a) an interest comprised in the Crown Estate, and the Crown Estate Commissioners;
(b) an interest belonging to Her Majesty in right of the Duchy of Lancaster, and the Chancellor of the Duchy;
(c) an interest belonging to the Duchy of Cornwall, and such person as the Duke of Cornwall or the possessor for the time being of the Duchy appoints;
(d) any other interest belonging to a government department or held on behalf of Her Majesty for the purposes of a government department, and the Minister in charge of that department.

(12) For the purposes of this section "long lease at a low rent" shall be construed in accordance with sections 7 and 8.

95. Chapters I and II shall not prejudice the operation of section 21 of the National Trust Act 1907, and accordingly there shall be no right under Chapter I or II to acquire any interest in or new lease of any property if an interest in the property is under that section vested inalienably in the National Trust for Places of Historic Interest or Natural Beauty.

96. There shall be no right under Chapter I or II to acquire any interest in or lease of any property which for the purposes of the Care of Cathedrals Measure 1990 is within the precinct of a cathedral church.

97.—(1) No lease shall be registrable under the Land Charges Act 1972 or be taken to be an estate contract within the meaning of that Act by reason of any rights or obligations of the tenant or landlord which may arise under Chapter I or II, and any right of a tenant arising from a notice given under section 13 or 42 shall not be an overriding interest within the meaning of the Land Registration Act 1925; but a notice given under section 13 or 42 shall be registrable under the Land Charges Act 1972, or may be the subject of a notice or caution under the Land Registration Act 1925, as if it were an estate contract.

(2) The Land Charges Act 1972 and the Land Registration Act 1925—

(a) shall apply in relation to an order made under section 26(1) or 50(1) as they apply in relation to an order affecting land which is made by the court for the purpose of enforcing a judgment or recognisance; and
(b) shall apply in relation to an application for such an order as they apply in relation to other pending land actions.

(3) The persons applying for such an order in respect of any premises shall be treated for the purposes of section 57 of the Land Registration Act 1925 (inhibitions) as persons interested in relation to any registered land containing the whole or part of those premises.

98.—(1) Where a claim to exercise the right to collective enfranchisement under Chapter I is made by the giving of a notice under section 13, or a claim to exercise the right to acquire a new lease under Chapter II is made by the giving of a notice under section 42, then except as otherwise provided by Chapter I or (as the case may be) Chapter II—

(a) the procedure for giving effect to the notice, and
(b) the rights and obligations of all parties in relation to the investigation of title and other matters arising in giving effect to the notice,

shall be such as may be prescribed by regulations made by the Secretary of State and, subject to or in the absence of provision made by any such regulations, shall be as nearly as may be the same as in the case of a contract of sale or leasing freely negotiated between the parties.

(2) Regulations under this section may, in particular, make provision—

(a) for a person to be discharged from performing any obligations arising out of a notice under section 13 or 42 by reason of the default or delay of some other person;
(b) for the payment of a deposit—
  (i) by a nominee purchaser (within the meaning of Chapter I) on exchange of contracts, or
  (ii) by a tenant who has given a notice under section 42; and
(c) with respect to the following matters, namely—
  (i) the person with whom any such deposit is to be lodged and the capacity in which any such person is to hold it, and
  (ii) the circumstances in which the whole or part of any such deposit is to be returned or forfeited.

99.—(1) Any notice required or authorised to be given under this Part—

(a) shall be in writing; and
(b) may be sent by post.

(2) Where in accordance with Chapter I or II an address in England and Wales is specified as an address at which notices may be given to any person or persons under that Chapter—

(a) any notice required or authorised to be given to that person or those persons under that Chapter may (without prejudice to the operation of subsection (3)) be given to him or them at the address so specified; but
(b) if a new address in England and Wales is so specified in substitution for that address by the giving of a notice to that effect, any notice so required or authorised to be given may be given to him or them at that new address instead.

(3) Where a tenant is required or authorised to give any notice under Chapter I or II to a person who—

(a) is the tenant's immediate landlord, and
(b) is such a landlord in respect of premises to which Part VI of the Landlord and Tenant Act 1987 (information to be furnished to tenants) applies,

the tenant may, unless he has been subsequently notified by the landlord of a different address in England and Wales for the purposes of this section, give the notice to the landlord—

(i) at the address last furnished to the tenant as the landlord's address for service in accordance with section 48 of that Act (notification of address for service of notices on landlord); or
(ii) if no such address has been furnished, at the address last furnished to the tenant as the landlord's address in accordance with section 47 of that Act (landlord's name and address to be contained in demands for rent).

(4) Subsections (2) and (3) apply to notices in proceedings under Chapter I or II as they apply to notices required or authorised to be given under that Chapter.

(5) Any notice which is given under Chapter I or II by any tenants or tenant must—

(a) if it is a notice given under section 13 or 42, be signed by each of the tenants, or (as the case may be) by the tenant, by whom it is given; and
(b) in any other case, be signed by or on behalf of each of the tenants, or (as the case may be) by or on behalf of the tenant, by whom it is given.

(6) The Secretary of State may by regulations prescribe—

(a) the form of any notice required or authorised to be given under this Part; and

(b) the particulars which any such notice must contain (whether in addition to, or in substitution for, any particulars required by virtue of any provision of this Part).

100.—(1) Any power of the Secretary of State to make orders or regulations under this Part—

(a) may be so exercised as to make different provision for different cases or descriptions of cases, including different provision for different areas; and
(b) includes power to make such procedural, incidental, supplementary and transitional provision as may appear to the Secretary of State necessary or expedient.

(2) Any power of the Secretary of State to make orders or regulations under this Part shall be exercisable by the statutory instrument which (except in the case of regulations making only such provision as is mentioned in section 99(6)) shall be subject to annulment in pursuance of a resolution of either House of Parliament.

101.—(1) In this Part—

"Business lease" means a tenancy to which Part II of the Landlord and Tenant Act 1954 applies;

"common parts", in relation to any building or part of a building includes the structure and exterior of that building or part and any common facilities within it;

"the court" (unless the context otherwise requires) means, by virtue of section 90(1), a county court;

"disposal" means a disposal whether by the creation or the transfer of an interest, and includes the surrender of a lease and the grant of an option or right of pre-emption, and "acquisition" shall be construed accordingly (as shall expressions related to either of these expressions);

"dwelling" means any building or part of a building occupied or intended to be occupied as a separate dwelling;

"flat" means a separate set of premises (whether or not on the same floor)—

(a) which forms part of a building, and
(b) which is constructed or adapted for use for the purposes of a dwelling, and
(c) either the whole or a material part of which lies above or below some other part of the building;

"interest" includes estate;

"lease" and "tenancy", and related expressions, shall be construed in accordance with subsection (2);

"rent assessment committee" means a rent assessment committee constituted under Schedule 10 to the Rent Act 1977;

"the term date", in relation to a lease granted for a term of years certain, means (subject to subsection (6)) the date of expiry of that term, and, in relation to a tenancy to which any of the provisions of section 102 applies, shall be construed in accordance with those provisions.

(2) In this Part "Lease" and "tenancy" have the same meaning, and both expressions include (where the context so permits)—

(a) a sub-lease or sub-tenancy, and
(b) an agreement for a lease or tenancy (or for a sub-lease or sub-tenancy),

but do not include a tenancy at will or at sufferance; and the expressions "landlord" and "tenant", and references to letting, to the grant of a lease or to covenants or the terms of a lease, shall be construed accordingly.

(3) In this Part any reference (however expressed) to the lease held by a qualifying tenant of a flat is a reference to a lease held by him under which the demised premises consist of or include the flat (whether with or without one or more other flats).

(4) Where two or more persons jointly constitute either the landlord or the tenant or qualifying tenant in relation to a lease of a flat, any reference in this Part to the landlord or to the tenant or qualifying tenant is (unless the context otherwise requires) a reference to both or all the persons who jointly constitute the landlord or the tenant or qualifying tenant, as the case may require.

(5) Any reference in this Part to the date of the commencement of a lease is a reference to the date of the commencement of the term of the lease.

(6) In the case of a lease which derives (in accordance with section 7(6)) from more than one separate leases, references in this Part to the date of the commencement of the lease or to the term date shall, if the terms of the separate leases commenced at different dates or those leases have different term dates, have effect as references to the date of the commencement, or (as the case may be) to the term date, of the lease comprising the flat in question (or the earliest date of commencement or earliest term date of the leases comprising it).

(7) For the purposes of this Part property is let with other property if the properties are let either under the same lease or under leases which, in accordance with section 7(6), are treated as a single lease.

(8) For the purposes of this Part any lease which is reversionary on another lease shall be treated as if it were a concurrent lease intermediate between that other lease and any interest superior to that other lease.

(9) For the purposes of this Part an order of a court or a decision of a leasehold valuation tribunal is to be treated as becoming final—

(a) if not appealed against, on the expiry of the time for bringing an appeal; or

(b) if appealed against and not set aside in consequence of the appeal, at the time when the appeal and any further appeal is disposed of—

(i) by the determination of it and the expiry of the time for bringing a further appeal (if any), or

(ii) by its being abandoned or otherwise ceasing to have effect.

102.—(1) Where either of the following provisions (which relate to continuation tenancies) applies to a tenancy, namely—

(a) section 19(2) of the Landlord and Tenant Act 1954 ("the 1954 Act"), or

(b) paragraph 16(2) of Schedule 10 to the Local Government and Housing Act 1989 ("the 1989 Act"),

the tenancy shall be treated for the relevant purposes of this Part as granted to expire—

(i) on the date which is the term date for the purposes of the 1954 Act (namely, the first date after the commencement of the 1954 Act on which, apart from the 1954 Act, the tenancy could have been brought to an end by a notice to quit given by the landlord under the tenancy), or

(ii) on the date which is the term date for the purposes of Schedule 10 to the 1989 Act (namely, the first date after the commencement of Schedule 10 to the 1989 Act on which, apart from that Schedule, the tenancy could have been brought to an end by such a notice to quit),

as the case may be.

(2) Subject to subsection (1), where under section 7(3) a tenancy created or arising as a tenancy from year to year or other periodical tenancy is to be treated as a long lease, then for the relevant purposes of this Part, the term date of that tenancy shall be taken to be the date (if any) on which the tenancy is to terminate by virtue of a notice to quit given by the landlord under the tenancy before the relevant date for those purposes, or else the earliest date on which it could as at that date (in accordance with its terms and apart from any enactment) be brought to an end by such a notice to quit.

(3) Subject to subsection (1), in the case of a tenancy granted to continue as a periodical tenancy after the expiry of a term of years certain, or to continue as a periodical tenancy if not terminated at the expiry of such a term, any question whether the tenancy is at any time to be treated for the relevant purposes of this Part as a long lease, and (if so) with what term date, shall be determined as it would be if there had been two tenancies, as follows—

(a) one granted to expire at the earliest time (at or after the expiry of that term of years certain) at which the tenancy could (in accordance with its terms and apart from any enactment) be brought to an end by a notice to quit given by the landlord under the tenancy; and

(b) the other granted to commence at the expiry of the first (and not being one to which subsection (1) applies).

(4) In this section "the relevant purposes of this Part" means the purposes of Chapter I or, to the extent that section 7 has effect for the purposes of Chapter II in accordance with section 39(3), the purposes of that Chapter.

103. This Part applies to the Isles of Scilly subject to such exceptions, adaptations and modifications as the Secretary of State may by order direct.

SCHEDULES 1 TO 5 ARE NOT PRINTED HERE.

SCHEDULE 6

PURCHASE PRICE PAYABLE BY NOMINEE PURCHASER

PART I

GENERAL

Interpretation and operation of Schedule

1.—(1) In this Schedule—

"the freeholder" means the person who owns the freehold of the specified premises;

"intermediate leasehold interest" means the interest of the tenant under a lease which is superior to the lease held by a qualifying tenant of a flat contained in the specified premises, to the extent that—

(a) any such interest is to be acquired by the nominee purchaser by virtue of section 2(1)(a), and

(b) it is an interest in the specified premises;

"the valuation date" means the date when the interest in the specified premises which is to be acquired by the nominee purchaser from the freeholder is determined either by agreement or by a leasehold valuation tribunal under this Chapter.

(2) Parts II to IV of this Schedule have effect subject to the provisions of Parts V and VI (which relate to interests with negative values).

PART II

FREEHOLD OF SPECIFIED PREMISES

Price payable for freehold of specified premises

2.—(1) Subject to the provisions of this paragraph, the price payable by the nominee purchaser for the freehold of the specified premises shall be the aggregate of—

(a) the value of the freeholder's interest in the premises as determined in accordance with paragraph 3,

(b) the freeholder's share of the marriage value as determined in accordance with paragraph 4, and
(c) any amount of compensation payable to the freeholder under paragraph 5.

(2) Where the amount arrived at in accordance with sub-paragraph (1) is a negative amount, the price payable by the nominee purchaser for the freehold shall be nil.

Value of freeholder's interest

3.—(1) Subject to the provisions of this paragraph, the value of the freeholder's interest in the specified premises is the amount which at the valuation date that interest might be expected to realise if sold on the open market by a willing seller (with neither the nominee purchaser nor any participating tenant buying or seeking to buy) on the following assumptions—

(a) on the assumption that the vendor is selling for an estate in fee simple—
   (i) subject to any leases subject to which the freeholder's interest in the premises is to be acquired by the nominee purchaser, but
   (ii) subject also to any intermediate or other leasehold interests in the premises which are to be acquired by the nominee purchaser;
(b) on the assumption that this Chapter and Chapter II confer no right to acquire any interest in the specified premises or to acquire any new lease (except that this shall not preclude the taking into account of a notice given under section 42 with respect to a flat contained in the specified premises where it is given by a person other than a participating tenant);
(c) on the assumption that any increase in the value of any flat held by a participating tenant which is attributable to an improvement carried out at his own expense by the tenant or by any predecessor in title is to be disregarded; and
(d) on the assumption that (subject to paragraphs (a) and (b)) the vendor is selling with and subject to the rights and burdens with and subject to which the conveyance to the nominee purchaser of the freeholder's interest is to be made, and in particular with and subject to such permanent or extended rights and burdens as are to be created in order to give effect to Schedule 7.

(2) It is hereby declared that the fact that sub-paragraph (1) requires assumptions to be made as to the matters specified in paragraphs (a) to (d) of that sub-paragraph does not preclude the making of assumptions as

to other matters where those assumptions are appropriate for determining the amount which at the valuation date the freeholder's interest in the specified premises might be expected to realise if sold as mentioned in that sub-paragraph.

(3) In determining that amount there shall be made such deduction (if any) in respect of any defect in title as on a sale of the interest on the open market might be expected to be allowed between a willing seller and a willing buyer.

(4) Where a lease of any flat or other unit contained in the specified premises is to be granted to the freeholder in accordance with section 36 and Schedule 9, the value of his interest in those premises at the valuation date so far as relating to that flat or other unit shall be taken to be the difference as at that date between—

(a) the value of his freehold interest in it, and
(b) the value of his interest in it under that lease, assuming it to have been granted to him at that date;

and each of those values shall, so far as is appropriate, be determined in like manner as the value of the freeholder's interest in the whole of the specified premises is determined for the purposes of paragraph 2(1)(*a*).

(5) The value of the freeholder's interest in the specified premises shall not be increased by reason of—

(a) any transaction which—
 (i) is entered into on or after the date of the passing of this Act (otherwise than in pursuance of a contract entered into before that date), and
 (ii) involves the creation or transfer of an interest superior to (whether or not preceding) any interest held by a qualifying tenant of a flat contained in the specified premises; or
(b) any alteration on or after that date of the terms on which any such superior interest is held.

(6) Sub-paragraph (5) shall not have the effect of preventing an increase in value of the freeholder's interest in the specified premises in a case where the increase is attributable to any such leasehold interest with a negative value as is mentioned in paragraph 14(2).

Freeholder's share of marriage value

4.—(1) The marriage value is the amount referred to in sub-paragraph (2), and the freeholder's share of the marriage value is—

(a) such proportion of that amount as is determined by agreement between the reversioner and the nominee purchaser or, in default of agreement, as is determined by a leasehold valuation tribunal to be the proportion which in its opinion would have been determined by an agreement made at the valuation date between the parties on a sale on the open market by a willing seller, or

(b) 50 per cent. of that amount,

whichever is the greater.

(2) The marriage value is any increase in the aggregate value of the freehold and every intermediate leasehold interest in the specified premises, when regarded as being (in consequence of their being acquired by the nominee purchaser) interests under the control of the participating tenants, as compared with the aggregate value of those interests when held by the persons from whom they are to be so acquired, being an increase in value—

(a) which is attributable to the potential ability of the participating tenants, once those interests have been so acquired, to have new leases granted to them without payment of any premium and without restriction as to length of term, and

(b) which, if those interests were being sold to the nominee purchaser on the open market by willing sellers, the nominee purchaser would have to agree to share with the sellers in order to reach agreement as to price.

(3) For the purposes of sub-paragraph (2) the value of the freehold or any intermediate leasehold interest in the specified premises when held by the person from whom it is to be acquired by the nominee purchaser and its value when acquired by the nominee purchaser—

(a) shall be determined on the same basis as the value of the interest is determined for the purposes of paragraph 2(1)(*a*) or (as the case may be) paragraph 6(1)(*b*)(i); and

(b) shall be so determined as at the valuation date.

(4) Accordingly, in so determining the value of an interest when acquired by the nominee purchaser—

(a) the same assumptions shall be made under paragraph 3(1) (or, as the case may be, under paragraph 3(1) as applied by paragraph 7(1)) as are to be made under that provision in determining the value of the interest when held by the person from whom it is to be acquired by the nominee purchaser; and

(b) any merger or other circumstances affecting the interest on its acquisition by the nominee purchaser shall be disregarded.

Compensation for loss resulting from enfranchisement

5.—(1) Where the freeholder will suffer any loss or damage to which this paragraph applies, there shall be payable to him such amount as is reasonable to compensate him for that loss or damage.

(2) This paragraph applies to—

(a) any diminution in value of any interest of the freeholder in other property resulting from the acquisition of his interest in the specified premises; and

(b) any other loss or damage which results therefrom to the extent that it is referable to his ownership of any interest in other property.

(3) Without prejudice to the generality of paragraph (b) of sub-paragraph (2), the kinds of loss falling within that paragraph include loss of development value in relation to the specified premises to the extent that it is referable as mentioned in that paragraph.

(4) In sub-paragraph (3) "development value", in relation to the specified premises, means any increase in the value of the freeholder's interest in the premises which is attributable to the possibility of demolishing, reconstructing, or carrying out substantial works of construction on, the whole or a substantial part of the premises.

(5) Where the freeholder will suffer loss or damage to which this paragraph applies, then in determining the amount of compensation payable to him under this paragraph, it shall not be material that—

(a) the loss or damage could to any extent be avoided or reduced by the grant to him, in accordance with section 36 and Schedule 9, of a lease granted in pursuance of Part III of that Schedule, and

(b) he is not requiring the nominee purchaser to grant any such lease.

PART III

INTERMEDIATE LEASEHOLD INTERESTS

Price payable for intermediate leasehold interests

6.—(1) Where the nominee purchaser is to acquire one or more intermediate leasehold interests—

(a) a separate price shall be payable for each of those interests, and

(b) (subject to the provisions of this paragraph) that price shall be the aggregate of—

   (i) the value of the interest as determined in accordance with paragraph 7, and

   (ii) any amount of compensation payable to the owner of that interest in accordance with paragraph 8.

(2) Where in the case of any intermediate leasehold interest the amount arrived at in accordance with sub-paragraph (1)(*b*) is a negative amount, the price payable by the nominee purchaser for the interest shall be nil.

Value of intermediate leasehold interests

7.—(1) Subject to sub-paragraph (2), paragraph 3 shall apply for determining the value of any intermediate leasehold interest for the purposes of paragraph 6(1)(*b*)(i) with such modifications as are appropriate to relate that paragraph to a sale of the interest in question subject (where applicable) to any leases intermediate between that interest and any lease held by a qualifying tenant of a flat contained in the specified premises.

(2) The value of an intermediate leasehold interest which is the interest of the tenant under a minor intermediate lease shall be calculated by applying the formula set out in sub-paragraph (7) instead of in accordance with sub-paragraph (1).

(3) "A minor intermediate lease" means a lease complying with the following requirements, namely—

(a) it must have an expectation of possession of not more than one month, and
(b) the profit rent in respect of the lease must be not more than £5 per year;

and, in the case of a lease which is in immediate reversion on two or more leases, those requirements must be complied with in connection with each of the sub-leases.

(4) Where a minor intermediate lease is in immediate reversion on two or more leases—

(a) the formula set out in sub-paragraph (7) shall be applied in relation to each of those sub-leases (and sub-paragraphs (5) and (6) shall also so apply); and
(b) the value of the interest of the tenant under the minor intermediate lease shall accordingly be the aggregate of the amounts calculated by so applying the formula.

(5) "Profit rent" means an amount equal to that of the rent payable under the lease on which the minor intermediate lease is in immediate reversion, less that of the rent payable under the minor intermediate lease.

(6) Where the minor intermediate lease or that on which it is in immediate reversion comprises property other than a flat held by a qualifying tenant, then in sub-paragraph (5) the reference to the rent payable under it means so much of that rent as is apportioned to any such flat.

(7) The formula is—

$$P = £\ \frac{R}{Y} - \frac{R}{Y(1 + Y)^n}$$

where—

P = the price payable;
R = the profit rent;
Y = the yield (expressed as a decimal fraction) from 2½ per cent. Consolidated Stock;
n = the period, expressed in years (taking any part of a year as a whole year), of the remainder of the term of the minor intermediate lease as at the valuation date.

(8) In calculating the yield from 2½ per cent. Consolidated Stock, the price of that stock shall be taken to be the middle market price at the close of business on the last trading day in the week before the valuation date.

(9) For the purposes of this paragraph the expectation of possession carried by a lease in relation to a lease ("the sub-lease") on which it is in immediate reversion is the expectation of possession which it carries at the valuation date after the sub-lease, on the basis that—

(a) (subject to sub-paragraph (10)) where the sub-lease is a lease held by a qualifying tenant of a flat contained in the specified premises, it terminates at the valuation date if its term date fell before then, or else it terminates on its term date; and
(b) in any other case, the sub-lease terminates on its term date.

(10) In a case where before the relevant date for the purposes of this Chapter the landlord of any such qualifying tenant as is mentioned in sub-paragraph (9)(a) had given notice to quit terminating the tenant's sub-lease on a date earlier than that date, the date specified in the notice to quit shall be substituted for the date specified in that provision.

Compensation for loss on acquisition of interest

8. Sub-paragraphs (1) to (4) of paragraph 5 shall apply in relation to the owner of any intermediate leasehold interest as they apply in relation to the freeholder.

Owners of intermediate interests entitled to part of marriage value

9.—(1) This paragraph applies where—

(a) the price payable for the freehold of the specified premises includes an amount in respect of the freeholder's share of the marriage value, and
(b) the nominee purchaser is to acquire any intermediate leasehold interests.

(2) The amount payable to the freeholder in respect of his share of the marriage value shall be divided between the freeholder and the owners of the intermediate leasehold interests in proportion to the value of their respective interests in the specified premises (as determined for the purposes of paragraph 2(1)(*a*) or paragraph 6(1)(*b*)(i), as the case may be).

(3) Where the owner of an intermediate leasehold interest is entitled in accordance with sub-paragraph (2) to any part of the amount payable to the freeholder in respect of the freeholder's share of the marriage value, the amount to which he is so entitled shall be payable to him by the freeholder.

PART IV

OTHER INTERESTS TO BE ACQUIRED

Price payable for other interests

10.—(1) Where the nominee purchaser is to acquire any freehold interest in pursuance of section 1(2)(*a*) or (4) or section 21(4), then (subject to sub-paragraph (3) below) the price payable for that interest shall be the aggregate of—

(a) the value of the interest as determined in accordance with paragraph 11,
(b) any share of the marriage value to which the owner of the interest is entitled under paragraph 12, and
(c) any amount of compensation payable to the owner of the interest in accordance with paragraph 13.

(2) Where the nominee purchaser is to acquire any leasehold interest by virtue of section 2(1) other than an intermediate leasehold interest, or he is to acquire any leasehold interest in pursuance of section 21(4), then (subject to sub-paragraph (3) below) the price payable for that interest shall be the aggregate of—

(a) the value of the interest as determined in accordance with paragraph 11, and
(b) any amount of compensation payable to the owner of the interest in accordance with paragraph 13.

(3) Where in the case of any interest the amount arrived at in accordance with sub-paragraph (1) or (2) is a negative amount, the price payable by the nominee purchaser for the interest shall be nil.

Value of other interests

11.—(1) In the case of any such freehold interest as is mentioned in paragraph 10(1), paragraph 3 shall apply for determining the value of the interest with such modifications as are appropriate to relate it to a sale of the interest subject (where applicable) to any leases intermediate between that interest and any lease held by a qualifying tenant of a flat contained in the specified premises.

(2) In the case of any such leasehold interest as is mentioned in paragraph 10(2), then—

(a) (unless paragraph (b) below applies) paragraph 3 shall apply as mentioned in sub-paragraph (1) above;
(b) if it is the interest of the tenant under a minor intermediate lease within the meaning of paragraph 7, sub-paragraphs (2) to (10) of that paragraph shall apply with such modifications as are appropriate for determining the value of the interest.

(3) In its application in accordance with sub-paragraph (1) or (2) above, paragraph 3(6) shall have effect as if the reference to paragraph 14(2) were a reference to paragraph 18(2).

Marriage value

12.—(1) Where any such freehold interest as is mentioned in paragraph 10(1) is an interest in any such property as is mentioned in section 1(3)(*a*)—

(a) sub-paragraphs (2) to (4) of paragraph 4 shall apply with such modifications as are appropriate for determining the marriage value in connection with the acquisition by the nominee purchaser of that interest; and
(b) sub-paragraph (1) of that paragraph shall apply with such modifications as are appropriate for determining the share of the marriage value to which the owner of that interest is entitled.

(2) Where—

(a) the owner of any such freehold interest is entitled to any share of the marriage value in respect of any such property, and
(b) the nominee purchaser is to acquire any leasehold interests in that property superior to any lease held by a participating tenant,

the amount payable to the owner of the freeholder interest in respect of his share of the marriage value in respect of that property shall be divided between the owner of that interest and the owners of the leasehold interests in proportion to the value of their respective interests in that property (as determined for the purposes of paragraph 10(1) or (2), as the case may be).

(3) Where the owner of any such leasehold interest ("the intermediate landlord") is entitled in accordance with sub-paragraph (2) to any part of the amount payable to the owner of any freehold interest in respect of his share of the marriage value in respect of any property, the amount to

which the intermediate landlord is so entitled shall be payable to him by the owner of that freehold interest.

Compensation for loss on acquisition of interest

13. Sub-paragraphs (1) to (4) of paragraph 5 shall apply in relation to the owner of any such freehold or leasehold interest as is mentioned in paragraph 10(1) or (2) and to the acquisition of that interest as they apply in relation to the freeholder and to the acquisition of his interest in the specified premises (and accordingly any reference in those provisions of paragraph 5 to the specified premises shall be read for this purpose as a reference to the property in which any such freehold or leasehold interest subsists).

PART V

VALUATION ETC. OF INTERESTS IN SPECIFIED PREMISES WITH NEGATIVE VALUES

Valuation of freehold and intermediate leasehold interests

14.—(1) Where—

(a) the value of the freeholder's interest in the specified premises (as determined in accordance with paragraph 3), or
(b) the value of any intermediate leasehold interest (as determined in accordance with paragraph 7),

is a negative amount, the value of the interest for the relevant purposes shall be nil.

(2) Where sub-paragraph (1) applies to any intermediate leasehold interest whose value is a negative amount ("the negative interest"), then for the relevant purposes any interests in the specified premises superior to the negative interest and having a positive value shall be reduced in value—

(a) beginning with the interest which is immediately superior to the negative interest and continuing (if necessary) with any such other superior interests in order of proximity to the negative interest;
(b) until the aggregate amount of the reduction is equal to the negative amount in question; and
(c) without reducing the value of any interest to less than nil.

(3) In a case where sub-paragraph (1) applies to two or more intermediate leasehold interests whose values are negative amounts, sub-paragraph (2) shall apply separately in relation to each of those interests—

(a) beginning with the interest which is inferior to every other of those interests and then in order of proximity to that interest; and
(b) with any reduction in the value of any interest for the relevant purposes by virtue of any prior application of sub-paragraph (2) being taken into account.

(4) For the purposes of sub-paragraph (2) an interest has a positive value if (apart from that sub-paragraph) its value for the relevant purposes is a positive amount.

(5) In this Part of this Schedule "the relevant purposes"—

(a) as respects the freeholder's interest in the specified premises, means the purposes of paragraph 2(1)(*a*); and
(b) as respects any intermediate leasehold interest, means the purposes of paragraph 6(1)(*b*)(i).

Calculation of marriage value

15.—(1) Where (as determined in accordance with paragraph 4(3) and (4)) the value of any interest—

(a) when held by the person from whom it is to be acquired by the nominee purchaser, or
(b) when acquired by the nominee purchaser,

is a negative amount, then for the purposes of paragraph 4(2) the value of the interest when so held or acquired shall be nil.

(2) Where sub-paragraph (1) above applies to any intermediate leasehold interest whose value when held or acquired as mentioned in paragraph (*a*) or (*b*) of that sub-paragraph is a negative amount, paragraph 14(2) to (4) shall apply for determining for the purposes of paragraph 4(2) the value when so held or acquired of other interests in the specified premises, as if—

(a) any reference to paragraph 14(1) were a reference to sub-paragraph (1) above; and
(b) any reference to the relevant purposes were, as respects any interest, a reference to the purposes of paragraph 4(2) as it applies to the interest when so held or acquired.

(3) References in paragraph 16 or 17 to paragraph 14(2) or (3) do not extend to that provision as it applies in accordance with sub-paragraph (2) above.

Apportionment of marriage value

16.—(1) Where paragraph 14(1) applies to an interest, the value of the interest for the purposes of paragraph 9(2) shall be nil, unless sub-paragraph (2) below applies.

(2) In a case where paragraph 14(1) applies to the freeholder's interest in the specified premises and to every intermediate leasehold interest—

(a) sub-paragraph (1) above shall not apply for the purposes of paragraph 9(2); and
(b) any division falling to be made on the proportional basis referred to in paragraph 9(2) shall be so made in such a way as to secure that the greater the negativity of an interest's value the smaller the share in respect of the interest.

(3) In a case where—

(a) paragraph 14(2) operates to reduce the value of any such superior interest as is there mentioned ("the superior interest"), and
(b) after the operation of that provision there remains any interest whose value for the relevant purposes is a positive amount,

the value of the superior interest for the purposes of paragraph 9(2) shall be the value which (in accordance with paragraph 14(2)) it has for the relevant purposes.

(4) In a case where—

(a) paragraph 14(2) operates to reduce the value of any such superior interest as is there mentioned ("the superior interest"), but
(b) after the operation of that provision there remains no such interest as is mentioned in sub-paragraph (3)(*b*) above,

the value of the superior interest for the purposes of paragraph 9(2) shall be the value which it has for the relevant purposes apart from paragraph 14(2).

Adjustment of compensation

17.—(1) Where—

(a) paragraph 14(2) operates to reduce the value of any such superior interest as is there mentioned ("the superior interest"), and
(b) apart from this paragraph any amount of compensation is payable under paragraph 8 to the owner of any relevant inferior interest in respect of that interest,

there shall be payable to the owner of the superior interest so much of the amount of compensation as is equal to the amount of the reduction or, if less than that amount, the whole of the amount of compensation.

(2) Where—

(a) paragraph 14(2) operates to reduce the value of two or more such superior interests as are there mentioned ("the superior interests"), and
(b) apart from this paragraph any amount of compensation is payable under paragraph 8 to the owner of any relevant inferior interest in respect of that interest,

sub-paragraph (1) shall apply in the first instance as if the reference to the owner of the superior interest were to the owner of such of the superior interests as is furthest from the negative interest, and then, as respects any remaining amount of compensation, as if that reference were to the owner of such of the superior interests as is next furthest from the negative interest, and so on.

(3) In sub-paragraph (1) or (2) "relevant inferior interest", in relation to any interest whose value is reduced as mentioned in that sub-paragraph ("the superior interest"), means—

(a) the negative interest on account of which any such reduction is made, or
(b) any other interest intermediate between that negative interest and the superior interest;

but sub-paragraph (1) shall apply in the first instance in relation to any amount of compensation payable to the owner of that negative interest, and then, for the purpose of offsetting (so far as possible) any reduction remaining to be offset in accordance with sub-paragraph (1) or (2), in relation to any amount of compensation payable to the owner of the interest immediately superior to that negative interest, and so on in order of proximity to it.

(4) To the extent that an amount of compensation is payable to the owner of any interest by virtue of this paragraph—

(a) paragraph 2(1)(*c*) or 6(1)(*b*)(ii) shall have effect as if it were an amount of compensation payable to him, as owner of that interest, in accordance with paragraph 5 or 8, as the case may be; and
(b) the person who would otherwise have been entitled to it in accordance with paragraph 8 shall accordingly not be so entitled.

(5) In a case where paragraph 14(2) applies separately in relation to two or more negative interests in accordance with paragraph 14(3), the preceding provisions of this paragraph shall similarly apply separately in relation to the reductions made on account of each of those interest, and shall so apply—

(a) according to the order determined by paragraph 14(3)(*a*); and
(b) with there being taken into account any reduction in the amount of compensation payable to any person under

paragraph 8 which results from the prior application of the preceding provisions of this paragraph.

PART VI

VALUATION ETC. OF OTHER INTERESTS WITH NEGATIVE VALUES

Valuation of freehold and leasehold interests

18.—(1) Where—

(a) the value of any freehold interest (as determined in accordance with paragraph 11(1)), or
(b) the value of any leasehold interest (as determined in accordance with paragraph 11(2)),

is a negative amount, the value of the interest for the relevant purposes shall be nil.

(2) Where, in the case of any property, sub-paragraph (1) applies to any leasehold interest in the property whose value is a negative amount ("the negative interest"), then for the relevant purposes any interests in the property superior to the negative interest and having a positive value shall, if they are interests which are to be acquired by the nominee purchaser, be reduced in value—

(a) beginning with the interest which is nearest to the negative interest and continuing (if necessary) with any such other superior interests in order of proximity to the negative interest;
(b) until the aggregate amount of the reduction is equal to the negative amount in question; and
(c) without reducing the value of any interest to less than nil.

(3) In a case where sub-paragraph (1) applies to two or more leasehold interests in any property whose values are negative amounts, sub-paragraph (2) shall apply separately in relation to each of those interests—

(a) beginning with the interest which is inferior to every other of those interests and then in order of proximity to that interest; and
(b) with any reduction in the value of any interest for the relevant purposes by virtue of any prior application of sub-paragraph (2) being taken into account.

(4) For the purposes of sub-paragraph (2) an interest has a positive value if (apart from that sub-paragraph) its value for the relevant purposes is a positive amount.

(5) In this Part of this Schedule "the relevant purposes"—

(a) as respects any freehold interest, means the purposes of paragraph 10(1)(*a*); and
(b) as respects any leasehold interest, means the purposes of paragraph 10(2)(*a*).

Calculation of marriage value

19.—(1) Where (as determined in accordance with paragraph 4(3) and (4)) the value of any interest—

(a) when held by the person from whom it is to be acquired by the nominee purchaser, or
(b) when acquired by the nominee purchaser,

is a negative amount, then for the purposes of paragraph 4(2) the value of the interest when so held or acquired shall be nil.

(2) Where, in the case of any property, sub-paragraph (1) above applies to any leasehold interest in the property whose value when held or acquired as mentioned in paragraph (*a*) or (*b*) of that sub-paragraph is a negative amount, paragraph 18(2) to (4) shall apply for determining for the purposes of paragraph 4(2) the value when so held or acquired of other interests in the property, as if—

(a) any reference to paragraph 18(1) were a reference to sub-paragraph (1) above; and
(b) any reference to the relevant purposes were, as respects any interest, a reference to the purposes of paragraph 4(2) as it applies to the interest when so held or acquired.

(3) In this paragraph any reference to any provision of paragraph 4 is a reference to that provision as it applies in accordance with paragraph 12(1).

(4) References in paragraph 20 or 21 to paragraph 18(2) or (3) do not extend to that provision as it applies in accordance with sub-paragraph (2) above.

Apportionment of marriage value

20.—(1) Where paragraph 18(1) applies to any interest in any property to which paragraph 12(1) applies, the value of the interest for the purposes of paragraph 12(2) shall be nil, unless sub-paragraph (2) below applies.

(2) Where, in the case of any property, paragraph 18(1) applies to every interest which is to be acquired by the nominee purchaser—

(a) sub-paragraph (1) above shall not apply for the purposes of paragraph 12(2); and
(b) any division falling to be made on the proportional basis referred to in paragraph 12(2) shall be so made in such a way

as to secure that the greater the negativity of an interest's value the smaller the share in respect of the interest.

(3) Where in the case of any property—

(a) paragraph 18(2) operates to reduce the value of any such superior interest as is there mentioned ("the superior interest"), and
(b) after the operation of that provision there remains any interest which is to be acquired by the nominee purchaser and whose value for the relevant purposes is a positive amount,

the value of the superior interest for the purposes of paragraph 12(2) shall be the value which (in accordance with paragraph 18(2)) it has for the relevant purposes.

(4) Where in the case of any property—

(a) paragraph 18(2) operates to reduce the value of any such superior interest as is there mentioned ("the superior interest"), but
(b) after the operation of that provision there remains no such interest as is mentioned in sub-paragraph (3)(*b*) above,

the value of the superior interest for the purposes of paragraph 12(2) shall be the value which it has for the relevant purposes apart from paragraph 18(2).

Adjustment of compensation

21.—(1) Where in the case of any property—

(a) paragraph 18(2) operates to reduce the value of any such superior interest as is there mentioned ("the superior interest"), and
(b) apart from this paragraph any amount of compensation is payable by virtue of paragraph 13 to the owner of any relevant inferior interest in respect of that interest,

there shall be payable to the owner of the superior interest so much of the amount of compensation as is equal to the amount of the reduction or, if less than that amount, the whole of the amount of compensation.

(2) Where in the case of any property—

(a) paragraph 18(2) operates to reduce the value of two or more such superior interests as are there mentioned ("the superior interests"), and
(b) apart from this paragraph any amount of compensation is payable by virtue of paragraph 13 to the owner of any relevant inferior interest in respect of that interest,

sub-paragraph (1) shall apply in the first instance as if the reference to the owner of the superior interest were to the owner of such of the superior interests as is furthest from the negative interest, and then, as respects any remaining amount of compensation, as if that reference were to the owner of such of the superior interests as is next furthest from the negative interest, and so on.

(3) In sub-paragraph (1) or (2) "relevant inferior interest", in relation to any interest whose value is reduced as mentioned in that sub-paragraph ("the superior interest"), means—

(a) the negative interest on account of which any such reduction is made, or
(b) any other interest in the property in question which is to be acquired by the nominee purchaser and is intermediate between that negative interest and the superior interest;

but sub-paragraph (1) shall apply in the first instance in relation to any amount of compensation payable to the owner of that negative interest, and then, for the purpose of offsetting (so far as possible) any reduction remaining to be offset in accordance with sub-paragraph (1) or (2), in relation to any amount of compensation payable to the owner of such interest falling within paragraph (b) above as is nearest to that negative interest, and so on in order of proximity to it.

(4) To the extent that an amount of compensation is payable to the owner of any interest by virtue of this paragraph—

(a) paragraph 10(1)(*c*) or (as the case may be) paragraph 10(2)(*b*) shall have effect as if it were an amount of compensation payable to him, as owner of that interest, in accordance with paragraph 13; and
(b) the person who would otherwise have been entitled to it in accordance with paragraph 13 shall accordingly not be so entitled.

(5) In a case where paragraph 18(2) applies separately in relation to two or more negative interests in accordance with paragraph 18(3), the preceding provisions of this paragraph shall similarly apply separately in relation to the reductions made on account of each of those interests, and shall so apply—

(a) according to the order determined by paragraph 18(3)(*a*); and
(b) with there being taken into account any reduction in the amount of compensation payable to any person by virtue of paragraph 13 which results from the prior application of the preceding provisions of this paragraph.

Index